THE DARKEST DAYS

THE DARKEST DAYS

The Truth Behind Britain's
Rush to War, 1914

Douglas Newton

VERSO
London • New York

First published by Verso 2014
© Douglas Newton 2014

1 3 5 7 9 10 8 6 4 2

Verso
UK: 6 Meard Street, London W1F 0EG
US: 20 Jay Street, Suite 1010, Brooklyn, NY 11201
www.versobooks.com

Verso is the imprint of New Left Books

ISBN-13: 978-1-78168-350-7
eISBN-13: 978-1-78168-657-7 (UK)
eISBN-13: 978-1-78168-351-4 (US)

British Library Cataloguing in Publication Data
A catalogue record for this book is available from the British Library

Library of Congress Cataloging-in-Publication Data

Newton, Douglas J.
The darkest days : the truth behind Britain's rush to
war, 1914 / Douglas Newton.
    pages cm
Includes bibliographical references and index.
 ISBN 978-1-78168-350-7 (alk. paper) – ISBN 978-1-
78168-351-4 (ebook)
1. World War, 1914–1918–Great Britain. 2. World
War, 1914–1918–Causes. 3. World War, 1914–
1918–Diplomatic history. 4. Great Britain–Foreign
relations–1910–1936. I. Title.
D517.N49 2014
940.3'2241–dc23

                    2014007134

Typeset in Garamond by MJ & N Gavan, Truro, Cornwall
Printed in the UK by CPI Group (UK) Ltd, Croydon, CR0 4YY

For Julie,
still loving

If men are *to do and die*, for mercy's sake let them *question why* as thoroughly as possible; else some other men are sure to be required *to do and die* as a consequence of this blindness and haste. If people had questioned why, not only this war, but nearly, perhaps, every other modern war would have been spared us.

Vernon Lee, *Satan the Waster* (1920)

Contents

Acknowledgements

I n researching and writing this book, I have sought assistance from many friends and contracted many debts. My family has been of great assistance to this project along the way. My love and gratitude go especially to Julie Newton for her encouragement and for her repeated close readings of the manuscript. I am grateful also to Joy Melhuish, who first introduced me to the captivating history of peace activism many years ago. She has always read and corrected each manuscript, and she made it possible for me to undertake such wide research in Britain on my many visits. I would like to thank my family for their constant encouragement: David Newton, Juliette Warren, Pamela Mary Newton, my mother, Michael Newton, Mary Anne Anastasiadis, Robert Newton, Richard Newton, and especially my sister Pamela Newton. For sharing with me her deep knowledge of the intriguing historical personalities in this story, and for reading early versions of this book, I must thank especially Belinda Browne. The following deserve warm thanks for reading versions of the manuscript and for offering both advice and constructive criticism: Gregory Bateman, Brian Brennan, Peter Butt, Daryl Le Cornu, Roderick Miller, Peter Henderson, Bruce Hunt, Robert Lee, Greg Lockhart, Andrew Moore, Alan Roberts, Youssef Taouk, and Dimity Torbett. For sharing his own passion, knowledge, and provocative insights into the subject of war and peace, I must thank Thomas Reifer. I have also benefitted from the inspirational advice of Keith Wilson, who encouraged me on my visit to Leeds long ago. His provocative work in British foreign and defence policy lit the way for me. I must thank him warmly. Early in my career, Ken Morgan and Cameron Hazlehurst were also especially encouraging to me, and I thank them sincerely. Colleagues and students at the University of Western Sydney, where I taught an Honours subject on the First World War for many years, have also helped in innumerable ways. For his special advice with regard to publication, I must thank Nicholas Jacobs. Of course, none of the above necessarily endorses the interpretation presented here, and all the blemishes in the work are mine.

I would like to thank Kate Russell, Laura Ponsonby, Ian Russell, and their family for their hospitality and generosity to me when I stayed with them at Shulbrede Priory. Kate Russell's guidance through the private papers of Arthur Ponsonby was invaluable. I must also thank Kate Russell and Laura Ponsonby for permission to reproduce material from the papers of their grandfather, Arthur Ponsonby, Lord Ponsonby of Shulbrede.

Dozens of dedicated archivists who manage the manuscript collections at many libraries and archival institutions have been of great assistance to me in my research over the past decade. I cannot list them all, but I wish to record my thanks to each and every one. I would like to thank especially Colin Harris and Elizabeth Turner at the Bodleian Library, for granting me access to new deposits in the Lewis Harcourt Papers and the Francis Hirst Papers before they were catalogued, and also Helen Langley for assistance with arranging permissions.

I would also like to thank sincerely the following individuals and institutions for making it possible for me to access personal papers, and for granting me permission to quote from personal papers over which they hold copyright: Robert Bell (Geoffrey Dawson); Allen Packwood at the Churchill Archives Centre (Maurice Hankey); Christopher Arnander (Reginald and Pamela McKenna); the Columbia Centre for Oral History Collection (CCOHC) project at Columbia University (Norman Angell); James Towe (Victor Cavendish, 9th Duke of Devonshire); the Bonham Carter Trustees (Herbert Henry Asquith and Margot Asquith); Christopher Osborn (for the unpublished diaries of Margot Asquith); the National Library of Scotland (Richard Haldane, Elizabeth Haldane, Arthur Murray); the Parliamentary Archives (Lloyd George, Herbert Samuel, Bonar Law); Charles Simon (Viscount Simon); Glennis Cripps (John Bruce Glasier); the Warden and Scholars of New College Oxford (Lord Milner); and the Surrey History Centre on behalf of the copyright holders (T. C. and J. A. Farrer). I am grateful to Helen Langley, Curator of Modern Political Papers at the Bodleian Library, for granting permission to quote from the unpublished diary of Lewis Harcourt, 1st Viscount Harcourt, on behalf of William Gascoigne, the owner of the Harcourt copyright. Quotations from the diary of Wilfrid Blunt are made by permission of the Syndics of the Fitzwilliam Museum. Extracts from the Manchester Guardian Archive are reproduced by courtesy of the University Librarian and Director, the John Rylands Library, the University of Manchester. For access to the papers of John Dillon, I would like to thank the Board of Trinity College in Dublin. Quotations from the papers of Charles Hardinge, 1st Baron Hardinge, and Robert Crewe-Milnes, 1st Marquess of Crewe, are reproduced by permission of the Syndics of Cambridge University Library. Quotations from the papers of Charles Trevelyan and Walter Runciman are reproduced by permission of the Librarian, Robinson Library, Newcastle University. Quotations from Sir Winston Churchill's papers are reproduced with permission of Curtis Brown, London, on behalf of the Estate of Sir Winston Churchill. © Copyright, Winston S. Churchill. Quotations from the papers of the Seventh Earl Beauchamp are reproduced by permission of the copyright owners. Quotations from the Times Newspapers Limited Archive at the News International Record Office, Enfield, are reproduced under license, and by permission of *The Times*/Newssyndication.com. For permission to quote from the papers of the 5th Marquess of Lansdowne, I would like to thank the Marquis of Lansdowne.

I have made every effort to contact copyright owners for the quotations from private papers contained within this book. Some of my enquiries have not been answered or have been returned from old addresses. If I have inadvertently infringed the copyright of any person I do apologise sincerely. On being informed, the publisher will endeavour to correct any such omission in future editions of this work.

Finally, for his faith in the project at the outset, and for his encouragement and support at many points, I would like to thank Leo Hollis. For their professional assistance in developing the book at Verso, I would also like to thank Mark Martin, Tim Clark, Chris Dodge and Avis Lang, whose sharp eyes were a blessing for me.

D. N.
Armistice Day, 2013

Keir Hardie addresses the 'War Against War' rally for neutrality and peace at Trafalgar Square, London, Sunday 2 August 1914.

Introduction

This book is meant to unsettle. It attacks the comforting consensus that has emerged in contemporary history regarding the British choice for war in August 1914. According to this consensus, the story is a simple one: Britain was wholly in the right, for she did all she could to avert war. Britain's choice for war was made on Tuesday 4 August, and was an irresistible response to the German aggression of that day – the invasion of Belgium. The choice for war was almost universally approved, and only a rump of 'pacifists' dissented.

In refutation, this book reveals a much more complex truth. Britain, like all the nations caught up in this tragedy, made errors. Her leaders made reckless decisions that only hastened the war, and left things undone that might have helped to avert it. Britain's choice for war was in fact made on Sunday 2 August, before Belgium was invaded, and was driven above all by a desire to show 'solidarity' with France and Russia. Some at the top looked upon the moment as favourable for war, for Britain could join with two other friendly Great Powers and ensure Germany's defeat. Turning to those activists who campaigned for Britain's neutrality during the crisis, it is clear they had significant support, far beyond the ranks of mere 'pacifists'. The apparent inability of Britain's peace activists in 1914 to prevent the nation's intervention testifies not to the futility of their cause but to the rapidity of the crisis.

The book argues that – just as the British people discovered in 2003 with regard to the decision for another war – even nations very largely in the right can make terrible mistakes in rushing into a conflict. This volume, then, is not in the heroic tradition of so many recent British histories of the First World War. It is in the tragic tradition, arguing that British errors made a significant contribution to the outbreak of the common European tragedy that was the Great War.

Dire Necessity

Over the last thirty years, it has become increasingly common for historians of Britain's Great War to stand up for the war. This school of history can be conveniently labelled the 'dire necessity' school. Its argument is straightforward: the war was horrible, but for Britain and its Empire it was a 'dire necessity'. Historians of this persuasion praise those British politicians who chose war in 1914, and are keen to revive the reputations of the British generals who directed the combat. They applaud the 'see it through' spirit that inspired the British national effort. They are impatient with those who opposed the choice for war, and with those historians who focus upon the cost in corpses. They tell the story of the Great War as a 'good' war. Authors loyal to this developing consensus openly announce their intention to challenge the grimly negative 'popular memory' of the Great War.[1]

Historians of the 'dire necessity' school have produced valuable studies of Britain's military effort,[2] but they often go further than merely analysing battles, typically offering full-throated endorsements of the war. They vehemently defend the British commitment to the war: It was 'a just war, and a necessary war', and 'there was no alternative'.[3]

With great passion, these historians object in particular to any notion that the war was 'futile'. Futility is old hat – victory shines through in its place. The big themes are the reality of victory, and the crucial contribution of British arms. The lessons that the West should take from the conflict are chiefly positive – the lessons of national resolve and readiness for sacrifice. Victory redeems the war.

Not surprisingly, historians from this new hawkish school lavish praise upon Britain's choice for war in 1914. They are in no doubt that, as one prominent military historian concludes, Britain took 'the right decision', and staying out 'would have courted national disaster'.[4] In such circles, fatalism about the choice for war is common. History could never have been other than it was. Britain did the only thing she could do. There was no alternative to war, and the people recognised this. For example, another historian argues that British Liberal Prime Minister Herbert Asquith's decision to intervene was 'inevitable' and his management of the crisis was something of a political 'triumph'.[5]

What If?

Of course, not all historians agree. Most notably, Niall Ferguson has dared to question the perceived wisdom of the commitment.[6] 'What if Britain had "stood aside" in August 1914?' he asks, speculating about the likely course of events if Britain had not intervened – and if Germany had won. The probable evils that might have flowed from a German victory, he suggests, could scarcely have been worse than the actual evils visited upon Europe by fifty-one months of catastrophic war. Of course, nothing about what did not happen can be proven – or disproven.

Much more provocative – and inspirational for this book – has been the work of Keith Wilson. As a critic of British foreign policy, Wilson is refreshingly objective. He contends that Britain's 'policy of the Entente' – the diplomatic alignment with France (in 1904) and then with Russia (in 1907) – was originally conceived as a stratagem to secure the British Empire from Russia and France, rather than as a far-sighted plan to contain Germany. He documents the imperial obsessions that drew Britain's decision-makers toward an ever more dangerous reliance upon the Ententes before 1914. He scorns the Liberal politicians, Prime Minister Asquith and his foreign secretary Sir Edward Grey, who declared that Britain had retained her 'free hand' up to 1914. He highlights how rushed, how closely contested, and how very 'political' was the final choice for war.[7]

However, none of the dissenting historians has succeeded in challenging the prevailing consensus that endorses the British choice for war. All wear a social black eye for having defied the 'dire necessity' school.

It is important to stress that the path of speculation about Britain 'standing aside' in 1914 is not essential to the debate. The question 'What if Britain had "stood aside" in 1914?' does not really help us to understand what happened. It hypnotises and misleads. It is the simplest of questions asked of great complexities. It is the last question posing as the first. A critic of Britain's role in 1914 does not need to go to the length of speculating about what might have happened if Britain had remained neutral at the *end* of the July–August crisis. Certainly, a case can be made that Britain 'did the right thing' on Tuesday 4 August. However, even accepting this, it is still essential to interrogate Britain's role up to this point, and to ask what might have been done differently. Logically, Britain's action on the last day of the diplomatic crisis cannot be assumed to vindicate all her actions over the preceding fourteen days.

A great many other 'What if?' questions might be asked of British actions along the twisted path from Thursday 23 July to Tuesday 4 August 1914. What if Britain's leaders and diplomats had sought determinedly to restrain Russia? What if Grey had put both the Russian and French ambassadors in London under real pressure on the issue of Russia's early mobilisation? What if Winston Churchill, the First Lord of the Admiralty, had not issued orders to keep the British Fleet concentrated, ready for deployment (on Sunday 26 July), a publicised initiative that heartened advocates of 'firmness' in Russia and France? What if Churchill had not been permitted to order the fleet to its war stations (on Tuesday 28 July), another initiative that incited hard-liners? These and a dozen other questions might be asked of British actions *before* Tuesday 4 August.

The historians of the 'dire necessity' school will have none of this. They argue that the end for which the British fought was right – the destruction of the German menace. The end was so shiningly right that the means scarcely merit close inspection. Any 'forcing the pace' on the Entente side is forgiven as prudent 'preparedness'. This keeps our understanding of the crisis in a state of perpetual adolescence.

Who – or What – Caused the War?

Readers may well ask where this book stands on the biggest question of all – who or what caused the war? In response, three statements must serve to outline the philosophic foundations of this study.

First, we have to accept that some things about the crisis will never be known. It is simply impossible to recover all the fingerprints on the fuse after such a conflagration. Caches of documents have vanished – most obviously documents on the French state visit to Russia in mid-July 1914.[8] Crucial figures, such as Maurice Paléologue, the French ambassador in St Petersburg, and Raymond Poincaré, the French President, sanitised their personal archives after the war.[9] The vital personal archives of Sir Edward Grey and German Chancellor Bethmann Hollweg perished in accidental fires.[10] Files everywhere have been subject to 'weeding', including vast numbers of War Office files in Britain.[11] Other crucial gaps remain. For example, we do not know what was *said* over telephone calls made between decision-makers in each nation in July–August 1914.[12]

Second, a key philosophic premise underpinning this work is that the search for eleventh-hour causes and the incontrovertibly guilty men of 1914 is fruitless – if the intention is to fix upon national 'guilt'. A focus upon wicked persons will produce such men in every capital city in 1914 – not just in Berlin. For example, recent research into the role of French politicians, diplomats and military figures during the July–August crisis is damning.[13] Most historians agree that in the last week of July, Paléologue 'did everything possible to block a compromise settlement'.[14] Similarly, early in the crisis, the French generals put intense pressure on their Russian counterparts to move from a partial to a general mobilisation.[15] One judicious summary of scholarship on the outbreak of war acknowledges that 'France barely tried to restrain Russia at all during the crisis.'[16] Alternatively, in his carefully documented recent work, Sean McMeekin has pointed the finger squarely at the Russians – Tsar Nicholas II, his foreign minister Sergei Sazonov, and the Russian generals. He puts the case that desire for conquest at Constantinople and the Straits lured the Russian elite on to risk world war.[17] But we cannot conclude from such work unmasking reckless men that either France or Russia was ultimately to 'blame' for the explosion.

Third, a focus upon guilty persons will only distract us from understanding the complex systemic causes of the war. Apportioning blame among those *who* were to blame does not help us to see *what* was to blame. The larger truth of the tragedy of 1914 is that the economic, political, and diplomatic systems across Europe were defective, and all the Great Powers shared in these systemic defects – the New Imperialism, social Darwinism, economic nationalism, ethnically conscious chauvinism, a creeping militarism that looted national treasuries, weak international institutions, and a new popular press that debased political culture and poisoned the popular mind. The febrile political atmosphere was also the creation of men of property who were engaged in a common revolt against new schemes of income-related taxation. Some of these men funded a dangerous radical turn in conservative politics that sought salvation from trade unionism, socialism and democracy in a histrionic ultra-nationalism and even in war itself. Finally, tilting the Continent toward tragedy was the presence of so many mediocre men in high places running the game of brinkmanship, the characteristic products of class-bound societies. These were the forces and perverse ideologies that built toward the disaster. And they were to be found across Europe, and beyond, in 1914.[18]

Even Fritz Fischer, the revered German historian who fifty years ago exposed the blunders of the German elite of 1914, did not imagine that those in the Kaiser's circle were solely to blame for the European catastrophe. In his path-breaking *Germany's Aims in the First World War* he wrote:

There is no question but that the conflict of military and political interests, of resentment and ideas, which found expression in the July crisis, left no government of any of the European powers quite free of some measure of responsibility – greater or smaller – for the outbreak of war in one respect or another.[19]

Indeed, it is galling to see the determinedly anti-militarist Fischer, who struggled to exorcise nationalist fantasies, to expose follies, and to confront errors in Germany's history, extolled by nationalist historians outside Germany who refuse to find any fantasies, follies, or errors in their own countries' records. Why, we should ask, should Fischer's searing indictment of corrupting imperialism, delusional militarism, and the recklessness and vainglory of right-wing elites be confined to Germany?

This book does not discount the work of those historians who, inspired by Fischer, have documented the errors made by the German elite before and during the July–August crisis. Many courageous authors have enabled us to peer inside the demon that was the Prussian elite.[20] But clearly these historians have come to quite different conclusions about the mix of fantastical ambition, on the one hand, and genuine fear for German security, on the other, that motivated Germany's decision-makers. Certainly all have exposed the often bewildered and sometimes mendacious men unhappily exercising authority in Germany's name in July 1914.[21] It was indeed the German people's profound misfortune to have at the helm in Berlin so many aristocratic incompetents and imperial fantasists, who were quite overwhelmed by the crisis. But such men stalked the gilded rooms of power across Europe.

There is no consensus that the German decision-makers were inexorably on a path to a hegemonic war.[22] 'Chaos and confusion rather than direction and design were the hallmarks of German decision making in late July 1914', writes Holger Herwig. The German elite, he observes, was 'beset by doubts, petty bickering, confusion and lack of vision'.[23] Clearly the political and military elite in Berlin was no monolith. Some in the Kaiser's circle calculated that a high risk of general war was acceptable as they guided the nation through the crisis; some even longed for war as a deliverance from a domestic political impasse; and yet others drew back in horror as they stared into the abyss, terrified that war would unleash revolution. There was panic and mutual recrimination among the German and Austro-Hungarian decision-makers.[24] As Sean McMeekin has argued most recently, 'So far from "willing the war," the Germans went into it kicking and screaming as the Austrian noose snapped shut around their necks.'[25]

Of course, this is not intended to exculpate the German decision-makers. The great body of research documenting German mistakes and worse is immensely persuasive. But it should not be cited as if it provides a final and authoritative vindication of all that British, French and Russian decision-makers did in their turn in 1914. German blunders do not blot out the blunders of others.

At the heart of this book is the belief that the war was not irresistible. The improbable can still rule in history. Fatalism, driven by knowledge of the outcome, blights many narratives of the crisis from the British perspective. It needs to be challenged. The purpose of this book is to re-examine the events of July–August 1914 in Britain, from the perspective of both those choosing war and those resisting it. It aims to reconsider both the British choice for war and the campaign waged for neutrality at the time by 'Radicals', as those on the progressive wing of the Liberal Party proudly called themselves in those days. It rejects the common assumptions that history could not have been otherwise and that Britain was bound to embark upon war on Tuesday 4 August. It accepts that Britain suffered from many of the same destructive forces in her politics and society as could be discerned in other nations. Europe was sick – and Britain was not free from the infections that disabled and disoriented others.

Disappointing as it is to the convinced moralists, there is no 'one true cause' to be discovered in this or other narratives of the July–August crisis. When the plague is upon all houses, as it was, it is only right to explore each house in that spirit. That is the spirit motivating this book. Britain is the house under examination here. Britain was not especially to blame – but neither was she free of blame – when in 1914 the tragedy of war engulfed a rotten system.

Prelude: Trafalgar Square
and 10 Downing Street
Sunday 2 August 1914

It was the biggest Trafalgar Square demonstration held for years; far larger for example than the most important of the suffragist rallies.

Manchester Guardian, 3 August 1914[1]

In one long moment, the people choosing war and the people resisting war almost collided in London on the warm and humid afternoon of Sunday 2 August 1914.

At about 2 p.m. four large processions were forming in different parts of London before marching to Trafalgar Square for a protest rally. The processions were scheduled to begin from outside Westminster Cathedral, in the west, from St George's Circus, in the south, from the East India Dock gates, in the east, and from Kentish Town, in the north. The purpose of the rally was proclaimed in bold letters on leaflets handed to passers-by: 'ENGLAND STAND CLEAR!' As the leaflets explained, the demonstration was being organised for all those who wanted a great people's gathering 'to demand that England shall not be dragged into a Continental War'.[2] The chief speaker was to be Keir Hardie, the most charismatic figure from the leading ranks of the British Labour Party. Listed with him were some of the most famous names in British trade unionism, the women's movement, and the wider internationalist fraternity. It was to be a rally for peace, and for Britain's neutrality.

Why this sudden apprehension of war? After all, more than a month had passed since the bloody event that was the immediate cause of renewed international tension in the Balkans. In Sarajevo on 28 June, a young Serbian nationalist had assassinated the Austrian heir-presumptive Archduke Franz Ferdinand and his wife Sophie, symbols of Austro-Hungarian domination over the southern Slavs. It was a dangerous provocation. In the international jostling that followed, Serbia had the support of Russia, Russia had the support of France, and Austria-Hungary had the support of Germany. But such crises had been negotiated away before. That a European war of enormous scale might suddenly erupt out of this incident had been glimpsed in London as a dangerous possibility only late in the afternoon of Friday 31 July. At this time, on the eve of the bank holiday weekend, news had arrived in Whitehall of Russian general mobilisation. Prime Minister Asquith had told the House of Commons of this ominous development just before the House rose on Friday 31 July.[3]

The demonstrators preparing to march toward Trafalgar Square were determined that Britain should not be sucked into a continental war arising from this dispute in Eastern Europe, in which Britain had no direct interest. They feared that British intervention might follow from her controversial diplomatic alignments, the famous 'Ententes' or 'understandings' with France and Russia. They would march in defiance of the editorials of the Conservative newspapers arguing on that very day that Britain must show 'solidarity' and intervene instantly on the side of her 'friends', France and Russia, if war erupted.[4]

A few minutes before 2 p.m., just as the processions across London began to march, ministers from Asquith's Cabinet began to leave Number 10 Downing Street. A momentous and rare Sunday Cabinet meeting had just ended. Perhaps the ministers and the demonstrators caught sight of each other? If the marchers from Westminster Cathedral took the traditional route via Whitehall, they would have passed by the entrance to Downing Street. None could possibly have known what had just happened in the Cabinet room at Number 10, barely 100 metres away: the key decision that would embroil Britain in the looming continental war had just been taken.

The exhausting Cabinet meeting had lasted from 11 a.m. until 2 p.m. After much passionate debate, the nineteen ministers had finally come to a decision: they agreed that Sir Edward Grey, the Foreign Secretary, should be empowered to grant to Paul Cambon, the French ambassador, a 'pledge' of British naval support for France in the current crisis. Cambon had been pleading for this for some days. Grey wasted no time in delivering it. In his study overlooking St James's Park, Grey met with Cambon just twenty minutes after the Cabinet meeting ended. He passed on an assurance that the British fleet would defend French shipping and ports if the German fleet came into the English Channel or the North Sea to attack France.[5]

This promise of British naval assistance to France had been vehemently opposed by a number of Cabinet ministers. They had insisted that it meant war. It was the action, they protested, of an already committed ally, not the mediating neutral power that Britain claimed to be. Germany might well declare war against Britain in retaliation, they warned. One minister, John Burns, announced to his shocked colleagues that he must resign in protest. Another, John Morley, confided privately to the Prime Minister that he too would have to resign. Other Radicals were known to be wavering. A small group of these dissenting ministers, some mulling over their own resignations, made their way to the home of Earl Beauchamp, Halkyn House in Belgrave Square, to debate their next move over lunch.[6]

Soon the marchers, accompanied by large banners and a band, joined the throng already filling Trafalgar Square. When Keir Hardie was assisted onto the plinth of Nelson's column and the rally for peace and neutrality began at 4 p.m., the crowd was estimated at between fifteen and twenty thousand people. 'It was the biggest Trafalgar Square demonstration held for years; far larger for example than the most important of the suffragist rallies', wrote the reporter from the *Manchester Guardian*.[7] But as these protestors strained to hear the speakers on that Sunday afternoon, the British government had already taken the decisive step to abandon neutrality if a wider war ignited. In this crisis, the peace activists had just one day – Sunday, the traditional day for outdoor protest – to demonstrate their opposition to war.[8]

Only two days later, deep in the evening of Tuesday 4 August, it was all over. Britain declared war on Germany.

ONE

The Myth of an Irresistible War

The perfect weather continued, and the dumb impotent feeling of the gulf between nature, the past, all beautiful true and gracious things and beliefs, and this black horror of inconceivability that nevertheless was true.[1]

Goldsworthy Lowes Dickinson, August 1914

'My God, Mr Page, what else could we do?' exclaimed King George V, throwing up his hands, as he explained Britain's declaration of war upon Germany to the American ambassador in early August 1914.[2] Could Britain have remained neutral? 'Thank God there were not half a dozen people in this country who wished this course.'[3] Such was the view of Edwin Montagu who, as a Financial Secretary to the Treasury and friend of the Asquith family, was very close to the key decision-makers in 1914.

There, in a nutshell, was the dominant narrative of Britain's 1914. It persists to this day. War was irresistible – there was no alternative – and the whole nation was practically unanimous in support. Is it true?

The Cabinet Crisis of Monday 3 August 1914

In the thick traffic of events leading up to the outbreak of the First World War, one significant development in Britain is now almost forgotten: on the very eve of the war there was a Cabinet crisis. It reached its climax at a Cabinet meeting at 10 Downing Street on the morning of Monday 3 August 1914 – just a day before Britain declared war upon Germany. Four resignations lay on the table.

To understand this, let us go back just a week to explore the origins of this internal political crisis. Over the preceding seven days, from Monday 27 July, there had been a series of tense Cabinet meetings to consider Britain's response to the Balkan affair. Only with difficulty had Asquith and his Foreign Secretary, Sir Edward Grey, held the nineteen ministers together on the basis of a policy of deliberate ambiguity for Britain. The idea was for Britain to don a mask of inscrutability: no promises to either of the great rival alliance systems regarding British action in the event of war – no promises to Germany and Austria-Hungary that Britain would stay out, no promises to France and Russia that Britain would intervene. Charles Hobhouse, a Cabinet minister, captured the governing idea: 'our influence for peace depended on our apparent indecision'.[4]

During that week Europe had moved from the certainty of a Balkan conflict, when Austria-Hungary had declared war on Serbia on Tuesday 28 July, to the possibility of something much bigger, when Russia's general mobilisation became known on Friday 31 July. Ministers were told to stay in London for more Cabinet meetings. It was the August bank holiday weekend. In a striking testament to the seriousness of the situation, a Cabinet meeting was held on Saturday 1 August, followed by two more the next day.

By the afternoon of Sunday 2 August, big cracks in the Cabinet had opened up. Between late Sunday evening and the morning of the Monday, Asquith received four resignation letters. All were lodged in protest against the Cabinet decision of Sunday afternoon – the decision that Grey should convey a guarantee of British naval support to France. That guarantee was seen by most around the Cabinet table as sealing Britain's choice for war.[5]

The first of the dissenting ministers to go was John Burns, an independent Liberal with a trade union background. Burns tearfully threatened immediate resignation as soon as the Cabinet ended on the Sunday afternoon. He confirmed his decision in a late-night letter to Downing Street denouncing the 'decision of the Cabinet to intervene in a European war'.[6] He did not come to the Monday Cabinet. Next to announce his determination to depart was the ambitious Attorney General, Sir John Simon. Simon sent his letter of resignation in to Downing Street very late on Sunday. Grey's pledge of naval support to France, he complained, was 'tantamount to a declaration that we take part in this war'.[7]

Next morning, Monday 3 August, a third letter of resignation arrived. This came from John Morley, the Lord President of the Council. He was a venerable figure, having been in every Liberal Cabinet since 1886. In his letter, Morley explained his objection not only to the pledge given to France on Sunday but also to the government's foreign policy as a whole. The gulf in the Cabinet on this issue, Morley explained, arose from an 'essential difference between two views of Neutrality'.[8] This was a reference to a long-running quarrel – Morley and like-minded Radicals on the left of the Liberal Party had long complained that the 'Liberal Imperialists' (as the Liberal enthusiasts for Empire were dubbed) in the Cabinet were allowing Britain to be tugged in the wake of her Entente partners, Russia and France.

When the next Cabinet gathered at 10 a.m. on the Monday morning, there was great anxiety. Asquith gave the Cabinet a summary of the latest information on the international crisis. But then he turned gravely to the immediate issue – the survival or collapse of the Cabinet itself. He told his careworn colleagues that overnight two Cabinet ministers had sent in their resignation letters followed by a third that morning. Then, when Asquith paused, a fourth minister passed his resignation letter across the table – Earl Beauchamp, a leading progressive in the Lords. The government's own 'successive acts', he complained, had made war 'inevitable'.[9]

Four – from a Cabinet of nineteen men. One minister recalled that at that moment tears stood in Asquith's eyes. He explained that

such serious dissent was unprecedented during his six years as Prime
Minister. Moreover, he told his men, it was not just the Cabinet but
also the wider Liberal Party that was 'still hesitating' with regard to
the impending war.[10] 'Seems as if I shall have to go on alone', he
declared sardonically.[11] Lewis Harcourt (known to all as 'Loulou'),
the leading neutralist minister, recorded more of Asquith's words.
Beyond the four resigning ministers, Asquith knew that 'many
others' were 'uneasy'. He might well choose to resign. But he could
not face it, he told the hushed Cabinet. 'Dislikes and abhors a coalition', Harcourt jotted down in summary of Asquith's explanation.
He chose to stay, even if it was a 'most thankless task to go on'.[12]
It was all 'very moving', wrote Herbert Samuel, another prominent
Cabinet minister.[13]

'That is 4 gone!' Asquith wrote later that day to Venetia Stanley,
the latest young woman with whom the Prime Minister was infat-
uated – and upon whom he rained a deluge of love letters, even
during this crisis.[14] No one knew for certain if the four resignations marked the high point of rebellion, or if more would follow.
Would Grey, who was to speak in the Commons that afternoon, find
the words to contain the unrest in Cabinet? Or would he inflame
the situation by arguing for British intervention? If more ministers rebelled against the policy of backing France, the government
would probably crash. More were expected. Harcourt, the organiser
of the neutralist faction, believed he had up to eleven ministers in
his camp.[15]

In fact, just one more resignation came in the aftermath of Grey's
speech, from a junior minister, Charles Trevelyan. The young Radical
told the Prime Minister he was shocked to hear that Britain was
bound to support France if war exploded. Trevelyan explained that
his objection was 'fundamental'. The government had been wrong in
the essentials of its foreign policy.[16]

Thus, by the early evening of Monday 3 August, Prime Minister
Asquith faced a total of five resignations – four from his Cabinet plus
one more from his wider ministry. All five reflected long-standing
hostility to the 'policy of the Entente'.[17] The dissident ministers' resignations were not submitted – as is often mistakenly reported – in

protest against Britain entering the war. That came the following day, Tuesday 4 August.

The gravity of this domestic political crisis cannot be doubted. And yet, by the evening of the following day, Tuesday 4 August, it seemed to have vanished. The same Liberal Prime Minister and a few of his closest colleagues, in this same Cabinet room, made the final decision that took Britain into the war. At about 10.15 p.m. they agreed to summon a Privy Council at Buckingham Palace that was instructed to declare war upon Germany, effective from 11 p.m.[18]

Few in Britain realised that their government had come so near to disintegrating. The crisis was carefully hidden, because the resigning Cabinet ministers had agreed to keep silent, for the sake of appearances.[19] Moreover, the sensational events of Tuesday 4 August – the German invasion of Belgium in the morning and the British declaration of war upon Germany in the evening – immediately smothered the story of a Cabinet crisis.

Yet the event was truly singular. It had no parallel among the other nations. Nowhere else in Europe did ministers resign with the hot breath of war on their faces. Not at any level. Not in Berlin, Vienna, Budapest, St Petersburg, Paris, Brussels, or Belgrade. Only in London. And yet few historians have even noticed it.[20] Fewer still acknowledge it as a remarkable protest.[21] Those historians keen to get to battle generally ignore it. If Britain had rebels against the war, such historians imply, they must have been a mere handful of cockeyed eccentrics indulging in a quixotic folly. This is far from the truth.

Moral Superiority and National Unanimity

The story of Britain's 1914 is often told as a kind of heart-warming morality tale. It was from the beginning pitched as a deeply flattering narrative. The decision-makers themselves certainly asserted from the outset that Britain's choice for war was both unavoidable and ethical. 'Standing aside' – the phrase itself alluding to the biblical lesson about those who shamefully 'passed by on the other side' – was portrayed as a self-evidently immoral thing to do. 'I do not believe

any nation ever entered into a great controversy – and this is one of
the greatest history will ever know – with a clearer conscience.'[22] So
proclaimed Asquith on 6 August 1914, two days after the declaration
of war. His speech focused almost entirely on the German invasion of
Belgium. This crime, Asquith explained, morally validated Britain's
entry into the war. It was a chest-swelling moment.

Why this high moral tone? In part it followed from the reality
that Britain was making a more adventurous choice than the other
European nations. The leaders of the continental powers all preached
the urgency of self-defence, and all claimed they were standing ready
to repel an invasion by land. On the face of it, the situation of Britain,
the world's greatest sea power, was different. Threats to her territory
were less pressing. Indeed, in the opening days of the war the British
government decided to send the great bulk of British land forces out
of the country. Britain went to war across the water, so her leaders
insisted, to save others. Therefore, the moral basis of Britain's declaration – the necessity for Good to intervene against Evil – was asserted
with tremendous emphasis.

In supporting the choice for war, editorial writers, clerics, and
activists of all kinds followed this same high-minded line, designed
to minister to the feelings of all drawing-room moralists. It was a
high-spiced elixir. As Charles Montague, a leader writer at the time
for the *Manchester Guardian*, recalled, 'All the air was ringing with
rousing assurances. France to be saved, Belgium righted, freedom
and civilization re-won … What a chance!'[23]

In this atmosphere it was easy to take the next step and assert
that the nation was unanimous. Many boasted that this unanimity was to be seen everywhere. The Military Correspondent of *The
Times*, Charles Repington, supplied a classic assertion of the dazzling
impact of the Belgian factor in fusing this unanimity. The invasion
of Belgium, he wrote, cured 'Gladstonian Liberalism' of its hatred
of war and ensured that 'all doubts and differences vanished, and we
went into the war wholly united and in a good cause'.[24]

The newspapers supporting the choice for war asserted it too. *The
Times*, vehemently pro-war, insisted that from Monday 3 August
'all remains of doubt and hesitation vanished.'[25] There was 'general

unanimity' in the House of Commons in favour of war.[26] After war was declared the next day, *The Times* found the parliament with 'its unanimity still unimpaired'.[27] 'Public opinion stands with absolute unanimity behind the government in this' war', declared the *Scotsman*.[28]

Radical Dissent

If the nation was unanimous, it followed that those dissenting must have been a mere Radical underground – a contemptible rump of opinion. Some historians evidently think this was the case. One writes that protest against war 'seemed irrelevant and unrealistic, merely the negative warblings of the Little Englander in the wilderness'.[29]

Observers on the eve of war did not see it that way. On Thursday 30 July, the Radical MP Arthur Ponsonby, chairman of the Liberal Foreign Affairs Group (or LFAG), formed by Liberal Party dissidents on foreign policy, warned Asquith in a formal letter that 'nine tenths of the party' supported his group's stand.[30] George Mair, the lobby correspondent of the neutralist *Manchester Guardian*, estimated 'that four fifths of the Government's supporters associate themselves informally with the position of Mr Ponsonby'.[31] Asquith himself wrote privately to Venetia Stanley that 'three quarters' of his MPs were opposed to Britain's intervention.[32] Could this majority have repented of its convictions overnight?

If unanimity prevailed everywhere, then surely all the rebellious ministers would have recanted. Did they? Certainly, the invasion of Belgium fragmented the dissenting group. Two of the four Cabinet ministers who had resigned, Simon and Beauchamp, rejoined the Cabinet on Tuesday 4 August. But two others, Burns and Morley, refused all inducements to return. Did the dissenters – of either stamp – change their critical opinions? Faced with the horror of the German invasions of both Belgium and France in August 1914, did they revise their opinions? They did not.

So far as the British public was aware, John Morley, the most senior Liberal to resign, disappeared into obscurity. He told supporters he would keep 'an iron silence'.[33] He gave no defiant speeches in the Lords. But he told friends that the Liberal Imperialist ministers had behaved abominably.[34] This conviction was not dissolved by the German assault on Belgium. Ten days into the war he told C. P. Scott, owner and editor of the *Manchester Guardian*: 'The crash is terrible, whether we think of the ideals of your life or mine; or of individuals to whom we have attached and trusted; or of the Liberal Party; or of European Humanity.'[35] His disappointment with other Radicals who clung to the Cabinet never diminished.[36] 'I do not flinch a hair's breadth from the stand I took when I quitted the Cabinet', Morley told Andrew Carnegie, the millionaire peace activist, in November 1914.[37] To visitors to his home at Wimbledon, Morley revealed his deep contempt for Grey, who had made a 'mess' of foreign policy by turning Ententes into alliances.[38]

In 1928, five years after Morley's death, it was revealed that he had prepared a slender memoir on 1914. It was published as *Memorandum on Resignation, August 1914*. In this he complained that Asquith, Grey and Churchill had manipulated their colleagues in their eagerness to intervene. Morley dismissed the 'blaze about Belgium'. He accused the Liberal leaders of using the Belgian factor quite dishonestly, as a mere pretext to cover a previous commitment to intervene in any war on behalf of France, made before 1914, and confirmed on Sunday 2 August.[39]

John Burns was restrained in public. 'Me and Morley has decided to keep an iron silence,' he told friends.[40] He shared no doubts in the Commons. But his private writings dripped with venom. His diary was filled with bitter denunciations of those who had chosen war. On 2 August 1915 he recorded: 'A year ago today since I resigned. After a year's waste of blood and treasure I rejoice that I had the wisdom, courage and knowledge of what would happen to register by my resignation my objection to this gratuitous and wanton war.' He attacked those who had allowed the Entente with France to blossom into an alliance: 'This alliance was entered upon by a secret coterie behind the back of the Cabinet, without the knowledge of Parliament and to the surprise of the country.'[41] He never retreated. Ten years after the war Burns told visitors to his home he was still 'very proud' of his resignation. One recorded that 'He fished out his diary of 1914 & read us bits on the cabinet at the end of July ... "There's no blood on my doorstep!" he said quietly, but with terrific emphasis.'[42]

What of those ministers who had reversed their decisions, Earl Beauchamp and John Simon? On rejoining the Cabinet, Beauchamp revealed his lively misgivings to only a few. For example, on the first anniversary of the outbreak of war, Beauchamp told former Radical colleagues that he should have stayed out. Burns recorded the conversation: 'I am afraid he [Beauchamp] is sorry he did not leave with us as I knew he felt as we did but was only persuaded to stay against his better judgement by PM.'[43] By 1916, Beauchamp had joined those openly agitating for a negotiated end to the war.[44]

When he returned to the Cabinet, John Simon also did not abandon his long record of criticism of Grey.[45] In his resignation letter he had written that 'I cannot agree in the policy pursued.'[46] Rejoining the Cabinet, he wrote to Asquith that he did so 'with goodwill; though with a heavy heart'.[47] Simon was a model of discretion ever after. But he told C. P. Scott privately that he rejoined Asquith's Cabinet 'without in the smallest degree, so far as he was concerned, withdrawing his objection to the policy [of intervention] but solely in order to prevent the appearance of disruption in the face of grave national danger'.[48] The Radicals still counted Simon as one of their number, and they turned to him in 1915 to defend their rights to free speech.[49] As Trevelyan put it privately, Simon 'might easily have been on our side of the fence with another ounce weight of moral courage'.[50]

Charles Trevelyan was in fact the only departing member of the Asquith ministry to go public.[51] The unfolding tragedy in Belgium and France did not sway him. He moved quickly to open defiance. On 5 August he invited Edmund Morel, the greatest progressive agitator in Britain, to join him in forging a new organisation for the 'body of Liberal members united for common action on war questions.'[52] He sought out allies. At midnight on the day war was declared, Ramsay MacDonald from the Labour Party washed up at the chambers of Norman Angell, the internationalist publicist, 'threw himself into a chair', and pleaded with him to lead action against war.[53] Within days

Trevelyan brought these ardent spirits together. Trevelyan, Morel, Angell and MacDonald then launched a new body, to be called the Union of Democratic Control (UDC). Aiming at the democratic reform of British foreign policy, the UDC soon attracted hundreds of supporters.[54] Trevelyan never walked away from his denunciation of British action in July–August 1914.[55]

One more ex-minister is important to this story – Robert Reid, Lord Loreburn. He did not resign in 1914; he was already in retirement. As Lord Chancellor he had been in the Liberal Cabinets from December 1905 until withdrawing from active political life in June 1912. He had revolted with other Cabinet Radicals against Grey's secret commitments to France in 1911.[56] Loreburn was the angriest former insider of them all. His resentment against the Grey–Asquith faction was unflagging. From retirement, he had encouraged the leading Cabinet Radicals to oppose any commitment to a war for Entente solidarity.[57] Once war was declared, he maintained a public silence about his former Liberal colleagues' culpability. But he laced his private letters with passionate indictments.[58] In September 1914 he wrote to his friend Francis Hirst, editor of the *Economist*: 'My opinion about the subject of the war is exactly what it was. I deliberately say nothing because I feel so deeply the danger.' But his contempt was clear. 'The only thing to wish for as regards the Government is that these men should all cease to be Ministers … I feel it keenly that I was misled … For the present I can only say that I have done with the so-called Liberal Party, the Party I mean, not the principles which have been betrayed.'[59] After a year stifling his anger, Loreburn began to campaign openly for a negotiated peace in November 1915.[60]

Then, in 1919, Loreburn published *How The War Came*. In this he roundly condemned the Liberal Imperialists for their secret dealings. These had 'left the peace of Great Britain at the mercy of the Russian court'. In particular, he lashed out at Asquith and Grey for having stealthily contracted alliances in all but name. These, Loreburn claimed, had robbed Britain of true freedom of action in 1914. 'We went to war unprepared in a Russian quarrel', he concluded, 'because we were tied to France in the dark.'[61] Such was the opinion of the former Lord Chancellor, a man with seven years' experience inside the Liberal Cabinets.

The mutinous British ministers thus held firmly to their critical views. For them, neither Germany's behaviour in the crisis of 1914, nor the atrocities of war that followed, wiped the slate clean for the Asquith government.

A deep revulsion against those who had chosen war was felt far beyond the ranks of the ex-ministers who knew the inside story. A very significant segment of progressive opinion in Britain shared the recriminations. Many believed that a great deception had taken place. It is true that few resorted to public action, especially in the first months of the war. But stern critics could be found in the ranks of the Liberal Party, among the cream of Liberal journalists, among elder statesmen, in the Irish Parliamentary Party, in the Labour Party, and among politically active British women.

The idea that all Liberal MPs rallied to a man behind their leaders, once war was declared and German evil exposed, is fantasy. Only a day before Britain's declaration of war, sixteen of them had spoken in the Commons against Britain's intervention.[62] During August 1914, a core of up to twenty Radical MPs continued to meet at the House of Commons, with a watching brief to discuss tactics 'and expedite a speedy settlement'.[63] Many of these same MPs were privately devastating in their criticisms of Grey. Percy Molteno, a Radical MP, was typical. He wrote to a fellow South African Radical decrying the war as 'purely a diplomatists' war'. As Molteno explained, 'we have been dragged in quite unnecessarily and automatically by arrangements made with France years ago of which the House and the country knew nothing'.[64]

Some railed against the war in their local press. Richard Denman, a Radical MP from Carlisle, had a letter published on the day war was declared. Should Britain fight for 'Slavonic civilization'? he asked. 'I can only answer an emphatic "No." '[65] The invasion of Belgium led to no public retraction. A few days later he wrote again: 'I am unable to justify or even to defend, the action of the Government in declaring war upon Germany.' He denounced the decision to send the British Expeditionary Force (BEF) to the Continent. Belgium's independence and the security of the Channel ports 'were both obtainable by diplomacy'. 'I resent the hypocrisy of pretending that we are fighting because Germany has violated Belgian neutrality', he added. The government 'knew all along that for strategic reasons Germany was bound to take the course she has taken'.[66]

Charles Trevelyan, too, was openly defiant. He published his reasons for resignation. He seethed. In this crisis, he explained, Britain ought to have adopted at the outset 'an attitude of strict neutrality', because the quarrels in the Balkans and Eastern Europe were irrelevant. The 'racial struggle between Serbia and Austria', he wrote, was 'not worth to us the life of a single British soldier'. He charged the Asquith government with deception in asserting that Britain was 'unfettered' and then insisting on obligations of honour. 'And remember it is for Russia first and foremost that we are fighting.' For Trevelyan, the disgraceful German attack upon Belgium was not a sufficient cause for plunging into war: 'if France had committed the offence I think we should have found some protest sufficient short of plunging our country into war'.[67]

Some of the most respected opinion-makers in the Liberal press were white-hot in temper. On 8 August, Leonard Hobhouse informed his sister Emily that Grey's handling of the diplomatic crisis had been disastrous; he had failed either to rein in Russia or negotiate with Germany to save Belgium. 'As to Liberalism it died last Monday ... We may write Finis to our work.'[68] C. P. Scott wrote in late August that Grey had never seriously pursued 'close and cordial' relations with Germany. 'It seems plain now', he added, 'that while formally reserving his liberty Grey felt himself absolutely bound to France in case she were threatened.'[69] In November 1914, Francis Hirst told his sister that in essence the war had arisen from the fact that 'the Liberal Imperialist Junta practised a deception on the Cabinet'.[70]

In the Irish Party were more angry men. One of the most critical was John Dillon, deputy leader of the Irish Parliamentary Party. His recriminations were kept private, but they were deep. Two days into the war Dillon told his friend, the Irish newspaperman T. P. O'Connor, that 'the world is now reaping the bitter harvest of the Triple Entente and Grey's foreign policy which for years I have denounced to deaf ears.'[71] Similarly, Dillon confided to C. P. Scott that in his opinion the war was 'the greatest crime against humanity'. He confessed: 'I cannot help feeling that England must bear a considerable share of the responsibility.'[72] Dillon wrote to Wilfrid Scawen Blunt, a former diplomat and veteran critic of British imperialism, a series of letters full of contempt for Grey, the Foreign Office 'set', and *The Times* for 'engineering this combination against Germany'. 'It was bound to end in war', he raged.[73] For political reasons, he kept silent – but he told trusted friends that Britain's war was the fault of the policy of the Entente and the Liberals' foolish faith in Grey as a man of peace.[74]

Unable to keep silent was Ramsay MacDonald. As chairman of the Parliamentary Labour Party, he was a casualty of the crisis. He voiced dissent from the outset, in his speech to the House of Commons on Monday 3 August. He wanted the Labour Party to register a protest by abstaining on the vote of credit on Thursday 6 August. The Labour MPs defied their leader. MacDonald promptly resigned as chairman,[75] and immediately vented his contempt for Grey. He travelled north to address supporters in Leicester on Friday 7 August. Belgium was a pretext. 'We are fighting because we are in a Triple Entente', he told supporters.[76] Soon after, on 13 August, MacDonald repeated his charges against Grey in the *Labour Leader*.[77] In his diary he was even more scathing, denouncing Grey as 'the abject tool of Russia and of France, who looks so solid and wise and who is simply prejudiced and short-sighted'.[78] MacDonald's revolt had strong support in the Independent Labour Party (ILP).[79]

So, too, was Britain's women's movement riven on the war. When the leadership of the National Union of Women's Suffrage Societies (NUWSS) opted to accept the government's explanations, support the war, and oppose activism in pursuit of peace, mutiny was barely contained. The idea that Britain was absolutely in the right, so that women should simply focus on mitigating suffering, was soon fiercely contested. Between February and April 1915, half the executive of the NUWSS resigned in protest. Almost all the younger leaders – including Maude Royden, Catherine Marshall, Kathleen Courtney, and Helena Swanwick – walked out.[80]

Some retired senior politicians caught the stink of something very corrupt in Britain's actions in 1914. They questioned the excuses given out. Lord Eversley, a Liberal veteran from the Gladstone era, told Burns that the Liberal Imperialist war-makers' vainglory had lost 'a large section of the Liberal Party'. He blamed 'the secret negotiations and understandings' that had led to the 'disaster'. Britain was at war 'on behalf of a cause in which we have no concern'. Victory for Russia and France would be 'far more hostile to our permanent interests than defeat', he wrote.[81] Similarly, George W. E. Russell, another Liberal veteran, shared his private doubts far and wide. In December 1914, Russell told his friend Edmund Barton, the former Australian Prime Minister, that the Asquith government had deceived the parliament and people. 'I deplore the defect – as I think it – in our Constitution, which enables Ministers to tie us up into Treaties and "understandings", of which the Parliament and the nation know nothing.'[82]

Grey was a punching bag for critics who had long despised him. Wilfrid Blunt, who was well informed about the current government through a network of friends that included both Churchill and Margot Asquith, exploded with fury in his diary. 'So here we are faced with the full consequences of Grey's pig-headedness', he wrote. And for whom was Britain fighting? 'For Russia, the tyrant of Poland, Finland, Persia and all northern Asia. For France, our fellow brigand in north Africa, and lastly for Belgium with its abominable Congo record [,] and this is what we call English honour.' He wrote off Grey as 'a dangerous fool who has been playing a gambler's game'. He denounced the stomach-turning 'hypocrisy' of the government's stand.[83]

Of course, many others did revise their positions as the battles exploded across Europe in August 1914. For example, James Bryce, ex-ambassador to the United States and an active neutralist during the crisis, put the pragmatic position: 'Being in, we must go straight through.' But he confessed quite freely that 'it was the behaviour of Germany to Belgium that made the Liberal Party acquiesce'.[84] His choice of the word 'acquiesce' was telling. Many in the Liberal Party did exactly that – but acquiescence should not be confused with enthusiasm for war, nor is it evidence of unanimous support for an irresistible conflict.

Agony was the common emotion. Arthur Ponsonby, for example, left memorable testimony to his own heartsickness. Under moonlight in London on 12 August 1914, Arthur watched in desperate dismay as his brother, General Johnnie Ponsonby, departed for France at the head of his battalion of the Coldstream Guards. In his diary, Ponsonby described this 'utterly incredible' scene:

> The long expected European war has come ... A dozen or so diplomats, a score of ministers, and two or three monarchs have been offending one another, so to make things straight they have ordered out millions of peaceful citizens to go and get massacred. The Government have been telling us lies and we believed them. We were committed and we did not know it, so without being attacked or our own interests in any way threatened we joined in. It is an end of Liberalism, of social reform, of progress itself for the moment.[85]

So too 'Goldie' Dickinson, a leading international theorist from King's College Cambridge, spoke for many Liberal intellectuals. He gave memorable expression to a suffocating sense of both horror and powerlessness. Embarking on a summer holiday with friends beside the River Wye near Hereford in mid-August 1914, he was haunted by knowledge of the industrialised slaughter let loose across the Channel:

> As we sat by the river, in that marvellous summer, it seemed incredible what was going on over the water in France ... The perfect weather continued, and the dumb impotent feeling of the gulf between nature, the past, all beautiful true and gracious things and beliefs, and this black horror of inconceivability that nevertheless was true.[86]

TWO

Mixing Signals
Thursday 23 to Sunday 26 July

Happily there seems to be no reason why we should be anything more than spectators. But it is a blood-curdling prospect – is it not?[1]

H. H. Asquith, 24 July 1914

Britain's first responses to the Balkan crisis were strangely mixed. Both diplomats and Dreadnoughts were deployed. On the one hand, Grey launched a series of diplomatic mediations, and he called upon others to refrain from all military steps to give diplomacy its chance. On the other hand, Churchill launched an important naval initiative, with Grey's endorsement. The First and Second Fleets of the Royal Navy were concentrated, in an advanced state of readiness for battle. Britain appeared to be signalling her devotion to diplomacy – and her preparedness to face war.

The Balkan Tangle

Let us dip back briefly into the first days of the crisis. Following the assassination of the Archduke Franz Ferdinand and his wife Sophie on 28 June 1914, the British Foreign Office expected some kind of 'punitive expedition' against Serbia.[2] Grey seemed resigned to it.[3] Every imperial power indulged in this kind of chastisement. When on Monday 6 July the German ambassador, Prince Karl Max Lichnowsky, gave broad hints that Austria-Hungary contemplated 'military action', Grey sought only an assurance that no annexation would follow. Lichnowsky gave it readily.[4] In the words of Lichnowsky, Grey 'seemed to understand' that Austria-Hungary must take 'energetic measures'.[5] Two days later Grey telegraphed very briefly to Francis Bertie, British ambassador in Paris, explaining that 'some *démarche* against Serbia' was imminent, and adding that 'in such an event, we must do all we could to encourage patience in St Petersburg'.[6] In a further interview with Lichnowsky on 9 July, Grey told him that the Austrian 'action' should be 'kept within certain bounds' so that Britain, once again, could 'encourage patience at St Petersburg'. He reassured Lichnowsky also that he would model his diplomacy on that adopted during the Balkan crisis of 1912–13, and 'do [his] utmost to prevent the outbreak of war between the Great Powers'.[7] This was a reference to the Ambassadorial Conference in London that had met intermittently under Grey as chairman from December 1912 to August 1913. In that setting, Britain, France, Russia, Germany, Austria-Hungary and Italy had negotiated their way through the tensions arising from the two Balkan Wars of 1912–13.

Lichnowsky reported this interview optimistically to Berlin, noting Grey's assurances about muzzling Russia. But even by 15 July, Lichnowsky was more anxious, reporting that Grey might not be able to hold Russia back. He noted that Grey had again specified that 'everything would depend on what kind of intervention was contemplated by Austria and that under no circumstances ought Serbia to be expected to forfeit a part of her territory'.[8] Thus, in various diplomatic interviews in early July, Grey had given the impression that he would tolerate a mild punishment for Serbia, but no annexation, and would try hard to stop any escalation of the crisis.

Then came the Austro-Hungarian ultimatum to Serbia. It was delivered, with its forty-eight-hour deadline, in Belgrade, the Serbian capital, at 6 p.m. on the evening of Thursday 23 July. The timing was planned very carefully: it was intended to prevent close consultation between the Russians and the French on the matter. For a French state visit to Russia, involving long negotiations at the Peterhof Palace, was just concluding. Poincaré, the French President, and René Viviani, his newly elected Prime Minister who was also Minister of Foreign Affairs, were in fact hosting the Tsar and his family at a farewell dinner on board the new Dreadnought-class battleship *France* in Kronstadt, the great naval base near St Petersburg, when the ultimatum was presented in Belgrade. No news of it reached the *France* before the Tsar departed. The *France* promptly left Kronstadt, resuming a planned cruise to Sweden, Norway and Denmark. Poincaré and Viviani learned of the ultimatum from 'garbled radio messages' while cruising the Baltic the next day, Friday 24 July.[9]

Grey first got wind of the ultimatum to Serbia from an interview with Count Mensdorff, the Austrian ambassador, on Thursday 23 July. Grey advised against a tight time limit. It would 'inflame opinion in Russia'. He observed that it would be difficult now for him and others to preach 'patience and moderation' at St Petersburg. Memorably, he warned Mensdorff of the peril of a wider conflict. War between 'four Great Powers' would be 'terrible'. Significantly, the use of the phrase 'four Great Powers', implying just Germany, Austria-Hungary, Russia and France, appeared to exempt Britain. Grey warned of revolution following war. He hoped that Austria and Russia could discuss the quarrel 'directly with each other'.[10]

As promised, next morning, Friday 24 July, Mensdorff delivered a copy of the ultimatum itself. Grey remonstrated with Mensdorff again. But the merits or deficiencies of the Austrian case were 'not our concern', said Grey. 'It was solely from the point of view of the peace of Europe that I should concern myself with the matter, and I felt great apprehension.'[11] From that moment, Grey certainly recognised the potential risk of a wider war arising from the Sarajevo murders and absorbed himself in the diplomacy of the crisis.[12]

The Cabinet first learned of the crisis at its meeting at 10 Downing Street in the afternoon of the same day, Friday 24 July. It came at the end of an exhausting debate on strategy over Home Rule. Civil war in Ireland was shaping up as a very real possibility. The Buckingham

Palace Conference, seeking a compromise, had just broken up without success. Naturally, all ministers at the Friday Cabinet were chiefly preoccupied with Ireland. When that was dealt with, there was a rustle indicating impatience to leave. 'Grey checked a general movement to rise and go', Masterman, a rising young minister, told his wife later. Grey swiftly surveyed the problem in the Balkans created by the ultimatum, and pronounced the situation to be 'very critical'.[13]

Grey warned the ministers that the ultimatum 'had brought us nearer to a European Armageddon than we had been through all the Balkan troubles'. Grey explained that he had asked Cambon, and would shortly ask Lichnowsky, for support in ensuring that Germany, France, Italy and Britain would 'jointly press Austria and Russia to abstain from action'. The aim was to localise any combat. But, he remarked, 'if Russia attacked Austria, Germany was bound to come to the latter's help'. Intriguingly, Grey also observed that 'Italy had already asked him to pair the U.K. off against herself in a general row'.[14] Two features of this are noteworthy. First, Grey had discerned that the initial danger of escalation might well arise from Russia. Second, Grey had mentioned the possibility that Britain would remain neutral, with Italy – as a 'pair'. The word 'neutral' was in the air.

Grey's presentation grabbed Asquith's attention. Already he saw the potential for ruinous complications. In his now almost daily letter to Venetia Stanley, Asquith borrowed Grey's most telling phrase: he told her of the danger of the Austro-German and Franco-Russian alliance systems leading to 'a real Armageddon'. But he reassured her: 'Happily there seems to be no reason why we should be anything more than spectators.'[15]

Grey's consistently anti-German advisers had a very different view. Arthur Nicolson, the Permanent Under-Secretary, and Eyre Crowe, the Assistant Under-Secretary, maintained close contacts with Paul Cambon and Alexander Benckendorff, the French and Russian ambassadors. Over the next week, Nicolson and Crowe relayed advice from Albert Gate House, the French Embassy in Knightsbridge, and Chesham House, the Russian Embassy in Belgravia. The mantra was well rehearsed: 'solidarity' with France and Russia was vital; German efforts to divide the Entente must be repelled. Therefore, they advised against counselling caution at St Petersburg and Paris, and they excused all Russian military moves as merely prudent. Britain must 'stand by her friends', lest Britain expose her Empire to danger in the future.[16]

St Petersburg and Paris repeated the familiar tough-guy argument: only Britain's explicit threat to make war in common with Russia and France could deter it. The first significant cable relaying this message came on Friday evening 24 July. George Buchanan, British ambassador in St Petersburg, reported on a historic gathering. Sergei Sazonov, the Russian Foreign Minister, had summoned him on the Friday morning for a meeting at the French Embassy with Maurice Paléologue, the French ambassador. Describing the talks, Buchanan included at the outset a quick summary of the outcome of the recent French state visit to Russia. There was, Buchanan reported, a 'perfect community of views' between France and Russia. Moreover, the two allies were united in taking action in Vienna against any 'demand for explanations' directed against Serbia, or indeed any 'intervention in the internal affairs of Serbia'. Sazonov denounced the Austro-Hungarian ultimatum as 'immoral and provocative'. In response, Paléologue immediately offered to Sazonov unqualified assurances of France's readiness to assist Russia – not just diplomatic support, but a readiness to 'fulfil all obligations imposed on her by the alliance'.

Buchanan reported that Sazonov and Paléologue had then applied significant pressure upon him to fall into line. Sazonov urged 'solidarity'. At this point, Buchanan noted, he gently explained there was little hope that the British government would offer such a 'declaration of solidarity', certainly not to the point of 'force of arms'. 'We had no direct interests in Serbia, and public opinion in England would never sanction a war on her behalf', Buchanan stated. Sazonov shot back that this was only part of the larger European question from which 'we could not efface ourselves'. If war broke out, Britain would soon be 'dragged into it'. If Britain 'did not make common cause with France and Russia from the outset', she 'should not have played a "beau rôle"'. Then came a critical military detail: Sazonov confided that, while the Tsar and his Council of Ministers were yet to decide, he 'personally thought that Russia would at any rate *have to mobilise*'. Buchanan left this unchallenged. He simply recommended joint diplomatic action to secure more time. Buchanan clearly sympathised with Sazonov and Paléologue. He held out some hope to them, suggesting that Grey 'might be prepared' to warn both Berlin and Vienna that an Austrian attack on Serbia 'would in all probability force Russia to intervene'. Then, he had added, 'if war became general, it would be difficult for England to remain neutral'.[17]

Asquith's reaction to this cable is fascinating. While loyal to the Entente and to Grey, Asquith showed an awareness of the danger of Britain being sucked into war by provocative Russian action. Again impressing his lover, he sent a copy of Buchanan's revealing cable of Friday 24 July to Venetia Stanley, commenting that 'it shows the Russian view, & how even at this stage Russia is trying to drag us in'.[18] This telegram ended up in the files of Edwin Montagu, with all the sentences showing Russian pressure underlined in red.[19]

But reports along the same lines kept coming from Buchanan in St Petersburg. The Tsar's 'great disappointment' at Britain's reluctance to declare 'solidarity' immediately was painfully reported on Sunday 26 July. Buchanan also sought to steer Grey: he should make it clear to the House of Commons and the press that it was Austria, and not Russia, that was chiefly at fault.[20] On Tuesday 28 July, Buchanan again reported Sazonov's insistence – which Buchanan clearly backed – that the 'only way to avert war was for His Majesty's Government to let it be clearly known that they would join France and Russia'.[21] This was the standard line among Nicolson's handpicked officials and ambassadors.

Grey's advisers reinforced the theme. They blanched at every indication that Grey might 'shirk' it. As early as Saturday 25 July, Eyre Crowe all too candidly advised: 'The moment has passed when it might have been possible to enlist French support in an effort to hold back Russia.' Supposedly, just two days after the Austro-Hungarian ultimatum, it was too late to check Russia. Sweepingly, he counselled against '*any* representation at St Petersburg and Paris'.[22] Crowe's emphasis was constantly on the need for Britain to *follow* France and Russia immediately into war. By 30 July he advised:

> If and when, however, it is certain that France and Russia cannot avoid the war, and are going into it, my opinion, for what it is worth, is that British interests require us to take our place beside them as Allies, and in that case our intervention should be immediate and decided.[23]

It would be difficult to find more eloquent testimony to the reality underpinning the 'policy of the Entente': that Britain's ultimate decision for or against war would be taken *after* the decision-makers in Paris and St Petersburg had made it for her.

A Conference of Ambassadors

Grey's most well-known initiative at the beginning of the crisis was to recommend four-power mediation of the Austro-Serbian quarrel. Just as Grey had foreshadowed to Lichnowsky, the idea was to revive the London Conference of Ambassadors of 1912–13. So, in the afternoon of Sunday 26 July, the Foreign Office sent out telegrams to the Foreign Ministers of those powers considered *not* to be directly involved in the Austro-Serbian quarrel, that is, Italy, Germany and France. It asked them to instruct their ambassadors in London to meet with Grey and get mediation underway – and 'to request that pending results of [the] conference all active military operations should be suspended'.[24] Lichnowsky responded very quickly, announcing that the German government 'accepts your suggested mediation à quatre'.[25]

How did this idea get airborne? It is worth looking very closely at events associated with the proposed conference in London. For Grey himself was to place great stress on the Germans' eventual decision, two days later, to reject his proposal. He pushed it as the explanation for everything during the war. According to Grey, peace 'could perfectly easily have been found' through the conference, but Prussian militarism wanted war.[26] Much later in his memoirs he explained that he 'really felt angry' that the Germans had 'vetoed the only certain means of peaceful settlement'.[27]

In fact, Grey's *original* idea had not been a conference at all but rather bilateral negotiations between Austria and Russia.[28] When Buchanan himself put this forward in St Petersburg on 22 July, it was the visiting French President Poincaré who had complained that 'a conversation à deux between Austria and Russia would be very dangerous at [the] present moment'.[29] In London on the same day, Grey found Benckendorff reluctant too.[30] So, with the French and Russians apparently wanting London to butt out, Grey did not press the point.

News of the Austrian ultimatum brought matters to a head, of course. On Friday 24 July and Saturday 25 July, Grey began to tell the London ambassadors of a *second* proposal: that the four disinterested powers should simply counsel moderation at both Vienna and St Petersburg, and, in particular, urge that there be no crossing of frontiers, even after mobilisation.[31] Again Benckendorff was very doubtful. He told Grey that he disliked the whole idea of the four disinterested powers working together because it 'would give Germany the impression that France and England were detached from Russia'.[32]

On the Saturday, Grey also called in at Buckingham Palace. Significantly, King George V noted in his diary that Grey passed on Benckendorff's views. Grey, the King recorded, conveyed chilly pessimism: 'Had a long talk with Sir Edward Grey about Foreign Affairs. It looks as if we were on the verge of a general European war. Very serious state of affairs.'[33] If at this point Grey used the phrase 'verge of a general European war', and included the word 'we', it was remarkable. If so, perhaps he already believed that he had little power to keep Britain out. Then Grey left London. He went straight to his fishing lodge at Itchen Abbas in Hampshire in pursuit of salmon.

It was on the Sunday afternoon that Grey, while fishing at Itchen Abbas, received a *third* proposal, for an Ambassadors' Conference. Sir Arthur Nicolson, on duty at the Foreign Office on the Sunday, relayed the idea, as a suggestion from the Russian Foreign Minister, Sergei

Sazonov. Russia and Serbia, it seemed, would favour an appeal to the powers. It was, wrote Nicolson, 'the only hope of avoiding a general conflict'.[34] In mid-afternoon, Grey quickly agreed, and returned to his fishing, while the telegrams launching the Ambassadors' Conference were sent from the Foreign Office.

The motives of Nicolson, a devout Russophile, were complex.[35] Nicolson proposed British sponsorship of this conference as a way of demonstrating that Britain was *not* indifferent to the crisis, and certainly not 'detached' from Russia. He wrote to Grey from his home a personal letter late on Sunday explaining all. It was steeped in pessimism. Such a conference was 'the only chance of avoiding a conflict – it is I admit a very poor chance – but in any case we shall have done our utmost'. He also announced his conviction that 'Berlin is playing with us'. Backing this up, he reported on his meeting that afternoon at the Foreign Office with Mensdorff. The Austrian ambassador had mentioned Ambassador Lichnowsky's apparent confidence that 'we [Britain] could stand aside and remain neutral – an unfortunate conviction'. Nicolson, of course, was determined to frustrate any expectation of neutrality. Britain must make it clear she could not stand out, wrote Nicolson, 'when all Europe was in flames'. This might exercise 'a restraining influence' on Berlin, he advised.

In the same letter, Nicolson complained also of the visit of Prince Heinrich of Germany, the Kaiser's brother, to Buckingham Palace on Sunday morning. The Prince had broken off his yachting at Cowes, and rushed to London, to breakfast with King George V. They had a brief conversation.[36] When Nicolson lunched on Sunday with Lord Stamfordham, the King's secretary, he heard scraps of it. Prince Heinrich had expressed Germany's confidence that Russia would not risk war because 'if Russia moved there would be an internal revolution'. Nicolson dismissed this as 'nonsense'. The Prince's visit, he explained, was part of a German plot. The Germans, because they were planning war, were 'anxious' to foster the illusion 'that Russia will remain quiet and to spread [it] about that we will be equally quiescent – a foolish procedure'.[37]

Nicolson's private letter reveals much. Ever the Entente loyalist, he pounced upon any opportunity to squash German illusions that neither Russia nor Britain would fight. In Nicolson's mind – and in Grey's mind if it could be influenced – the proposal for an Ambassadors' Conference in London was not to be read as an indication of Britain's status as a disinterested power. Rather, it was to advertise her continental consciousness – and keep Germany guessing.

In any case, on Sunday 26 July, the proposal for an Ambassadors' Conference was up and running as Britain's first response to the crisis.

Weekend Retreats

Various British Cabinet ministers sought solace in the countryside over the weekend of Saturday 25 and Sunday 26 July. More troubles in the coming week were expected to arise from a predictable quarter – Ireland. It was still *the* issue. It was to his own weekend retreat, 'The Wharf', humbly tucked away in the village of Sutton Courtenay near Oxford, that the Prime Minister repaired with his family and a few close friends. On Saturday, Asquith walked by the Thames with Lady Ottoline Morrell, wife of Philip Morrell, a leading Radical. He told her that the quarrel between Austria and Serbia was not serious. Lady Ottoline preserved her impressions. Asquith 'did not seem worried'. He told her 'with a laugh' that the Balkan crisis would 'take the attention away from Ulster, which is a good thing'.[38]

But others were disturbed. Among the few guests that weekend was Edwin Montagu, a fixture in Asquith's family circle – and his rival for the affections of Venetia Stanley over the last two years.[39] Montagu mused on the potential for an escalation of the Balkan dispute. He 'feared it would lead to a world war'. He burst out as he paced the room: 'Of course, I suppose we shall have to go to war sooner or later with Germany about the Navy, and this may be a good time as any other – they are probably not so well prepared now as they would be later.' Morrell recorded the conversation that followed. When the subject of Belgium came up, Asquith gave his view that Britain was 'under no obligation' to assist the Belgians.[40]

Next morning, Lewis Harcourt, the Colonial Secretary, motored over to 'The Wharf' from his nearby grand residence, Nuneham Park, to discuss with Asquith the Cabinet meeting of the previous Friday. Naturally, the two men first discussed Ireland. Then, Harcourt turned the discussion to 'the probable Austro-Serbian War'. Speaking as a leading Radical, Harcourt warned the Prime Minister sharply. 'I told him', Harcourt recorded, 'that under no circ[umstance]s could I be a party to our participation in a European War.' He also cautioned him against entrusting anything to Churchill's judgement in this crisis:

> I warned him that he ought to order Churchill to move no ship anywhere without instructions from the Cabinet. I have a profound distrust of Winston's judgment and loyalty and I believe that if the German fleet moved out into the Channel (against France – not us) he would be capable of launching our fleet at them without reference to the Cabinet. The PM pooh poohed the idea – but I think he is wrong not to take this precaution.[41]

Harcourt's warnings to Asquith, of course, were confided privately. But on that same weekend John Simon gave public voice to the Radical view. Here at the start of the crisis, before Cabinet confidentiality on Britain's stance kicked in, Simon was quite definite as he addressed a meeting of Altrincham Liberals on the evening of Saturday 25 July. Simon asked his audience to resolve, with him, that 'whatever may be the difficulties and dangers which threaten peaceful relations in Europe, the part which this country plays shall *from beginning to end be the part of a mediator* simply desirous of promoting better and more peaceful relations.'[42]

In any case, Ireland immediately returned to centre stage. While ministers relaxed in the countryside, an explosion of violence in Dublin took place on the same Sunday. Three people were killed and thirty-eight wounded on Bachelor's Walk when troops from the King's Own Scottish Borderers fired upon a crowd following the landing of guns at Howth for the Irish Volunteers. The Labour and Radical press criticised the government for double standards, because the Ulster Volunteers had successfully landed a much larger number of guns at Larne in April 1914.[43] More bloodshed was an imminent danger.

The Concentration of the Fleets, Sunday 26 July

Over the same weekend of 25–26 July, there were significant developments at the Admiralty. The British Fleet was advanced to a state of readiness for war. Some background is vital here. That summer the British Navy had performed a test mobilisation. More than 400 ships took part, and these were assembled at Portland Harbour on the Dorset coast by 16 July. The exercise was concluded on Thursday 23 July, and the fleets were then scheduled to disperse. This was to have been completed by Monday 27 July.[44]

Churchill was ultimately responsible for a vitally important change in this schedule. While enjoying a brief 'paddling' holiday at the seaside in Cromer on the Norfolk coast over the weekend, at noon on the Sunday Churchill granted permission over the telephone to his First Sea Lord, Prince Louis of Battenberg, to take 'whatever steps' he thought necessary in light of the Balkan crisis – the Austrian ultimatum had expired on the Saturday. When Churchill did return to London at 10 p.m., he found that at 4.05 p.m. on the Sunday afternoon, Battenberg had indeed acted. He had ordered that no ships of the First Fleet or its attached Flotillas were to disperse from Portland. The 'stand-fast' order came 'at the eleventh hour' for Admiral Callaghan, Commander-in-Chief of the Home Fleets, but the dispersal was effectively halted. Thus, naval forces were held in an advanced state of readiness. The First Fleet was ordered also to complete stores of coal, and soon after the Second and Third Fleets received similar orders.[45]

That same evening Churchill walked around to his former house at 33 Eccleston Square, which Grey was renting. He sought Grey's support for the stand-fast order, and for a public announcement. According to Churchill, Grey agreed to a newspaper announcement on the Monday, so that it 'might have the effect of sobering the Central Powers and steadying Europe'.[46] This decision was, of course, defended as a measure designed to deter Germany and Austria without at the same time encouraging Russia and France to be reckless – logically unlikely, but steadfastly argued. It was a first instalment of British naval mobilisation. It came before any declaration of war or clash of arms, even in the Balkans. Most importantly, the decision to publicise the move flaunted Britain's loyalty to the Entente.

Was it really possible for such a measure to deter one side while not inciting the other? There was, plainly, no chance for the Cabinet to debate this. It was done – and formally reported in the press on Monday 27 July. There is no doubt that Churchill provided the drive here. Masterman remembered Churchill saying, 'I have ordered the Fleet not to disperse on my own responsibility. If the Cabinet disapprove, I am prepared to resign.'[47] Harcourt's warnings to Asquith were in vain.

The Russian and French ambassadors could hardly fail to read about the British naval move. *The Times* carried the report: 'Orders have been given to the First Fleet which is concentrated at Portland, not to disperse for manoeuvre leave for the present. All vessels of the Second Fleet are remaining at their home ports in proximity to their balance crews.'[48]

For good measure, Grey told Benckendorff, the Russian ambassador, the joyful news on the Monday – in one of his few interviews with Benckendorff during the crisis. As Grey put it, the naval initiative was intended to help deflect the charge that the Germans were being belligerent because they were certain Britain 'shall stand aside in any event'. Next day Grey spoke to Cambon on the subject. Cambon also 'expressed great satisfaction'. Grey told his ambassadors in St Petersburg and Paris to relay the news.[49] In this way Britain was sending mixed signals: she was attempting to mediate, certainly – *and* she was ready for war. *The Times* – stridently prointerventionist – hailed the naval move as exactly the 'earnest' signal required.[50]

What was its effect? Did it incite the wilder men to risk more? The biggest danger, of course, was that early naval moves on the part of Britain would serve as an incitement of Russia, inspiring her to act boldly in support of Serbia. For there were indeed those at St Petersburg determined to reverse Russia's humiliations in 1908 (when Russia had been forced to accept Austria's annexation of Bosnia-Herzegovina) and in 1913 (when Serbia, Russia's protégé, had been forced to give up some territorial gains from the First

Balkan War). Russia's most dangerous initiative was already under way, as decided upon by the Council of Ministers on Friday 24 July, 'a *secret* large-scale mobilisation of Russia's army – and its navy'.[51] And the key French decision-makers were falling upon their faces in servility to the Russian alliance. As one historian puts it, the French were acting 'as if the nation had no options at all'.[52] Desperate for a speedy Russian attack upon Germany in the event of war, the French exercised no brake upon Russia. As Trachtenberg writes, 'Russia, in fact, had effectively been given a blank check.'[53]

The French response to the British naval move can be easily traced. As mentioned above, Poincaré and Viviani were aboard the battleship *France* on Friday 24 July. Here they studied cables giving details of the Austro-Hungarian ultimatum. The two men came to the crisis from different perspectives. Poincaré, believing passionately in the need to fortify the Franco-Russian alliance, was concerned that Russia might show weakness by not backing the Serbs. Viviani, a left-republican, was less belligerent. He had been Prime Minister only since mid-June. On this trip he had been unwell, and was slow to resist Poincaré's dominance. Every key decision was taken, as Poincaré wrote in his diary, 'on my advice'. The first telegram from the *France* to St Petersburg on 24 July was practical. It urged Serbia to accept as many terms as possible consistent with her independence, advised that more time be sought, and suggested an international investigation of the assassination to avoid a humiliation for Serbia. News of the diplomatic break between Austria-Hungary and Serbia – the prelude to war – reached the *France* when it berthed in Stockholm on Saturday 25 July. First reports from Paléologue in St Petersburg disappointed Poincaré. Sazonov appeared to be prepared for mediation of some kind. There was no news on Russian military measures. Poincaré described Sazonov's attitude as an 'abdication'. In irritation he wrote, 'We can assuredly not be more Slav than the Russians.'[54]

Then, as the *France* headed for Copenhagen on the morning of Monday 27 July, Poincaré decided that he must embolden the Russians – and he took heart from diplomatic telegrams describing the British stance. Poincaré highlighted one telegram showing that, in response to German pleas for localisation of war, 'Sir Edw[ard] Grey gave a firm reply that if war breaks out in the east, no nation could avoid being implicated.'[55] This stimulated Poincaré. Claiming that Grey was showing 'firmness' – his watchword – Poincaré prodded Viviani into sending another telegram at noon. 'I point to this firmness as an example to Viviani', he wrote in his diary. He pleaded with Viviani to authorise a telegram to St Petersburg promising the Russians that 'France will second her action.'[56] So the telegram was sent. It assured the Russians that France saw the need for the two allies to 'affirm their perfect *entente*' and that France was 'prepared, in the interests of general peace, *to back fully the action of the imperial government*'.[57] Only 'firmness', Poincaré maintained, could save the Franco-Russian alliance, save the Tsar's government from its internal troubles, and save Sazonov – who might be replaced if Serbia was humiliated.[58]

On the same day, Monday 27 July, the government in Paris contacted the *France* and requested that the remainder of the cruise be abandoned. The French decision-makers were returning to Paris.

THREE

'Apparent Indecision'
Monday 27 July

Our influence for peace depended on our apparent indecision.[1]
Charles Hobhouse, 27 July 1914

'Behind this catastrophe there lies what surely must be the briefest chapter of diplomatic history in European records.'[2] Such was the verdict of one Radical editor. Indeed, many at the top in Britain experienced the crisis as quite overwhelmingly rapid. On Monday 27 July, war was just wind in the rafters. A week later, on Monday 3 August, Grey would make the case in the House of Commons for British intervention in a European war. The next day, Britain would declare war. How did it happen that the last great Liberal Cabinet in British history chose war so quickly in 1914?

Nineteen Liberal ministers sat in the Asquith Cabinet in the last week of July 1914. There were some very famous names among them: Prime Minister Asquith, Edward Grey, David Lloyd George, Winston Churchill, Richard Haldane, and Herbert Samuel. Which way did the Liberal ministers lean? Who were the immoveable Entente loyalists? Who were the firm neutralists? Historians differ in their counting of heads – as did the ministers themselves. However, most agree that, at the beginning of the crisis, a clear majority of ministers, probably eleven of the nineteen, were leaning decisively against Britain's intervention in a European war.[3]

To understand how these men jumped in 1914, we have to unearth some earlier quarrels from their collective memory.

Cabinet Revolts, 1911–14

Britain had come near to war in July 1911, when Britain backed France in a dispute with Germany over Morocco – the so-called Agadir crisis. It had shocked the Radical faction. Walter Runciman told Harcourt it was time to 'check the mad desire for war which has overtaken some even reliable politicians'.[4] Then it was revealed that Grey had authorised 'military conversations' with the French as early as 1906. These 'conversations' had been hidden from the majority of the Cabinet.[5] The government's inner circle had carelessly allowed these exchanges with the French to blossom, fostering firm expectations in Paris of British military assistance in any crisis. Soon it was known that on 23 August 1911 the Committee of Imperial Defence (CID) had actually discussed the details of despatching the British Expeditionary Force to France. Outraged at this, Morley wrote to Harcourt: 'They must surely be mad. A very short Cabinet will pulverize them.'[6]

In fact, two long Cabinet meetings were required, in early November 1911. The Radical faction – a majority led by Morley, Harcourt, Runciman, Burns, Loreburn and Reginald McKenna – won a complete victory. Morley fumed that it was time for the Cabinet to 'tell Fr[ance] that we can't give her military help at the commencement of a war'.[7] After long debate, Asquith, Harcourt, Morley and Loreburn negotiated on a double-barrelled resolution for the Cabinet. First, it was agreed that 'no communications should take place between the General Staff here and the staffs of other countries which can directly or indirectly commit this country to naval or military intervention'. Second, any 'conversations' about war operations must have the 'previous assent of the Cabinet'.[8] Henceforth, the Cabinet's supremacy was secure – or so the Radicals believed.

But less than a year later the Cabinet was rocked again. This time the dispute originated with the First Lord of the Admiralty, Winston Churchill. Appointed only in October 1911, Churchill had decided to reduce British naval forces in the Mediterranean and concentrate strength in the North Sea, against Germany. The Cabinet debated his proposals over three months. In the House of Commons on 22 July 1912, Churchill finally announced the changes. But, critics asked, was this redistribution of naval forces being *coordinated* with France? In fact, a new draft 'Anglo-French Naval Agreement' had been drawn up. It was presented to the French naval attaché, the Comte de Saint-Seine, on 23 July 1912 – the day after Churchill's address in the House. According to this document, the French and British navies divided their responsibilities in the Channel and the Mediterranean. But there was a crucial addition to the document: a political pre-amble, inserted by Churchill. It aimed to dispel any suggestion of a British obligation to fight in a French war. It specified that the move-ments of the fleets were being 'made independently'.[9] Britain would retain her 'freedom of choice', Churchill assured Asquith and Grey. In a crisis, Britain could not be accused of 'bad faith' by France 'if [and] when the time comes to stand out'.[10]

Still, the suspicion that Britain was being further entangled haunted the Cabinet discussions. The Radicals saw ghastly portents of war. During the debates in the Cabinet on 15 July, Harcourt led the Radical charge. 'I spoke very strongly against "conversations" with French attachés except on express declaration that we are in no way committed', he wrote in his Cabinet journal. Grey offered to draft a form of words for a letter to Paris specifying 'that renewal of con-versations does not *commit* either party to joint action without [the] decision of Gov[ernmen]t at [the] time'.[11] But Grey complained later that the Radicals wanted 'to cold-shoulder France'.[12]

Compromise followed. Grey and Harcourt agreed that a formal letter should be despatched to Paris. They negotiated over the wording, from July to November 1912.[13] The objective of the Radicals in these exchanges was clear: to avoid any suggestion that Britain had con-tracted moral obligations to France. During debates in Cabinet, one minister sketched a cartoon depicting two figures, a crouching frog surveying a crouching lion, under the caption 'FROGGY WOULD A WOOING GO'.[14] In this strange atmosphere, Grey's formal letter was finalised. Harcourt proudly recorded that it *makes it clear that we are not committed to any common action*.[15]

The letters were formally exchanged between Grey and Cambon in November 1912. Grey's letter included the essential phrases demanded by the Radicals. It was specified that military consultation 'does not restrict the freedom of either Government to decide at any future time whether or not to assist the other by armed force'. The recent naval moves were mentioned specifically: 'The disposition, for instance, of the French and British fleets respectively at the present moment is not based upon an engagement to co-operate in war.' Finally, it was acknowledged that if either nation faced 'an unprovoked attack by a third Power', then they would 'take in to consideration' the plans of the General Staffs.[16]

It had taken four months of negotiation, but the Radicals were more than happy with the outcome. There was only one disappointment. Harcourt had recommended in Cabinet that the Cambon-Grey letters should be shared with the newly appointed German ambassador, Prince Lichnowsky, and 'eventually published'.[17] Grey appears to have quietly ignored this. Thus, the letters remained an 'unpublished agreement'. But the Radicals believed they had saved Britain's 'free hand'.

A 'devil of a row' erupted again during the winter of 1913–14.[18] This time tempers frayed over Churchill's determination to boost naval spending to over £50 million for 1914–15. Lloyd George led the 'economists' against Churchill,[19] complaining that Churchill was 'like a man who buys Rolls Royce motor cars and dines at the Carlton with other people's money'.[20] So serious was the quarrel that Asquith contemplated dissolving the parliament to avoid a 'smash-up & resignation'.[21] Asquith noted that Simon, Samuel, Beauchamp and Hobhouse were 'aggressive' for economies, and he was struck by the 'hostility & suspicion Winston excites'.[22] In the compromise eventually struck, Churchill got his money, with only minor concessions – as Asquith had persuaded Churchill to 'throw a baby or two out of the sledge' to satisfy 'the critical pack'.[23]

To summarise, by 1914 Asquith had learned that the factions inside his Cabinet were 'miles apart' when they debated issues of foreign policy and defence.[24] On the one side were the interventionists. They were unfalteringly loyal to the Entente in diplomacy, and favoured the despatch of a British Expeditionary Force to the Continent in war. On the other side were the neutralists. Some wanted cuts in the navy. But not all. Some Liberals favoured a 'big navy' as the best argument against a 'continental commitment' and conscription.[25] The common ground for the neutralists was a demand that there be no subservience toward France and Russia as Entente partners, and a continuing effort to find a reconciliation with Germany.

The Cabinet Interventionists

Eight ministers were likely to agree to a British intervention in a continental war, essentially for reasons of solidarity with Britain's diplomatic partners, France and Russia – especially if their innocence in any crisis situation was clear. These eight included some of the most powerful men in the Cabinet. First, the group included three dyed-in-the-wool Liberal Imperialists from the Right of the party, Herbert Asquith (Prime Minister and, since March 1914, Secretary of State for War), Sir Edward Grey (Foreign Secretary), and Viscount Haldane (the Lord Chancellor, a former Secretary of State for War). To the circle of interventionists must be added two more recent converts to the 'policy of the Entente', Winston Churchill (First Lord of the Admiralty), and Charles Masterman (Duchy of Lancaster). Finally, inside this group there were three men whose loyalty to Grey and Asquith weighed heavily. In this moderate camp were Augustine Birrell (Chief Secretary for Ireland), Lord Crewe (India Office), and perhaps Reginald McKenna (Home Office).

It was a stronger possibility still that all in this group would advocate British intervention if Germany threatened Belgium in war. In this context, it is important to note that a German invasion of Belgium in any western conflict was widely anticipated in London among the political class. Since at least the summer of 1911, this had been discussed quite openly as a probability among leading men in Britain, both Liberal and Conservative.[26]

Asquith himself was personally devoted to Grey. He would back him in any crisis, even though he had his own doubts over Russia.[27] Moreover, he was personally alienated from many of the neutralists – 'our extreme peace lovers'.[28] He would describe them as pursuing 'the *Manchester Guardian* tack'. That paper's editor, C. P. Scott, was a former MP and rival whom he had long disliked.[29]

McKenna's situation is worth explanation. As First Lord of the Admiralty from 1908 to 1911 he had favoured the 'big navy'. But, like his naval chiefs, he disapproved of plans for continental intervention. In October 1911, Asquith decided to move against McKenna, and to replace him as First Lord of the Admiralty with the more pugnacious Churchill. McKenna was transferred to the Home Office. The move was widely seen as payback for McKenna's defiance of the 'continentalists'.[30] From that point, McKenna was linked to the Radicals – but on the margins. For he was fatalistic. He wrote later: 'When the issue of our intervention was first raised I had no doubt that we were committed to France, and that in the event of war being declared between France and Germany we should join in.'[31]

Churchill's situation was complicated too. The former Tory had been a Radical when he first joined the Liberal Cabinet. After his appointment to the Admiralty, he was a changed man. His noisy advocacy of increased naval spending exasperated many. Margot Asquith could not keep pace with his 'extraordinary changes of conviction'. She thought him 'pathetically ungrown-up'. In May 1913, both Herbert and Margot Asquith accompanied him on a tour on board the Admiralty yacht *Enchantress*. Soon Margot had had enough: 'His vanity is a canker: it spreads and destroys.' The Prime Minister's opinion was milder: '*no* one will ever have confidence in him'. Margot also recorded in her diary one memorable instance of his devotion to the navy. Taking the salute from battleships at Malta, Churchill declared: 'Isn't it fine Margot? It's a priesthood! That's what it is this service.'[32]

Churchill confounded his former Radical colleagues with his new trigger-happy enthusiasms. He surprised a Cabinet in April 1913 by announcing his own support for conscription.[33] His colleagues ribbed him that he supported the Channel Tunnel only in order 'to land troops in France without the cooperation of the Admiralty'.[34] His fascination with weaponry repelled the Radicals. When Morley expressed doubt over his proposal to mount an air attack on tribesmen in Somaliland in March 1914, Churchill denounced this as 'pious sentiment' and scribbled a note to him: 'In politics vice & violence always prosper & the path of virtue is hedged with anxious thorns.'[35] Runciman complained that Churchill's 'real blood feeling' for armaments was a 'sincere unembarrassed declaration of faith as well as policy'. Runciman dubbed him 'this brilliant unreliable Churchill who has been a guest in our party for eight & a half years'. By 1914, his Radical critics wished he would go.[36]

The Cabinet Neutralists

On the other side of the argument were men determined to resist the idea that Russia and France were Britain's 'allies' – an assumption which they suspected lurked behind the mask of Entente. As Morley told McKenna in 1912: 'My own mind is quite made up. No alliance, with or without a mask.'[37] Who were these convinced neutralists? How many were there? Churchill, writing in his memoirs, was sure that the neutralists made up at least 'three quarters' of the Cabinet in 1914.[38] In his memoirs, Grey thought the Radicals 'sufficient in number and influence to have broken up the Cabinet'.[39]

The man most familiar with mustering the neutralist faction was Lewis Harcourt. Morley recalled that during the crisis of 1914 'Harcourt had been busy in organising opinion among his Cabinet colleagues in favour of neutrality.'[40] Harcourt's private memoranda on Cabinet meetings show that at various points in the crisis he tallied up his men. On Monday 27 July he listed eleven names as pledged disciples in the 'Peace party', in this order: Lewis Harcourt (Colonial Office); John Morley (Lord President); Walter Runciman (Agriculture); T. McKinnon Wood (Scotland); 'Jack' Pease

(Education); Reginald McKenna (Home Office); Lord Beauchamp (Commissioner of Works); John Burns (Trade); John Simon (Attorney General); Charles Hobhouse (Postmaster General); and Augustine Birrell (Ireland). He added two more names as 'probably' inside his camp, Herbert Samuel (Local Government), and Charles Masterman (Duchy of Lancaster), because both were Radicals in domestic policy. That made a total of thirteen.[41] Two days later, he claimed that only nine of these were so solid they were likely to resign with him on the issue of neutrality.[42] Most notably, Lloyd George, the Radical celebrity, at least on domestic issues, did not appear on any list. He was still suspect. Most Radicals believed that his belligerent 'Mansion House speech' at the time of the Moroccan crisis in July 1911 had revealed him to be a strong interventionist – with just a gambler's eye on the main chance.

But, as can be seen, there was some unpredictability. For instance, both camps counted Birrell and Masterman. Moreover, several on Harcourt's list were wavering. Runciman appears to have played something of a double game. In touch with the Radicals throughout the crisis, he later claimed that 'Grey, Pease, Churchill, Crewe, Asquith and me held what may be called the Grey-Asquith view.'[43] Samuel was pessimistic about a major European war. As early as Sunday 26 July he wrote to his mother that 'since Friday night I have felt it probable that by the end of this week, Europe may be engaged in, or be on the brink of, the greatest war for a hundred years'.[44] And Britain's position? 'I hope that our country may not be involved', he wrote. 'But even of that one cannot be sure. At this stage I think it will not be.'[45] This was scarcely rock-solid conviction.

The Times, the Cabinet, and the Balkan Crisis

The first meeting of the Asquith Cabinet to discuss the Balkan crisis at any length was held in the early evening of Monday 27 July. Casting a shadow over it was a very controversial leader entitled 'Europe and the Crisis' that had appeared in *The Times* that morning. In this editorial Lord Northcliffe, the greatest of the press barons,

challenged the Cabinet on the Balkan affair. The politicians could
not ignore him.

The composition of this particular editorial had caused some controversy at Printing House Square, the main building of *The Times* at
Blackfriars, on the Sunday evening. There had been a fierce dispute
over authority. Geoffrey Dawson was chief editor of *The Times*.[46] But
Dawson was out of London on this day, leaving George Freeman, his
deputy editor, in command. However, according to Henry Wickham
Steed, the foreign editor and a Northcliffe favourite, Northcliffe
himself telegraphed *The Times* on the Sunday asking Freeman to
allow Steed to write a special editorial on the crisis. Conflict erupted
between Steed and the chief leader-writer John Woulfe Flanagan. In
an atmosphere of great tension Steed's editorial took shape.[47]

There is no doubt that Steed fashioned the editorial to reflect
Northcliffe's dogged anti-Germanism and his own conviction that
Britain must intervene in any war. Britain's agonising between peace
and war, he wrote later, produced 'a period of crisis severer than any
through which the British people had passed since the Napoleonic
era'.[48] Steed seized his opportunity to boom a policy of absolute
loyalty to Britain's 'friendships':

> Our friendships are firm, as our aims are free from all suspicion of
> aggression. While we can hope to preserve peace by working with
> the Great Powers who are not immediate parties to this dangerous
> quarrel, we shall consider that end above all else. But should there
> arise in any quarter a desire to test our adhesion to the principles
> that inform our friendships and that thereby guarantee the balance
> of power in Europe, we shall be found no less ready and deter-
> mined to vindicate them with the whole strength of the Empire,
> than we have been found ready whenever they have been tried in
> the past. That, we conceive, interest, duty, and honour demand
> from us. England will not hesitate to answer to their call.[49]

From the moment this inflammatory editorial appeared in *The
Times*, the extreme interventionist position was on the table. It
appalled advocates of neutrality. C. P. Scott and John Dillon, for

example, agreed about its 'monstrous character'.[50] Radical MPs were concerned *The Times* might be seen as speaking for the government. Edmund Harvey, for example, wrote to his father on 30 July that 'the articles in *The Times* must do harm abroad'.[51] Thus, among the 'surfeit of problems and worries' assailing Asquith as the crisis opened was the pugnacity of *The Times*.[52]

Before turning to the Cabinet's reactions, we must note Grey's first announcement on the crisis in the House of Commons. In the mid-afternoon of Monday 27 July, Grey offered a 'short narrative' of the Balkan tangle – in just over 700 words. This was in fact the most information he was to give the Commons during that whole week. In essence, he told the Commons of his first diplomatic initiative, on Friday afternoon 24 July, to urge that the four Powers 'not directly interested in the Serbian question' – Germany, France, Italy and Britain – should press both Vienna and St Petersburg 'to suspend military operations while the four Powers endeavoured to arrange a settlement'. He then outlined his more precise proposal on the Sunday – the Ambassadors' Conference. Grey explained that he was awaiting 'complete replies' to his invitations.

There was some interest in Grey's more general remarks about the crisis. But he gave no clues to British action should war erupt. He made no mention of the British naval orders issued overnight – the holding together of the First and Second Fleets. This move, of course, was publicised in the newspapers. He did not grandstand about Britain's readiness to fight for 'our friends', as *The Times* had done. On the other hand, he did not rebuke *The Times*. And most significantly, he did not dismiss the quarrel in Eastern Europe as arising from a bad cause – the assassination – and therefore of no interest to Britain. He declared that if relations between Austria-Hungary and Russia 'became threatening, the question would then be one of the peace of Europe: a matter that concerned us all'. This was the line that encouraged the Russians and the French. Crucially, as many Radicals noted, he did not rule out a British military response of any kind – he simply made no mention of it.[53]

Two hours later the ministers on the front bench moved down to Asquith's room for a rare Cabinet meeting at the House of Commons.

It lasted just an hour. Ireland took precedence. The ministers discussed in a 'desultory way' the problem of gun-running. To give time for parliamentary tempers to settle, the Cabinet resolved to postpone consideration of the Amending Bill to the Home Rule Bill from the coming Tuesday to the Thursday.[54]

This left only minutes to consider the Balkans. Accounts of the discussion vary a good deal. Did Grey put the Cabinet under pressure immediately, as Morley later suggested? Probably not.[55] In Grey's memoirs he explained that he knew at an early point 'that to press the Cabinet for a pledge to France would be fatal'. So instead he urged both factions 'to work together for the one object on which both were heartily agreed, to prevent a European war.'[56]

Grey explained to the Cabinet his mediation proposals. Pease, in his diary, recorded Grey criticising the 'unreasonable' Austrian attitudes, which showed his instincts. Then Grey explained his policy: he was 'anxious not to disclose that as [a] Gov[ernme]nt we intended if possible to keep out of all war, lest his influence as mediator might be thereby diminished'.[57] In this way, Grey implied that he and the neutralists were not so far apart – keeping out of the war was the common goal. But, while the Radicals might prefer an unequivocal disavowal of war, Grey insisted that doubt helped him as a mediator. Grey did alert the Cabinet to pressures arising from French and Russian expectations – Morley says he read to the Cabinet a telegram from Buchanan showing Russian pressure – but Grey did not barrack for solidarity.[58]

In his diary, Hobhouse summarised Grey's case:

If she [Britain] kept aloof from France and Russia we should forfeit naturally their confidence forever, and Germany would almost certainly attack France while Russia was mobilising. If on the other hand we said we were prepared to throw our lot in with the Entente, Russia would at once attack Austria. Consequently our influence for peace depended on our apparent indecision.[59]

The Cabinet was impressed. As Samuel informed his wife Beatrice after this Cabinet meeting, he was 'inclined to be pessimistic about

the outlook', but he conceded that 'we are doing our best to localise the conflict'.[60] Harcourt was confident in Grey: 'Grey is working
hard for peace and not belligerent.'[61]

Churchill then dominated. He reported that he had met the
German shipping magnate Albert Ballin, the Kaiser's confidante, at
the home of the banker Ernest Cassel on Friday evening 24 July.
Churchill dwelt on one aspect of his conversation. Ballin had asked
Churchill directly 'if England w[oul]d remain neutral if Germany
promised when she defeated France to take no French soil but only
some of her colonies'. This put the worst face on the exchange.
Expressed this way, Ballin appeared as the emissary of German plot-
ters, intent on aggression and trying to buy Britain off. In fact, Ballin's
mission was prompted by press leaks of Anglo-Russian naval conversations. This was the heart of the discussions as he met with various
British politicians in London that week. Ballin's report to Berlin was
focused on the assurances he had been given – untruthful assurances
– that Britain had no intention of making a naval convention with
Russia.[62] But Churchill's tale wrong-footed the Radicals. They could
scarcely push for neutrality on Britain's part if it appeared to be at
German prompting, and at France's expense. Harcourt reacted pre-
dictably: 'I said it was inconceivable that we should take part in a
European war on a Serbian issue, but still more inconceivable that
we should base our abstention on such a bargain.'[63] Clearly Churchill
was eager to discredit neutrality as dishonourable – always a German
snare to facilitate aggression. Grey would soon do the same.[64]

Perhaps Churchill's depiction of Ballin's approach as clearly dishonourable helped him notch up a clear win with regard to the
naval initiative he had taken on Sunday. Retrospectively, the Cabinet
endorsed the stand-fast order. 'The action of the First Lord in postponing the dispersal of the First and Second Fleets was approved',
as Asquith advised the King.[65] Of course, it was simply a done
deed, already publicised in the press, and reported to the Entente
ambassadors. It would have been extremely difficult for the Cabinet
to overturn.

The most important result of the Cabinet meeting was its endorsement of Grey's policy of deliberate ambiguity. Undoubtedly it

appealed because it put off potential squabbles. Asquith depicted it as strictly even-handed. He told the King as much: the Germans were urging Britain to declare that 'in no conditions' would she come into war, in order to dissuade Russia; the Russians were urging Britain to declare unconditional 'solidarity', and threatened to declare Britain's friendship 'valueless' unless she did so. Under Grey's policy of deliberate ambiguity, Britain would do neither thing. Asquith explained also that this Cabinet had decided to postpone any discussion of 'our precise obligations in regard to the neutrality of Belgium'.[66] It was clever, and expedient. The politically safer course at home, preserving Cabinet unity, matched the diplomatically safer course abroad, preventing war. Inscrutability on Britain's part was best. It might dissuade both sides in Europe from risky action. Ambiguity and postponements preserved Cabinet unity – for the moment.

FOUR

Manoeuvring in the Dark
Monday 27 and Tuesday 28 July

After the Cabinet I had talks with several colleagues in order to form a Peace party which if necessary shall break up the Cabinet in the interest of our abstention. I think I can already count on 11.[1]

'Loulou' Harcourt, 27 July 1914

Soon after the Cabinet meeting of Monday 27 July, the Cabinet factions began to manoeuvre and polarise. The Radicals met together, looking for a stronger commitment to a strictly neutral diplomacy. The Liberal Imperialists on the Right of the Cabinet made plans in the opposite direction, for a drive in favour of greater 'preparedness'. The public policy of 'apparent indecision' only temporarily veiled this growing divide.

The Radicals' Push for Neutrality

For the Radicals, the Cabinet on Monday 27 July 1914 had included some painful revelations. Harcourt was disappointed that Asquith had not followed his advice so emphatically given on Sunday at Sutton Courtenay – no naval moves pre-empting Cabinet. Churchill, with Grey at his side, had done exactly that. 'Apparent indecision' was all to the good, but Churchill had compromised it already. Harcourt's record of the Cabinet meeting shows a mood of resignation about a local war in the Balkans. 'It looks as if war there were certain. But will Russia come in: followed by Germany and France[?]', he mused in his Cabinet journal.[2] In this context, the neutralists hankered for something more definite: the Liberal leaders should rule out the possibility of Britain being sucked into war over an obscure quarrel in the Balkans.

After the Cabinet was over, Harcourt rallied his men in his room at the House. They shared their disquiet over the Cabinet meeting, and the odd mixture of diplomatic mediation and advanced naval preparation then under way. Harcourt was ready to contemplate drastic action. 'After the Cabinet I had talks with several colleagues in order to form a Peace party which if necessary shall break up the Cabinet in the interest of our abstention.' How many stood with him? 'I think I can already count on 11', Harcourt wrote.[3]

Certainly Morley was thinking along the same lines. At the Privy Council Office the next day, he told his friend Sir Almeric FitzRoy, the Council's Clerk, that if Britain's preliminary preparations were followed by actual mobilisation he would resign. Morley pleaded that he could not tolerate Britain joining 'a Slavonic movement against Teuton influence'. Russia represented 'barbarism'.[4]

Most importantly, Lloyd George was not in Harcourt's 'Peace party'. On the afternoon of Monday 27 July, just before the Cabinet meeting, Lloyd George had been testing arguments in favour of Britain's intervention. In discussion with a very worried C. P. Scott, Lloyd George decried *The Times'* recklessness and assured Scott that 'there could be no question of our taking part in any war in the first instance'. But he frightened Scott with his thinking aloud. He warned that 'a difficult question would arise if the German fleet were attacking French towns on the other side of the Channel'. Reviewing various possibilities, he explained that Britain might support France and Russia diplomatically, just enough to pressure Austria; then Britain could back out, making it easier for Italy to back out too, with Britain 'as it were pairing' with Italy – the same image Grey would use. Italy's defection, said Lloyd George, would be a valuable bonus for France. Scott warned against this dangerous game of bluff. Showing his familiarity with the analyses of Henry Wilson and other 'continentalists', Lloyd George then prophesied Germany's tactics: there would be a rapid attack on France, including a 'German invasion across Belgium', he predicted, before the Germans turned to face Russia. In response to C. P. Scott's objections, Lloyd George observed, 'You know I am much more pro-French than you are.' Scott pressed the neutralist case. Britain should 'make it plain from the first that if Russia and France went to war we should not be in it'. If Grey led the Liberals into war, Scott predicted, the future would belong to 'Radicalism and Labour'.[5]

Lloyd George, no doubt, took stock of Scott's advice. Nonetheless, at the Cabinet of Monday 27 July, Harcourt had found Lloyd George in a 'belligerent' mood in comparison with Grey.[6] The Chancellor, it appeared, was unwilling to make common cause with the Radicals.

The Foundering of the Ambassadors' Conference

Grey's commitment to his plan for an Ambassadors' Conference was genuine. As early as 6 July, Grey had told Lichnowsky of his hopes that his mediation would be the key to the crisis. Grey had explained, 'If trouble did come, I would use all the influence I could to mitigate difficulties and smooth them away, and if the clouds arose to prevent the storm from breaking.'[7]

However, on Monday 27 July, Grey's plan for an Ambassadors' Conference began to fall apart. It is important to emphasise here that *both* Russia and Germany found fault with the plan. In the afternoon of Monday 27 July, Buchanan reported that Sazonov had changed his mind yet again: he wanted direct negotiations instead between Vienna and St Petersburg. Arthur Nicolson, pro-Russian as he was, complained, 'One really does not know where one is with Mr Sazonov.'[8]

In the evening, the Germans famously replied to Grey's proposal with a 'no'. They could not accept what would amount to a 'court of arbitration' in London, unless it was called together at the request of Austria and Russia.[9] Grey did not respond immediately with horror. The plea that the German 'no' had tilted the balance of probabilities inexorably toward war was something for the future. By the afternoon of Tuesday 28 July, Grey himself backed away from the Ambassadors' Conference. Lining up with Sazonov, he described an exchange of views between Austria and Russia as 'the most preferable method of all'. If the talks could be brought off, he wrote, he would 'suspend every other suggestion'. Therefore, it is important to stress that German reluctance *and* Russian initiatives at St Petersburg and Vienna had changed the game.[10]

Early on the Wednesday morning a second telegram from Berlin arrived, confirming Bethmann Hollweg's opposition to a conference of ambassadors in London.[11] Grey was still not angry. On that same day, he told Lichnowsky that a conference between the Austrian ambassador and the Russian officials in St Petersburg was 'the best possible solution'.[12] By this time, of course, the news of the Russian response to the Austrian ultimatum, Russia's partial mobilisation, followed by the Austrian declaration of war against Serbia about midday on Tuesday 28 July, had severely disabled any prospect of the Austro-Russian talks bearing fruit.[13]

The foundering of Grey's proposal was not a surprise to everyone in British diplomatic circles. In Paris, Lord Bertie had been wary at the start, warning of Austrian sensitivities.[14] Bertie also offered memorable advice on the main issue. Bluntly, he urged Grey to encourage France to restrain Russia in this crisis. St Petersburg should be warned against pursuing her 'absurd' pan-Slavic ambitions.[15] Bertie sided also with his German colleague in Paris, Baron Schoen, who was complaining over French reluctance to stress in their communiqués the desire of *all* the Great Powers to prevent escalation of the dispute.[16] At the Foreign Office, this was exceptional advice.

Lichnowsky had backed Grey's plan for an Ambassadors' Conference in London. Berlin's decision against it – overruling Lichnowsky – was a serious mistake. The move offended Grey, who, egged on by his advisers, chalked it up as evidence of German bad faith. It was certainly the case that some in the German elite had weakened Grey's efforts for mediation by offering only qualified

endorsements or by surreptitiously preaching against their accept-
ance at Vienna.[17]

But other factors also contributed to the German decision to turn
aside Grey's proposal. One was fear that Italy would side with the
Entente, so that three ambassadors would line up against one in
London.[18] Another was fear that Britain was not to be trusted in
chairing a conference of mediation. This arose in part from German
apprehension that Britain and Russia were moving closer to a naval
agreement – 'the last link in the chain' of encirclement, as Bethmann
Hollweg described it. The Germans knew about these talks, and yet
Grey had denied them.[19] This added to the perception that Britain
was dishonest and clingingly loyal to the Entente. In addition,
there was little trust in Lichnowsky as the German representative.
'Lichnowsky is much too gullible. He allows himself to be taken in
by the English', the Chancellor told his secretary Kurt Riezler on
7 July 1914.[20] But behind it all stood Britain's record, eroding her
credibility as a mediator. As Zara Steiner asks, 'How could Britain be
a bridge when she had already bargained away a good measure of her
diplomatic freedom for fear of German ambitions?'[21]

The significance of the conference that never was can be over-
stated. Some saw it as pointing to an insatiable German hunger for
war. Yet Russia's attitudes toward the London conference at the time
seemed to be as confused as Germany's. Benckendorff was cool.[22] As
even Crowe minuted, 'the rapid succession of fresh proposals and
suggestions coming from St Petersburg made it easier for Germany
to find fresh excuses for her inactivity'.[23] It was less than honest of
British observers to act as if the German decision put her perma-
nently in the wrong. Some in Whitehall looked upon it as a winning
card to be kept for the future. Certainly Grey allowed his sense of
hurt to grow into a passion. In mid-August Hobhouse noted that
'Grey, who has never forgiven Germany for attempting to play with
him, is the fiercest of all of us to destroy her once and for all.'[24]

Certainly the collapse of Britain's key proposal for mediation
put extra pressure on Grey. The chorus demanding some display of
Entente solidarity grew louder. Hectoring came from Grey's own
advisers, especially Nicolson and Crowe, that is, those officials who

had done most to build the 'policy of the Entente'. They pleaded that loyalty to Russia as much as to France was required.[25] Benckendorff and Cambon, of course, chimed in. Then came prodding telegrams from George Buchanan, the British ambassador in St Petersburg. Buchanan advised Grey early in the crisis that 'we shall have to choose between giving Russia our active support or renouncing her friendship. If we fail her now we cannot hope to maintain that friendly cooperation with her in Asia that is of such vital importance to us.'[26] This was advice that struck Harcourt as astonishing.[27] Lord Bertie, British ambassador in Paris, also advised absolute loyalty to France – leavened by suspicion of Russia's cause.[28] The message was loud and clear: the Entente was indispensable; Britain could not risk abandonment by her partners. She must fight to preserve their loyalty.

Grey acted in this spirit. He warned Lichnowsky in the aftermath of Austria's ultimatum, on Friday 24, Saturday 25 and Monday 27 July, that honouring the Entente would be Britain's first priority. Lichnowsky was certainly persuaded. Courageously, he repeatedly directed plain advice back to the German Foreign Office. He implored Berlin to back up Grey's efforts at mediation and warned that, if not, 'all confidence in us and our peaceful intentions here will be shattered'.[29] On Saturday 25 July he cabled: 'I do not think that England could possibly remain disinterested should France be drawn in.'[30] Later he added that any brusque dismissal of Grey's mediation would 'probably have the result of driving England unconditionally to side with France and Russia'.[31] He reported on Monday 27 July that it was certain that Britain 'would place herself unconditionally by the side of France and of Russia, in order to show that she is not willing to permit a moral, or perhaps a military, defeat of her group. If under these circumstances it should come to war, we shall have England against us.'[32] But he was not believed. Sadly, not for the first or last time, those who told the truth in Berlin would be smeared as the dupes of London – just as those who told the truth in London would be smeared as the dupes of Berlin.

The Fleet Moves to War Stations, Wednesday 29 July

Was Britain focused upon diplomacy or Dreadnoughts? The foundering of the Ambassadors' Conference clearly gave the edge to those who favoured further military preparations. It was Churchill who once again pushed forward the pace of naval 'precautions'. Soon after the Cabinet of Monday 27 July, Churchill had sent to all his naval commanders a secret telegram, beginning with the observation that the 'European political situation makes war between the Triple Entente and Triple Alliance Powers by no means impossible.' Tellingly, the provocative expression 'Triple Entente' was used – in defiance of many Cabinet instructions.[33] Churchill's telegram carefully specified that 'this is *not* the warning telegram' – the official first signal of war. Rather, commanders were ordered to 'be prepared to shadow hostile men-of-war' and to consider the disposition of their ships with that shadowing task in mind. 'Measure is purely precautionary', explained the telegram. 'The utmost secrecy' was to be maintained regarding all these preparations.[34]

The next day the Admiralty took another leap forward. At 10 a.m. on Tuesday morning 28 July, Churchill, Battenberg and the Chief of the Staff together decided that the First Fleet, now concentrated, should be ordered north to its war stations. 'I feared to bring this matter before the Cabinet', Churchill explained brazenly in his memoirs, 'lest it should mistakenly be considered a provocative action likely to damage the chances of peace.'[35] Moreover, he pleaded, the movement of ships from one British port to another was not something that necessarily came to Cabinet. Therefore, as Churchill told the story, he informed only Asquith, 'who at once gave his approval'. Secret orders were sent at 5 p.m. on the Tuesday evening for the rapid movement of the First Fleet to Scapa Flow, beginning under cover of darkness and passing through the Strait of Dover early next morning without lights. Only officers were to be told the destination. In addition, the Second Fleet was to assemble at Portland.[36]

Accordingly, very early on Wednesday morning 29 July, the First Fleet steamed out at speed from Portland. The warships passed through the Channel and then turned north, toward the fleet's war stations.[37] Why did the First Fleet take the eastern route to the north? In the official history, Julian Corbett explained that, under war plans, the fleet would normally have taken the safer, western route. It would only 'face the risk of going east-about up the North Sea' if there were a 'sudden crisis' and 'a chance of bringing on a fleet action'. Corbett claimed 'that chance was clearly in view'. Naval Intelligence believed that the German High Seas Fleet was 'concentrated off the coast of Norway' and, therefore, that the First Fleet might face action.[38] Whether or not the fleet was hoping for action, or merely preparing for action – the passage north was uneventful.

In all of this Churchill's demeanour was a worry, even to himself. At midnight on Tuesday 28 July, Churchill wrote to his wife Clementine exposing his strange inner turmoil. A spirit of gruesome jauntiness had taken hold:

> Everything tends toward catastrophe & collapse. I am interested, geared up & happy. Is it not horrible to be built like that? The preparations have a hideous fascination for me. I pray to God to forgive me for such fearful moods of levity. Yet I w[oul]d do my best for peace, & nothing w[oul]d induce me wrongfully to strike the first blow.

In the inner folds of his conscience he found some anger for the 'stupid Kings & Emperors'. He lamented that 'we all drift on in a kind of dull cataleptic trance'. But sparking the apparatus of naval warfare into life clearly excited him. 'We are putting the whole Navy into fighting trim (bar the reserve)', he told Clementine. 'The sailors are thrilled and confident.' All was primed and 'ready as it has never been before'. If a sea battle were to begin 'we shall give them a good drubbing'.[39]

Later in his memoirs Churchill painted the manoeuvring of the First Fleet to Scapa Flow in the dead of night in vivid word pictures. He described the grand sight, as he imagined it, of 'the scores of gigantic castles of steel wending their way across the misty shining sea, like giants bowed in anxious thought'. He proudly conjured up the vision of 'eighteen miles of ships running at high speed and in absolute blackness through the narrow straits'.[40]

This romantic war writing distracted from the facts. The most obvious was that this latest naval initiative was ordered very early in the crisis. The decision to move the ships to their war stations was made at the Admiralty on the morning of Tuesday 28 July and the orders were issued at 5 p.m. This was *before* news reached London, at 7.20 p.m., of the Austrian declaration of war against Serbia. Similarly, it came before news confirming that Grey's Ambassadors' Conference was dead, which arrived, as mentioned, on the Wednesday morning. Therefore, Britain's mighty navy was almost wholly mobilised and the fleet ordered to war stations before it was clear that war would explode, even in the Balkans, and before diplomacy to avoid it was exhausted.[41]

Moreover, by Churchill's own admission the two preparatory naval moves pre-empted Cabinet decisions. Churchill acted between Cabinets. Both decisions had the effect of accelerating the 'march of events', a phrase Churchill was fond of employing as if events were pushed forward by some quite preternatural power.[42] The truth is that Churchill succumbed to a temptation to frogmarch events.

This may be contrasted with the relative calm of General Sir Henry Wilson, the Director of Military Operations, at this same time. Wilson was a devoted fan of the BEF, and just as keen to see Britain mobilise the moment Russia or France did so. Nevertheless, over the three days Sunday 26 July to Tuesday 28 July, when Churchill pushed forward his naval preparations, Wilson was in no hurry. He was constantly in touch with Nicolson at the Foreign Office and was permitted to read all the key telegrams. On Sunday 26 July he wrote in his diary that, because there was 'no news of Germany moving', war was unlikely. On Monday, and for the same reason, he wrote 'there will not be any war'. Only on Tuesday 28 July did he concede that Russian mobilisation was imminent. But he wrote that it was 'impossible to say what will follow'.[43] Even to General Wilson it was evident that Britain was forcing the pace.

What was Churchill's purpose? In his memoirs he explained that he moved forward pre-emptively on naval preparations to make certain that 'the diplomatic situation did not get ahead of the naval situation'. The danger of the reverse happening appears not to have troubled him. In his own words, he was determined that the British Grand Fleet should be in its war station before Germany knew whether or not Britain would intervene, and *'therefore if possible before we had decided ourselves'*.[44]

Of course, Churchill calculated that if war broke out his early preparations would be praised as merely prudential. Incitement of Russia and France did not bother him. The second naval move, like the first, was publicised. On Thursday 30 July the newspapers reported the departure of the First Fleet from Portland.[45] The Liberal newspapers loyally insisted there was no 'sinister inference' to be drawn. It was all precautionary, to meet 'all emergencies'. The 'free hand' was safe, because Britain's relations with Russia and France 'do not bind us to join in any war which either of them chooses to make'.[46] So they imagined.

But the latest naval initiative certainly had an international impact. It was on display in the Channel. As the First Fleet surged through the Strait of Dover to its war stations, it passed the French battleship *France*, returning to Dunkirk from the Baltic with the two French leaders, Poincaré and Viviani. Vice Admiral Sir George Warrender, temporarily commanding the First Fleet, was on HMS *Iron Duke*, and he exchanged salutes with the French battleship.[47] The incitement to the Entente could not have been more dramatically signalled.

In Russia there was a dramatic reaction. On Thursday 30 July, a Reuter's correspondent in St Petersburg reported: 'The sailing of the British fleet from Portland has created an immense impression, and, coupled with Japan's assurances [that she would not oppose Russia], has more than confirmed Russia's determination to stand to her guns.'[48] Next day came the public announcement of Russia's general mobilisation. In the press, the British fleet's movement was cited along with mobilisation as providing the spark to public hysteria. 'The war fever seized St Petersburg when the mobilisation was announced, and it increased almost to delirium upon receipt of the news of the sailing of the British fleet.'[49]

In these murky events, three points deserve emphasis. First, in ordering the fleet to war stations, Churchill had again evaded the Cabinet. Second, evidence of the German Navy's aggressive preparations, such as might have justified these measures, was nowhere to be found. Churchill himself conceded, in a memorandum to Asquith in November 1914, that during the July–August crisis 'the movements of the German fleet were such as normally take place at that season of the year'. There was 'no concealment of them: they were continuously and accurately known'.[50] Third, an unspoken motive was at work: to make it more likely that Britain would send the BEF to the Continent. As Churchill was a convinced 'continentalist', it would be remarkable if this never entered his head. The official naval historian boasted of it: 'So far, then, as naval readiness could secure the country against invasion, there was now no reason why part at least of the Expeditionary Force should not now leave. The Germans seemed to be more concerned with meeting a descent than with making one.'[51]

Small wonder the Tories looked upon Churchill as their man in the Liberal Cabinet. As Admiral Fisher told Churchill on 31 July, 'Arthur Balfour rushed into my arms as I walked out of the Admiralty and he thanked God that you were First Lord!'[52]

FIVE

Facing Both Ways
Wednesday 29 July

We nineteen men round the table at Downing St may soon
have to face the most momentous problem which men can face.
Meantime our action is held in suspense, for if both sides do not
know what we shall do, both will be the less willing to run risks.[1]

Herbert Samuel, 29 July 1914

The next crucial Cabinet meeting came at 10 Downing Street
on the morning of Wednesday 29 July, amid disturbing news.
The newspapers carried details of the Austro-Hungarian
declaration of war on Serbia, announced the previous day. War in
the Balkans was a reality – although intense fighting was many days
away. What would Russia do? Foreign Office telegrams had reported
Russia's partial mobilisation as early as Saturday 25 July.[2] Grey's
report to the Cabinet, no doubt, was eagerly awaited. His plan for
an Ambassadors' Conference had just collapsed. And the Cabinet's
factions were firming up. What should Britain do?

Grey, Belgium, and the Gladstone Precedent

Grey was half an hour late for Wednesday morning's Cabinet, explaining that he had just come from an interview with the German ambassador. When he arrived, he reported on the perilous international situation. Harcourt penned this summary:

> European situation very bad – Austria declines to continue communications by her Ambassador at St Petersburg. Russia has said she will mobilise if Austria declares war – before end of Cab[inet] we heard Russia *had* mobilised in cert[ain] towns on her *Southern* frontier. Germany has s[ai]d she will not mobilise unless Russia does so on her (*Russia's*) Western frontier.[3]

Grey's report certainly highlighted the dangers in the east, and acknowledged the critical role already played by Russia.

But, tellingly, Grey's focus in the Cabinet moved west. Just hours after war was declared in the Balkans, Grey began to speak of conflict in Belgium. Here was the bridge over which the 'Peace' majority of the Cabinet might travel into his interventionist camp. Therefore, purely for the education of the Cabinet, Grey distributed some carefully prepared printed material on the seventy-five-year-old Treaty of 1839 on Belgium's neutrality. Grey spoke of 'our liabilities for the guarantee of Belgian neutrality & independence'.[4] The text of the treaty, which Grey presented, indisputably bound five monarchs to respect Belgium as 'an independent and perpetually neutral state'. It also imposed upon Belgium herself an obligation to observe that neutrality in her dealings with all powers. All of the provisions of the treaty, including Belgium's neutral and independent status, were 'placed under the guarantee of their said Majesties', that is, the monarchs of Great Britain, Austria, France, Russia and Prussia. Next Grey presented material showing Liberal Prime Minister Gladstone's actions during the major crisis over Belgium at the time of the Franco-Prussian War of 1870. Needless to say, the example of the great Liberal premier in 1870 still counted for a great deal among Liberals in 1914.

Gladstone now stalked the Cabinet table. Ministers travelled back forty-four years. They were reminded that in 1870 Britain did *not* rely on the old Treaty of 1839. Rather, Britain had undertaken fresh diplomatic initiatives and concluded two new treaties. On 30 July 1870, two weeks after the outbreak of the Franco-Prussian War (15 July), Lord Granville, Gladstone's Foreign Secretary, made proposals to both France and Prussia (as the leading power in the 'North German Confederation' – united Germany did not yet exist). Negotiations quickly produced identical British treaties that were signed with France on 9 August and with Prussia on 11 August, that is, more than three weeks after the war had begun. The timing is significant. At that point, neither side had yet set foot on Belgian territory. Both powers accepted the British treaties as strengthening that situation. Nonetheless, British diplomatic skill was in evidence. The British treaties were scrupulously even-handed. Under their terms, Britain threatened war against either France or Prussia if either invaded Belgium, and promised to cooperate with the other power toward the limited objective of defending Belgium. Most significantly too, the terms were limited to a period of twelve months after peace. After this time, 'the independence and neutrality of Belgium', as the treaty stipulated, would rest again on the original Treaty of 1839.[5] It is vital to note that the old treaty did *not* require Britain to undertake war against any power that might violate Belgian neutrality – only the 1870 treaties threatened such a war.

With this material on the Cabinet table, Asquith's ministers debated the meaning of the Treaty of 1839. Harcourt recorded some of the questions that were raised: 'Is it a joint or several Guarantee? Are we bound to observe it if other parties do not? Is it an undertaking to Belgium? If so what are we to do if Belgium does not ask or wish for our action?' Harcourt recorded the crucial advice given by the legal officers of 1870, namely, that the treaty was 'a several guarantee – hence [the] Anglo-French and Anglo-German treaties of that year declaring its [Belgium's] neutrality'.[6] The most critical question was clear: would Britain make war, in 1914, in Belgium itself, in order to prevent a signatory power invading? France as well as Germany? Harcourt recorded the consensus reached in the Cabinet on this question: 'Everyone agreed we would not land troops *in* Belgium.'

The debate that followed was very intense. Some ministers clearly favoured intervention on the Continent. For others it was anathema. McKenna, the former First Lord of the Admiralty, took the lead in proposing that Britain should contemplate only a limited naval war. If 'German aggression on Belgium' was to be countered, argued McKenna, this could be done more effectively 'by our Fleet sealing up German ocean traffic'. A food crisis in Germany would follow, he predicted.[7] This attractive idea, that Britain's war might be strictly limited to naval action, was to have an impact over coming days.

But Radicals in the Cabinet were much more interested in the possibilities of averting war altogether. The parallel of 1870 offered that possibility. Could Grey not follow in the footsteps of Lord Granville? On this issue, the contributions of Grey and Asquith were the vital ones. Grey – who often personalised the issues – spoke about his own imminent difficulties in diplomacy with France. He predicted that two questions would shortly be directed to him from France: he explained that 'at any moment' the French might ask Britain directly for her support in a coming war, and then 'if we said No, whether we would renew the 1870 treaty to prevent [the] violation of Belgium'. Asquith pitched in at this point. He revealed his own conviction that in any coming conflict in the west 'the Germans, if they attacked France would go through Belgium'. Therefore, Asquith explained, with respect to Grey's two questions, a no to France's direct request for support would be provocative enough, but a yes to the request for a renewal of the treaty of 1870 would be 'almost equally provocative'.[8] In Asquith's mind, therefore, the kind of even-handed negotiations that Britain undertook in August 1870 – which had saved Belgian and British neutrality – was impossible now. There would be no attempt to renew Gladstone's treaties. The reality of the Entente prevented it.

Again, it is important to recall the exact terms of Gladstone's treaties negotiated with both Prussia and France in 1870. Both strengthened the neutrality of Belgium. First, Britain had promised to cooperate with France, to restore Belgian neutrality, if Prussian armies entered Belgium. Second, Britain had promised to cooperate with Prussia, to restore Belgian neutrality, if French armies entered Belgium. Most importantly, under Article I of both of Gladstone's treaties, Britain declared that she was under no obligation 'to take part in the general operations of the war'.[9] Asquith had ruled out such treaty-making in 1914, because France would regard Britain's 'non-participation' in a wider war 'as an unfriendly act'.[10] This made it plain that eight years of Entente diplomacy had snuffed out the possibility of a truly disinterested foreign policy for Britain – just as Radicals complained.

Asquith and Grey wanted more: a commitment to war on the basis of the Belgian issue. They did not get it. Would Britain 'stand by France'? Harcourt insisted the question 'cannot be answered without a Cabinet decision: we do not decide that today; new circ[umstance]s may arise'.[11] The neutralist majority rallied to refuse a decision at this Cabinet. The teach-in on 1839 and 1870 had high-lighted a crucial fact: Britain was not *obliged* to make war on a power violating Belgium's neutrality. Therefore, the Radicals argued, there should be no decision in advance to fight on behalf of Belgium. The Cabinet resolved that 'the matter if it arises will be rather one of policy than of legal obligation'.[12]

Asquith made the best of this. He entertained his Cabinet by sati-rising Britain's critics: both sides in the European power balance, as he put it, were calling on Britain to do opposite things to safeguard peace. Both sides pretended to believe that *Britain* would be most to blame if war broke out. 'Russia says we can prevent Europ[ean] war by saying we shall support France – Germany says we can prevent it by saying we shall *not* do so', Asquith observed. 'Evidently we could do nothing right', he explained wryly.[13] Asquith's clever wordplay served to highlight his claim that Grey was uncommitted and even-handed – even though his rejection of the Gladstonian diplomacy of 1870 had established that he was not. Harcourt took heart: 'Grey does not believe that our action w[oul]d be a real deciding element in the outbreak (or not) of war.'[14]

'Apparent Indecision' Revisited

Next Grey shared with the Cabinet his disappointment at the demise of his Ambassadors' Conference. He remarked that 'if it had not been for his intervention they were hopelessly drifting into war'.[15] He continued to press for mediation, he explained. Offering guidance to Grey, the Cabinet then agreed that the Foreign Secretary should give a similar message to the French and German ambassadors, Cambon and Lichnowsky, that afternoon. He promised to restate the Cabinet's policy of ambiguity:

> Grey said he must tell Cambon that our people thought the Austro-Serbian quarrel did not directly concern us, and that he would say to Cambon [']Don't count upon our coming in['], and to Lichnowsky [']don't count on our abstention['] – and neither could then regard our inaction or action respectively as an Act of Treachery. This was assented to.[16]

The Cabinet clearly wanted Britain to hold fast to inscrutability.

Here in a nutshell was Grey's policy. As he stated it, it was the policy most likely to preserve the peace. The Radicals accepted it at face value. It was, wrote Harcourt, 'a sound strong & honest diplomatic position so long as we in Cabinet *do not commit ourselves to a decision. When (and if) we do, Grey's position will be hopelessly weakened.*'[17] Herbert Samuel still believed in the policy. He explained that it might just frighten the contending European forces into a more cautious path: 'Meantime our action is held in suspense, for if both sides do not know what we shall do, both will be the less willing to run risks.' Not that Samuel was very confident of the outcome. He told Beatrice that 'the probabilities are that the fuse which has been fired will quickly bring a catastrophic explosion'.[18]

The policy of 'apparent indecision' was only just preventing a split inside the Cabinet. Dedicated men on both sides still threatened to walk. On the Radical side, Harcourt recorded in his notes his still-steadfast opposition to war: 'I am determined not to remain in the Cab[inet] if they decide to join in a war – but they cannot so decide as I am certain now that I can take at least 9 colleagues out with me on resignation, viz Morley, Burns, Beauchamp, McK[innon] Wood, Samuel, Hobhouse, Runciman, Simon.'[19] For his part, Morley also spoke openly of resignation. According to Pease, at one point Morley responded to Grey by reasserting that 'I shall not be a party to any intervention between Austria and Serbia', but he added that 'France may be a different thing.'[20]

Resignations from the Liberal Imperialist side were also mooted. According to Morley, it was during this Cabinet that Grey threatened to depart if the Cabinet opted in advance for a declaration of neutrality.[21] 'If the Cabinet was for Neutrality, he did not think he was the man to carry out such a policy', Grey told them all. This provoked a collective sigh on the part of the Cabinet, 'and a moment or two of breathless silence fell upon us'.[22] It was worth a sigh. Cabinet had just rejected the idea that any military advance into Belgium must be a trigger to war. Grey then made it plain that he personally ruled out neutrality. The armour of his mind was implacable: he was convinced that Britain *must* intervene in a European conflict, based ultimately on loyalty to the Entente, whether or not Belgium was invaded. Projecting an inscrutable diplomacy might hold the Cabinet together – but not if diplomacy collapsed.

The 'Warning Telegram', Wednesday 29 July

Next the discussion in Cabinet turned to military preparations. Here the Cabinet made a decision scarcely reconcilable with 'apparent indecision' – it decided that the official 'Warning Telegram' should be sent out across the Empire. The neutralists had gained their victory over Belgium; the interventionists now prevailed on the matter of Britain cranking up her military machine – just in case.

In this discussion, Churchill played the key role. He explained that the First Fleet's move to its war stations had begun overnight, while his Cabinet colleagues slept. On his orders, and with Asquith's assent, the ships were by now half-way to their war stations. Perhaps to soften this, he found time to decry the 'calamity' of war and the stupidity of monarchs. This peroration led Harcourt to record his impression that Churchill was somewhat 'less bellicose' than on Monday.[23]

But Churchill then returned to the fray. German possession of the Belgian ports, which his ships were passing as he spoke, would be a disaster. Grey was right, insisted Churchill. Belgium was a trigger. But, failing that, another precaution was instantly required, he demanded: the official 'Warning Telegram' must be sent immediately to all governors, naval and military commanders throughout the Empire. This was the first 'button', as it were, in the famous 'War Book' composed by the Committee of Imperial Defence.

Here was a very significant step: British military preparations would be set in motion across the globe. Emotions would be roused. The Cabinet needed persuading. Pease pleaded that nothing should be done 'of a provocative character'. Grey backed Churchill, defending the naval initiatives he had taken. The Foreign Secretary summarised his own stance: he would 'leave nothing undone to promote Peace, but to make no preparations would lose us all our influence with all the Powers' – suggesting that he meant both enemies to be deterred and friends to be encouraged.[24]

At length, the crucial decision was made. The Cabinet resolved that the 'Precautionary Stage' in this crisis had arrived. Therefore, that afternoon London would despatch the 'Warning Telegram' throughout the British Empire. The 'War Book' was 'to be opened'. As Asquith explained to the King, this step was instigated immediately after the Cabinet rose, just before 2 p.m.[25] This was an event of signal importance in this story. Britain was preparing to unleash huge military forces, largely naval. It is worth stressing that, while diplomatic events rushed forward, Wednesday 29 July was arguably still an early point in the crisis for Britain, an early point for her to build military steps on top of the naval movements already undertaken. There was no apprehension of an imminent threat to Britain. At this point, actual war was still confined to the Balkans: Belgrade was shelled on the evening of the Wednesday.[26] Only Russia among the major powers had moved to 'partial mobilisation'. Germany was not to issue her comparable 'Danger of Threatening War' proclamation (*Kriegsgefahrzustand*) until Friday 31 July.[27] France and Germany would not announce their general mobilisations until the coming Saturday 1 August. Yet Britain, on Wednesday 29 July, with her navy already at war stations, was advancing and widening military preparations. Even General Wilson wrote in his diary: 'I don't know why we are doing it, because there is nothing moving in Germany.'[28]

When the Cabinet concluded, Grey crossed Downing Street and returned to the Foreign Office. Still bound to the Cabinet policy of 'apparent indecision', Grey faced two tense interviews, with the French and German ambassadors. Grey told Paul Cambon that Britain might stand aside from an *eastern* war, and that Britain had not decided on her position in the event of German and French involvement in war. Cambon was disappointed. In response, he made it plain that France *had* decided, and absolutely: if Russia came to blows with Germany, France would not remain neutral. She would rush to Russia's aid. In this way Cambon made it clear that, for France, unwavering loyalty to her alliance came before all other considerations – exactly the policy he recommended to Grey.[29] Grey saw Lichnowsky on the same afternoon. Grey was not without hope. But the warning was stern. He told the Prince that he had a 'friendly and private communication' to make to him, as '*he did not wish later to be reproached with insincerity*'. Britain 'could stand aside' in the event of an Austro-Russian war, Grey explained. But in the event of a Franco-German war, he warned, Britain would have to 'make up its mind quickly. In such an event *it would not be practicable to stand aside and wait for any length of time.*' The British government, Grey explained, had '*to reckon with public opinion*' which, initially sympathetic to Austria, 'was beginning to veer round completely'.[30] Lichnowsky understood the gravity of the new warning.

Opening the 'War Book'

While Grey was meeting the two anxious ambassadors, other Liberal ministers busied themselves in Whitehall despatching the Warning Telegram. How was it that the Cabinet had agreed to this next big military step?

It was a victory for the government's military advisers, especially Maurice Hankey, secretary of the Committee of Imperial Defence (CID) and chief architect of the 'War Book'. He had been especially active on the matter on Tuesday 28 July. He had met with Asquith and urged the declaration of the 'Precautionary Stage', arguing that it was only of a 'defensive character'. But Hankey had found Asquith 'reluctant to take any further step which might be interpreted as warlike'. So Hankey pressed the two key Entente enthusiasts, Nicolson and Churchill, to shoulder Asquith into action. It worked. Hankey was much encouraged on the morning of Wednesday when Churchill asked him to bring a copy of the War Book to Downing Street. Soon after the Cabinet ended, he was summoned to come instantly to help 'start the ball rolling'.[31]

Hankey was happy: 'I am thankful to say that the Gov[ernmen]t are taking no chances', he wrote to his wife.[32] But he found the politicians still anxious that the appearance of mobilisation be avoided. During the day and evening, Hankey 'had two or three interviews with the P. M., and I tackled Winston, who was in Njinski [sic] pyjamas'. The politicians wanted 'to keep the press quiet', so a 'doping' order was required, he explained.[33] Hankey prepared one. On Thursday 30 July the newspapers duly reported an official announcement that disavowed any 'mobilisation' and insisted that all measures were 'purely precautionary and of a defensive character'.[34] The same newspapers also reported the First Fleet's dash from Portland 'yesterday morning'. *The Times* commented soothingly that Britain's naval measures were 'a natural outcome of the trend of events and can in no way be regarded as alarming or provocative'. Of course, some in the Cabinet were alarmed. The Radical faction had been twice surprised to learn, after the event, of big decisions: the decision to concentrate the fleet at Portland, and then the decision to move the First Fleet to its war stations. The neutralists had already learned how much could be smuggled into precautionary measures.

What was the reaction at 10 Downing Street to the grave decision to 'open the War Book'? There was a mixture of apprehension – and excitement. Asquith's fatalism was now dominant. He had already written to Venetia Stanley in the morning that the 'whole Irish business' had been 'put into the shade by the coming war – "coming" for it seems now as if nothing but a miracle c[oul]d avert it'.[35]

Margot recorded in her diary that evening an extraordinary scene in her bedroom. Asquith came to tell her that the Warning Telegram had been sent. She sat in the evening abandon of newspapers and bed-clothes. He sat on the bed. Margot noted the change in Asquith's demeanour. She could tell 'that something momentous had happened'. 'This is what the Committee of [Imperial] Defence have been discussing and settling for the last 2 years', he explained. He was 'curious' to see how it turned out. The telegrams had gone out 'marvellously quickly'. Margot noted that she had never seen him 'so keen'. She in turn felt 'passionately moved' and '10 feet high'. 'How thrilling! Oh! Tell me weren't you [e]x[c]ited darling[?]', said Margot. He kissed her and told her it would all be 'very interesting'.[36]

At dinner that evening there was one subject of discussion. 'War! War!' exclaimed Margot in her diary. 'Everyone at dinner discussing how long the war might last.' Margot carefully recorded that the average estimate around the table was '3 weeks to 3 months', and that 'H[enry] said nothing which amazed our [guests?]!'[37] There were no expressions of reluctance, regret or horror.

The Radicals had different experiences that same evening. After lunch at Downing Street, Harcourt had crossed to the Colonial Office and, with a heavy heart, gave orders for the 'Warning Telegrams' to be sent to all Dominions and colonies. He was careful to note that the 'Search' of German ships was *not* yet to be undertaken. His last telegrams left the Colonial Office at 6 p.m.[38] Harcourt was then detained at the House of Commons until 2 a.m. As he made his way to his home in Berkeley Square, he saw that every light in the Admiralty building was burning. Harcourt committed to his Cabinet journal his mounting fears regarding Churchill's evident desire to bump the Cabinet into war. 'I fear he is carrying his preparation on too far', wrote Harcourt, '& getting prematurely in the war stage'.[39]

Then, early on Thursday morning 30 July, Harcourt's suspicion deepened. He learned that a 'Search' *had* been undertaken on German ships at Gibraltar during the previous evening. Fearful that Churchill had overreached his authority, Harcourt sent for copies of the telegrams from the Admiralty to Gibraltar and Malta to check the instructions. They were correct and had properly warned against 'Search' at this stage. To be on the safe side, Harcourt ordered that fresh telegrams be despatched. He was 'much afraid of an "incident" over [a] search on some German vessel'.[40]

Later that morning, more disturbing information came from a contact at the Admiralty.[41] Overnight Churchill had instituted moves for the Admiralty to hire the Cunard liner *Aquitania*. Harcourt speculated that Churchill might already be preparing transports for troops to Belgium, in defiance of Cabinet. In addition, Harcourt learned that Churchill had 'commandeered all coal in South Wales – Cardiff paralysed'. This provoked Harcourt to an explosion in his journal against Churchill: 'I think he has gone mad.'[42]

SIX

Drum-Taps
Monday 27 to Friday 31 July

Russia is now defending a vital interest. France, who is bound to Russia by alliance, and still more by the necessities of her European situation, and political independence, is compelled to support Russia. England is bound by moral obligations to side with France and Russia, lest the balance of forces on the Continent be upset to her disadvantage and she be left alone to face a dominant Germany. A vital British interest is therefore at stake.[1]

The Times, 31 July 1914

Events inside the Cabinet need to be seen in the context of the continuing campaign in the Conservative press for British intervention. The newspapers normally hostile to the government, such as *The Times*, the *Morning Post*, the *Daily Mail*, and the *Daily Telegraph*, raised a clamour for intervention. Their editorials thundered out their demand: Britain must proclaim her resolve to intervene from the moment war ignited in Europe. They barracked for immediate mobilisation, as soon as Britain's partners did so. In promoting war, the task of the Conservative press was to counsel the people that there were worse things than war – national dishonour, for one. The many veteran spruikers for the Entente went about this task with a ferocious consistency.

The Clamour for Intervention in *The Times*

As noted previously, from Monday 27 July onward, *The Times* in particular urged that Europe should be told of Britain's intentions to join instantly with her 'friends', Russia and France, in the event of war. *The Times* did announce its hopes for peaceful mediation. After all, the plan for an Ambassadors' Conference had originally been Arthur Nicolson's, and he was close to Geoffrey Dawson, the chief editor of *The Times*. Moreover, at first, the Berlin correspondent, J. E. Mackenzie, accepted that Germany was 'certainly, and no doubt sincerely, working for peace'.[2]

The Times editorial of Tuesday 28 July sided explicitly with Russia. Even if *Russian* action led to war, Britain still had no alternative but to fight. Localising war was a chimera. War simply could not be confined to the Balkans, *The Times* argued, 'if Russia feels constrained to answer the appeal of her Slav kinsmen, as almost certainly she would feel constrained to answer it'.[3] Similarly, Colonel Repington, the military correspondent of *The Times*, appeared to accept a rolling sequence of mobilisations, kicked off by Russian action, as 'with a line of tin soldiers'. War was 'terribly automatic'. 'We shall all support our friends because we must', predicted Repington, 'and in a very short time after a Russian mobilisation is announced it will be a miracle if all Europe is not aflame'.[4]

As the week unfolded, *The Times* battered its readers with a noisy advocacy in favour of solidarity with Russia and France. *The Times* gave unflinching editorial support to the message coming from both the Russian and French embassies in London: if Britain wanted peace, she should announce her absolute loyalty to her 'friends'. On Wednesday 29 July, *The Times* argued that 'the surest way to preserve that peace for which [the British people] long, and perhaps the only way, is to make clear to all that if their friends are forced into such a war England for her part will support them to the full'.[5]

Significantly *The Times* did not attach any special significance at this stage to the Germans' decision to decline Grey's Ambassadors' Conference. This was not 'in any sense a rebuff', argued the editor, for Germany was supporting the Austrian-Russian talks in St Petersburg.

The Times repeated its assurances that in Germany 'the maintenance of European peace is warmly and honestly desired'.[6] But the very next day *The Times* repeated arguments for immediate British intervention in the event of war. Preserving the balance of power and the safety of Belgium were both advanced as sufficient considerations. Britain could not afford 'to see France crushed by Germany, or the balance of power upset against France'. *The Times* further growled: 'If France is menaced, or the safety of the Belgian frontier, which we have guaranteed with her and with Prussia by treaties that Mr Gladstone's government in 1870 confirmed, we shall know how to act'. Britons would 'strike as one man'.[7]

With this editorial *The Times* sought to foster the view that Britain was *obliged* – legally and morally – by diplomatic treaty, to go to war to defend Belgium. This line, advocated eagerly by interventionist politicians, sought to conflate in the public mind the original Treaty of 1839 and the Gladstone treaties of 1870. Of course, Gladstone's treaties had long expired. The Treaty of 1839 was the only applicable treaty. Therefore, *The Times*' description of the Belgian frontier as still 'guaranteed' in 1914, in the same sense that it had been 'guaranteed' in 1870, could be misleading. The claim that Gladstone had simply 'confirmed' this 'guarantee' in 1870 was certainly misleading.

It is important also to note that it was news of *Russia*'s partial mobilisation that brought about a distinct sharpening in tone in the pages of *The Times*. News of that awesome step had been filtering into London for some days, as noted above, but had not been reported in the press and was not confirmed in parliament by Grey until Thursday 30 July.[8] Steed was given the chance to write an editorial on the subject for *The Times* of Friday 31 July. He did not hold back:

> Russia is now defending a vital interest. France, who is bound to Russia by alliance, and still more by the necessities of her European situation, and political independence, is compelled to support Russia. England is bound by moral obligations to side with France and Russia, lest the balance of forces on the Continent be upset to her disadvantage and she be left alone to face a dominant Germany. A vital British interest is therefore at stake.[9]

There was not a word urging Russia, or France, to be cautious; there was not a word urging the British government to restrain Russia or France. Rather, Belgium dominated. If the Germans advanced through Belgium, warned Steed, Germany might take Antwerp, Flushing, Dunkirk and Calais and build bases against England. Britain would have to enter the war for 'the safety of the narrow seas'. It was, therefore, 'the instinct of self-preservation' which compelled Britain 'to be ready to strike with all our force for our own safety and for that of our friends'.

Over the same week Northcliffe's *Daily Mail*, based at Carmelite House off Fleet Street, blared out the same message. The alliance system was the first point of reference – Triple Entente versus Triple Alliance. As early as Saturday 25 July, the *Daily Mail* advocated Britain's linking arms with Russia and France the moment conflict broke out.[10] But, as the week unfolded, there was a telling addition to the usual arguments: the Liberals were to blame for Britain's apparent dependence on Russia and France. For it was the Liberals who had failed to spend enough on the Royal Navy, and the Liberals who had funked it over conscription, so that Britain had no massive army to match her navy. So, in this crisis, argued the *Daily Mail* on Friday 31 July, 'We must stand by our friends, if for no other and heroic reason, because without their aid we cannot be safe.'[11]

The Men Behind *The Times*

What lay behind this extraordinary crusade for intervention? Lord Northcliffe, the legendary press baron – 'the Chief' – directed it from his rooms at *The Times* building, Printing House Square. His senior writers were in contact with the key men in the Foreign Office and the embassies of the Entente powers, who in turn fed the campaign for intervention with both fact and fiction. Intervention was the essential conviction. Geoffrey Dawson, who had been chief editor of *The Times* for two years, embraced it. Dawson's keenest allegiance, after all, was to Lord Alfred Milner and his influential Round Table movement, which was devoted to the expansion of the British

Empire, hostile to Germany as an imperial rival, and absolutely loyal to the Entente for the sake of the Empire.[12] Equally anti-German and pro-Entente in outlook was Valentine Chirol, the retired former foreign editor. Chirol was a close friend of both Nicolson and Charles Hardinge (Viceroy in India), both zealous promoters of the Entente in Foreign Office circles. According to Chirol, he was able to bring his influence to bear at the paper at this time because Dawson 'made a personal appeal to me to stand by him in this crisis'.[13]

Why were the editorials so stridently pro-interventionist? In part, the cause lay in tensions at *The Times*. Dawson, the idealistic Milnerite, and Northcliffe, the blunt-speaking tycoon, were impatient with each other. Who ruled at Printing House Square was a contentious question. The sources also show attempts to marginalise Dawson from the story – so that Northcliffe and Steed could share more of the 'glory' for driving Britain toward intervention.[14] Steed, who enjoyed Northcliffe's special esteem, certainly managed to increase his influence at this time, by means of a tragic event. On the evening of Friday 24 July, as Dawson left London for Oxford, his car was involved in 'a ghastly accident' on the Embankment. A child was killed and Dawson was 'much knocked up'.[15] The incident preyed on his mind. But from Oxford, his phone calls over the weekend revealed 'such obvious chaos in P.H.S. [Printing House Square]' that he determined to return quickly. 'N [Northcliffe] had paralysed the office', wrote Dawson on Sunday 26 July, and he arrived at Blackfriars 'just in time to get things straight'.[16] Indeed, '*The Times* Editorial Diary' for 1914 recorded Dawson as the overall editor of the edition of Monday 27 July.[17] On that day he was 'v[ery] seedy as the result of overwork and the shock of Friday'. But he had time to touch some of the usual bases, revealing something of the network in London rallying for intervention. For instance, he lunched on Monday at the Travellers Club with Nicolson, the key advocate for intervention among Grey's intimates. He also had 'a weary talk with N[orthcliffe]'.[18] Next day, he gave evidence at the inquest into the death of the little boy killed by his car. It was, he wrote, 'a trying time, w[ith] the v[ery] poor, drunken family'.[19] But again Dawson was listed as overall editor of the paper on the Tuesday.[20] So, Steed definitely was not in sole charge of *The Times* during the week of diplomatic crisis.[21]

It was Dawson who remained the chief guiding light at *The Times*. By Wednesday 29 July he was back working 'practically all day' at Printing House Square, and glad to find on a visit to the Commons that 'this morning's article had made a great impression'.[22] Only late that day did Dawson leave London for a rest, leaving George Freeman in command of *The Times*.[23] On Friday 31 July he returned. This time he encountered 'considerable excitement and confusion in the Office' and he found that Steed was especially 'incoherent'.[24] Certainly the sources show tensions between Dawson and Steed, Northcliffe's protégé, and doubtless these tensions had an effect at *The Times* during that week. Both men were confirmed intervention-ists. But because they competed for the favour of 'The Chief', an out-and-out Germanophobe and unflinching interventionist, the editorials of *The Times* grew in vehemence. Whatever the precise stimulus, a whole week of editorials in *The Times*, penned mostly by Flanagan but shaped by Steed, Dawson, and Northcliffe, bawled for British intervention in solidarity with the Entente.

The Tory Press Falls in Behind *The Times*

Other leading Conservative newspapers provided solid support for the interventionist case. It is true that in the early days of the crisis Lord Burnham's *Daily Telegraph* was relatively dispassionate. Burnham's editor, John M. Le Sage, offered no sympathy for Serbia in its quarrel with Austria-Hungary, declaring that Germany was perfectly entitled to help her ally 'in exacting her vengeance' for the assassination.[25] The moderation of the paper irritated pro-interventionist firebrands like Leo Amery, who detected in it 'the Jewish influence generally' – a reference to Lord Burnham's ethnicity.[26]

But once Russia's partial mobilisation was publicly known on Thursday 30 July, the *Daily Telegraph* suddenly altered its stand. The 'Triple Entente' was rediscovered as a sacred cause to which Britain must 'remain faithful'.[27] The following day, Friday 31 July, Le Sage strangely found 'one bright spot' in the fact that it was now 'abundantly clear in foreign capitals that France, Russia and Great Britain mean resolutely to stand shoulder to shoulder, whatever the ultimate cost may be'. The *Daily Telegraph* wheeled out the old 'necessity of a Balance of Power' to justify British intervention. Britain must 'be loyal to those whom we ask to be loyal to us'. Astonishingly, Russia's chief role in provoking the intensification of the crisis was admitted, without a hint of reproof: 'The whole of the fatal chain of consequences follows from the fact, or the suspicion that Russia is about to take up arms.'[28]

The *Morning Post*, owned by Lord and Lady Bathurst, was the third of the trio of influential Conservative daily papers. It, too, pressed for a British dash into war. The 'stand by our friends' refrain was repeated in a series of grave editorials. The editor, H. A. ('Taffy') Gwynne, a devout conscriptionist, appealed to Britain's warlike virtues. War was just around the corner; the vital requirement, then, was simultaneous mobilisation: 'If the word mobilisation is pronounced in St Petersburg, Berlin and Paris, it will have to be pronounced in London also.' The Entente was an engagement of honour, to Russia as much as to France. According to Gwynne, Britain was bound by her diplomatic and military conversations – whatever might have been said in parliament about a 'free hand'. On Monday 27 July, frothed Gwynne, 'Engagements, written or unwritten, formal or moral, have been made which cannot now be evaded'.[29]

Lord Astor's *Pall Mall Gazette* propagated the same message. Here the editor, the intimidating J. L. Garvin, also preached instant intervention. One typical editorial, that of Wednesday 29 July, advised: 'Our duty is clear. We must stand by our friends with the most prompt resolution, and with the whole of our might.'[30]

The passionate advocacy of intervention struck a great many observers as pure delirium – and not just Radicals and Liberals. For example, Sir William Tyrrell, Grey's private secretary, confided in a private note to Arthur Ponsonby on 31 July his personal view that 'the "new style" and line *The Times* takes make me fairly sick'.[31] This was not so surprising, because Tyrrell was the one man in Grey's constant company who cherished hopes of reconciliation with Germany.[32]

Many in the Radical camp fumed that the press barons had such power to move opinion in this way. Charles Trevelyan recalled that, as the diplomatic crisis of the week worsened, the Northcliffe press 'was beginning to shriek for war'.[33]

Again it is important to stress how early in the crisis this extreme position – instant intervention and immediate mobilisation – was put by the Conservative press. The editorials preaching this line appeared from Monday 27 July. During the next week, only Russia was known to be mobilising. Even at the seat of the Balkan War, Austria-Hungary did not move to a general mobilisation until Friday 31 July. The clamour for Britain's intervention had been running for a whole week in the Tory-aligned newspapers before it became clear that complications between the Great Powers were imminent. In this way did some newspapers grease the Gadarene slope.

SEVEN

Hope and Dread
Monday 27 to Friday 31 July

But the suggestion that we should spend British lives and British treasure to establish Russia in the Balkans would be an inconceivable outrage to a democratic country. Our hands are free in the business and we must take care to keep them free.[1]
Alfred Gardiner, *Daily News*, 29 July 1914

The British Cabinet was not under some kind of irresistible pressure for war from Britain's Conservative press empires. The vehemence and consistency of the Liberal newspapers in offering opposite advice was quite remarkable. They strongly urged Britain to pursue a strictly neutral diplomacy during the crisis, underpinned by a blunt refusal to depart from neutrality if war broke out. This was not a demand for *mere* neutrality – it was a demand for active neutrality during this crisis, so that Britain, and Europe, had the best chance of averting war.

British Liberals in 1914 took solace chiefly from four daily newspapers. First in importance was the *Westminster Gazette*, edited by J. A. Spender, close ally of the Liberal leaders. Second came the statesmanlike *Manchester Guardian*, the voice of northern liberalism as interpreted by the editor, Charles P. Scott. Third came the Cadbury-owned *Daily News*, edited by Alfred Gardiner, a Radical in outlook. The fourth Liberal masthead was the *Daily Chronicle*, edited by Robert Donald, a temperate voice. Labour readers had two newspapers to comfort the soul, the new *Daily Citizen* and the weekly *Labour Leader*.

The Liberal Press Urges a Neutral Diplomacy

The stance of the *Westminster Gazette* was closely watched in the crisis, for J. A. Spender was known to socialise with both Asquith and Grey. From the outset, Spender's position was complex. He expressed understanding for Austria-Hungary's case against Serbia, but then unease at the very heavy Austrian demands addressed to Serbia. He thought the quarrel 'remote' from British interests.[2] That Austria-Hungary was recklessly spoiling for a war to punish Serbia, encouraged by Germany, remained a consistent theme in his editorials.[3] He supported Grey's proposed Ambassadors' Conference. He urged also that Austria-Hungary must promise no annexation of Serbian territory, a promise that should 'satisfy Russia that her interests are not imperilled'.[4] For Spender, Britain's 'free hand' gave her the credentials to lead a successful mediation.

As the crisis developed, following the Austro-Hungarian declaration of war on Serbia on Tuesday 28 July, Spender's editorials continued to tilt toward British neutrality. He developed four themes: the horror of all Europe being hauled into war through the alliance system; the danger of a Russian over-reaction to Austria's provocation; the importance of Britain maintaining a focus absolutely upon mediation; and a refusal to speculate on British intervention so that Grey's mediation could retain credibility.[5]

But, most significantly, Spender depicted a land war for Britain on the Continent as highly unlikely. Britain had wider 'interests and liabilities', Spender argued – India, the Dominions, the Empire, and vast trade routes requiring protection. He did not support the idea of a BEF scampering across the Channel: 'It is idle at such a moment to speak as if we had an unlimited force which could be committed wholly to military enterprise in Europe without thought of the immense interests elsewhere of which we are the trustees.'[6]

On Friday 31 July, Spender highlighted the Russian danger. Mediation efforts must continue to 'enable the Russian mobilisation to stop'. Significantly, he emphasised again 'the necessity of keeping the free hand for our Government'. He recalled that Asquith in the Commons had stressed that, in this crisis, Britain 'has no interests of its own directly at stake'.[7] The editorials reflected Grey's position: Britain was free, she was mediating, and she cultivated a deliberate ambiguity in her position. But in his stout opposition to the BEF's deployment Spender was closer to the Radicals than to Grey.

The editorial columns of the *Manchester Guardian* were sharper in tone. The paper was even more fervently against British intervention, more hostile toward Russia, and it dogmatically repudiated the idea that Britain had 'obligations' toward the Entente. The principal leader writer on foreign policy was Herbert Sidebotham, C. P. Scott's close friend, who shared the role with L. T. Hobhouse.[8] On Saturday 25 July the *Manchester Guardian* indicated sympathy with the Austro-Hungarian case against Serbia, and denounced Russia's threats on her behalf as 'a piece of sheer brutality'. The British ambassador in St Petersburg should give 'no sort of encouragement to Russian policy'. Grey's task was 'not to destroy our influence for good in Europe by marching us into the Dual Alliance [the Franco-Russian alliance], or for that matter into any camp'.[9]

The *Manchester Guardian* argued from the outset that Britain was not just free but *neutral*. Not only should Britain pursue mediation, she should also rule out military intervention in Russia's cause. A Balkan war might be two weeks away. In that time Britain must pursue an absolutely neutral diplomacy. This would strengthen Britain's 'reputation for impartiality'. Other powers might be roped together in defensive alliances, but Britain had 'no such commitments. Not only are we neutral now, but we could and ought to remain neutral throughout the whole course of the war.'[10]

The *Manchester Guardian* criticised both the Asquith government and the Tory press as the crisis developed. The editorial of Tuesday 28 July found 'one conspicuous omission' in Grey's statement to the

Commons on the Monday: he had not stressed Britain's neutrality. The Tory newspapers made matters worse by undermining 'that reputation for impartiality on which the success of our efforts for peace must chiefly depend'. The *Guardian* took aim at *The Times*' provocative leaders. 'These swelling phrases' masked a militarist spirit, for 'if certain people had their way we should be dragged into the war as members of the so-called Triple Entente'. Liberals must stand firm against the spirit of English militarism: 'The whole future of England depends on the suppression of that spirit. It is war to the knife between it and Liberalism. Either it kills us or we kill it.'[11]

Once war was declared between Serbia and Austria, the *Manchester Guardian*'s editorials grew angrier. The *Guardian* focused on the danger of a Russian leap into war, and denounced the pro-Russian cheer-leading in the Northcliffe press.[12] On Thursday 30 July, Grey and Asquith were criticised for speaking so briefly in the Commons: 'Sir Edward Grey walks deliberately past opportunities of saying that we are and will be neutral in the quarrels of Europe.' But the *Guardian* still reserved its heaviest fire for Russia and the Northcliffe press. Loyalty to Russia in a coming war between Teuton and Slav, as preached by *The Times*, was a 'grotesque conception of our national policy'. Russia was the root cause of the war: 'If Russia makes a general war out of a local war it will be a crime against Europe.'[13]

News of Britain's naval movements and the 'precautionary steps' rang alarm bells. The *Manchester Guardian* denounced the military moves as eroding Britain's impartial stance: 'Either the Government are bluffing or they are preparing to take an active and not merely a defensive part in the war.' The worst aspect of this, the editor warned, was that it may 'have the effect of stiffening Russia in her demands and of destroying our main chance of influencing the councils of Europe for good'. If the government was planning intervention, it was 'a policy that would surpass folly and approach criminality'. And who was pushing this? The *Guardian* warned that 'in the newspapers there is visible the working of a conspiracy to drag us into war'.[14]

The following day, Friday 31 July, a terrible premonition gripped the editorial team at the *Manchester Guardian*. On many occasions Grey and Asquith had assured the House of Commons that Britain had 'a free hand' – yet military preparations were proceeding apace. Was it that the two Liberal leaders had contracted obligations in secret? The *Manchester Guardian* railed against 'the almost unthinkable supposition that by some hidden contract England had been technically committed, behind her back, to the ruinous madness of a share in the wicked gamble of a war between two militarist leagues on the Continent'. Had the Asquith government 'led the country into a calamitous foreign entanglement' after all?[15]

The views of the *Daily News* also evolved during the crisis, but the stress on Britain's neutrality as the key to successful mediation, the need to restrain Russia, and the paramount need to avoid British military intervention were constant themes. Like his fellow editors on the Liberal side, Alfred Gardiner also attacked the Northcliffe press. Gardiner stressed from the beginning of the crisis that there was never a moment when 'the detachment of this country from the European camps was a fact of more momentous consequence'. Grey should use 'the disinterestedness of this country' to bring about successful mediation, he advised. France's task was to 'make it clear to Russia that she will have no share in a war to save Serbia from a proper punishment for her part in the crime of Sarajevo'.[16] Serbia's guilt was 'too flagrant to admit of dispute'.[17]

By Wednesday 29 July, following Austria's declaration of war against Serbia, Gardiner immediately targeted Russia. 'The hope of isolating the struggle depends on Russia', Gardiner argued. France must find the courage to say firmly that she would not back Russia, 'the most barbaric power in Europe'. Gardiner reminded his readers that Russia was 'not the champion of the freedom of anybody', and was justly infamous for the crushing of liberty in Finland and Persia. 'Not a British life shall be sacrificed for the sake of Russian hegemony of the Slav world.' The advocacy of Russia's cause in *The Times* was disgraceful. To 'spend British lives and British treasure to establish Russia in the Balkans would be an inconceivable outrage to a democratic country'.[18] For Gardiner, it was essential that 'the free peoples of France, England and Italy' remain neutral. 'We must not have our Western civilisation submerged in a sea of blood in order to wash out a Serbian conspiracy.'[19]

From Friday 31 July the letters page of the *Daily News* lit up. Dozens of brief statements and special articles arguing against intervention testified to the dread now filling many Liberal hearts. In a transparent attempt to increase pressure on the Liberal Cabinet, famous Liberal names spoke out on neutrality. Some pertinently reproduced Asquith and Grey's answers to questions in parliament over the preceding two years, when both had assured the nation, time and again, that there were no 'unpublished agreements' obligating Britain's intervention on the Continent.[20]

Gardiner's quarrel with *The Times* also produced a special *Daily News* editorial on Friday 31 July in which he defiantly rebutted the argument to be found in the Northcliffe papers that Britain must line up with Russia and France from considerations of honour, principle and interest. If Britain assisted Russia in the defeat of Germany it would 'strike a blow at Western culture in order to bolster up the infinitely lower culture of Eastern Europe'. Britain must not come to the aid of 'the forces of ignorance, reaction and tyranny'. Gardiner mocked the proposition that Britain must rush to war to protect that 'hollow and disastrous' concept of the balance of power. Moreover, he insisted that 'to help Russia to crush Germany and Austria' would upset any balance, make Russia 'the dictator of Europe', and create a real threat to India. He concluded with this advice to the Liberal Cabinet:

> Honour, principle and interest all alike dictate one course – to maintain an absolute neutrality should this lamentable dispute, in which we have neither lot nor part, bring war to the great Continental Powers. By maintaining that attitude now, and making it plain to the world, we shall do much to avert the colossal infamy of war; for we shall dissipate all suspicion as to the sincerity of our efforts for peace, and we shall disillusion any Power which is tempted to drive matters to a crisis because it counts upon our aid. By standing apart from any conflict, we preserve for Europe in the worst event the precious possession of an impartial mediator.[21]

Robert Donald's *Daily Chronicle* took a moderate line across the week: Serbia should yield, Austria-Hungary was largely in the right, Russia should act moderately, and Germany had quite reasonably declined the Ambassador's Conference in favour of direct talks. Britain's Liberal leaders should renounce any intention to intervene.[22]

'BRITAIN MUST HOLD ALOOF'

For Radicals, the stance of the Labour press was heartening too. The new daily Labour Party newspaper, the *Daily Citizen*, launched in October 1912, stood full-square for neutrality.[23] The *Daily Citizen* pleaded for the Foreign Office to work steadfastly against any escalation. 'Once let the fire break out, and who can tell how far the conflagration may spread', warned the paper as early as 22 July.[24]

With much insight, the *Daily Citizen* stressed that Russia's internal situation was a perilous factor in this crisis. Danger arose from the fact that the quarrel with Austria, and the visit of the French delegation to Russia in mid-July 1914, were both taking place at a time of major strikes in Russia. The Tsarist autocracy might be tempted to distract the population with a flag-waving adventure.[25] 'A war between Austria and Serbia would rock all Europe. Russia and Germany would be drawn in, and the battlefield might then extend far enough', cautioned the *Citizen* on Saturday 25 July. But the *Citizen* stressed that 'Russia's attitude is the most sinister feature of an alarming situation.'[26] Russia remained at the centre of the paper's coverage. Thus, the *Citizen* was probably the first newspaper to introduce to the British people the face of the Russian Foreign Minister. On Monday 27 July, the caption under a front-page portrait of Sergei Sazonov declared bluntly, 'Upon Russia and her action rests the fate of Europe.'[27]

What should Britain do? On Thursday 30 July, the paper's front-page headline was 'BRITAIN MUST HOLD ALOOF'. The editorial hissed at Grey: 'Sir Edward Grey will be a traitor to the present and future interests of the country if he allows himself to be drawn in except as a keeper of the peace.'[28] The following day, Friday 31 July, a special box appeared on the front page of the *Daily Citizen* with the headline 'BRITAIN HER OWN MISTRESS – NOT BOUND TO AID ANY EUROPEAN POWERS'. Here Asquith was pinned down by his own statement to the House of Commons of 24 March 1913, specifically promising that there were no engagements that had compromised Britain's free hand.[29] In this way both the Labour and the Liberal press sought to hold Asquith and Grey's feet to the flame on their many assurances that there were no 'unpublished agreements' compromising Britain's freedom to choose between peace and war.

The ILP weekly newspaper *Labour Leader* took the same strong position against intervention. In a guest editorial on Thursday 30 July, Will Anderson, a prodigious new talent in the Labour Party, urged localisation of any conflict. 'It is impossible to exaggerate the issues that tremble in the balance', he wrote. War on a wide scale would see 'the smashing up' of the European socialist movement's plans for social reform for years to come. 'How can war be prevented? For the moment nothing else matters.' Diplomats must not be permitted 'to throw a lighted brand' into the 'powder magazine of Europe'. But to secure peace, the people must demonstrate. What was needed were 'gigantic gatherings' against war, such as the Germans had organised in 1911, to frighten the statesmen. British workers had to 'make it clear to the Government and to Sir Edward Grey that the workers have no intention of letting the country be dragged into war over some Hapsburg quarrel'.[30]

In this way, the leading Liberal and Labour newspapers lined up for neutrality – an active neutrality. In their view, Britain had quite rightly *not* gone to war in July 1911 when France and Germany were quarrelling directly over colonial territory in Africa. For Britain to threaten war in July 1914, when Austria and Russia were quarrelling over an assassination, was unthinkable.

EIGHT

Smearing Neutrality
Thursday 30 and Friday 31 July

But apart from that, for us to make this bargain with Germany at the expense of France would be a disgrace from which the good name of this country would never recover.[1]

Grey to Goschen, 30 July 1914

Very late in the evening of Wednesday 29 July, Bethmann Hollweg, the German Chancellor, made a diplomatic mistake – a serious one, that was easily exploited. He attempted to start negotiations with Britain over her neutrality in any coming conflict. Such negotiations, after all, had taken place in August 1870, when Gladstone achieved the two treaties with Prussia and France. But this time the Germans would begin crudely, by seeking Britain's reaction if Germany promised to take no European territory following the defeat of France in war.

The German Offer – and the British Rebuff

The German approach began with a summons to the British ambassador in Berlin, Sir Edward Goschen, to meet the Chancellor very late in the evening of Wednesday 29 July at the Chancellery in

Berlin. This came after the Chancellor had returned from an exhausting day at Potsdam. Here he and the other German decision-makers had become increasingly agitated by reports of Russia's widening mobilisation.[2]

Bethmann Hollweg spoke with much emotion. He told Goschen that he fully appreciated the 'key-note of British policy', namely, that Britain 'would never allow France to be crushed'. Therefore, he explained, Germany was willing to rule that out. If war happened, and if Britain pledged her neutrality, Germany would make no annexations in Europe. However, responding to a question from Goschen, the Chancellor explained that he could give no assurance with regard to French colonies. Similarly, 'provided that Belgium did not take sides against Germany, her integrity would be respected after the conclusion of the war'. Indicating his own diffidence in making this approach, he then hazarded a question: he asked Goschen how he thought Grey might react. Goschen replied that Grey was unlikely to bind himself: 'personally I thought that you [Grey] would like to retain full liberty of action'.[3] Goschen had a very late night. He cabled a summary of this discussion to London from the British Embassy at 1.20 a.m. on Thursday 30 July. It was marked as received at the Foreign Office at 9 a.m. on the Thursday.

Knowing its consequences, it is easy to agree that the German approach was a serious diplomatic blunder. It revealed the extent to which the German elite was a prisoner of its military planners' decisions. They were proposing to safeguard German security through a military strategy that included a diplomatically disastrous element: an attack in the west via Belgium, ignoring the Treaty of 1839.[4]

Grey saw Goschen's telegram soon after its arrival at the Foreign Office on the morning of Thursday 30 July. He immediately wrote out a reply that constituted an unambiguous rejection and took it across to Downing Street to consult Asquith. Asquith agreed that the German approach should be promptly spurned, 'without waiting for the Cabinet', the next meeting having been set down for Friday. 'Time pressed, and it was certain that the Cabinet would agree that this bid for neutrality could not be accepted', Grey explained later. So, Grey took it back to the Foreign Office, 'and showed the telegram to those whom I was in the habit of consulting there'.[5] This meant, of course, Nicolson, Crowe and Tyrrell. They were luckier than the Cabinet members – for at least they saw the German approach before Grey killed it. Thus, between Cabinets, another critical decision was made: a telegram to Goschen, rejecting the German offer out of hand, was despatched at 3.30 p.m. The German blunder was real enough – and Grey was choosing to capitalise upon it.

Certainly Grey's telegram to Berlin conveyed a spirit of high dudgeon. Goschen was instructed to tell the Chancellor that his proposal – treating it as singular and final – was rejected: 'that we should bind ourselves to neutrality on such terms cannot for a moment be entertained'. The Chancellor, argued Grey's cable, was asking Britain to 'stand by while French colonies are taken and France is beaten'. France would be 'crushed', even if only her colonies were taken. 'But apart from that, for us to make this bargain with Germany at the expense of France would be a disgrace from which the good name of this country would never recover.' Britain similarly could not undertake 'to bargain away whatever obligation or interest we have as regards the neutrality of Belgium'. The word 'bargain' – used in the negative sense of a sordid pursuit of a venal man's price – was employed three times. Britain's leaders preferred to 'preserve our full freedom to act as circumstances may seem to us to require'.[6] In diplomatic terms, these phrases were intemperate. The Chancellor of Germany was being openly accused of asking the British leaders to do shameful things – things that would disgrace Britain's name. There was no hiding the force of the rebuff. In this way, Grey and Asquith slammed the door on the possibility of negotiating to achieve the neutrality of either Belgium or Britain – before any but a handful of Asquith's and Grey's Cabinet colleagues even knew of the German approach.

In the aftermath of the crisis, contempt was heaped upon the German 'bid for neutrality'. It was, critics claimed, self-evident proof of German perfidy. Later, on 6 August, Asquith would wince in horror in the Commons as he related 'this infamous proposal'. Infamous? He was milder at the time. He told Venetia Stanley that the amateurs in Berlin had launched 'a rather shameless attempt on the part of Germany to buy our neutrality'. He noted 'something crude and almost childlike about German diplomacy'.[7] Also, as Radical critics complained later, neither Grey nor Asquith told the House of Commons about this allegedly 'infamous' German offer when each spoke on Thursday 30 and Friday 31 July.[8]

Should this have ended negotiations? The Germans quickly explained their misstep. Foreign Minister Gottlieb von Jagow insisted that the Chancellor would 'not have spoken' in the way he did with Goschen at midnight on Wednesday 29 July if Lichnowsky's cable of the afternoon had arrived in time. It contained Grey's most emphatic warning so far, that there was no chance of British neutrality if war broke out in the west.[9] Why the German leap into such a blunder? The Radical MP Francis Neilson correctly saw the motive behind the German 'bid for neutrality': 'Why, panic is large in every paragraph of it; and that is not surprising.'[10] Recent analyses agree: fear of Russian mobilisation undoubtedly prompted it.[11]

Radical Planning to Resist War

Meanwhile the Cabinet Radicals planned their tactics for the Cabinet of Friday 31 July. Harcourt, Pease and Simon were in touch with their supporters on Thursday morning. A solid core of ministers was firming up for peace, including Birrell, possibly Samuel, and – prodded by Simon – even Lloyd George, who was *entirely* with us' having been bowled over by 'the business view of Manchester'.[12]

In the afternoon, Harcourt lunched with his supporters at the House. Suddenly war seemed close. All were expecting the second reading of the Amending Bill on Irish Home Rule. But Asquith rose to announce its postponement, in light of the 'almost unparalleled' gravity in European affairs.[13] In fact, the Tories had sought postponement, to show Europe a 'solid front'.[14] Asquith's dramatic announcement suddenly raised fears of war. In the Ladies' Gallery sat Margot Asquith. She permitted herself to gloat over the discomfort of the 'Ulster ladies' whose civil war in Ireland was being eclipsed.[15]

Grey then managed the German 'bid for neutrality' of that day with great skill. He spoke confidentially to Harcourt on the front bench. He told the tale, slanting the facts to justify the peremptory rejection:

> Grey told me he had rec[eive]d from Bethmann Hollweg (I suppose thro[ugh] Goschen at Berlin) [a] shameful proposal that we should declare our neutrality on promise from Germ[an] Govt that they would respect [the] neutrality of Holland: ditto of Belgium after they had violated it to attack France: w[oul]d no[t], after crushing France annex European territories (though take her colonies): subsequently offers us a European neutrality & friendship in general affairs. Grey of course without hesitation rejected offer with (I think) some contumely.[16]

Grey must have realised that in exposing this 'shameful proposal' he had an unmatched opportunity that could be exploited to weaken Radical resolve. Harcourt's reaction was encouraging: he instantly acknowledged that Grey had done the right thing. This would guide Grey's tactics. The German gambit could always be represented as the defining moment, evidence that German diplomacy was the work of blackguards, pitted against moral pillars. The option of neutrality for Britain could now be smeared as part of a German plot, and those supporting it the unwitting tools of Berlin.

But Grey also assured Harcourt he was maintaining his stance of deliberate ambiguity. Cambon was coming shortly to the Foreign Office. Again, as Grey predicted, he would put '*the* question: "Are we going to help France if war breaks out[?]"' Grey told Harcourt that he would dutifully stick to the usual reply, namely that he 'cannot answer without a Cabinet (tomorrow morning)' and that 'in pres[ent] circ[umstance]s public opinion here [would] not support or enable H.M.G. to give an affirmative answer'.[17] Clearly, in Grey's judgement, a disappointing answer to France required the endorsement of a Cabinet – but the emphatic refusal already given to Germany had required no such Cabinet.

Harcourt was shocked at Grey's revelation of the German

approach, but it did not shake loose his commitment to neutrality. He continued to prepare his Radical allies. He met again with his colleagues in his room at the Commons that afternoon: Simon, Morley, Hobhouse, Beauchamp, Pease, Runciman and Birrell. Seven ministers were still with him, he believed, and possibly Lloyd George. Seven or eight resignations was not a majority, but it would sink the government. John Morley told Harcourt that 'he was prepared to resign at my signal, but I don't think it will be tomorrow'.[18]

Harcourt spent much of this unhappy Thursday trying to slow the wheels of war in his role as Colonial Secretary. For example, in the morning he confronted more tasks arising from the Warning Telegram. The Admiralty asked him to request the Australian government to place its naval fleet under the command of the Admiralty. He declined, on the grounds it was 'premature, unnecessary, & that I wanted [the] initiative to be taken by Australia'. He did agree to a private message to the new Governor General, Ronald Munro Ferguson, with a request that he should 'try to produce it'. Then, at 5 p.m. he received a response from Australia, acknowledging the Warning Telegram of Wednesday and making an 'unofficial offer of their fleet for our purposes' before Harcourt's request had even reached Munro Ferguson. The Admiralty was pleased, and swiftly asked Harcourt to telegram to Australia again instructing the Australian ships to go immediately to 'war stations'. 'I did so with regret', Harcourt recorded. Again he thought it 'premature', and only 'possibly justified on ground of great distances for their fleet. e.g. The [battle-cruiser] *Australia* has got to go to coast of West Australia.'[19] The incident typified an exquisite difficulty for Harcourt over the coming days: as a leading neutralist he resisted steps toward war at home, while as Colonial Secretary he confronted the eagerness of the Dominions to contribute immediately to any war. Harcourt clung to his position. He ended his private journal for Thursday 30 July with the fighting words: 'War situation I fear much worse tonight. Pray God I can still smash our Cabinet before they can commit the crime.'[20]

On the eve of the Friday Cabinet the atmosphere at 10 Downing Street was quite the reverse. Rupert Brooke, the famous poet, a friend of Violet Asquith, was among dinner guests on Thursday 30 July. He would be forever dead within a year. Later his mother would write to Violet:

> My Rupert hated the idea of war; I shall never forget his misery when he came home last 31 July. He had been dining at your home the night before and had felt very strongly that war was on us; he wouldn't go anywhere and sat almost in silence.[21]

'Neutrality' at the Cabinet of Friday 31 July

Asquith appeared to believe that Britain was now on the eve of combat. Just prior to the Cabinet that began at Downing Street at 11 a.m. the next morning, Friday 31 July, Asquith dropped into Margot's bedroom. Asquith 'said that tho[ugh] he himself had no hope there was an idea that things were better', and then immediately he went 'down to the Cabinet'.[22] This was an astonishing declaration – 'no hope'. Certainly there was mounting financial panic, paralysing the London markets. That morning the Stock Exchange was closed until further notice.[23] But it should be recalled that by that Friday morning no *major* power had yet declared war on another.

If both Asquith and Grey had 'no hope', it may explain their tactics. For when the Cabinet ministers met at 11 a.m. on Friday morning 31 July, Grey led a charge by the interventionists to break the neutralists' refusal to promise anything to France – based on the supposedly transparent dishonour of the German 'bid for neutrality' on the previous day.

The Cabinet embarked upon yet another debate on Britain's stance. Updating the Cabinet, Grey reported that at his Thursday interview with Cambon he had loyally clung to the Cabinet's position: he had 'told him he c[oul]d not answer about our support to France till he had consulted Cab[inet] today'.[24] But then came the real surprise – another ambush. Excepting Harcourt, whom Grey had informed on the Thursday, most ministers learned only here for the first time of the German offer to begin negotiations on the matter of British neutrality, the offer that had been rejected by Asquith and Grey the previous afternoon.

As Grey had pre-empted the Cabinet's decision, he had every motive to play up his revulsion at German wickedness.[25] Harcourt recorded his narrative:

> Grey reported [the] monstrous proposal of Bethman [*sic*] Hollweg of yesterday that we sh[oul]d declare neutrality on promise that Germany w[oul]d not violate neutrality of Holland *now* and guarantee neutrality of Belgium *after the war*! If [Germany] was successful French territory not to be annexed but *this not to apply to Fr[ench] colonies*, & an offer of some permanent German neutrality afterwards.[26]

The indignation over Germany wishing to leave open her option to seize French colonies was largely confected – unless all clean forgot that Britain had often seized colonies in the context of a European war. And indeed she would soon do so again, guided by these same men. In any case, adopting Grey's horrified tone, Harcourt led off for the Radicals, approving Grey's 'admirable telegram' rejecting the 'monstrous' German offer. Harcourt's siding with Grey probably prevented a Cabinet revolt against what Grey and Asquith had done, in the name of all, without Cabinet sanction.

However, Grey's effort to exploit the German blunder did not sway Radical opinion on the main issue. Certainly, the German approach reflected badly on the German leaders. But the Radicals still resisted the claim that all the duplicitous villains were in Berlin. Those in St Petersburg still worried many. Herbert Samuel, for one, was still fearful of Russia's provocative actions and was impressed with the patience of Bethmann Hollweg, notwithstanding Grey's revelations.[27] The neutralists were disappointed with Berlin – but not disgusted.[28]

Discussion turned once again on what Grey should tell the French ambassador at his now daily afternoon interview. Churchill was 'bellicose and aggressive', according to Pease. Lloyd George, however, was in a moderate temper. Having been closeted away during the past few days with Britain's business leaders, Lloyd George spoke effectively of their strong opposition to any war.[29] The Chancellor of the Exchequer was, wrote Harcourt, 'hotly & earnestly on our (peace) side'. He warned of the massive disruption if mills, factories and mines were to close upon the outbreak of war, leaving the 'population starving'. One businessman had told him, 'England will be in revolution in a week.' Harcourt conceded that Lloyd George had 'impressed Cabinet'. But he still did not count on him, because 'as he depends on public opinion he may wobble over again in 2 days'.[30]

At length, the majority against intervention held firm. Grey was fastened down: in his afternoon interview with Cambon he undertook 'definitely that he w[oul]d make no promises as to our action in hypothetical circ[umstance]s'. But, in Harcourt's words, while forced to stick to 'no promises' in his talks with Cambon, Grey proposed to add a morsel of hope:

[Grey p]roposes to tell him this afternoon that present Engl[ish] opinion w[oul]d not support our participation. If Belgium [was] violated, [this] *might* change public opin[ion]. But in any case we could never promise assistance without [the] assent of H of C e.g. vote of credit w[oul]d be necessary.[31]

This last suggestion also introduced a new theme. The Liberal leaders were beginning to speak more about democracy and parliament. The House of Commons, it appeared, would choose between war and peace – *before* any declaration. This pleased the Radicals. Public opinion was cited in Pease's summary of the Cabinet's final resolution: 'British opinion would not now enable us to support France – a violation of Belgian neutrality might alter public opinion, but we could say nothing which could at the moment commit ourselves.' The most important result of the meeting therefore was entirely satisfactory to the Radicals. Harcourt was ebullient: 'It is now clear that *this* Cabinet will not join the war', he scrawled in pencil to Jack Pease.[32]

However, several notes exchanged by neutralists during the Cabinet meeting showed chinks of doubt. 'This is going very well so far', wrote Harcourt to Pease. But Pease betrayed impatience in reply: he was tired of endless debates about Britain being non-committal in 'hypothetical circumstances'. Harcourt counselled him: 'But Grey is not proposing to commit us to any hypothetical position.' Simon's note to Harcourt showed him still solid: 'One large consideration not mentioned today is the importance of Great Britain being in a position in the latter stages of a European war (1) to mediate as a friend all round (2) to re-establish European finance.' Harcourt replied: 'I think our abstention is vital but I don't think anyone will regard us as a friend.'[33] At the end of the day, Harcourt was buoyant. Again he jotted down his conviction: 'I feel now that *this* Cabinet will never join in *this* war – though several colleagues are uneasy on the subject of our treaty obligations about Belgium.'[34]

Two Telegrams – and the Russian Escalation

One more puzzle arises. After the Cabinet meeting of Friday 31 July, at 5.30 p.m., Grey sent two remarkably brief telegrams. They directed Britain's ambassadors in Paris and Berlin to ask the French and German governments *the* crucial question about Belgian neutrality: whether 'in view of [the] prospect of mobilisation in Germany' and 'in view of existing treaties', each respective government 'is prepared to engage to respect [the] neutrality of Belgium so long as no other Power violates it'.[35]

Had the Cabinet of the morning approved this? No.[36] Again, Grey was acting on critical matters between Cabinets. In his memoirs, Grey recalled that on the Friday 'I took a step that contemplated the contingency of war', and sent the two telegrams.[37] In discussion with Cambon earlier in the afternoon, Grey referred to the idea as his own: 'Parliament would wish to know how we stood with regard to the neutrality of Belgium, and it might be that I should ask both France and Germany whether each was prepared to undertake an engagement that she would not be the first to violate the neutrality of Belgium.' Grey floated the idea in light of 'the latest news' just arriving – news of *Russian* general mobilisation.[38]

Were the telegrams prompted by the report of Russian mobilisation? That dreadful news came from the German Embassy in London at about 4.30 p.m. on Friday 31 July. When *exactly* London knew is shrouded in mystery. Tyrrell assured the German Embassy during the afternoon that London had no news of it.[39] Then, dramatically, a few minutes after 5 p.m., Asquith announced it in the Commons, citing 'Germany' as the source.[40] Possibly the facts were confirmed in a brief telegram from Buchanan in St Petersburg that arrived in London at 5.20 p.m.[41] In any case, it is remarkable that, following Asquith's announcement of general *Russian* mobilisation, signalling a crisis in the *east*, within half an hour the Foreign Office despatched the two telegrams to Paris and Berlin, referring to a mooted *German* mobilisation, and fixing upon the central issue in the *west* – the neutrality of Belgium! Clearly, a determination to find the chief fault in Berlin was at work.

London's political priorities were also evident in both the timing and the content of the telegrams. A war in the west, in which Belgium displaced all other anxieties, might unify the Asquith Cabinet. Answers to the two telegrams might be politically useful in Cabinet. They might help the interventionists to shift attention to considerations of British *interests* in Belgium and away from the more controversial matter of British *obligations* to France. Politics was dictating diplomatic tactics.

Clearly Grey was preparing to argue that German bad faith was again self-evident. In making this case, it can be said that he blurred the historical record. In his memoirs he claimed that in sending these two telegrams he 'was in close accord with the attitude of Mr Gladstone's Government in the Franco-Prussian War of 1870'.[42] Of course, the parallel was not so neat. For in 1870, both France and Prussia had been promised something in the negotiated treaties additional to that of 1839: a degree of security if each respected Belgian neutrality, because Britain would remain neutral; but if either violated Belgian neutrality, that belligerent was threatened with military complications on Belgian soil from British forces, despatched only for the purpose of maintaining Belgian neutrality. This time the promises of security and the threats of military complications were not spelled out, not negotiated, and did not confront France and Germany with equal military hazards. In late July 1914, in the context of the public revelation of Russian general mobilisation, and with Germany facing the danger of invasion on *two* fronts, Grey's diplomacy amounted to a gesture that was only apparently even-handed. Of course, none of this excuses the resort to force in the west by the panic-stricken German elite in 1914.

At dinner at Downing Street on that Friday night, Russia's sudden escalation of the crisis must have been in every mind. Asquith had only just told the Commons of it. Now he sat down to dinner with his sons Raymond and Cyril, along with Churchill and Edwin Montagu, junior minister at the Treasury. Margot Asquith found she could scarcely look at the 'self-centred' Churchill, and fled from his emphatic flow of remarks – 'mind you, *mark my words*, make *no* mistake Margot. *I. I.*' Enthusiasts for intervention were in the majority when Grey, Haldane and Crewe joined the company for bridge. Montagu outshone them all in his eagerness for war. Jumping up from the cards, he seized Margot's arm 'and in a violent whisper said "We ought to mobilise tomorrow and declare it!"' He fumed with hatred for the neutralists holding Britain back. 'How I wish Simon c[oul]d be crushed right out! His influence is most pernicious. He and Lloyd George my chief are against this.'[43]

For Britain the undertow of the crisis was now keenly felt. In the space of a week, the Cabinet had travelled from a desultory discussion of war across remote frontiers in the Balkans, to nerve-jangling discussions over the fate of Belgium and France. As Friday ended, Russia's bombshell sank in.

NINE

The Internationalists Awake
Tuesday 28 to Friday 31 July

Great Britain in no conceivable circumstances should depart from a position of strict neutrality and [this meeting] appeals to His Majesty's Government to give effect to this view while continuing to offer its good offices in every promising way to secure the restoration of peace.[1]

> Resolution signed by eleven Liberal MPs and
> sent to Sir Edward Grey, 29 July 1914

Over the weekend of 1–2 August, advocates of neutrality would come to the realisation that during the preceding week of international crisis they had been duped. The Radicals at Westminster would suspect that the Liberal leaders had misled them in a deliberate effort to muzzle their dissent. Suddenly, by the end of the week, Britain's internationalists both inside and outside parliament were preparing to mount a public campaign for neutrality.

The Muzzling of the Radical Backbench

One Radical most anxious about Grey's management of the crisis from the very beginning was Charles Trevelyan. He got drips of information from several ministers, including Runciman and Pease. But it was Trevelyan's personal encounters with Grey that most troubled him. Probably on Friday 24 July, just after news reached London of the Austro-Hungarian ultimatum to Serbia, Trevelyan had a difficult exchange with Grey at the House of Commons:

> I went up to him and asked him for news. I said something quite politely about the matter not concerning us at all, and that I presumed we should be strictly neutral. He replied in an extraordinarily hard, unsympathetic way. He seemed to be coldly angry with me, and insisted on perverting my words into the meaning that under all circumstances we should necessarily stand aside. So obvious was it that he disliked the idea of neutrality, that I got extraordinarily uncomfortable … It created a profound distrust in my mind.[2]

In these early days, however, in common with most MPs, Radicals believed the crisis in Ireland 'far outweighed' that in the Balkans.[3] For example, Arthur Ponsonby, the ex-diplomat, passionate advocate of a more 'democratic' foreign policy and Chair of the Liberal Foreign Affairs Group (LFAG), immersed himself in the Irish crisis from late June.[4] Poignantly, he still found time for internationalist gestures: on 9 July he hosted thirty German schoolboys on their visit to Westminster – part of the doomed generation.[5] He did not mention the European crisis in letters to his wife Dolly until Monday 27 July. Ponsonby observed simply that 'European war I hope may still be prevented.'[6]

Inside the House of Commons, the Radical MPs convoked their first LFAG meeting on the Balkans only on Wednesday 29 July. But with Ireland still centre-stage, few MPs could be mustered. Just eleven Radical MPs deliberated, with Ponsonby in the Chair.[7] A resolution was composed, deploring the recklessness of *The Times* for demanding British intervention. The LFAG urged that 'Great Britain in no conceivable circumstances should depart from a position of strict neutrality and appeals to His Majesty's Government to give effect to this view while continuing to offer its good offices in every promising way to secure the restoration of peace.'[8] It was signed by all eleven MPs present.

In forwarding this resolution to Grey, Ponsonby wrote an accommodating covering letter. He informed Grey that the group had expressed 'the most complete confidence' in his diplomacy. He promised to do nothing publicly that might 'embarrass' him in his 'delicate negotiations' to preserve the peace. The resolution would 'not be reported to the press'. This must have appealed to Grey very much. But Ponsonby also pointed to 'alarmist reports of the mobilisation of our forces' – the naval movements, publicised since Monday. Ponsonby stressed the Radicals' key demand: 'It was felt that if both France and Russia were informed that on no account would we be drawn into war even though they and other European powers were involved it would have a moderating effect on their policy.'[9]

A promise on Britain's part that 'on no account' would she intervene, of course, clashed with the Cabinet's policy of 'apparent indecision'. It was the opposite of Grey's own fundamental conviction, that if war commenced Britain was obliged to intervene as the virtual ally of France and Russia. But Grey replied immediately, summoning Ponsonby for a private talk. Both were excruciatingly cordial. For the moment, Grey assured Ponsonby that he could make 'no open statement of our determination not to be drawn in'. Grey explained soothingly that 'doubt on this point was useful to him in negotiating'. Britain was 'absolutely free and working for peace'. As Ponsonby recorded, Grey made it clear he 'would prefer our keeping quiet this week'.[10] Grey's intentions were clear: to stifle the Radicals for as long as possible so that he might escape domestic pressures to declare neutrality. Grey's reassurances percolated through Radical ranks. Edmund Harvey, a Radical MP, wrote,

> I believe that the great majority of the Cabinet are absolutely sound on keeping England out of the war, but there is a minority of a different view and one dreads the influence of Churchill. Grey is anxious to do what we can to restrain Germany by not announcing that we do not intend to fight ... I believe Grey is working his hardest and doing his utmost to prevent a general war.[11]

Grey was not the only pro-interventionist Cabinet member seeking to throw dust in the eyes of the Radicals. Churchill was also in the game. Ponsonby wrote to him on 31 July, pleading with him to 'use all your influence toward moderation'. Churchill could scarcely have failed to notice Ponsonby's observation that the Radicals had 'held back so far in our desire not to do anything which might embarrass Grey in the slightest degree'. Churchill replied, 'So long as no treaty obligation or true British interest is involved I am of your opinion that we sh[ould] remain neutral.' In Cabinet, of course, Churchill had already argued that neutrality was impossible. But, appearing to reinforce Grey's policy of fostering doubt as Britain's best contribution to peace, Churchill explained that it would be 'wrong at this moment to pronounce finally one way or another as to our duty or our interests'.[12] So, the Radicals should be quiet.

Asquith, too, was using his influence behind the scenes to discourage the Radicals from going public, even enlisting the Archbishop of Canterbury, Randall Davidson, in this cause. The Radical MP J. Allen Baker, who was about to travel to a Christian internationalist conference at Lake Constance in Germany, had approached Davidson on Thursday 30 July, seeking his signature for a manifesto to be published in favour of British neutrality.[13] The Archbishop refused his signature and the next day consulted Asquith, who assured Davidson that such public manifestos would be 'actively harmful'.[14] The Radicals, and Christians, should keep silent for the sake of Britain's inscrutability – so politically convenient and diplomatically necessary.

At question time in the House of Commons on Thursday 30 July, the Radicals were true to their promise of restraint. No Radical asked a question. Bonar Law, the Conservative leader, simply asked for the latest information. Grey answered briefly, assuring the Commons that, notwithstanding the Russians' partial mobilisation of their forces on the previous day, Britain continued 'to pursue the one great object, to preserve European peace'.[15]

The LFAG met immediately afterwards, attracting twenty-two members. Apprehensive of escalation of the war in Serbia, the group decided that Ponsonby should write again – this time to Asquith.

In his letter Ponsonby again cited the Radicals' restraint so far as proof of their good faith. But now he wrote boldly. The Radicals wished to record, wrote Ponsonby, their 'strongest possible conviction that Great Britain on no account should be drawn into a war in which neither treaty obligations, British interests, British honour or even sentiments of friendship are at present in the remotest degree involved'. A threat followed. If Britain entered the war, Radical MPs would contemplate 'the actual withdrawal of support from the Government'. Ponsonby estimated that 'nine tenths of the party' were behind his group. He warned Asquith that at question time next day, Friday 31 July, he planned to direct a question to Grey on behalf of the Radicals, seeking assurances of neutrality from the government.[16] Clearly the Radicals wanted to hear Grey or Asquith disavow the 'stand-by-our-friends' line being run by *The Times*.

Grey responded for Asquith. He summoned Ponsonby on Thursday evening. Grey reassured him that Britain was still pursuing even-handed diplomacy and that he had 'made no promises and used no "threats" to anyone'.[17] But Grey dodged the foreshadowed inconvenient question in the House. When the LFAG met again the following morning, Friday 31 July, Ponsonby informed the group that he had just received a letter from Tyrrell. He advised Ponsonby that Grey would not be in his place in the Commons on that day to answer any questions. He would be swallowed up by his duties at the Foreign Office. Tyrrell pleaded, on Grey's behalf, for patience. The LFAG Radicals again drew back, deciding to delay Ponsonby's question.[18]

Cabinet discussed the Radicals' threat to ask a question of Grey on that same Friday morning. Grey told Cabinet he was 'inclined to give the answer A. P. [Ponsonby] wants, but not till Monday'. Harcourt noted that some ministers were 'rather unwilling', and others dismissive, declaring that 'it amounts to nothing!' Harcourt urged that an answer be given 'as it helps our peace friends to keep quiet – most important they should do so and we in Cab[inet] still remain uncommitted so as to strengthen Grey's hands diplomatically'.[19] Later, Asquith sent a suitably respectful letter to Ponsonby, assuring him of the government's pacific intentions.[20] The incident illustrates how the policy of supposed inscrutability could be used to induce the Radicals to 'keep quiet'.

Indeed, for a week the Radical faction at Westminster had kept quiet. Believing in the assurances offered them, the Radicals withdrew themselves as a factor on the floor of the parliament itself. Moreover, they were still confident in their allies inside the Cabinet, especially Harcourt and Runciman.[21] For instance, on Thursday 30 July both Lord Bryce and Percy Molteno consulted Harcourt to exchange views 'on behalf of Radicals'. Molteno was prominent in the LFAG, and Bryce was regarded as a sympathetic Radical elder. Harcourt proudly recorded that 'they were confident in me and as long as I stayed in Cabinet they w[oul]d assume that peace was assured'.[22] The impenetrable diplomatic fog protected Grey too. Some Radicals admitted that they were groping forward, with few firm facts that might have emboldened them. It was a roller-coaster ride in the gloom. For example, Christopher Addison, a member of the LFAG, recalled that most members of the group 'felt so much in the dark'.[23]

By the end of the week, the more ardent were tired of waiting. After all, neither Grey nor Asquith had moved an inch in their direction. Neither man had publicly breathed a word of caution at Russia. Neither man had disavowed *The Times*. On Friday 31 July, Morgan Philips Price, a young Liberal lion, wrote to Hirst:

> Should Sir Edward Grey be hounded on by the Foreign Office and those devils of the 'Times' to involve us in a European war, I hope a *great outcry* will be raised all over the country by those Liberals who still hold true to the traditions of Liberalism as enshrined in the lives of Bright, Gladstone and Cobden ... This is the supreme crisis of Liberalism. Is everything we hold dear to be sacrificed to the '*Moloch*' of the '*European Power Balance*'? Are these barbarian Slavs to rule not only Asia but Europe also, in order that Jingo Editors may fatten, armament dividends increase, and the poor plunged further into social misery. I feel the gravity of the situation profoundly.[24]

On the same day, Charles Trevelyan remembered that he became 'really alarmed'. Runciman counselled him: 'One thing was clear that Grey was insisting on keeping our hands free. That, it was said, was the best way of putting pressure on Germany.' But Trevelyan now had grave doubts and believed the situation was 'extraordinarily unsatisfactory'. A second personal encounter with Grey heightened his fears. Late in the evening of Friday 31 July, Trevelyan met Grey on the little blue bridge across the lake in St James Park. Grey, no doubt, was on his way to Haldane's house at 28 Queen Anne's Gate, where he had been staying since Monday in order to be just a short walk from the Foreign Office building:

> I felt how hard he was, nothing but cold distance. I remember a feeling coming over me as he spoke that he was of a different world, and that I almost regarded him as an enemy. I parted from him sick with the feeling that he was concealing things I should hate.[25]

The Neutrality Committees

Outside the House of Commons, internationalists and peace activists of various kinds had also been stirred into life. Two committees were formed almost simultaneously, with the aim of mounting a public campaign for neutrality.

Norman Angell's British Neutrality League was the first, launched on Tuesday 28 July. Angell, author of the liberal internationalist classic *The Great Illusion* (1909), was perhaps the most gifted publicist of the age. For the best part of a decade, Angell had sedulously promoted his vision of peace secured by international understanding and economic integration. He ran an organisation called the Civil Union, and the journal *War and Peace*.[26] In mid-July 1914, Angell had led an international conference for students at Beaconsfield. Back in London, as he recalled, 'I found myself surrounded by these youngsters who'd come from Beaconsfield – American, French, German – wanting to know what was to be done.' Angell founded 'in twelve hours' the British

Neutrality League. 'I had the feeling that if we could only *get a little time* we might even yet stop this disaster.'[27] He soon had a staff based at the Salisbury Hotel.[28] The group initiated a publicity campaign and money rolled in. On Friday morning 31 July, Trevelyan visited Angell and found him 'preparing for a press demonstration next week in favour of neutrality'. He recalled that Angell was 'buying up whole sheets of newspapers for advertising neutrality'.[29]

Angell was also the first to challenge *The Times* in its own columns. His special target was Russia. His letter appeared on Saturday 1 August, neatly summarising the Radical critique.

> The object and effect of our entering into this war would be to ensure the victory of Russia and her Slavonic allies. Will a dominant Slavonic federation of, say, 200,000,000 autocratically governed people, with a very rudimentary civilisation, but heavily equipped for military aggression, be a less dangerous factor in Europe than a dominant Germany of 65,000,000 highly civilised people and mainly given to the arts of trade and commerce?

In the Crimean War, Angell reminded his readers, Britain had fought for the purpose of preventing Russian aggrandisement. 'We are now asked to fight for the purpose of promoting it.' He concluded that Britain could 'best serve civilization, Europe – including France – and ourselves by remaining the one power in Europe that has not yielded to the war madness'.[30]

A second dissident group, the British Neutrality Committee, appeared on Friday 31 July, launched by Graham Wallas, a leading political scientist, and John Hobson, the renowned Radical economist. Starting work on the same day, the two men drafted a declaration urging Britain's neutrality. In Wallas's view, Britain should emulate the United States and Italy, proclaim absolute neutrality, and work single-mindedly upon mediation.[31] Wallas and Hobson were joined by a small number of supporters at the National Liberal Club over the weekend, including journalists like Sam Ratcliffe of the *Manchester Guardian*. Charles Trevelyan looked in. He thought the Wallas-Hobson group was slow moving.[32] Wallas took rooms on the Strand for his committee, and prepared for a long period of agitation. The group attracted big names, such as Lord Courtney, the Quaker peer, and the academics Lowes Dickinson and Gilbert Murray. Hobson attempted to gain the allegiance of the Liberal elder statesman Lord Bryce, but, like some other Liberals, he urged the Radicals not to make waves in public but rather to trust the government's peaceful intentions.[33]

Angell's group was the more dynamic. Over the weekend his advertisements began to appear. He composed a number of 'Neutrality League Announcements' for the press and for distribution as handbills in the street. These attacked the 'War Party' in Britain and warned that intervention would help catapult Russia to European mastery. According to Angell, one military officer rushed to agree: 'I think it will take us five years to get the Russians into Europe and fifty to get them out.'[34] Angell's handbills also stressed that under existing treaties Britain 'was not bound to join in a general European war to defend the neutrality of Belgium'.[35]

The International Women's Movement

The fervent internationalists of the women's movement were also spurred into action. Internationalism had become an important ingredient in the ideology of the women's movement over recent years.[36] For example, at Rome in May 1914 the International Council of Women (ICW) had warmly commended international arbitration. The conference also recognised the special vulnerability of women in regions of conflict. The problem of rape in wartime was talked about quite openly.[37]

In part the energy of the women's movement in Britain in July 1914 came as a result of a happy chance: the fact that the International Women's Suffrage Alliance (IWSA) happened to be meeting in London under the presidency of the American suffragist Carrie Chapman Catt. The IWSA, in which twenty-six nations were represented, was the most important women's suffrage organisation in the world. On its board were formidable propagandists for the cause of female equality.[38] The British were strongly represented. Millicent Garrett Fawcett, the famous leader of the National Union of Women's Suffrage Societies (NUWSS), and Chrystal Macmillan, the Scottish lawyer, were there. The headquarters of the IWSA was also in London. Naturally there was close fellowship between officers of the IWSA and the NUWSS.

The mostly younger British women pushed forward the issue of peace in July 1914. Mary Sheepshanks, Kathleen Courtney, Catherine Marshall, Maude Royden, and Helena Swanwick were devoted to that cause. Some of these women had experienced some German education or had family connections in Germany, which led them to question British nationalist simplicities.[39] They were influential within both the NUWSS and the IWSA and were keen to mount a public campaign for peace.[40]

The IWSA board met in London on 9 July to prepare the next conference on women's suffrage, to be held in Berlin in 1915.[41] Over the next weeks, Rosika Schwimmer, a visiting Hungarian suffragist, gave events a new twist. She had just been appointed press secretary of the IWSA.[42] She had an eye for propaganda and a passion for peace. For instance, over breakfast at 11 Downing Street on Thursday 9 July she had told Lloyd George to watch for war escalating from the Balkan crisis.[43] During July she turned heads when she attacked London's billposting firms for refusing a suffragist poster on child mortality, which happened to feature a mother and naked child.[44] During her visit to London, Schwimmer shared digs with Sheepshanks and Marshall in Westminster. There a plan took shape. As the Balkan crisis unfolded, the women decided to urge the IWSA to sponsor a high-profile action against war, even though President Catt had only just departed for America.[45]

Prodded by these younger activists, the British branch of the IWSA met in London on Wednesday 29 July. Fawcett and Macmillan, for the IWSA, deliberated with Emily Hobhouse, Courtney, Swanwick, Marshall and Sheepshanks. The women agreed to Schwimmer's plans. The first step was to draw up an IWSA manifesto.[46]

The manifesto implored European governments to negotiate a solution to the crisis. The tone was emphatic and moving. It did not neglect the fundamental object of the IWSA: the women's claim for suffrage. It railed against the stark injustice that voteless women faced the 'threatened unparalleled disaster' of war. The manifesto combined this with a prophetic denunciation of war itself: 'Whatever its result the conflict will leave mankind the poorer, will set back civilisation, and will be a powerful check to the gradual amelioration in the condition of the masses of the people, on which so much of the real welfare of the nation depends.' The manifesto called on all the governments 'to leave untried no method of conciliation or arbitration for arranging international differences which may help to avert deluging half the civilised world in blood'.[47] Fawcett and Macmillan signed for the IWSA. As these two women spoke for the international body, the appeal was directed to all governments, and did not specifically promote British neutrality.

The manifesto and the moment were historic. The international organisation for women's suffrage, speaking for the women of the world – half of humanity – was shouting a protest against war as the horrific event hurtled towards them.

But how was this manifesto to be distributed? It was sent to the press, of course. But then Fawcett insisted that a delegation should meekly deliver copies to the doorways of the various London embassies and not seek interviews with the ambassadors. This disappointed Macmillan and Schwimmer, who pressed for some eye-catching gesture.[48] The manifesto did appear in full in most Liberal newspapers, such as the *Manchester Guardian*, on Saturday 1 August, but with much shorter reports – or none – in the Conservative press.[49] On that same day, the IWSA sent an appeal directly to Queen Wilhelmina of Holland, seeking her intervention for peace on behalf of the women of the world. This, too, gained publicity for the manifesto.[50] But Schwimmer and her friends looked for an opportunity for more defiant propaganda.

They got their chance. Over the weekend, European women's organisations urged the IWSA in London to make a more spectacular demonstration for peace.[51] Marshall and Sheepshanks advocated a large public meeting.[52] By Monday 3 August, the NUWSS had agreed. Acting with great haste, the NUWSS booked the new Kingsway Hall in London – for the evening of the very next day, Tuesday 4 August. The purpose of the demonstration, explained Royden in *Common Cause*, was to provide 'a public platform in London upon which women of various societies could voice the women's claim to be heard on questions of peace and war'.[53] But time was short.

TEN

Doing Diplomacy in a Dressing Gown
Friday 31 July and Saturday 1 August

I felt quite helpless as far as Russia was concerned, and I did not believe any Power could exercise influence alone.[1]

Sir Edward Grey, 24 July 1914

The Russian decision to order general mobilisation had been made between 7 p.m. and 9 p.m. on Wednesday 29 July. The decision came at a meeting attended by Sazonov, the Foreign Minister, Sukhomlinov, the Minister of War, and General Yanushkevich, the Chief of Staff. It was endorsed immediately by the Tsar over the telephone and 'received with enthusiasm' by the Russian military planners in St Petersburg.[2] As one expert has argued, it was this decision that 'effectively shattered any prospect of averting a great European war'.[3] Pink posters announcing general mobilisation appeared all over the city of St Petersburg early on Friday 31 July.[4] Reliable news of this catastrophic development, as remarked previously, reached London late in the afternoon of Friday 31 July. How did Britain respond?

Buckingham Palace in the Small Hours

Russia's move represented a huge difficulty for Asquith and his government. Would not Russia now be exposed as in the wrong? Would not Germany be acting in self-defence? It was an obstacle for those hoping to manoeuvre Britain to action in lockstep with her Entente partners. Grey certainly realised this. He told Cambon on Friday that the Russian move 'would precipitate a crisis, and would make it appear that German mobilisation was being forced by Russia'.[5]

The problem pursued the Liberal leaders late into the evening. Soon after midnight, a special communication, in German, was rushed to the Foreign Office from the German Embassy in London. William Tyrrell considered it so important that he brought it to Downing Street. The message detailed the Kaiser's effort to have the latest British and German proposals for mediation accepted at Vienna. Then it outlined complaints that the Tsar's peremptory resort to general mobilisation had sabotaged this. Next were indications that two ultimata – although the word did not appear – had already been sent from Berlin to St Petersburg and Paris. The message explained that the Germans had been forced by the Russian action to demand that Russia halt her mobilisation and that France proclaim her neutrality.[6] War loomed.

Asquith considered the message so serious that, in spite of the late hour, he sat down immediately with Grey's assistants, Tyrrell and Eric Drummond, and his own secretary, Maurice Bonham Carter, to plan a response. They composed the text of a telegram, in the form of a personal appeal from King George V to Tsar Nicholas II, imploring the Tsar to keep negotiating for peace. Then Asquith and Tyrrell drove to Buckingham Palace to obtain the King's consent, arriving at about 12.30 a.m. on the Saturday morning. George V's Equerry in Waiting woke the King and he met Asquith in the Audience Room at 12.45 a.m.[7] 'The poor King was hauled out of bed', as Asquith explained, 'he in a brown dressing gown over his night shirt & with copious signs of having been aroused from his first "beauty sleep" – while I read the message and the proposed answer'. In Asquith's suggested text, King George urged Tsar Nicholas to clear away any 'misunderstanding' that must have produced 'this deadlock' in the negotiations. The King suggested some more personal touches to be included in the message: 'My dear Nicky' at the beginning and his childhood pet-name 'Georgie' at the end. In his diary later, King George recorded simply that Asquith 'showed me the draft of a telegram he wanted me to send to Nicky as a last resort to try to prevent war, which, of course, I did'.[8] This plea to the Tsar was duly telegraphed from the Foreign Office to the British Embassy in St Petersburg at 3.30 a.m. on Saturday 1 August, with instructions that Buchanan should seek an audience with the Tsar 'at once' to pass on George V's personal appeal.[9]

Asquith was back at 10 Downing Street at about 2 a.m. Still wakeful hours later, he eventually found a vision of his beloved Venetia Stanley 'floating about me' and this 'brought me rest and peace'.[10]

The Restraint of Russia

These events naturally prompt the question, Did Britain do its best to restrain Russia? The question was asked at the time. Had the government 'pressed Russia not to go on mobilising her troops while negotiations were going on?' enquired Aneurin Williams in the Commons on Monday 3 August. 'Did we bring such pressure upon Russia? We have had no assurance of it today.'[11] Later the Radicals would complain that Grey 'had failed utterly to influence Russia's military preparations'.[12] Did he try?

In fact, during the crisis Grey paraded his inability to restrain Russia. The whole relationship with Russia was fraught. A massive British government investment in the Anglo-Persian Oil Company, to secure oil for the Admiralty's newest oil-fired ships, had been finalised only weeks beforehand. Plans to exploit oil resources in the neutral zone of Persia would be put at risk if relations with Russia soured.[13] Very early in the crisis Grey had warned Lichnowsky that he 'would be quite unable to put a curb on Russian policy', because Anglo-Russian relations were very sensitive at the time.[14] On Friday

24 July, after news of the Austrian ultimatum, Grey remarked to Cambon that he 'had not contemplated anything being said in St Petersburg until after it was clear that there must be trouble between Russia and Austria'.[15] Similarly, he informed Lichnowsky on that same day that he could no longer 'endeavour to exercise a moderating influence at St Petersburg'. 'I felt quite helpless as far as Russia was concerned', Grey explained.[16]

But he was not powerless to raise Russia's hopes. As mentioned previously, on Monday July 27 Grey had flourished the 'stand-fast' order to the fleet at Portland.[17] In Paris, Lord Bertie was underwhelmed. Alone among Grey's advisers, he urged London and Paris 'to put pressure on the Russian Government not to assume the absurd and obsolete attitude of Russia being the protectress of all Slav States whatever their conduct, for this will lead to war'.[18] Lichnowsky coaxed Grey in the same direction. On Wednesday 29 July, he 'begged' Grey to counsel moderation in Russia and 'to prevent a general mobilisation there'. This time Grey had replied that he 'would use his influence in this direction and try to get them to keep as cool as possible'.[19]

Did he? This raises the more general issue of relations between Grey and the Russian ambassador, Benckendorff. In May 1914 Benckendorff had told St Petersburg of his confidence that 'the real leaders of the Cabinet' would always 'carry the day' against the Radicals in ensuring Britain marched with Russia. 'I doubt whether a more powerful guarantee for common military operations could be found in the event of war, than this spirit of the Entente'.[20] During the whole course of the crisis, Benckendorff appears to have sent directly to Grey one solitary note, on Saturday 1 August – a note denying Russian responsibility for the disaster.[21] Grey saw Benckendorff only six times during the crisis. From the moment it grew serious, on Thursday 23 July, Grey saw Benckendorff only three times – on Saturday 25 July, Monday 27 July and Thursday 30 July – and not once after Russian general mobilisation was known.[22] This compares with a total of ten interviews with Paul Cambon and fourteen with Prince Lichnowsky across the same period. Benckendorff was scarcely under any pressure from Grey.

The issue of reining in Russia troubled Grey long into the future. For example, in April 1918, Grey explained to Gilbert Murray that it was the German 'veto' against his proposed Ambassadors' Conference that had disabled him with regard to Russia. 'I could not protest against Russian preparation for the event of war,' Grey pleaded, 'especially as the German preparations were far ahead of the Russian, and I could not promise the support of this country to Russia.'[23] Ten years later Grey clung to the same explanation. 'After Germany refused the Conference', Grey told Gooch, 'I could not put pressure on Russia.'[24] In Grey's memoirs also he explained his impotence in the matter. After 31 July, he wrote, 'Germany ceased to talk of anything but the Russian mobilisation. I could do nothing to stop that.' Indeed, he was irritated. 'I felt impatient at the suggestion that it was for me to influence or restrain Russia. I could do nothing but express pious hopes in general terms to Sazonov.'[25]

What was done *after* news of general mobilisation arrived in London? What became of the late-night plea from George V to Nicholas II? In that cable, sent to Buchanan at 3.30 a.m. on Saturday 1 August, there was no direct request for a reconsideration of Russia's mobilisation. It reached Buchanan at 5 p.m. and he did not see the Tsar until 10.45 p.m. Then, stunningly imposing his own choices upon national decision-making, Buchanan assisted the Tsar in composing a reply rebuffing George V. The return cable explained that the plea was too late – the German ambassador in St Petersburg had given notice of the formal declaration of war at 7 p.m. Asquith's first effort to restrain Russia, therefore, fizzled out.[26]

But a second, related effort was in process, and this went straight to the matter of Russian mobilisation. At 6.30 p.m. on the same day, Saturday 1 August, more than six hours after the German ultimatum to Russia had expired, Grey sent another cable to Buchanan. This time he had a direct proposal, bearing upon Russia's mobilisation: he requested him to inform Sazonov that Austria had indicated readiness to accept mediation in Vienna, assuming Britain would 'urge upon [the] Russian Government to stop the mobilisation of troops directed against Austria'. In light of this, Buchanan was directed to ask specifically if 'Russia can agree to stop mobilisation'.[27] There was no direct response. As noted above, just a half-hour after Grey sent this cable, Germany declared war against Russia.

Had Britain sought to 'hose down' Russia? Grey had settled for the wave of a watering can. He retained a kind of indefatigable naïveté about the capacity of the Entente – as something less than a defensive alliance – to restrain both Russia and France. Apparently, he could rely on the fact that Britain's position was not quite certain. 'They might hope for our help,' he wrote later, 'but they knew that any aggressive policy on their part would destroy that hope.'[28]

There was always the possibility that Britain might contemplate getting at Russia via France. But Paris repelled any such pressure. The French leaders beamed one message at Grey and the Cabinet: Britain had the responsibility to deter war – by threatening to make war. There was no question of a joint approach to Russia to reverse her military steps.[29] A special effort to keep Britain straight on this point came on Friday 31 July. With his government's backing, Poincaré addressed a personal letter to George V. At the heart of the letter was a blunt warning. If Germany believed Britain would 'stand aloof', then war was inevitable. But if Germany 'realises that, should occasion arise, the Entente Cordiale would be affirmed on the battlefield', then peace might be saved. There was no talk of holding back Russia. Quite to the contrary, Poincaré rebuffed the very idea. Britain, France and Russia must show '*complete unity in diplomatic action*'.[30] This appeal was delivered to Buckingham Palace, via the French Embassy, in the evening. Of course, it was meant for the Cabinet as much as the King.[31]

Certainly Grey was not the man to urge Paris to restrain St Petersburg. Grey's standard line, maintained even in the House of Commons on Monday 3 August, was that Britain knew nothing about the inner workings of the Franco-Russian alliance.[32] This, of course, beggared belief, and Radicals expressed amazement.[33] But ignorance was all to a purpose: not knowing the terms of the Franco-Russian alliance, Grey could scarcely be expected to pressure France or Russia on the subject.

The Cabinet ministers appear to have been equally acquiescent, even though details of Russia's mobilisation were slowly revealed to them. The issue of restraining Russia does not seem to have gripped the Cabinet. The letters of Herbert Samuel, in the centre of the Cabinet factions, are telling in this regard. On Tuesday 28 July Samuel wrote to tell his wife Beatrice that there was 'a strange silence from Russia'. Either she 'intends to keep quiet', or 'she is carrying out the preliminaries of her mobilisation without alarming the Germans prematurely'.[34] The next day he wrote, 'Russia will mobilise her southern armies tomorrow'.[35] Then, on Thursday 30 July, he wrote, 'Russia is mobilising her northern armies now. Germany will probably mobilise tomorrow.' Moreover, Samuel entertained no hope at all that France could resist the tug of alliances: 'The French, most unwilling of all, are dragged in by their Russian alliance, and cannot abstain without treachery.'[36] 'Russia has mobilised all her forces', he reported to Beatrice on Friday 31 July.[37] Samuel's only record of British action to nudge Russia was his account of Asquith's visit to the Palace in the early hours of Saturday 1 August to arrange the fruitless cable to the Tsar.[38]

Did not Radicals in the Cabinet press hard for the restraint of Russia? Morley wrote later of having warned the Cabinet repeatedly of the danger of supporting Russia, and of Russian aggrandisement in Europe. He claimed that Lloyd George, for one, was impressed by this argument.[39] Historians did ask surviving ministers in the late 1920s if they shared with Morley a 'fear of supporting an evil despotism like Russia'. Some turned the question aside. Crewe replied bluntly, 'No'.[40] Samuel replied, 'Certainly the Cabinet would not have entered into the war for the sake of Russia. But that was not at any time the issue.'[41] Runciman was equally dismissive. 'I do not think there were many men in the Cabinet who were influenced by the fact that we would, in effect, be supporting Russia. If that was Lord Morley's view I can only say that I never heard him express it during the time that he was a member of the Cabinet.'[42] This is wildly inconsistent with Morley's account and other records. In any case, the neglect of the issue of Russian mobilisation by the Cabinet, and the apparent assumption that Britain was quite without the duty or the power to restrain Russia, is truly astonishing.

As the crisis unfolded over the week beginning Monday 27 July, the nub of the Radical critique of Britain's 'policy of the Entente' was being borne out: Britain's decision for or against war was likely to be pre-empted by the actions of others. The special nightmare of the Radicals was that the decision would be pre-empted by others in the *east*. And that was exactly what happened.

Grey chose to support last-minute efforts to defuse the Austro-Russian quarrel by promoting direct negotiations between Austria and Russia in St Petersburg and between Austria and Serbia in Vienna. But in practice this meant that Britain's participation in the war hung on the success or failure of diplomatic negotiations to smother war in the east. If they failed, war in the west would follow – and Britain would fight. Britain's decision effectively was dependent on talks between the most reactionary and obstinate of Europe's diplomatic elite in faraway eastern capitals. As Herbert Butterfield has written, 'so far as Grey was concerned, there was a sense in which the French and the Russians, in the extreme eventuality, would have the last word'. And so they did.[43]

ELEVEN

The Russian Jolt
Saturday 1 August

Let us announce that neutrality to the world. It is the one hope ...
We can save Europe from war even at this last minute. But we can
only save it by telling the Tsar that he must fight his own battles.[1]

Alfred Gardiner, 1 August 1914

The Saturday morning papers splashed the biggest news of the
crisis so far – Russia's general mobilisation. But the editorial
pages were still sharply divided. Most notably, the right-
wing papers lifted their barracking for intervention a notch. A 'now
or never' spirit pervaded. Some began to argue quite openly that
the moment was favourable for Britain to join in a war, when she
could fight alongside two formidable allies, and crush her imperial,
commercial and naval rival – Germany.

The Times Preaches Solidarity with Russia

The willingness of *The Times* in particular to urge solidarity with
Russia is no mystery. Robert A. Wilton, *The Times* correspondent
in St Petersburg, had contacts at the highest level. His confidantes
included Ivan Goremykin, the newly appointed, seventy-five-year-old

ultra-conservative Prime Minister, Sazonov, the Foreign Minister, and Prince Gregory Trubetskoy, a diplomat and close ally in the ministry. In a series of letters to Steed in the early months of 1914, Wilton conveyed an image of Russia beginning to swagger in expectation of war. He stressed that all sides of Russian politics looked forward eagerly to the eventual possession of Constantinople through conflict.[2] In the clash that was coming, Germany would only be intimidated, advised the Russians, by 'a more firm and united attitude of the three Entente Powers'.[3] Prince Trubetskoy told Wilton in March 1914 that the combination of 'British Navy, the Russian army and French money' was irresistible. 'We are much stronger than the Triple Alliance and there is no reason why we should wait upon them.' Wilton noted that 'Russia is displaying a much more energetic attitude that has been noticeable for a long time past.' The Russian leaders wanted 'to infuse greater activity into the Entente'.[4] Steed replied to Wilton to stress in his talks that 'we are as anxious as ever to maintain harmony and unity of aim between the powers of the Entente'.[5]

Wilton sent an account of a long interview with Goremykin in April 1914. He reported that Goremykin was obligingly pro-Tory, pro-Entente, and very much pro-solidarity. He wanted 'much closer' relations with Britain. He offered Wilton the unblushing assurance that 'there was never any serious intention of invading India on our part'. British India was safe, so long as Britain could retain Russia as a friend. Wilton added that Goremykin, Sazonov and the Russian military all wanted the Entente with Britain upgraded to a formal alliance. Wilton too backed the idea, but recognised the obstacle: 'But what would our [British] Radicals say?'[6] Clearly the Russian correspondent of *The Times* had 'gone native'. So complete was Sazonov's confidence in him that he offered to send Wilton's letters to London in the Russian diplomatic bag.[7] On Wilton's side, when war did come, he applauded it, and was delighted by his son's serving in the Russian Army.[8]

Thus were Steed, Dawson and the staff at *The Times* well primed to preach the dogma of 'solidarity' in 1914. They were, of course, aware of the great wrestle going on inside the British Cabinet. For example, on Friday 31 July Dawson had recorded in his diary: 'British position quite undefined. A deep schism in the Cabinet. Grey struggling for peace – Winston making early disposition for war.'[9] In this context, the proprietor and staff of *The Times* redoubled their efforts to stop the government's shilly-shallying in the aftermath of the Russian mobilisation.

The tone was that of a great moral crusade. Solidarity was writ large on the battle banner, but also, quite plainly – war. In its editorial of Saturday 1 August, written by Lovat George Fraser, a much-travelled imperial correspondent, *The Times* announced unashamedly, 'Peace is not, at such a moment, our strongest interest.' As always, *The Times* treated Russia and France as inseparable twins – 'our friends'. Neutrality was a cowardly betrayal: 'We dare not stand aside with folded arms and placidly watch our friends placed in peril of destruction', for it would be 'our turn next'. Therefore, advised *The Times*, the people of Britain must be prepared to 'play our part in this unprecedented encounter'. British patriots should 'shrink from no sacrifice'.[10]

In a special editorial on the same day, written by Dawson's friend and fellow-Milnerite Edward Grigg, the case for intervention was laid out methodically: firstly, 'we must stand by our friends'; secondly, Britain had 'a vital interest in seeing that France is not overwhelmed by Germany'; thirdly, Britain must ensure that Belgium and Holland were not absorbed, to ensure the safety of Britain's food and commerce. Then, awkwardly slapping on democratic paint, *The Times* announced a fourth reason: intervention was 'A Democratic Duty'. Britain was 'the leading partner in a democratic Empire'. The 'democracies of the Empire' had to stand against depraved civilisations that were bullying Serbia, and denying 'to a little nation the elementary rights of an Independent Government'.[11] In speaking up boldly for Serbia, this editorial epitomised the determination of the Northcliffe press to make no distinction between a crisis in the east and one in the west.

Lord Northcliffe's personal influence in favour of British intervention at this time was unflagging. At Carmelite House and Printing House Square during the week preceding the war, he had gathered about him his most trusted vassals: Dawson, Steed, Thomas Marlowe, the editor of the *Daily Mail*, and H. W. Wilson, the *Mail*'s chief writer on naval issues.[12] They reinforced his rabid interventionism.

On the other hand, Northcliffe had received more cautious advice from the banking oligarchy. For example, on the afternoon of Friday 31 July, at Northcliffe's daily editorial conference, Hugh Chisholm, *The Times*'s City Editor, outlined the views of Lord 'Natty' Rothschild and Leopold Rothschild. In their opinion, *The Times* was 'hounding the country into war'.[13] Chisholm himself had reported that the City was 'full in favour of the preservation of peace'.[14] But, he explained to Northcliffe, he did not agree with these peace-mongers. Indeed, he had turned 'white with rage at so gross an attempt to interfere with the independence of *The Times*', and vowed he would never speak to the Rothschilds again.[15] Steed offered an anti-Semitic rant. 'I felt quite as angry as Chisholm, and burst out "it is a dirty German-Jewish international financial attempt to bully us into advocating neutrality, and the proper answer would be a still stiffer leading article tomorrow."' Instantly 'The Chief' had come down on the side of Chisholm and Steed.[16]

The next editorial conference was held at Printing House Square on Saturday 1 August, at 4 p.m. Dawson, Steed, and Charles Duguid, City editor of the *Daily Mail*, were summoned.[17] According to Steed, Northcliffe spoke to him first, acknowledging that he had been 'chiefly responsible' for the steadfastly interventionist line in *The Times*: 'I have trustworthy information that the Government are going to "rat".'[18] Then, turning to all his troops, Northcliffe continued, 'We have taken a strong line in favour of intervention on behalf of France and Russia. What do we do if the government give way?'[19]

The 'trustworthy information' had come from George Lloyd – a young Empire-besotted Conservative MP (not to be confused, of course, with Lloyd George the Liberal). On visits to the French Embassy, Lloyd had heard from Paul Cambon's own lips of an imminent British betrayal. Lloyd had been agape with wonder. He had obediently repeated to Northcliffe Cambon's plea: all friends of France must pull every wire to frighten the Cabinet of Liberal ditherers away from neutrality.[20] Steed also remembered Lloyd visiting him two days earlier with the same warning.[21]

What to do? Steed suggested the Northcliffe newspapers should 'go bald-headed' against Asquith. Duguid and Dawson were more cautious. A roaring attack might risk their papers' patriotic credentials. The financial crisis was also discussed. As Dawson wrote, 'Astonishing things were happening in the City.'[22] During this conversation, Northcliffe took a telephone call from Lord Rothschild himself, requesting a meeting. Northcliffe halted the conference and instructed his staff to ponder the situation overnight.[23]

Steed was in a highly emotional frame of mind. He denounced those urging Britain's neutrality as 'partisans of Germany'.[24] *The Times*, he believed, must fight them tooth and nail. He trusted Marlowe to hold the line, but had doubts about Dawson. He left the conference 'feeling more miserable than I had ever felt before'. He contemplated resignation. Neutrality, he wrote, 'would mean the ruin of England'.[25]

Steed looked for consolation that night at the Russian Embassy. The path to Chesham House was well worn, for Benckendorff was as keen as Cambon in imploring for the aid of the Tory press. Steed arrived all zeal and notebook, and spent two hours condoling with Benckendorff on Britain's contemptible flirtation with neutrality. 'From nine till eleven I sat with him discussing the outlook from every angle', Steed recalled. Benckendorff was at his most inventive, pleading that he, Sazonov and Buchanan were all at their wits' end. He told the heart-rending tale of the 'fifty thousand Russians' singing 'Rule Britannia' outside Buchanan's windows in St Petersburg. He had not 'the faintest indication' of what Grey would do, just a feeling that he was 'straight'.[26]

Next day, Steed visited the French Embassy at midday. Much the same tearing of hair and rending of garments took place. Cambon confirmed that the wretched Liberal Cabinet was tilting toward neutrality – by the evening the word 'honour' might have 'to be struck out of the English vocabulary'.[27] Steed vowed to stand fast against neutrality.

'The Moment Is Favourable'

In some Conservative papers, it was not just loyalty that was urged – but war itself. The *Morning Post* advocated immediate British action in a series of hairy-chested editorials. On Saturday 1 August, H. A. Gwynne, the editor, preached the pure dogma of synchronised mobilisation. 'There is only one thing that can be imagined worse than a war, and that is a European war in which England did not play the game.'[28]

Gwynne also sent his ferocious opinions to the Foreign Office directly, in the shape of a personal letter to William Tyrrell, on 1 August. In this Gwynne worked all the familiar themes. Britain *was* committed, for 'even if France may not have been assured formally of our military help, she has always counted on our fleet'. Grey held 'the honour of England in his hands', Gwynne pleaded. Neutrality was shameful. 'We have worked hard to prepare public opinion for it and now when we get to the jump, as it were, we are refusing it' – as if war were a gymkhana.[29]

The *Spectator*, which appeared on the morning of Saturday 1 August, openly crusaded for war in a let-us-have-it-now spirit. 'If the worst comes to the worst, we shall stand loyally by our friends', wrote St Loe Strachey, the editor. The moment mobilisations began in Russia, in Germany and then in France – again, the order of events was quite clear to him – then Britain should immediately send the BEF to assist the French. But there was a new twist – now was the longed-for opportunity for Britain to crush her German rival:

> We can also feel, though we do not care to dwell upon such a point, that as far as we are concerned, the moment is favourable. The Fleet actually mobilised, is, we believe capable of fulfilling all the requirements of the nation. It never was in better heart. The Army is sound and well-equipped, if small. It is, indeed, not too much to say that for quality, both of officers and men, it is now the best in the world. The harvest which is being reaped, is a very bountiful one, and thus if war comes it will find us with our food supplies at the maximum.

There it was. Britain was apparently bursting with both heroes and grain. If she let down France and Russia, an isolated British Empire would face perils. It was time for all that pent-up British heroism to be released – in Europe.

> If we are going to rely upon the chance of Germany and Austria being beaten, is it not madness not to make that chance a certainty by fighting on the side which we not only want to see victorious, but which must win if we are to be safe? The truth is that neither from the point of view of honour and good faith, nor from that of national safety is it possible for us to stand out of the war if war comes.[30]

The Liberal Press Stands Firm Against Intervention

The Liberal papers crusaded with equal passion for neutrality. The Russian jolt horrified the *Manchester Guardian*. On Saturday 1 August, the *Guardian* attacked the 'organised conspiracy to drag us into war should the attempts of the peace-makers fail'. This was no invention to frighten readers. Those in C. P. Scott's circle genuinely believed that the Conservative Party and the Tory press were conniving in an organised movement against neutrality. L. T. Hobhouse told his sister Emily, 'The Jingoism of *The Times* clique baffled [the] imagination and we are evidently in the greatest danger.'[31]

In its editorial of Saturday 1 August, the *Guardian* rubbished Tory arguments concerning the defence of the Balance of Power, the neutrality of Belgium, and national honour. A victory won by Russia would be 'the greatest disturbance of the Balance of Power that the world has ever seen'. On Belgium, the *Guardian* reminded readers that Gladstone's short-term treaties struck with France and Prussia in August 1870 were long dead. As for the Treaty of 1839, the *Guardian* cited Lord Derby in 1867 to establish that Britain was under no legal obligation to make war. 'We are, therefore, absolutely free; there is no entanglement in Belgium', announced the *Guardian*. On the matter of honour, the Liberal leaders' own statements were invoked.

Britain could not be held under any moral pressure to fight because, as Asquith and Grey had assured the nation, there were 'no engagements with European Powers that should take away our perfect freedom of choice'. The real national dishonour, the *Guardian* concluded, was to choose war. It would be a breach of faith with the British people.[32]

Elsewhere in the *Guardian*, George Mair, the political correspondent, did his best to spur on the movement against war. He documented rising alarm.[33] The Radicals must go public, to establish 'the weight of this Liberal anti-war movement'. 'What is wanted', Mair wrote, 'is an open demonstration which can serve as a rallying point for public opinion outside.' The Radicals must force a debate in the House.[34] The *Manchester Guardian* also reproduced dozens of letters urging neutrality from Liberal MPs and peace activists.[35]

Across at the *Daily News*, Alfred Gardiner too was filled with dread. The manufactured agitation for intervention was clear to him. Gardiner supplied a special additional editorial, 'Why We Must Not Fight', on Saturday 1 August. 'It is because England is free that Europe hesitates', Gardiner reasoned. 'Let us announce that neutrality to the world. It is the one hope. There is no other.'[36] Asquith and Grey ought to have declared Britain's 'rigorous neutrality', he argued. Their 'tardiness and hesitations are not only encouraging Russia to appeal to the sword, but are also stimulating our own Jingoes'. He urged a parliamentary revolt, a public campaign, and even strikes. Organised labour, the workers in 'every factory and mill and workshop', should 'strike for their homes'.[37]

A spirit of open rebellion could also be glimpsed in the Rowntree-owned Radical weekly, the *Nation*, which appeared on Saturday 1 August. The tone adopted by the relieving editor, J. L. Hammond, was one of extraordinary urgency.[38] Hammond stressed how broad was opposition to war in Britain. It was the view of 'ninety-nine out of every hundred Liberals in the country'. Grey's 'disastrous' devotion to the Entente meant that 'our mediation carries much less than its proper moral weight'. The Tory press was inciting war, for every hint 'that our sword may be thrown into the Russian scale' worked against mediation. Britain had no interest in 'the crime of a racial war' between Germans and Slavs. 'The more we deplore the tragedy,' Hammond concluded, 'the more clear is our duty to keep aloof from it.'[39] The *Nation* found it 'stupefying' that Britain, in common with the other Powers, had begun precautionary measures leading to mobilisation. Most alarming was the decision to send the First Fleet to sea, 'a step which, according to Reuter, has greatly encouraged Russia'.[40]

J. A. Spender of the *Westminster Gazette* carried most weight in Liberal circles. On Saturday 1 August, he too was pacific. It was 'a catastrophe' that the 'diplomatic system' was driving Europe to war. 'Is there no one to break the spell, no gleam of light on this cold, dark scene?'[41] 'What of ourselves?' Spender asked. Like his brother Liberal editors, Spender rejected the notion of obligations of honour. Asquith had assured the Commons that Britain had made 'no unpublished agreements' committing her to war. This, he argued, 'secures us the free hand and sweeps away the various theories and hypotheses which assume us to be bound by engagements which it would be dishonourable to break'. Moreover, Berlin must know there were 'certain public treaties' that should not be breached, and 'certain possible developments' in a struggle between Germany and France 'which might kindle British opinion and drive us out of our present resolution to remain neutral if we possibly could'. This served as a mild warning to Germany.

Much sharper were Spender's criticisms of the Tory newspapers. They were trying 'to kindle a war fever' and 'drive us into the reckless project of embarking our Expeditionary Force on Continental warfare'. The Royal Navy was sufficient to defend Britain and keep any war limited. 'We have strong hopes', he concluded, 'that this country may be able to maintain her position as the rallying ground for those who desire peace in Europe.'[42]

Controversially, Spender also printed in the late edition of the *Westminster Gazette* on Saturday a cable sent to him from the German Chancellor, Bethmann Hollweg. It showed him instructing his ambassador in Vienna on Thursday 30 July to urge the Austrians to negotiate with the Russians, or else Germany would 'refuse to be drawn into a world conflagration'.[43] The lesson was plain: the Germans were sincerely trying to hold back Austria.

But which newspapers were being read at 10 Downing Street? Asquith sometimes dismissed the Liberal papers as 'reptile journals'.[44] Did he take account of their advice during this crisis? We can only speculate. But two weeks later Margot Asquith scrawled in her diary a bizarre retrospect: 'All the papers on 1st August made it pretty sure we were going to join with France to crush Germany.'[45] *All* the papers?

TWELVE

'Pogrom'
Friday 31 July and Saturday 1 August

The overwhelming mass of the Tory party seem to regard war as inevitable and some seem to be eager to take the best chance of smashing Germany.[1]

Edmund Harvey MP, 30 July 1914

I t is often imagined that all sensible people oppose war. In fact, in July 1914, many people in Britain looked forward to war with relish. Influential people given to portraying themselves as keepers of the national flame – in politics, the press, the Foreign Office, and the military – urged British military intervention from the very first days of the crisis. Some proudly documented their efforts later, claiming the credit for having helped guide the nation away from shameful neutrality.[2]

General Wilson Launches the 'Pogrom'

In some Conservative circles, the idea that Britain might not fight provoked nausea. Too many promises had been made to the French. Leo Maxse, editor of the right-wing and fanatically anti-German *National Review*, was one such Tory. For example, in May 1914 he had told Ludovic Naudeau, an influential Parisian journalist, that 'this Government would have to be mad as well as bad if it stood aside while France was attacked by the common enemy'.[3] In order to defend assurances like these, during the last ten days of peace a network of Tory men had laboured frantically against neutrality. Even a day's delay was remembered as dishonour. For example, in Paris in mid-August General Sir John French told George Adam, the Paris Correspondent of *The Times*, 'that for twenty four hours he did not know whether he would ever show his face again in France'.[4]

To avoid this apprehended shame, such men crusaded for war. Among them were some high-ranking British officers, but none more active than General Sir Henry Wilson, the Director of Military Operations. The Conservative-aligned press had already begun crusading. Among the activists at the top of the Conservative Party were Lord Lansdowne (leader of the party in the House of Lords), his son-in-law Victor Cavendish (the Duke of Devonshire), Arthur Balfour, former Prime Minister and Tory leader, and Andrew Bonar Law, the new leader of the party. Among the younger men, Leo Amery, an apostle of Lord Milner and friend of many journalists, was especially energetic. In the Foreign Office, Nicolson, Crowe and Tyrrell were personally close to members of this network.

In these circles, as was often said, everyone knew everyone.[5] In this golden gallery, common school and university experience, personal friendships, and family connections made the links tight. The lines of communication binding the fanatical supporters of the Entente in the Foreign Office, the War Office, the newspaper empires, and the Conservative Party were strong too. For example, Nicolson and Wilson were in the habit of exchanging views almost every day. Wilson thought nothing of subjecting the Foreign Office men to his bombast.[6] Tyrrell and Gwynne were regular correspondents.[7] Georgina, Lady Buchanan, wife of Sir George Buchanan, was the sister-in-law of Lady Bathurst, owner of the *Morning Post*.[8] It was a powerful network that could be swiftly energised.

In late July 1914, perhaps the headquarters for those eaten-up with anxiety that Britain might miss the war was 7 Draycott Place, close to Sloane Square, the home of General Wilson. The General was an authoritarian Ulsterman, a doctrinaire believer in universal service and an Entente loyalist. A reactionary in politics, he ridiculed 'that awful thing "an open mind"'.[9] He was close to many leading Conservative politicians, Foreign Office grandees, and editors of the right-wing press. Wilson made daily visits to Nicolson at the Foreign Office during the week of the diplomatic crisis. Interventionism was the shared faith. Moreover, they were almost neighbours: Nicolson lived at 53 Cadogan Gardens, just around the corner from Draycott Place. Similarly, Lieutenant-Colonel L. Vicomte de la Panouse, the Military Attaché at the French Embassy, was constantly in company with Wilson.[10] Both were determined to resist Britain's choice for neutrality.

Wilson, as remarked previously, had not seen any danger of a wider European war earlier in the week. But in the late afternoon of Friday 31 July, Crowe showed Wilson Buchanan's cable confirming Russian mobilisation. On the cable itself, Wilson wrote:

> Eyre Crowe brought this over at 5.45 p.m. … He told me he had had 3/4 of an hour with Grey and he thought the case was quite hopeless. Grey spoke of the ruin of commerce, etc., and in spite of all Crowe's arguments appeared determined to act the coward. Crowe begged me to see Asquith or Grey, but of course they would not see me. Crowe was in despair.[11]

Liberal cowardice was, of course, the canker in the Cabinet that explained everything. Wilson wrote that it was on this day that 'we began to suspect that the Cabinet was going to run away'.[12]

Wilson threw aside all restraint. Excitable, indiscreet, and given to 'stand-and-deliver' conversational stunts, Wilson deployed all these talents in an attempt to reverse the Cabinet's flight. He recorded in his diary on that same evening that he had given this advice to Panouse: Cambon should 'go to Grey tonight and say that, if we did not join, he would break off relations and go to Paris'.[13] The French, of course, rejected this madcap idea. But it revealed the atmosphere of panic among the ultra-patriotic elite in London.

That Friday evening Wilson decided to raise a 'pogrom' – summoning visions of the massacres perpetrated against Jews inside the Tsarist Empire. Wilson, Amery, and others in this circle used 'pogrom' to describe an orchestrated agitation to achieve some political object.[14] This particular 'pogrom' aimed to jolt sympathetic Conservatives, Foreign Office personalities and newspaper editors into joining Wilson's manufactured movement for intervention. The 'pogrom' was whipped up in order to intimidate the Liberal ministers. In addition, it would counter the 'pacifist' influence of the City men, those offering 'generally timid' and 'pusillanimous counsels', as Crowe put it to Grey.[15] In Wilson's mind, as in Steed's, of course, the City's peace-mongering was not just cowardice. It raised the spectre of Jewish-German interests – 'the hidden hand', as they dubbed it – working for British neutrality.

Wilson went to work on that same Friday evening to launch the 'pogrom'. He made a series of phone calls, egging on like-minded agitators to raise hell inside the Conservative Party. First, he contacted George Lloyd and Leo Amery. They were invited to link up with Lord Lovat, a Scottish aristocrat and military man, and Leo Maxse. Amery, Lovat, Maxse and Wilson had all worked together before, promoting conscription in the National Service League.[16] The object of their agitation on this occasion was to shake the Tory leadership out of its torpor, and to frighten Asquith. But there was an immediate obstacle; many of the Tory magnates had already left London for the bank holiday weekend. Bonar Law, Sir Edward Carson, F. E. Smith, and Max Aitken (later Lord Beaverbrook) had gathered together for a weekend of tennis at Wargrave Hall near Henley. Lord Lansdowne, a grand *seigneur*, had gone to his family's historic home, 'Bowood' in Wiltshire, for a number of social events with 'the tenantry' and 'the cottagers'.[17] The immediate task for the men of the 'pogrom' was to persuade the Tory leaders to return to London. Letters, telegrams, phone calls and personal appeals were organised. Unless neutrality was scotched, Wilson warned all his Tory friends that night, 'We are in the soup.'[18]

The French Embassy men rode with the 'pogrom' from the beginning. Wilson's young friends, Amery, George Lloyd, Maxse, and Steed, were all frequent visitors at Albert Gate House. Cambon, François Charles-Roux, his First Secretary, and Panouse all cried up the need for action against the treacherous Liberals.[19] General Wilson's French contacts were quite shameless in their appeals. For example, knowing of Wilson's sympathy for the cause of Ulster, Colonel Victor Huguet, the former military attaché and key figure in the 'military conversations', advised Wilson that war in Europe might be 'good for you, should you decide to join us[,] as you will never find a better diversion to your internal difficulties'.[20]

The Conservatives, the 'Pogrom', and Churchill

The Conservative young gun George Lloyd was especially prominent in the 'pogrom'. His interest was sparked when on Friday 31 July, that is, just after Asquith's announcement of Russia's general mobilisation in the Commons, he overheard the Prime Minister say to the Speaker: 'But Sir, this is no concern of ours.'[21] Such chilling portents of Britain remaining at peace sparked him into action. Much agitated, Lloyd visited both the Russian and French embassies on the Friday evening for the latest news. Cambon reported on his latest interview with Grey. Cambon had reminded Grey – stretching the truth to breaking point – that it was 'on your advice and under your guarantee that we moved all our ships to the south and our ammunition to Toulon. *Si vous restez inertes, nos côtes sont livrés aux Allemands* [If you do nothing, our coasts will be handed over to the Germans].' Cambon next told the wide-eyed Lloyd – as he did every Tory emissary – that England's honour rested in his hands. Cambon also brought Lloyd up sharp with the rumour that even the Tories were hesitating. Grey had told him so. After leaving Cambon, Lloyd dropped off at Draycott Place to share all this with Wilson.[22]

According to Steed, George Lloyd was still active in the cause shortly before midnight. He burst into Steed's room at *The Times* office just as Steed was revising proofs of the next morning's editorial column preaching intervention. A frantic conversation followed. 'The Government are going to "rat"', cried Lloyd, citing General

Wilson as his source. 'You don't mean that they are going to back down and betray the country?' asked Steed. Utterly distraught, Lloyd explained that the Tory leaders 'are going in to the country to play lawn tennis'. Steed responded that it was Lloyd's duty immediately to 'go in cars and fetch them'.[23]

Well and truly gingered up, Lloyd embraced this mission to rescue the honour of England and the Tories. On arriving home, he wrote to Austen Chamberlain alerting him to the 'ruinous and suicidal' prospect that 'the Government are going to back down and fail in their adherence to the Triple Entente'. He invited Chamberlain to help him 'to get our leaders to do their share in stiffening the Government's spine'.[24] Next he contacted both Amery and Maxse. The pace of the 'pogrom' was quickening.

Amery, because of his connections at *The Times*, the *Morning Post* and the *Observer*, was to prove indispensable. General Wilson put steel into his friend Amery, telling him on the Friday evening 'that the Government was absolutely rotten and in favour of betrayal all along the line'.[25] Immediately Amery wrote to both Chamberlain and Lord Milner pleading for their speedy return to London, and phoned Dawson and Gwynne pleading for still stronger editorials. Next morning, Saturday 1 August, Lloyd and the young diplomat Eustace Percy, on leave from Washington, joined Amery. Over lunch at Amery's house in Eaton Square, Lloyd repeated his horror stories from Chesham House and Albert Gate House. The French felt 'completely betrayed and were in an awful state of mind'.[26] The rumour of Tory wavering scandalised them all. This had to be knocked on the head. Jews in the press and party were suspected.[27] This was characteristic thinking at *The Times* too. For example, Valentine Chirol, the former foreign editor, wrote later to Lord Hardinge railing against the pernicious influence of 'Cosmopolitan finance' during the crisis and claiming that 'every German Jew has been hanging around Downing Street'.[28] The 'pogrom' was no accidental title.

From Amery's luncheon party sprang more efforts to bring the holidaying Conservative leaders back to London. Amery took a train to Westgate-on-Sea to retrieve Austen Chamberlain.[29] Lloyd telegraphed Lord Lansdowne at 'Bowood'. Lloyd also telephoned

Admiral Charles Beresford, another Benckendorff confidante. They decided on a personal mission to retrieve Bonar Law, and the two set off for Wargrave Hall.[30] By late afternoon they were waiting on a grassy bank for Bonar Law to finish a set of tennis – which, absurdly, reminded Lloyd of Francis Drake.[31] Then, faced with these two agitated emissaries bringing their tidings of imminent national shame, Bonar Law surrendered. The party set off for London.

Simultaneously in London, concerned members of the Diplomatic Service were straining to 'work' their connections inside the Foreign Office and the Conservative Party. Two diplomats were active in this cause: Sir Cecil Spring-Rice, on leave from Washington, and Louis Mallet, on leave from Constantinople. Both were devoutly pro-Entente and anti-German.[32] Their most important contact in the Tory party was the Duke of Devonshire. On Friday 31 July Devonshire dined with 'Springy'. Devonshire found him 'very much distressed' because 'we are going back on our word' – in other words, that the Cabinet might choose neutrality. Spring-Rice also reported he had heard the rumour of Conservative wobbling. This prompted Devonshire to contact Sir Edmund Talbot, the Conservative Chief Whip. Talbot immediately joined the 'pogrom'.[33] So too did Louis Mallet. On Saturday he telegraphed to Leo Maxse assuring him that he had written 'strongly' to Lord Lansdowne, pleading with him to galvanise the party behind intervention by Monday or the situation would be 'helpless'.[34] The actions of Spring-Rice, Mallet and others reflected the pro-Entente culture at the Foreign Office, encouraged by both Hardinge and Nicolson in the decade before 1914. Just after the outbreak of war, Hardinge was honest enough to admit that missing the chance to fight Germany, with Russia and France as firm allies, would have been a tragedy. 'It would have been an universal misfortune', wrote Hardinge, 'if we had been unable to profit by the miscalculation of Germany and had allowed her to choose a more favourable moment.'[35] Here was a sample of the 'now-or-never' spirit animating some in the Foreign Office and the Tory Party during the crisis.

In this concerted crusade, the Tory members of the 'pogrom' found they had one important ally working within Asquith's

Cabinet – Churchill. He was active behind the scenes in working up pressures upon his own colleagues. He had been in touch with F. E. Smith, his Tory friend from 'The Other Club'. Acting as Churchill's emissary, Smith had visited Wargrave Hall on Friday 31 July as the leading Tories arrived. Here Smith relayed to Bonar Law a truly astounding approach from Churchill. He asked if the Conservative leader would care to offer the names of Conservatives available to replace any Liberal ministers who might resign. Clearly a coalition was welcome in Churchill's eyes. Bonar Law was unwilling to nominate ministers. But he agreed that Smith should convey to Churchill an assurance in more general terms of Conservative support in war.[36] Churchill soon had a letter, which he would flourish at the Cabinet on Saturday. He penned a thank-you note to Smith: 'Very grateful for your letter with its generous and patriotic offer.'[37]

A Midnight Conclave at Lansdowne House

During Saturday 1 August the Tory leaders returned to London. Lord Lansdowne set off from 'Bowood' to host a gathering at Lansdowne House near Berkeley Square. Meanwhile, Devonshire was active all day in London preparing his men. He recorded the details in his diary: 'Interesting talks all afternoon. Apparently no troops are to be sent to France. Afraid everybody will be displeased with us.' To head this off, Devonshire had begun to round up the Tory leaders still in London for the crisis talks. He visited Balfour at his grand home at 4 Carlton Gardens in the mid-morning, and found him still in bed. Once roused, Balfour heard from Devonshire of Spring-Rice's warnings. Devonshire arranged for Spring-Rice himself to visit Balfour to reinforce his views. Balfour was persuaded to attend the talks.[38] In the early evening, Devonshire dined with Edmund Talbot, and then took him to the Savoy Hotel. Here they teamed up with Bonar Law and F. E. Smith. A roll-call of the very powerful was gathering.

Devonshire collected Lansdowne upon his arrival at Paddington Station and reported on his activities at the head of 'the movement' to head off neutrality.[39] Not until midnight were all gathered at Lansdowne House. Lloyd later recalled the scene in the famous drawing room: Lansdowne 'sitting primly at his table in the middle of the room facing us', while Devonshire, Balfour, Talbot and Bonar Law gathered around. Two star witnesses appeared: George Lloyd and General Wilson. Lloyd had persuaded Wilson to come, and he arrived 'following me in a black [I]nverness cape and an opera hat, looking for all the world like a gaunt conspirator', as Lloyd recalled.[40] Lloyd was invited because, as Lansdowne explained, he had been 'in intimate relations with the French Embassy'.[41] Lloyd and Wilson 'gave a detailed description of their interviews at the French Embassy. Apparently they are dreadfully sore with us for not sending the military force.'[42]

The failure to mobilise the BEF in support of France was the most galling fact. 'I feel we ought to back them up,' wrote Devonshire, 'but it will soon be too late to do anything on land.'[43] Lansdowne agreed, appealing for instant action. Turning to his party leader, he exclaimed, 'Bonar, we must get hold of the Prime Minister tonight.' But the Downing Street staff turned aside the phone call because Asquith was asleep.[44] Before dispersing at about 1 a.m., all agreed they would meet again next morning to plan an approach to Asquith.

Lloyd's night was not over. He was back at Charing Cross Station to collect Austen Chamberlain soon after 1 a.m. He pleaded with Chamberlain that he was 'the only person' who could inspire the Tories to resolute action and save the nation from dishonour. General Wilson, he added, was 'in despair' at the Liberals' unforgivable delay in issuing mobilisation orders. Chamberlain and Lloyd did not part until 2 a.m., with Chamberlain promising to do all he could the next morning.[45]

THIRTEEN

The High Tide of Neutralist Hope
Saturday 1 August

I said that we had come to a decision: that we could not propose
to Parliament at this moment to send an expeditionary military
force to the Continent. Such a step had always been regarded here
as very dangerous and doubtful. It was one that we could not
propose, and Parliament would not authorise unless our interests
and obligations were deeply and desperately involved.[1]

Sir Edward Grey to Paul Cambon, 1 August 1914

While the Conservative power brokers made their way
to London on Saturday 1 August, the Liberal Cabinet
ministers faced off yet again at the Cabinet table. The
immediate setting – Russia's general mobilisation – scarcely assisted
the interventionists. If one Entente partner was provocatively
rushing to war, it could be argued, why should Britain support the
other? Shocked by the news from Russia, the neutralist majority in
Asquith's Cabinet roused themselves to resist.

In doing so, it should not be thought that the Radicals defied
the popular will. In a sense, their efforts matched the mood of the
people. As Hankey observed on that Saturday, 'The people have not
the smallest enthusiasm for war.'[2]

The Cabinet of Saturday Rejects the BEF

The fractious Cabinet met again at 11 a.m. at Downing Street. Grey began by focusing the attention of the ministers once again on the Belgian issue. If there was no majority for intervention in support of France, then perhaps there was for Belgium. He produced the replies to his two telegrams of the previous day – that he had unilaterally decided to send. These had arrived in the small hours. The French had replied positively, agreeing to respect Belgian neutrality; the Germans had replied evasively, pleading that no commitment could be given in advance for reasons of Germany's military safety, faced as she was by two antagonists, in east and west.[3]

Grey may also have revealed that on Friday evening, forty-five minutes after sending his telegrams to Paris and Berlin, he had also approached the Belgians. Through the British ambassador in Brussels, Sir Francis Villiers, Grey had informed the Belgians of the terms of those two telegrams. Even more important, Grey had asked Villiers to tell the Belgians that 'I assume Belgium will to the utmost of her power maintain neutrality and desire and expect other Powers to observe and uphold it.'[4] This inquiry, of course, was a little more forceful than a simple request for the Belgians to state their position. It contained a warning: Belgium herself could not play safe and tolerate any passage of troops. Rather, Belgium must fight – or forfeit her neutrality in British eyes. King Albert certainly felt intimidated by it.[5]

The Belgian reply to Britain, indicating that Belgium was prepared to resist, was not received in London until 12.20 p.m. on Saturday, while the Cabinet was still in session, and probably too late for Grey to use.[6] But an overnight telegram from Villiers had arrived in time. This broke the news of the Belgians' own order for the general mobilisation of their forces.[7] The danger that Britain might be perceived as more Belgian than the Belgians was receding.

The Cabinet next discussed the varying French and German replies to Grey's telegrams – one so accommodating and one so ambiguous. For the interventionists, French faultlessness and German knavery were on display. Haldane began. Grey should tell Lichnowsky of Britain's 'feeling about Belgium [as the] "deciding factor", but promise our neutrality if France [was] not invaded'. If Haldane said exactly this, it would have surprised many: because to promise neutrality to either side was, of course, exactly the opposite of Grey's policy. But it pointed the way to a path not taken. The refusal to use Britain's neutrality as a bargaining piece was an essential element in Grey's stance of 'ambiguity'. In any case, Harcourt scribbled down the fundamental point, as the Radicals saw it: 'Grey not committed to Cambon.'[8]

Churchill then swung the conversation back to Belgium. He produced his letter from F. E. Smith, written at Wargrave Hall. On behalf of Bonar Law, Smith declared that 'the Government can rely upon the support of the Unionist party in whatever manner that support can be most effectively given'. His confidence was based, wrote Smith, 'on the assumption (which we understand to be certain) that Germany contemplates a violation of Belgian neutrality'.[9] Later Churchill told Smith his reading of the letter to Cabinet 'produced a profound impression'. One can well imagine that it did. Churchill also acknowledged his own deep pessimism: 'I cannot think war will be averted now.' Even more significantly, he agreed with Smith that 'Germany must march through Belgium, and I believe that the bulk of both parties will stand firm against that.'[10] Smith's letter served no doubt to heighten the pressure on the Radicals – for clearly the Tories were waiting in the wings to choose war, alone or in coalition, if the Radicals unhorsed Asquith.

Political calculation was *the* factor at work now. For Grey declared once again that he would resign if Cabinet chose an 'out-and-out and uncompromising policy of non-intervention'. Asquith, in his turn, warned that if Grey went, he too would tumble out. Others made the same threat. Harcourt sent a note around the table to Beauchamp: 'I must resign today if there *is any decision* to take part automatically under certain circ[umstance]s without previous reference to the Cabinet.' To comfort his ally, Beauchamp shot back: 'There will be nothing of the kind'.[11] Prominent men on both sides were thinking of walking away. In Asquith's words, 'We came, every now and again, near to the parting of the ways.'[12]

Eventually the Cabinet did agree that Germany must be warned emphatically that her reply on Belgian neutrality was unsatisfactory. Grey got his instructions: to caution Lichnowsky that Belgium might be the 'deciding factor' for British public opinion.[13] The words were fixed:

> The reply of the German Government with regard to the neutrality of Belgium is a matter of very great regret, because the neutrality of Belgium does affect feeling in this country. If Germany could see her way to give the same positive reply as that which has been given by France, it would materially contribute to relieve anxiety and tension here, while on the other hand, if there were a violation of the neutrality of Belgium by one combatant while the other respected it, it would be extremely difficult to restrain public feeling in this country.[14]

These were simple words of warning for the Germans to construe as they dared.

What more should Britain do? 'Preliminary steps' were again debated. The issue was fiercely contested. Harcourt's men were perturbed by the provocative Russian action of Friday, and the stiff-necked loyalty of France toward Russia. In their turn, the interventionists pressed for a full and immediate British mobilisation, on the plea of demonstrating 'solidarity'.

So confident was Churchill of winning the debate over mobilisation that, before leaving the Admiralty to attend this Cabinet, he had told his staff: 'It seems certain to me that the order to mobilise will be issued after the Cabinet this morning. Have everything in readiness.'[15] At Cabinet, Churchill put the case for calling out the Naval Reserve, completing the full mobilisation of the navy. Pleading the nearness of war, Churchill was 'very violent', Harcourt complained. 'Grey supports Churchill', he added.[16] But on this occasion Asquith backed away, complaining later of Churchill's vast ego.[17] With regard to the Naval Reserve, Asquith decreed there would be 'no proclamation before Monday'.[18] Thus, the Cabinet rejected Churchill's demands. As Churchill put it coyly in his memoirs, his colleagues judged full mobilisation of the navy at this stage to be 'not necessary to our safety'.[19]

Next, the Cabinet surveyed the possibilities of land battles on the Continent. Should Britain begin the process of embarking the BEF? The Cabinet endured a 'long speech on tactics' from Churchill in favour. Lloyd George replied, again impressing Harcourt that he was on the side of moderation – perhaps because he had just received a letter pleading for neutrality from Robertson Nicoll, editor of the *British Weekly*, the Nonconformist religious newspaper with a hold over Lloyd George's political base.[20] Here was the most critically important debate of the day – perhaps of the whole diplomatic crisis, as some imagined. At this crucial moment it provided an indicator of the balance of forces between the neutralists and interventionists in the Cabinet. Finally, the Cabinet resolved the matter: in the event of war, Britain would *not* send an Expeditionary Force to France.[21]

Plans for the embarkation of the BEF had, of course, caused rows before. The issue reminded all at the Cabinet table of the serious disputes that had rocked Asquith's Cabinet during 1911: 'military conversations', the war scare over Agadir, the replacement of McKenna by Churchill at the Admiralty, and the Cabinet revolt against the presumption of an alliance with France. In the wake of the shocking revelation of Russian general mobilisation, and inspired perhaps by Churchill's defeat on full naval mobilisation, the neutralists had chosen to stand firm. The civilians were defying the War Office. They were defying the 'pogrom' too.

For the Radicals, this was a tonic. Runciman had informed Charles Trevelyan earlier in the crisis 'that the great thing was to refuse to send an expeditionary force onto the Continent'. Naturally he was 'very proud' when he told Trevelyan the news on the Saturday.[22] Trevelyan certainly was elated, concluding that it was now absolutely clear that 'we are not going to war at once'.[23] Next morning, encountering his fellow Radical MP Francis Neilson in Whitehall, Trevelyan reassured him. 'There'll be no war', he said. 'There'll be no war.'[24] The Radicals now expected that Britain might yet pursue the role of the truly neutral mediator and avoid war.

In the hours following the Cabinet meeting, the leading neutralists boldly explained their victory in the corridors of Whitehall.
For example, Morley told FitzRoy at the Privy Council Office that
now 'the only thing we could do was to press France to exercise
restraint on Russia'. Moreover, Morley asserted, the power of money
in Britain was against any war. With regard to Belgium, continued
Morley, even a German military incursion there would not necessarily involve Britain in 'any treaty obligation'. He insisted that Britain
had no obligations whatsoever to Russia, and strictly limited agreements with France. Over luncheon, Lord Beauchamp told FitzRoy
that he was even more adamant than Morley 'in opposing our
participation in the struggle'.[25]

It is important to stress that the apparent victory of the neutralist
ministers on Saturday 1 August may have actually worked against
them. Paradoxically, it may have lessened the chances of avoiding
some ultimate commitment to war. For the decision against the BEF
fuelled expectations that any war for Britain would, after all, be a
limited naval commitment. This had seductive power.

Asquith loyally supported his Cabinet's decision. He told Venetia
Stanley that sending the BEF 'at this moment is out of the question
and w[oul]d serve no object'.[26] Asquith was to tell the Conservative
leaders on the morning of Monday 3 August 'that neither on military nor on political grounds ought the Expeditionary Force to be
sent at once'.[27] Lord Crewe, deputising for Asquith, informed the
King of the Cabinet's decision in a formal letter on Sunday 2 August.
Cambon had been informed, wrote Crewe, 'of the reasons which *at
the present juncture* make it impossible for Your Majesty's Government
to send our military force out of the country, *without pledging themselves either way for the future*'.[28] Crewe's carefully chosen words left
the door ajar.

The Radical victory on the BEF was no secret. It was reported
in newspapers on Monday 3 August. The *Daily Chronicle*'s well-
informed parliamentary correspondent, Harry Jones, wrote that the
Cabinet ministers had 'definitely decided not to send the expeditionary force abroad. Every honourable effort will be made to prevent
Britain being drawn into the war.'[29] On Monday 3 August, in a

friendly editorial that softened the paper's opposition to intervention, the *Daily Chronicle* carried to the Liberal faithful the beguiling
idea that if war came, Britain's war would be a naval war in any case.[30]
This prettified the war – tying it up in navy blue ribbon.

This was seized upon in strange quarters. For example, from Paris
on Monday 3 August came a supportive telegram to Grey from
Ambassador Bertie. He was loyal to the Entente with France, but
quite understood the government's decision. It was better to rely
on the navy, wrote Bertie, for it would bring war to an end sooner
'by starving Germany' and preserving Britain's strength to dictate
the peace.[31] Even more surprisingly, Lord Northcliffe embraced the
idea. In spite of his enthusiastic support for British intervention, he
had given hints to his intimates that he did not want the case for
a land war pressed too hard. On Friday 31 July he had privately
ticked off Repington, his military correspondent, for advocating the
immediate despatch of the BEF. This was too much in the spirit of 'a
political declaration' and would only encourage the Radicals in their
accusations that *The Times* was part of a pro-war conspiracy.[32] For
Northcliffe, a genuine believer in the danger of invasion, the BEF's
departure might imperil Britain. As late as Wednesday 5 August
Northcliffe's staff at Carmelite House would hear with 'surprise and
dismay' that 'the Chief', while all for war, was opposed to the idea of
a single British soldier being transported to France.[33]

If interventionists such as Bertie and Northcliffe grasped at this
notion, many others must also have done so. Perversely then, the
neutralists' apparent victory in the Cabinet on 1 August may have
damaged their cause. For a naval war – as the shop-front for intervention – made war easier to sell.

But for the moment, the Radicals in the Cabinet believed they
had achieved a win to be banked. Repelling the plan for the BEF
was a moment to savour. On this day, Harcourt must have been
gratified to receive a note from his former Radical Cabinet colleague,
Lord Loreburn, urging him to stand firm against the danger of war.
For this, he blamed as always 'the foolish coquetting with France'.
He encouraged Harcourt to resist the inevitable 'recriminations
and charges of perfidy' when Britain chose neutrality. The crucial

consideration was that France and Russia would be 'wholly untrust-worthy allies'.[34] Harcourt and his Radical supporters appeared to be following this advice exactly.

Two Interviews

Following the latest Cabinet, Grey had his two usual appointments, one with Lichnowsky and one with Cambon. Belgium was at the top of the agenda. This time Grey would disillusion the German ambassador while offering the French ambassador some grounds for hope.

In his interview with Lichnowsky at 3.30 p.m., Grey read the words of warning that had been agreed upon by the Cabinet. This provoked Lichnowsky to attempt some remarkable diplomacy on the run. He sought to find out the value to Germany in respecting the Belgian borders: if Germany undertook to respect Belgian neutrality, he asked Grey, would Britain then promise to remain neutral? Lichnowsky even asked if Grey could not formulate his own terms, there and then, under which Britain would remain neutral. Lichnowksy 'even suggested that the integrity of France and her colonies might be guaranteed'. Here was an intriguing proposition. So eager did the German ambassador seem to win a promise of British neutrality that he was willing to raise the offer made by Bethmann Hollweg with a pledge that Germany would not seek territorial gains at the expense of France in Western Europe or overseas.

On the face of it, Britain might have been able to secure the safety of both Belgium and France from any threat of German annexation, perhaps safety from the threat of war itself, if Britain chose to negotiate over the terms of her neutrality. For earlier in the day, as we shall see in the next chapter, both Grey and Lichnowsky had been flirting with the idea of discovering some means of confining the hot war to Eastern Europe. Under the vague conditions of the Entente, Britain was supposedly free to negotiate with Germany. But Grey would not do so. He simply closed the door.

In response to the German ambassador's anxious inquiries, Grey would make no promise. He stood still. Even if Germany did respect

Belgian neutrality, he told Lichnowsky, he could make no promise that Britain would remain neutral.[35] So Germany would gain nothing. Lichnowsky reported the exchange to Berlin in the late afternoon. He recorded that in response to his direct question 'whether he could give me a *definite declaration on the neutrality of Great Britain* on the condition that we respected Belgian neutrality, the Minister replied *that would not be possible for him*'.[36]

In this way Berlin was told of Britain's inflexible position: a German decision to respect Belgian neutrality would win Germany neither credit nor advantage. Britain would probably still rush to the assistance of France and Russia if it came to war. The Entente was sacred. Britain would not begin to negotiate over Belgium. From Berlin's point of view, saving Belgium from invasion would not save Germany from facing a phalanx of enemies.

These exchanges between Lichnowsky and Grey would provoke much soul-searching when the British diplomatic documents were published a few days later, on 5 August. For the exchange of conversation in Grey's study, even as reported in Grey's summary, showed quite clearly that Britain's decision to enter the war was *not* dependent on a German violation of Belgian neutrality. The German offer to respect the Treaty of 1839 had not moved Grey at all – because it was linked to British neutrality. He was, quite openly, beholden to Paris and St Petersburg.

Grey's interview with Paul Cambon must have struck him as the easier of the two that afternoon. After all, Grey had no statement of warning over Belgium to read to him. But the interview turned out to be very tense. Grey was still required to stick with the Cabinet policy of no promises to either side. Moreover, the Cabinet that had just ended had seen the interventionists take two hits: the Cabinet had rejected Churchill's plea for complete naval mobilisation and, even more important, it had rejected the plan for the despatch of a BEF to the Continent. Grey put to Cambon the hard fact: France must 'take her own decision at this moment without reckoning on an assistance that we were not now in a position to promise'.

The crestfallen French ambassador then took a risk. Cambon complained dramatically that 'he could not transmit this reply to his

Government'. He implored Grey for permission to report to Paris only that the British had made no decision as yet. For him, salvation might yet lie in delay. But Grey remained firm. The BEF was not going to France: 'we could not propose, and Parliament would not authorise [it] unless our interests and obligations were deeply and desperately involved'.[37]

Cambon responded with an attempt to embarrass Grey. He made an appeal based on the new dispositions adopted by the British and French fleets in the autumn of 1912. Adventurously distorting the historical record in a well-rehearsed speech, Cambon pleaded that 'the French coasts were undefended', and he bluntly asserted that this followed from the coordination of British and French naval planning in 1912 – something the Liberals had strenuously denied. But Grey weakened. The emotional blackmail assisted intervention. So he did not quarrel with Cambon's self-serving history of the 'redistribution of the fleets'. In reply, he simply suggested that an attack on the French coasts, and a violation of Belgian neutrality, 'might alter public feeling here'.

Then Grey bent further. He offered a strong hint to Cambon that a lifeline for him *was* being prepared. He told Cambon that at its next meeting he would seek Cabinet agreement on a pledge of naval assistance to France. In addition, he explained, he would seek a commitment that Britain would oppose any German invasion of Belgium. This indicated plainly to Cambon that, beneath the veneer of 'apparent indecision', Grey was personally committed to Britain fighting alongside France if it came to war. Cambon had learned already of Grey's rejection of all German offers to negotiate on British neutrality.[38] So, he had grounds for hope.

Nonetheless, after the interview Cambon performed some theatrics in the Foreign Office building. He made his way to Nicolson's door. Nicolson received Cambon in his office 'white and speechless' and guided him to a chair. Cambon stared up at him with eyes of accusation and told him Grey was immoveable. Nicolson then bounced upstairs in a rage. Here, in Grey's study, he put his protest to him crisply, as if Grey were an erring schoolboy. As a matter of honour, he pleaded, Grey could not show such faithlessness: he surely could not abandon France, not after all she had been led to expect. 'You will render us a by-word among nations.'[39] Grey was already painfully aware of the simmering indignation among his advisers at the Foreign Office. Those pressing him for 'solidarity' found the Cabinet decisions of Saturday devastating. The atmosphere was poisonous. For example, when General Wilson visited Crowe at the Foreign Office that evening he found him 'very pessimistic, all countries mobilising except us'.[40]

The men of war were right to be worried. On Saturday 1 August, the chances had firmed for Britain's neutrality.

FOURTEEN

Kite-Flying
Saturday 1 August

I suppose [the] French Government would not object to our engaging to be neutral as long as [the] German army remained on [the] frontier on the defensive.[1]

Sir Edward Grey, 1 August 1914

Τ here were more surprising turns of events in London on that crowded Saturday. Grey had long maintained that British intervention would be necessary the moment a major war broke out on the Continent. But the Cabinet had stood in the way on Saturday. And so, Grey was to be caught up in a curious episode of 'kite-flying' – a kite borne aloft on the hope that perhaps war could be penned up in the east.

Grey's Feelers on 'Neutrality' for Britain and France

The idea appears to have arisen in late-night conversations between Haldane and Grey. It must be remembered that Grey was living at Haldane's house at 28 Queen Anne's Gate throughout the period of the diplomatic crisis.[2] It appears that, prompted by Haldane, Grey momentarily flirted with an improbable compromise. This was the idea of Britain remaining neutral, if indeed France herself could remain 'neutral' – in the sense of remaining passive on Germany's western front, if war broke out in the east between Germany and Russia.

The germ of this idea can be glimpsed in Haldane's correspondence. On Tuesday 28 July he told his mother, 'I believe there is no Power that really wants war' and he took comfort from the fact that 'no act of violence has occurred so far'. Avoiding actual violence on the ground appears to have become his focus. On Friday 31 July, he wrote to his mother, 'Things look black, but there is hope so long as the frontiers are not actually crossed.'[3] As Haldane's guest across the same week, Grey was constantly consulting him, long into the evenings. To Haldane's sister Elizabeth, Grey 'spoke most gratefully of having been with R[ichard Haldane] all the time & of the help it had been'.[4] It appears that Haldane's special concern that the frontiers not be crossed inspired a brief diplomatic adventure on Grey's part.[5]

In the mid-morning of Saturday 1 August, Tyrrell, acting on Grey's instructions, sent a special message to Lichnowsky. It was an offer from Grey to make a statement after the morning Cabinet that 'may prove helpful in preventing the great catastrophe'. As Lichnowsky reported to Berlin, 'this seems to mean that in the event of our not attacking France, England, too, would remain neutral and would guarantee France's passivity'. This, of course, raised the possibility of quarantining the war in Eastern Europe. Then, while Lichnowsky was composing his cable to Berlin, Grey telephoned. Lichnowsky added the details:

> Sir E. Grey has just called me up on the telephone and asked me whether I thought I could give an assurance that in the event of France remaining neutral in a war between Russia and Germany, we [Germany] should not attack the French. I assured him that I could take responsibility for such a guarantee and he will use this assurance at to-day's Cabinet meeting.[6]

The cable was sent to Berlin at 11.14 a.m., while the Cabinet was in session. But Grey did not 'use this assurance' in Cabinet. There was no talk of Lichnowsky's 'guarantee' against a German attack in the west. Harcourt for one would have been electrified by news of Lichnowsky's assurance. His account of the Cabinet is silent on this point.[7] Grey appears to have changed his mind during the discussions. On the one hand, the Cabinet rejected the proposal for a BEF, which indicated Grey was losing the argument for intervention. But on the other, the Cabinet agreed to deliver a formal warning to Germany over Belgian neutrality, which indicated he might yet win the argument, for the sake of Belgium. Probably Grey failed to mention Lichnowsky's latest offer because opinion in Cabinet on Belgium was drifting in Grey's direction. So, he put his hopes on a German blunder in Belgium rather than on a German offer to spare the west.

Nevertheless, Grey was still putting out feelers in the afternoon. For Tyrrell called personally at the German Embassy again in the early afternoon. Lichnowsky reported to Berlin just after 2 p.m.:

Sir William [Tyrrell] has just called on me to tell me that Sir E. Grey wanted to make proposals to me this afternoon regarding England's neutrality, *even in the event that we should have war with France as well as Russia.* I am to see Sir E. Grey at three-thirty and will report at once.[8]

Was this British proposal real? The discussion when Grey saw Lichnowsky at 3.30 p.m. gave little hope. As shown in the previous chapter, it was at this tense meeting that Grey read to Lichnowsky the Cabinet's warning to Germany over Belgium. Weirdly, in spite of his own and Tyrrell's earlier dramatic contacts with the German Embassy, Grey closed up. He had no proposals to make on British neutrality, even when Lichnowsky disavowed German territorial ambitions. When the discussion turned finally to the idea of 'passivity' for France, as Lichnowsky reported to Berlin, Grey was elusive. 'He had also been wondering whether it would not be possible for us and France to remain facing each other *under arms, without attacking each other, in the event of a Russian war.*' This now appeared to be just a thought that Grey was taking out for a walk. Lichnowsky probed:

> I asked him if he were in a position to say whether France would agree to a pact of that sort. Since we intended neither to ruin France nor to conquer any territory, I could imagine that we might enter upon that sort of an agreement, if it assured us of Great Britain's neutrality.

The Minister said that he *would inform himself*, but he did not fail to realize the difficulty of restraining the soldiers of both sides in a state of inactivity.[9]

Here were shades of August 1870 – Gladstone's even-handed diplomacy, in pursuit of Belgian and British neutrality. Was that a real possibility? Or was Grey just musing?

Similarly, in the interview with Cambon later in the afternoon, the idea of neutrality was discussed almost casually. Grey did touch on the proposal floated with Lichnowsky in the morning, but he did not present it as a live option:

> Now the position was that Germany would agree not to attack France if France remained neutral in the event of war between Russia and Germany. If France could not take advantage of this position, it was because she was bound by an alliance to which we were not parties, and of which we did not know the terms.[10]

Cambon did not contradict him. As mentioned, Grey simply went on to advise that France must make her own decisions.[11]

When these interviews were over, however, Grey did make one more effort to 'inform himself' on the viability of 'passivity'. He cabled Lord Bertie, British ambassador in Paris, at 5.25 p.m. He noted first that he had loyally 'refused all overtures to give Germany a promise of neutrality'. Then he added a spectacular item that must have leapt off the page at Bertie. Grey noted his own suggestion, which Lichnowsky thought 'not impossible', namely, the idea of French and German forces after mobilisation remaining on the defensive in the west, 'neither crossing the frontier' – Haldane's phrase. Grey added a mysterious sentence, observing that, if this suggestion was compatible with the Franco-Russian alliance, then 'I suppose [the] French Government would not object to our engaging to be neutral as long as [the] German army remained on [the] frontier on the defensive.'[12] Neutrality was just hinted at – but there it was.

Three hours later the idea was still alive. At 8.20 p.m., Grey sent his usual telegram to Bertie in Paris, describing in detail his latest interview with Cambon. He again mentioned the proposal, and again described it as resting on the possibility that France and Britain might remain 'neutral'. But he immediately softened this by noting his assumption that France could not make use of the offer.[13]

These two telegrams to Paris may have been vague. But there was the word 'neutral', in both telegrams, in black and white, and it rasped the eye. Bertie reacted with predictable horror. In his response to the first telegram, dated 'midnight' and sent at 1.15 a.m. on the Sunday, he barely suppressed his anger. He argued that if France remained on the defensive in the west, then Germany would simply attack Russia first and then turn upon France. He made no reference whatever to Grey's suggestion of British neutrality. Pointedly, Bertie asked if it could be true that he was required to 'enquire precisely what are the obligations of the French under the Franco-Russian Alliance?' This missive from Paris would not be received in London until 4.30 a.m. on the Sunday morning.[14]

A Summons to Buckingham Palace

Long before that hour, the effort had been given up. Grey retreated. There is an indication in the diary of Arthur Murray, Grey's parliamentary private secretary, that Grey decided in the early evening of Saturday 1 August that he should ditch the proposal. In the billiard room at Brooks's – exactly when is not clear – Grey told Arthur Murray that the moment had come to confront the Cabinet with a do-or-die choice for intervention. 'Spent all day at the Foreign Office as usual. Edward Grey and self dined at Brooks's and played billiards', wrote Murray. 'He told me that he would have his "tussle" with the Cabinet tomorrow.'[15]

Murray, a passionate interventionist, was pleased. He recalled later in his memoirs that Grey was solid for intervention too. According to Murray, in conversations with Grey at the Commons, the Foreign Office, and at Brooks's during the last days of peace, Grey had 'constantly laid stress on the disastrous position into which a policy of non-intervention would lead us'.[16] Presumably Grey spoke in this vein to Murray on this Saturday evening. Murray buttressed Grey's conviction. For Murray had been doing his best all week to discredit neutrality. For instance, over lunch earlier in the week, also at Brooks's, he had urged Baron von Kühlmann, a Councillor at the German Embassy, to give up hope of British neutrality. Kühlmann had 'fished' and 'fished' for any hint that Grey might 'keep England out of it', especially on account of the 'Irish trouble'. Murray killed the idea. He told Kühlmann that the Asquith government was not a 'peace at any price' government. He warned him that 'you are making the biggest mistake you ever made in your life' if he imagined that the trouble in Ireland would lead Britain to choose neutrality.[17]

In any case, soon after 8 p.m. Grey suffered an unforgettable indignity that sealed his choice. He was summoned from Brooks's to Buckingham Palace to explain an astonishing cable from the Kaiser.[18] The Germans had reacted quickly to Lichnowsky's news of Grey's feelers regarding neutrality.[19] This prompted the Kaiser to send a cable to King George V. It referred to Britain's approach of that day 'offering French neutrality under guarantee of Britain'. In return, the Kaiser offered to 'refrain from attacking France'.[20]

What did the cable mean? Was Grey abandoning Russia? At the Palace, Grey was deeply embarrassed to be confronted with this. The King, of course, was emotionally committed to his much-loved cousin Nicky and obviously hostile to his troublesome cousin William. He had done almost nothing to reconcile the cousins, beyond the telegram to Nicholas prompted by Asquith early on Saturday morning. George V recalled later that it was Grey who was reluctant to embrace war, while he the King stood firm for intervention, arguing, 'If we kept out of the war it would mean ruin.'[21]

Grey had to choose, suddenly. Would he assist the King in replying to William II? He chose to help the King repel the German offer, and save his reputation at court. The penitent Grey concocted in pencil the draft of a telegram in reply. It amounted to expiatory soft soap. The whole episode was explained away, most unconvincingly, as a 'misunderstanding' on Lichnowsky's part. 'I think there must be some misunderstanding', began the King's reply. A fiction was invented, that neutrality had never been mentioned.[22]

In fact, both Tyrrell and Grey had suggested neutrality itself for Britain, and behind it loomed an even more significant possibility – that the western Entente partners might cut Russia adrift if France was willing. In ditching the approach, Grey abandoned any effort to test France's determination to gallop into combat alongside Russia. It followed with absolute certainty: Britain would fight too. On Sunday morning he cabled this simple message to Bertie, reeling in his neutrality kite: 'No action required now.'[23]

The German Response – and the 'Misunderstanding'

Could the war have been contained if the British had pursued the matter? Or would negotiation have incited the Germans to begin aggression on both fronts, sure of Britain's neutrality? We cannot know for certain, either way.

But indications are that the Kaiser and others in Berlin were very keen to avert Germany's exposure to war on two fronts. In the early evening of Saturday 1 August, at the very time that Grey was following up his afternoon approaches to Lichnowsky with his two telegrams to Bertie, there were bizarre scenes around the Kaiser at the Schloss, the palace in Berlin. At 5 p.m. he had signed the decisive order for 'war mobilisation'. Then, soon after 8 p.m., two telegrams from Lichnowsky were decoded and presented to the Emperor. They gave hopeful details of Grey's feelers regarding 'neutrality' in the west.[24]

Here was an offer of tempting palpability. The Kaiser amazed his advisers. He pleaded with his generals to hold back their plans for war in the west. Hopeful of securing neutrality on this frontier, he questioned the great mobilisation plan itself. 'So we simply deploy the whole army in the East!' he urged.[25] Moltke was devastated. He told General Falkenhayn that he was 'absolutely cut up because the Kaiser's decision showed that he still had hopes for peace'.[26]

The Kaiser even reversed preliminary military steps already under way to secure key railways in Luxemburg. The deployment of the Sixteenth Division, commissioned to leave Trier for the strategic occupation of Luxemburg, was actually halted by a telephone call from an aide-de-camp, on the Kaiser's order. Instead, the Kaiser decreed that Moltke must redirect German mobilisation against Russia only. For some hours the Kaiser insisted with a terrible urgency that the war could be and must be limited to Eastern Europe, against the shrill complaints of his military advisers. Clearly, even the whiff of a continuing possibility of British neutrality led him to demand sweeping changes in the German war plan – saving both Belgium and France from invasion – changes that his exasperated generals maintained would jeopardise the whole scheme.[27]

The negative interpretation of these events is that the Kaiser's relief at the news from London, and the champagne-fuelled joy of others in his entourage, points only to German determination to wage aggressive war from a position of advantage, first against Russia, then against France and Britain.[28] The more generous interpretation – which both Falkenhayn and Moltke believed and lamented – was that the Kaiser *was* anxious to avoid war.[29] In any case, soon after midnight, with the arrival of 'further reports' from London showing that the idea of neutrality was a phantom, the German war machine was ordered back into life on Germany's western frontiers. The events of the day in London, and the events of the evening in Berlin, point in every direction. This is tiresome for those who want events to yield a neat, indictable pattern – but this is how it was.

Grey and Churchill Choose War

Soon after Grey's painful hour at the Palace, news began to circulate in London of the next tragic development: the German declaration of war against Russia.[30] At this news, Grey appears to have embraced the policy of instant British intervention. But could he persuade the Cabinet? Many recalled 'the perfect misery of Sir Edward Grey' at this time.[31]

Grey resolved to press with all vigour for British entry into war. Elizabeth Haldane recorded in her diary that it was late in the evening of Saturday at Haldane's house, with Haldane and Crewe at his side, when Grey made the momentous decision: a pledge of naval support to France *must* be secured the next day. All three men then set off for Downing Street. Elizabeth preserved in her diary Grey's account of what happened next:

There [at 10 Downing Street] he found the P. M. & ladies playing bridge – and Lord Crewe said it was like playing on the top of a coffin. They waited till they had finished – about an hour. Then E. G[rey] wrote to the French Ambassador a note to say [he] would hear from him after the Cabinet next day, a personal note but one which indicated his view. He would of course have resigned & so would R [Haldane] had the Cabinet gone against him. He read the note to those present & the P. M. agreed to sending it.[32]

This note was of tremendous importance. It gave to the French ambassador advance notice of the precise promise that Grey hoped to squeeze from the Cabinet on Sunday morning. Grey entrusted the note to a messenger, who disappeared into the night.

The tormenting pressures of the evening were not yet over for Grey. He confessed later to Elizabeth Haldane that he had suddenly awoken with a start in the dead of night, terrified his message to Cambon had gone astray. 'He told me afterward that he woke at 4 a.m. & thought he had given it to the messenger in the dark. The German Embassy was nearest & he might have misread it. He could sleep no more at the thought.'[33] This tale again testifies to the confusions, the high-handed actions, and the midnight terrors that were characteristic of the lives of the crucial players as Britain plunged toward disaster in 1914.

Grey's note did indeed arrive safely at Albert Gate House just after 10 p.m. on the Saturday evening. On sighting it, Cambon was deeply relieved. Later he would recall that it '*sufficed to involve England against Germany*'.[34] On the previous day he had told Paris that Grey was truly 'a partisan of immediate intervention'.[35] Now he had proof.

News of the German declaration of war against Russia on the evening of Saturday 1 August sparked one other minister into late-night action. Churchill seized the opportunity to nullify at least one of the victories achieved by the Radicals in the Cabinet earlier that same day – their blocking of complete naval mobilisation.

When the news came to him about 9.30 p.m. on that Saturday evening, the First Lord was at the Admiralty. Churchill immediately walked to Downing Street. Most of the guests from a dinner party had departed. It speaks of the milieu in Asquith's home on this famous night that among the guests had been 'old Benck' – Benckendorff, the Russian ambassador.[36] Still with Asquith were key Cabinet interventionists, Grey and Haldane, plus Crewe, all of whom had just driven around from Haldane's house. Churchill grasped at his chance. 'I said that I intended instantly to mobilise the Fleet notwithstanding the Cabinet decision', Churchill recalled. Asquith 'said not a single word' but Churchill believed he wore a silent corroborative 'look'.

Something else bucked up Churchill. As he walked with Grey away from Downing Street into the night, Grey blurted out: 'You should know I have just done a very important thing. I have told Cambon that we shall not allow the German fleet to come into the Channel.'[37] This description, of course, assumed he would be successful in Cabinet the next morning. Naturally the news confirmed Churchill in his determination. He returned immediately to the Admiralty. At 1.25 a.m. on Sunday morning the Admiralty ordered the complete mobilisation of the Naval Reserves across the Empire.[38]

Now the full significance of Britain's two naval initiatives was revealed, both the retention of the fleets in a near-to-mobilised state at Portland on Sunday 26 July, and then the dramatic move to 'war stations' in the early hours of Wednesday 29 July. These made the final step, full naval mobilisation, just a small swift step. The mood in the Royal Navy itself was reflected in Julian Corbett's official history. He described the early naval movements as driven by loyalty to France: 'Seeing what our engagements were to France, no less could be done.' And the path was clear for the BEF.[39]

Were there alternative paths Britain might have taken? Yes, there were. Grey's contacts with the German Embassy during the day illustrated these. Lichnowsky had the highest hopes. He had penned a private note to Grey during Saturday telling him he had sent 'the contents of our letter' to Berlin, and that if 'we' avoid war 'it will be due essentially to your help'.[40] Might there have been different outcomes? The momentary change in the German war plan on Saturday evening is suggestive. But the truth is that nobody knows. To borrow from Dickens: 'and the moment shot away, into the plumbless depths of the past, to mingle with all the lost opportunities that are drowned there.'[41]

It is important to underscore the vital point: London had leapt to fateful decisions as peace crumpled in Eastern Europe. Two more vital steps on the path to war – Grey's communication to the French Embassy of his proposed pledge of naval support, and Churchill's orders for full naval mobilisation – were made in response to Germany's declared war on *Russia*. Again, the Cabinet had been sidelined. Again, Churchill and Grey had sprung forward.[42]

FIFTEEN

Tightening the Screws
Sunday 2 August

Lansdowne came down at 9.30. I found him as much alive as I was to the perils of the situation, and convinced, like myself, that for England to hang back now was for her to incur indelible disgrace and lasting danger and insecurity.[1]

Austen Chamberlain, Sunday 2 August 1914

As Sunday dawned, the results of the 'pogrom' that had been under way since Friday were on display in the pages of the Tory newspapers. For example, the *Observer*, a Sunday paper, sounded a great trumpet blast for war. Amery had been in the ear of the editor, J. L. Garvin, on Saturday, 'telling him to write all he could in the *Observer* to stiffen things'.[2]

In his major editorial of that day, Garvin, always histrionically proficient, did his very best. There was a riot of headlines: 'THE WAR OF WARS' – 'EUROPE'S ARMAGEDDON AND THE SUPREME QUESTION' – 'SHALL WE STAND BY FRANCE?' The subheadings shouted too: 'GERMANY'S TRIUMPH MEANS ENGLAND'S DOWNFALL.' 'THE NEMESIS OF BETRAYAL.' 'OUR NEUTRALITY IMPOSSIBLE.' The editorial argued that the German declaration of war on Russia overnight had signalled the moment for plain speaking. Peace would mean 'doom'. Neutrality was 'desertion'. If Britain chose peace the Empire was lost, for 'all the combatants in the end would compose their quarrels at the expense of the ample assets of the British Empire. He who is no friend will have no friend.'

Garvin painted a nightmarish future: German 'mastery of Europe', including the occupation of the Low Countries. Britain must awaken to the 'deadly peril' that she would confront if Germany triumphed 'so near to our own coasts'. Any feeble effort to retain Britain's neutrality 'would mean, a little later, the end of our Empire in the East'. Russia would swallow up India. Britain's duty was clear, Garvin pleaded: 'Since France mobilises we must mobilise without loss of a day.' War, it seemed, was here already. 'We fight as every great people must fight', he wrote, for both Britain's 'insular safety and our Imperial existence'. Loyal to an interpretation that would live forever in Conservative ranks, Garvin next attacked Grey's policy of sowing 'doubt' about Britain's stance. This had been the 'enfeebling element in the Councils of Europe'. It was 'doubt' that had made Vienna 'more peremptory' and Berlin 'more insistent'. Doubt should be ditched and war should be embraced. 'If England flinches now, she will have to make fatal diplomatic surrenders at a later stage or be forced into war under far worse conditions.' It was time for Britain to 'declare our unhesitating resolve to uphold the *entente cordiale* with our whole might by sea and land'.[3] This matched perfectly the arguments that the Conservative leaders were about to place before the Prime Minister. All were locked in heartfelt adoration of foreign policy clichés as old as the age of Queen Elizabeth – the 'balance of power' and the safety of 'the narrow seas'.

John Burns caught sight of newspaper placards advertising the *Observer* on his way into Westminster from Battersea that morning. Poignantly, he was travelling in 'a taxicab that had just come from a wedding smothered in confetti'. From the colourful cab hallowed by a loving couple's dreams of the future, Burns noticed the contingents of Territorials marching in Chelsea. He soon got a copy of the *Observer*. Burns jotted down his reaction in his diary: 'Garvin as usual roaring, tearing his passion to tatters and shouting calamity at the top of his voice. It is impossible to exaggerate the evil this lunatic has done to English politics over the last 10 years.'[4]

The Conservatives' Letter to Asquith

Austen Chamberlain, who had been too late for the midnight con-clave, was the first of the Conservative leaders to arrive at Lansdowne House at about 9.15 a.m. on the Sunday morning. Waiting for Lansdowne to descend to the drawing room, and then to finish break-fast, Chamberlain penned the first draft of a letter to Asquith and a statement to be read to him by a delegation. Then Chamberlain and Lansdowne swapped banter and agreed that 'for England to hang back now was for her to incur indelible disgrace and lasting danger and insecurity'. They discussed Chamberlain's various drafts.

The letter pressed Asquith to avoid 'any hesitation' in support-ing the French and Russians, 'our intimate friends', as they were described. The letter also reminded Asquith of the 'concerted naval and military measures' that had been agreed with France. Crucially, it offered 'the united support of the opposition in all measures required by England's intervention in the war'.[5] Britain's entry into this coming war was taken for granted. Another statement was drawn up too, as suggested by Henry Wilson the previous evening, demand-ing Britain's immediate general mobilisation and an ultimatum to Germany on Belgium.

At 10 a.m. Lansdowne and Chamberlain took these various drafts around to Bonar Law's house, 'Pembroke Lodge', in Edwardes Square in Kensington. Here the three Tory potentates drew up a final version of the letter. This was rather more muted than the first draft – deliberately so, as Bonar Law told Amery, because 'too much pres-sure' might 'rally the coalition in opposition to the war'.[6] Thus, the final version of the note (according to the handwritten copy in Lloyd George's papers) simply offered Asquith the blankest of cheques:

> Lord Lansdowne and I feel it our duty to inform you that in our
> opinion as well as in that of all the colleagues whom we have been
> able to consult, it would be fatal to the honour and security of
> the United Kingdom to hesitate in supporting France and Russia
> at the present juncture; and we offer our unhesitating support to
> the Government in any measures they may consider necessary for
> that object.[7]

Significantly, the Conservative leaders' letter made no mention of
the necessity of a violation of Belgian neutrality by Germany as a
casus belli.[8] The igniting of war on the Continent would be enough.
The group agreed that the note should *not* be endorsed as 'Private'.[9]
Under the conventions of the age, this preserved the Conservatives'
right to use it against Asquith if they so chose. The letter was signed
by Bonar Law and Lansdowne and taken in Lansdowne's car to
Downing Street. According to Chamberlain, it must have arrived in
time for the crucial Cabinet meeting beginning at 11 a.m. on Sunday
2 August.

A revealing subplot in this story also emerged during the conference at Bonar Law's house. How had the rumour got started that the
Conservatives were wavering? Grey, who saw Bonar Law each day
during that week, was doubtful that the Tories were united for intervention.[10] Rumours persisted. For example, Valentine Chirol told
Hardinge that some unionists 'were thoroughly rotten until actually the eleventh hour'. Bonar Law, Lord Curzon and Lord Midleton
were said to have been reluctant to face war.[11] Wherever the truth lay,
Bonar Law was braced up for war now.

The Tories discussed whether Balfour was the source. He had
confessed to an indiscretion at a large dinner party with both
Nicolson and Benckendorff during the week. Playing the entertaining contrarian, Balfour had 'characteristically' challenged Nicolson
when he 'had spoken as if it were a matter of course that we should
join in [a war] at once with France and Russia'. Balfour had told
Benckendorff that Britain had to consider the 'danger to India' if
Britain helped Russia to a great victory over Germany.[12] Balfour
then sent a personal note to Tyrrell, explaining that his offhand

remark had been quite misunderstood. It was a mere conversational prank.[13]

Similarly, during these same discussions, Robert Cecil phoned Law to say that he had snuffed out another potential source of the rumour. His brother 'Linky', Hugh Cecil, a strong Christian and a dissident on foreign policy, had written to Churchill favouring neutrality. Robert Cecil explained that he had countered this by assuring Churchill that the Conservatives were overwhelmingly in favour of intervention and the despatch of the BEF. Churchill passed this assurance on to Asquith.[14]

These discussions reveal much of the atmosphere prevailing at the heart of the Conservative Party: not a fleck of doubt was to be allowed to spoil the promises of absolute commitment to war on the part of the Conservative Party, which the leaders were determined to convey to the Liberals.

The Steering of the Liberals to War

Churchill's critical role in these events is again worth stressing. The sources show personal contacts on his part not just with F. E. Smith, but also with Bonar Law, Balfour and Lansdowne. Lansdowne recorded in a letter to his wife that on the morning of Sunday 2 August he fielded an early telephone call from Churchill 'begging me to see him as soon as possible'. Churchill then called around at Lansdowne House and saw him privately at 9.20 a.m., according to Lansdowne, just before he descended to meet Chamberlain.[15] In this way Churchill advised the Tories on their approach to Asquith on that same day. These contacts were revealed to all during the Conservatives' discussions at Bonar Law's house. Seeking confirmation that the proposed letter to Asquith was a good idea, Law suggested that F. E. Smith might telephone Churchill and check.[16] Churchill also visited Balfour on the morning of Sunday 2 August, before the vital Cabinet meeting of that day.[17] According to Devonshire's diary, Churchill's role was vital: 'The most important point is that Winston saw AJB [Balfour] and B-L [Bonar Law]. He has done very well.'[18]

Thus, two letters in two days from the Conservative Opposition reached the Liberal Cabinet: F. E. Smith's letter of Saturday 1 August, and the Tory leaders' letter of Sunday 2 August. Churchill had advised the Tories on both. The message was unmistakeable: the Conservative Party was strongly committed to military intervention. But there was an unspoken threat dramatised by these approaches too – a political threat left dangling over the heads of the Radicals in Cabinet during the key days of decision-making in this crisis. The spectre of coalition took shape. Indeed, all ministers in the Cabinet were aware that one of their own was in touch with the Opposition, perhaps even smoothing the way to a coalition. As we shall see, when at the height of the crisis John Simon was to send in a resignation letter to Asquith, he would make a veiled reference to Churchill's disloyalty, observing, 'It may be that a Coalition Government will be best (and one of your colleagues, I think, desires and intends it).'[19]

During the July–August crisis, on the Right of British politics – among some Conservatives, ultra-nationalists, and all those hoping to build a strong protectionist Empire – there was considerable eagerness for war. Deep frustration was felt in the week leading up to war, that the Liberals might 'shirk', as their critics saw it, this historic opportunity to crush Britain's chief competitor. Belgium, the Conservatives correctly discerned, was not the defining issue for their party, or indeed for the more keyed-up among the Liberal interventionists. Crusading for war *preceded* the materialisation of any threat to Belgium. For Conservatives the issue was simple: would Britain stand by France and Russia – or betray them?

In the months and years that followed, leading Conservatives would frequently express pride that their agitation in general, and the Conservative leaders' letter to Asquith of Sunday 2 August in particular, had helped steer the Liberal Cabinet into the war.[20] They depicted the Liberals as bloodless, indecisive 'fainthearts'. The Conservatives clung to the self-serving opinion that an early British proclamation of unconditional solidarity with Russia and France might have deterred Germany and saved Europe from war. This soon gained the status of a received truth. The Duke of Devonshire told an American reporter in 1915: 'The truth is that Grey held back too long. Perhaps if he had shown his teeth earlier, there would have been no war.'[21]

When British intervention was eventually achieved, just as the Conservative leaders desired, they were in a glow of virtuous exultation. Some allowed themselves momentary generosity. In the short term, they applauded Grey, for he had carried his party – but they praised Churchill to the skies. The party-hopper was forgiven. The Duke of Devonshire, for example, told his Conservative friends on 2 August that Churchill had played the key role, threatening to resign 'if we did not stand by France'.[22] Carson wrote to Churchill lauding 'the patriotic & courageous way you have acted in the present grave crisis'.[23] Geoffrey Dawson wrote that Churchill, fortunately, had 'been acting all the time ahead of the Cabinet and the Parliament'.[24] He told friends that Churchill deserved 'the greatest possible credit' for having got the fleet ready for war so early.[25] Chirol repeated the tale that Churchill had vowed to push the Cabinet along, telling Nicolson, 'By God, I will make them fight.'[26] Nicolson himself confirmed that Churchill had been 'in direct negotiations with the leaders of the Opposition for a Coalition Cabinet'.[27]

The Radicals saw it differently. They were painfully aware of the new cachet Churchill had gained during the crisis. For example, Hirst happened to run into Admiral Beresford a week after the war began. Beresford announced that he had 'made it up' with Churchill. He related the uplifting tale 'that Winston had forced the Cabinet to agree to mobilisation by threatening to resign'. Hirst replied, 'Yes, it is Winston's war or at least he is mainly responsible.' Beresford instantly agreed: 'Yes, you are about right.'[28]

SIXTEEN

'To the Square!'
Sunday 2 August

STAND CLEAR, ENGLAND! AUSTRIA AND SERBIA ARE
AT WAR ... We will allow nothing short of a direct attack upon
us to draw us into this quarrel.[1]
>Handbill distributed at the anti-war demonstration,
>Trafalgar Square, 2 August 1914

Not only the Radical wing of the Liberal Party but also the forces of internationalism as a whole in Britain were suddenly alive to the imminent danger of war by Friday 31 July. The two neutrality committees had been created, and the women's movement was active on the issue. It was the Labour Party that then moved most quickly to mount a public demonstration in central London.

The Awakening of Labour Internationalism

The demonstration was to be international in spirit – as it was in origin. In fact, it was to be one of a series beginning across Europe that weekend. The push for this came from a crisis meeting called by the International Socialist Bureau (ISB) in Brussels, a kind of

'Security Council' of the Second International – the body to which most of the European social-democratic parties belonged in 1914. On Tuesday 28 July, a small party of British socialists, including Keir Hardie for the Labour Party and Bruce Glasier for the ILP, had travelled to Brussels to represent Britain on the ISB.[2]

The crisis meeting of the ISB opened the next morning, Wednesday 29 July, at the Maison du Peuple, headquarters of the Belgian Socialist Party in Brussels. Many of the famous European socialist leaders were present: Jean Jaurès for France, Hugo Haase for Germany, Victor Adler for Austria, and Emile Vandervelde for Belgium. The ISB decided upon a campaign of rolling demonstrations in the European capitals.[3] The socialist leaders launched it that evening at the grand Cirque Royal theatre in Brussels, packed with 7,000 people. Hardie spoke with great fervour. 'In a few strong loftily pitched sentences', wrote Glasier, 'he poured burning condemnation on the ruling classes and the press' as 'the makers of war'.[4]

Next morning Glasier attended a second meeting of the ISB, at which he spoke optimistically. 'The British wanted peace. The whole of the Cabinet wanted peace', he told the meeting.[5] Later he mixed with the European socialist leaders. 'Jaurès shook hands all round', wrote Glasier in his diary. 'How robust and unconquerable Jaurès looked.' All looked forward to the coming International Socialist Congress, which the ISB had just moved from Vienna to Paris. As Glasier wrote confidently, 'we all go our ways to meet in Paris in the days of the Congress'. Having promised to stage anti-war demonstrations in Britain, the British delegates then returned to London on the evening of Thursday 30 July.[6]

The idea for a big demonstration on Sunday at Trafalgar Square was first proposed in George Lansbury's *Daily Herald* on Friday 31 July. In a front-page article entitled 'WORKERS MUST STOP THE WAR', the *Daily Herald* announced the plan. It urged 'every section of the working-class movement' to assist.[7] The ILP's *Labour Leader* on Thursday 30 July had already called for big demonstrations in a full-page boxed editorial, under the heading 'THE WAR MUST BE STOPPED. AND WE MUST STOP IT.'[8] On Friday 31 July the *Daily Citizen* also supported the proposal.[9]

On that same day the 'British Section' of the ISB – which meant in practice the Labour Party leaders and some socialists – then met at the House of Commons. Hardie and Glasier reported on the plans made in Brussels for protests across Europe. British socialists must do their share. All agreed. A second emergency meeting was held later on the same day to finalise plans. 'News that Russia is mobilising!' Glasier wrote in his diary. 'Outlook *suddenly* very grave.'[10] The meeting accepted Lansbury's plan for a Trafalgar Square rally.[11] The 'British Section' also decided to insert advertisements for the Trafalgar Square protest meeting in seven major London dailies. Plans for events beyond London were activated too. Francis Johnson, the ILP secretary, telegraphed fifty ILP branches on that same day, urging demonstrations as soon as possible against British intervention.[12]

MacDonald supplied a resolution for the rallies in the name of the 'British Section'. As a dedicated critic of the 'policy of the Entente' and of the Tsarist autocracy, he focused upon these twin evils. War to support Russia, to keep faith with the Entente, would be 'offensive to the political traditions of the country'. Therefore, 'the Government of Great Britain should rigidly decline to engage in war, but should confine itself to efforts to bring about peace as rapidly as possible'.[13]

That evening, Hardie helped draft an appeal entitled 'To the British People' on behalf of the 'British Section', to publicise the call for rallies.[14] The manifesto called for the people to 'HOLD DEMONSTRATIONS EVERYWHERE'. The tone was urgent: 'There is no time to lose. Already by secret agreements and understandings of which the democracies of the civilised world know only by rumour, steps are being taken which may fling us into the fray.'

There was clearly an effort to broaden the appeal beyond the ranks of labour. On Saturday 1 August the advertisements for the rally appeared under the headline 'WAR AGAINST WAR' in Liberal newspapers and even in *The Times*.[15] The *Daily Herald* editorial of Saturday 1 August sought to drum up wide support. It focused upon themes that Radicals could instantly recognise. It denounced 'secret diplomacy' and 'the theory of the continuity of foreign policy'.[16] The

Herald looked to middle-class allies: 'One set of people can alone prevent this act of criminal folly. It is the great Middle Class and Trade Unions.'[17]

The plans for the Sunday afternoon rally showed that Labour was dominant, but a broader coalition was being assembled. There were to be four processions converging on Trafalgar Square. Trade unionists were to come from the East India Dock Gates.[18] Marchers under the banner of the 'Daily Herald League' were to set off from St George's Circus. The small British Socialist Party (BSP) planned a procession from Kentish Town.[19] The Civil Union, Norman Angell's internationalist pressure group, planned a fourth procession from Westminster Cathedral. This would attract the middle-class internationalists.[20]

The handbills prepared for distribution on the day were printed by Norman Angell's magazine *War and Peace*. The text indicated the common threads linking socialist and Radical critiques at this time. 'STAND CLEAR, ENGLAND! AUSTRIA AND SERBIA ARE AT WAR', announced the handbill. What, then, should Britain do? 'The right course may be summed up in one word: – NEUTRALITY!' The handbill went on to offer eight reasons why Britain should remain neutral. Among the reasons given, the handbill argued that Britain had 'no direct interest in the war', 'no object in preserving the Balance of Power unless it secures peace', and 'no interest in helping Russia to dominate the Continent of Europe'. The conclusion offered this booming plea: 'It is therefore the duty of every Briton to urge upon the Government that : – we will allow nothing short of a direct attack upon us to draw us into this quarrel.'[21]

But overnight came news that could only have dampened spirits. The same Saturday newspapers carrying advertisements for the Trafalgar Square rally also printed the horrifying news that Jean Jaurès had been assassinated in Paris. Bruce Glasier was devastated when his wife told him. 'Katharine wakes me with the dreadful news that *Jaurès* was assassinated last night', he wrote in his diary. 'What a cruel deed – what a calamity to our movement. Our brave generous friend. I have wept today.'[22]

War Against War: Trafalgar Square, Sunday 2 August

Between 2 p.m. and 4 p.m. in the afternoon of Sunday 2 August, Trafalgar Square quickly filled to overflowing. The *Labour Leader* put attendance at the rally at 15,000.[23] The *Daily Herald* estimated that the 'colossal' crowd reached 20,000 people.[24]

The Labour newspapers were not talking up the figures. Even the *Scotsman* conceded that the demonstration was 'remarkable for its size' and that 'long before the advertised time the Square was packed with people of all classes'.[25] The friendly Liberal newspapers confirmed this. The reporter for the *Daily News* noted that the demonstration attracted 'a vast gathering to Trafalgar Square', with crowds spilling onto the pavements outside St Martin's in the Fields and the National Gallery, and with the 'densely crowded' roadway between the Square and the Admiralty Arch blocked to traffic.[26] Similarly, the *Manchester Guardian* reported that the crowd 'over-flowed into Whitehall and some distance up the Strand'. It was 'the biggest Trafalgar Square demonstration held for years', and 'far larger, for example, than the most important of the suffragist rallies'.[27] The *Daily Citizen*'s reporter also described the surging demonstration as 'wonderful even for Trafalgar Square'. The mass of people 'swelled up the Strand, down Parliament Street, and into Pall Mall. It surged around St Martin's Church, climbing the steps in eager search for a vantage ground. It sought the roofs of surrounding buildings.'[28]

The speakers were hoisted up onto the usual three 'platforms' in Trafalgar Square – the northern, eastern and western plinths of Nelson's Column. Policemen stood beneath the plinths, facing the crowds. Journalists stood there too, scribbling in their notebooks. Photographic evidence shows that the crowd was a mixture of middle-class and working-class men and women, with some children too.[29] The hats worn advertised the broad alliance of classes: straw hats, boaters, bowlers, soft hats, and cloth caps. The speakers crowded together on their plinths, flanked by the great bronze lions, under ominously darkening skies. A thunderstorm was brewing. The major speakers included Keir Hardie and Arthur Henderson, representing the Labour Party. With Henderson stood prominent trade unionists such as Ben Tillett and Bob Smillie. On another plinth was R. B. Cunninghame Graham, the veteran Scottish nationalist and socialist. On another stood Charlotte Despard, Marion Phillips, Mary Macarthur, and her friend Margaret Bondfield, representing the labour women's movement.

The main platform was the crowded northern plinth facing the National Gallery. Here Keir Hardie was the first speaker. Behind him was the bronze relief panel of the battle of the Nile in 1798, cast from captured French guns – spoils of war. The *Daily Citizen* caught the moment:

> When Mr Keir Hardie MP walked to the front of the plinth from which he was to speak with Mr Arthur Henderson a storm of cheering swept over the great square. He had to wait several minutes while a long procession with bands and banners poured into the already dense throng singing 'The Internationale'. Enthusiasm was intense, but the first words of the veteran Socialist brought an impressive stillness. M. Jaurès was in his thoughts.[30]

In this dramatic manner, Hardie began his address by reminding his listeners of the tragic news: 'Our hearts today are sorrowful for the loss of our great comrade, Jaurès. His silver voice is now stilled and the great white fire of his moral enthusiasm quenched forever.' There was silence and every head in the Square was bared in honour of Jaurès.

Hardie then launched into an attack on the absurdity of the impending prospect of mutual slaughter among the workpeople of Europe:

> Tonight there are millions of hearts in every country in Europe filled with sadness and foreboding. What is the cause of the war? You have no quarrel with Germany. German workers have no quarrel with you. German workers have no quarrel with their French comrades. The French workers have no quarrel with their Austrian comrades. Then why are we on the verge of the greatest calamity Europe has ever seen?

Then he turned to his main subject: the abominable possibility that diplomatic deals and military agreements, contracted in secret, might drag Britain into fighting in a Russian quarrel.

> Are we going to allow the Courts and the ruling classes to make treaties leading into war without our having a word to say? We should not be in this position but for our alliance with Russia. Friends and comrades, this very square has rung with denunciations of Russian atrocities. Surely if there is one country under the sun which we ought to have no agreement with, it is the foul Government of anti-democratic Russia.
>
> Our shores are not being attacked. Our liberties are not being menaced. Why, then, should we fight? We are here to say that, so far as we can decree, there shall be no shot fired, no sabre drawn in this war of conquest.
>
> The only class which can prevent the Government going to war is the working class. We shall have no great anti-war campaign by the Liberals – as we should have had if the Tories had been in office. The church will not lead in this holy war against crime and bloodshed. The task is left to the workers.[31]

Arthur Henderson then introduced the official resolution, drawn up by MacDonald. But it now included a special preliminary section. In this the London rally was called upon to denounce the 'secret alliances and understandings which, in their origins, were never sanctioned by the nations'. In his speech, Henderson declared that it was 'a day of humiliation for the democracy of Britain', because the British people were in danger of being flung into war without their consultation. Margaret Bondfield followed with a 'burning speech', urging every man and woman to 'fight Jingoism with every ounce of intelligence they possessed'.[32]

From an adjacent plinth Cunninghame Graham spoke, in his strong Scottish accent. The idea that war was inevitable was 'a damnable lie', he shouted. He pointed down Whitehall, to Downing Street: 'Our Ministers sitting now in conclave want the encouragement of a great popular movement to throw their weight into the scale for peace.' Russia must be shunned, declared Graham. Britain must not fight on the side of the 'Cossack outrager of women and the torturer of men'. Nor should Britain seek to advance 'the knout of the procurer and the Holy Synod of Russia'. Then, on this plinth, a Russian, a German, a Frenchman and a Swiss linked arms across each other, 'the crowd cheering wildly'.[33]

Several other speakers also denounced Russia. Pointing to news-paper posters displayed on the street corners of Trafalgar Square, George Lansbury noted that the *Observer* and *The Times* were shout-ing the message of war for 'honour'. 'We take up the challenge', declared Lansbury. 'It will be to the indelible dishonour of Great Britain to back up the autocracy of Russia.' Ben Tillett reminded the crowd that 'the whole career of the Russian Tsar is one of sordidness.' 'The feeling of all the speeches and of the gathering', reported the *Manchester Guardian*, 'was that of disgust at the prospect of being dragged into Russia's quarrel'.[34]

A dramatic moment came at about 4.30 p.m. when a short down-pour descended upon Trafalgar Square. In the face of this 'the solid core of the meeting stood gallantly to their umbrellas and cheered for the war against war'.[35] The rally resumed. 'Rain came, and still it stood, now singing, now cheering, now listening with an almost intense solemn silence, to firm denunciations of the madness of the nations.'[36]

The Demonstrations for Neutrality Beyond London

London was not alone, and Labour was not alone, in this awakening of a public movement against the threat of war. The beginnings of protest could be seen in many centres of local Liberal power in the North of England, and in Scotland, during the crisis. Events in two northern towns, Huddersfield and Carlisle, must serve to underline the point.

Huddersfield exemplified the potential for a broad movement to build when there was a close alignment between the views of the local Radical MP and local Liberal worthies. In Huddersfield, opposition to Britain entering the war was strong. The local Radical MP, Arthur Sherwell, a friend of the Rowntree family, voiced his opposition. The discussion circle known as the Liberal Five Hundred – the centre of local Liberal organisation – declared for neutrality. The Liberal-leaning newspaper the *Huddersfield Examiner* urged neutrality. At public meetings in and around the town, local ministers, Quakers, and the Adult School all condemned the prospect of British intervention.[37] Active too were the ILP, the BSP, the local Labour Party and trade unions. These organised two large demonstrations in St George's Square in Huddersfield on Sunday 2 August that 'filled the square'. There were protest meetings in the nearby towns of Matlock, Blackburn, Knutsford and Holmfirth. A gathering outside the church in the village of New Mill attracted 'about five hundred people, probably the entire adult population of the village'.[38]

Events in Carlisle also showed the potential for cooperation between Radical Liberals and the local labour movement in the cause of peace. The local Liberal MP, Richard Denman, was a strong Radical. The town newspaper the *Carlisle Journal* favoured neutrality. 'The tide of public indignation against the suggestion that this country should take part in a general European war is rising fast', commented that paper on Tuesday 4 August. Certainly Carlisle witnessed a remarkable gathering. On Sunday evening 2 August, there was a large demonstration in the Market Square in Carlisle, after evening church services concluded. Liberals, socialists, women and leading churchmen organised the rally, which attracted 'a large crowd'. Speakers insisted that 'the vast mass of opinion in our country' favoured neutrality. A resolution demanding neutrality was passed and telegraphed to Downing Street. Reporting this demonstration, the *Carlisle Journal* observed that such resolutions had been passed over the weekend across the nation 'wherever there was a Liberal gathering'.[39] Certainly from Scotland came a flow of telegrams to 10 Downing Street from Liberal and church meetings.[40]

The Labour and socialist press reported demonstrations for peace in many parts of Britain over the weekend. The *Labour Leader* devoted two full pages to short reports of protest meetings at forty-two locations, from Thursday 30 July to Tuesday 4 August.[41] At

Leicester Market Place 'large crowds responded'; at the Bigg Market in Newcastle 'huge crowds assembled'. Clapham claimed 'an enormous crowd', Ipswich recorded a crowd of 'four thousand' on the Cornhill, and Norwich's crowd was 'large and enthusiastic'. Exeter reported 'the biggest open-air meeting the Exeter ILP has ever secured'. In Oldham there was 'a magnificent meeting'. There were two large protest meetings in Manchester, in Stevenson Square and Milton Hall. In Bolton, 6,000 people joined a march against war on the Saturday and another 2,000 filled the Bolton Town Hall and passed a motion urging British neutrality.[42] Similarly, a crowd estimated at 3,000 filled the Bull Ring in Birmingham on Sunday.[43] Various trade union gatherings over the weekend denounced war.[44] In addition, the Scottish ILP claimed that more than 100 meetings took place in Scottish towns and villages.[45]

The Significance of the Public Rallies for Peace

How significant was it that there were so many demonstrations calling for Britain to remain neutral? Turning to the main rally in Trafalgar Square, it was hardly a surprise that the pro-interventionist newspapers were dismissive. Using this evidence, some historians also have continued to diminish the significance of the rally.[46] *The Times* supplied a hostile report. It suggested that the crowd in the square was made up of mere loafers, stragglers – and Germans. Crowning this report, *The Times* was full of praise for an impromptu counter-demonstration begun at the Admiralty Arch, which it insisted had 'far outdone' the efforts of those in Trafalgar Square.[47] This is contradicted by all other reports.[48]

Personal accounts vary. One seventeen-year-old participant remembered it as 'quite a thrilling meeting, with about ten thousand people there, and certainly very definitely anti-war'.[49] However, Beatrice Webb, the famous socialist intellectual, provided an entry in her diary, full of haughty contempt. She disliked the 'hooligan warmongers' on the edge of the crowd, but also thought the main demonstration 'undignified and futile'.[50]

It is important to remember that the demonstrations over that weekend were meant to be the first in a series. It was a big beginning, and had drawn in both Radicals and socialists. This suggests that if the neutralist forces had been able to gain more time to arouse public opinion on the issue, then there was potentially a deep well to draw upon. For the best part of a decade, Radical and Labour critics had warned against the danger of Britain's entanglement in war by secret diplomacy. Even more widely felt was revulsion at the prospect of Britain fighting as comrade-in-arms with Russia. The movement for neutrality was not built upon last-minute sentimentalism against war.

Three points deserve emphasis. First, many reports of the demonstrations outside London mentioned that big meetings had been achieved in spite of the very short notice. For example, Birmingham's Bull Ring meeting was called 'at less than 24 hours notice'. Second, many examples were given of a new spirit of cooperation animating the various sections of the progressive movement – Liberals, ILP, BSP, Labour Party, local trade councils and even Free Church Councils. Third, the weekend demonstrations were dress rehearsals. Plans were made for more and larger demonstrations, well advertised, for later in the week.[51]

In London, too, time had been very short for organisation and publicity. Yet the great rally succeeded. The Liberal press argued that Labour had acted for the very many concerned Liberals. The *Manchester Guardian* emphasised that 'the whole thing has come upon us so quickly that there has been no organised public protest, and it was left to the socialists this afternoon to hold the first anti-war meeting in the country'.[52] Many more rallies lay ahead – so those resisting war imagined. In the *Daily Herald*, the editor concluded on Tuesday 4 August, 'There is not the slightest sign of enthusiasm for this war in England.'[53] Again this underlines the fact that the dash toward war simply outpaced the peace movement.

Evidence from the streets is debatable. Certainly, the well-known evening balcony scenes before Buckingham Palace attracted thousands on Sunday 2, Monday 3 and Tuesday 4 August. They were incited by the Royal Family's appearances and the King and Queen's excursion through London on Monday afternoon. But even *The Times* conceded that well-to-do Londoners were prominent among those thronging in the streets and before the Palace. Reports on the revelries noted the frolicking of expensively dressed men and women in private motor vehicles that cruised through the milling crowds. Describing the fizzy crowds of revellers on the evening of Tuesday 4 August, *The Times* reported, 'Scores of motor-cars carrying men and women in evening dress wound slowly through them.' At Buckingham Palace, *The Times* noted, 'Numbers of motor-cars were drawn up near the Palace gates.' Flags, including 'the Royal Standard', were everywhere. 'Flags were waved from cabs, omnibuses, and private cars.' Clearly, shiny rich Londoners were among those entertaining themselves on these historic evenings, touring the scenes of revels, and indulging in some memorable skylarking, jovially impervious to the approaching disaster.[54] These were not ordinary Britons transported to passion by the prospect of righteous war.

Observers in the streets away from the Palace saw different things. As she walked through London on Tuesday 4 August, Elizabeth Cadbury was 'watching the crowds who were gathered together at any point where they thought there was a chance of hearing news, quietly and anxiously waiting. There seemed an extraordinary silence and sense of oppression over the whole of London.'[55] Many newspapers recorded that the tone of the crowds in the streets was strikingly different to that evident at the time of the Boer War.[56] There was deep anxiety rather than eagerness for war. Observers from all sides of politics noticed this. 'Here in London there has been no trace, or hardly any, of "music hall patriotism"', Chirol reported to Hardinge on Tuesday 4 August.[57] Jim Middleton, a Labour Party official, wrote to his parents observing, 'There is no jingoism here in London – bits of youths march about with their silken sweated flags, but there is a dull heavy thoughtfulness in people's faces that is altogether new.'[58]

The same spirit dominated after war was declared. On 5 August Beatrice Webb recorded that 'there is no enthusiasm about the war: at present it is, on the part of England, a passionless war, a terrible nightmare sweeping over all classes, no one able to realise how the disaster came about.' Again, on 6 August: 'There is still no enthusiasm for the war but a good deal of quiet determination.'[59] Arthur Acland, a senior Liberal, told Morley on 6 August that 'never were the working classes of this country less possessed of any war fever than now – at least so it would appear.'[60] On the same day Elizabeth Haldane was in London to attend a meeting of the Territorial Force. She stressed the lack of pro-war passion: 'the crowd serious & not carried away.'[61] From the North came similar reports. An industrialist based in Yorkshire told Harcourt: 'The calm round here is wonderful. No panic, no excitement, only quiet confidence in the issue.'[62]

Those who made the choice for war in Britain liked to imagine that it stood on the secure foundations of overwhelming public support – even unanimity – both in the last days of peace and in the first days of war. Few historians agree.[63]

SEVENTEEN

'Jockeyed'
Sunday 2 August

> Beauchamp feels we were 'jockeyed' this morning over the German fleet; Simon agrees & thinks we ought to have resigned with Burns.[1]
>
> Lewis Harcourt, Cabinet Memorandum, 2 August 1914

On the afternoon of Sunday 2 August, Britain took the highway to a catastrophic war. As outlined in the prelude to this book, while Trafalgar Square was filling with demonstrators urging neutrality, at Downing Street the choice for war was being made. It was indeed to be the decisive day – and exceptionally tense. A year later, Asquith would look back on these events in a private letter, recalling 'the all-day Cabinet, and the resignations: and the infinite kaleidoscopic chaos of opinions and characters'.[2]

Tears Before Cabinet

The day began memorably with tears. Prince Lichnowsky visited 10 Downing Street while the Prime Minister was still at breakfast. Lichnowsky put the German case, and he was soon in tears. Germany was in danger of being crushed by 'two opponents', he pleaded,

France and Russia. Britain 'would be in a much stronger position to mediate as a neutral'. If she chose neutrality she could avert 'a war of annihilation for the entire civilization of Europe'. Asquith replied by pointing to lines that Germany must not cross. Britain's 'neutral attitude', he explained, would be 'greatly hindered by two things': 'the violation of the neutrality of Belgium' and 'any attack by German war-ships on the totally unprotected northern coast of France'.[3]

In his cable to Berlin later that day, Lichnowsky reported that 'tears repeatedly stood in the eyes of the old gentleman and he said to me: "A war between our two countries is quite unthinkable."' Lichnowsky emphasised that the British leaders were still 'friendly', and 'holding back'. It seemed that 'for the present' they had not 'the slightest intention of declaring war upon us'. Lichnowsky was not under any illusion, but was clearly talking up a last chance for Britain's neutrality. His purpose was plain: to persuade Berlin it was worth making a huge concession to Britain, respecting at least one of Asquith's two conditions to preserve Britain's 'neutral attitude' – a promise not to use the German Navy against France's northern coast.[4]

A short while later, Margot Asquith went with her daughter Elizabeth to the morning service at St Paul's Cathedral. After the service Margot called around to the German Embassy at 9 Carlton House Terrace to see Lichnowsky and Princess Mechtilde. Both greeted her in the smoking room. 'I found them in a state of white despair', wrote Margot. Lichnowsky was 'like a Goya picture'. Margot described the scene, with Mechtilde weeping and Lichnowsky 'walking up & down in silence. He caught me by the hands & said. "Oh: say there is surely not going to be a war (pronouncing it like far)."' The two denounced the Kaiser as '*ill informed, impulsive, mad.*' When the moment came to part, the ambassador 'had large tears rolling down his thin cheeks.' He requested, 'Do come again'.[5]

At exactly this time, the leaders of the neutralist group of ministers were preparing carefully for the next crucial Cabinet. Plans for a pre-Cabinet caucus had been made the evening before. Simon had visited Harcourt at midnight with a request that he come to Number 11 Downing Street at 10 a.m. on the Sunday morning, to decide upon strategy. But when Harcourt awoke on Sunday he learned of another incident overnight showing how the Cabinet was being overridden. He heard that at 3 a.m. the Admiralty had directed his Colonial Office to send telegrams across the Empire calling up the Naval Reserve. This placed the Royal Navy in a state of complete mobilisation – the precise proposal rejected by the Cabinet on Saturday. The Admiralty officials had cited a 'Naval Reserve Proclamation', already signed by the King.[6]

When Harcourt appeared at 11 Downing Street at 10 a.m. he was no doubt exasperated. But he found seven ministers still firm for neutrality: 'Pease, McK[innon] Wood, Beauchamp, Simon, Runciman, Ll[oyd] Geo[rge] and self.' The key decision was soon made. 'Settled we w[oul]d not go to war for [a] mere violation of Belgian territory and would hold up if possible any decision today.' Lloyd George, significantly, joined Harcourt in a two-man delegation to see Asquith next door, a few minutes before Cabinet. Here, in the Ante Room, Birrell asked that his name be added to the list of dissidents. Probably in Asquith's sitting room, Lloyd George and Harcourt then told him that they 'represented 8–10 colleagues who would not go to war for Belgium'. Harcourt recorded Asquith's astonishing response: 'PM listened and s[ai]d nothing.'[7] All filed downstairs for the fateful Cabinet.

The Morning Cabinet Pledges Naval Aid to France

The morning Cabinet sat from 11 a.m. until almost 2 p.m. It was truly historic. As Walter Runciman wrote afterwards at the top of his usual printed invitation to this Cabinet: 'The Cabinet which decided that war with Germany was inevitable.'[8]

The nineteen men at the Cabinet table focused naturally upon the big news overnight: the German declaration of war on Russia. The Russian jolt of Friday had been displaced by the German jolt of Saturday. In conveying news to the Cabinet of each development in the crisis Asquith, Grey and Churchill were in a very strong position. They occupied the key Cabinet posts – the War Office, the Foreign

Office, and the Admiralty – with access to the latest intelligence. This was a huge advantage. Other ministers felt starved of facts. 'I have little more news than is in the papers', Samuel had complained on Friday 31 July.[9] Grey and Churchill were able to tell the Cabinet that the latest information pointed to premeditated German aggression: not only had Germany declared war upon Russia but German troops had also occupied strategic centres in Luxemburg.[10] But Grey was not without hope, for 'German troops are moving *south* as if they did not mean to enter Belgium'. He recapitulated that he had told Cambon 'we should not send troops to France to defend the Franco-Belgian frontier'. So, at this stage, it appeared the Cabinet's decision against deploying the BEF was holding.[11]

But Grey then shifted ground. He was suddenly vehement. 'Grey is much stronger than before for joining in war and would like to promise France our help *today*', wrote Harcourt. Grey told the Cabinet that 'it was *vital* to him that he should today assure Cambon that if the German fleet attacked [the] French coast we w[oul]d prevent it & use all our naval power and he must say this in Parl[iamen]t tomorrow'. He was again willing to say nothing to Cambon on Belgium, but he demanded a decision on naval assistance before he saw Cambon at 2.30 p.m.[12]

Other Cabinet ministers heard Grey turn the dial up. He announced that Cambon had 'appealed that morning very pathetically for a decision and we must give one'. Grey demanded to know 'what we should do to help them [the French] in war'. Grey employed a cascade of emotive arguments: the French 'had been relying on the entente'; the French had 'kept their Northern coast undefended'; France 'might be crushed from that quarter' [the sea]; 'Cambon had twice wept over our statement that we were not committed.' Finally, Grey produced his red flag of warning: 'he could not stay in office unless we blockaded the German Navy into the Baltic'.[13] Runciman recorded Grey's direct threat to walk out: 'Either we must declare ourselves neutral, or in it. If we are to be neutral he will go.' Grey 'asks for a sharp decision'.[14]

Samuel detected a new anti-German edge of passion. Grey was 'outraged' at German and Austrian dishonesty. They had 'played with the most vital interests of civilisation, have put aside all attempts at accommodation made by himself and others, and while continuing to negotiate have marched steadily to war'.[15] Next, Asquith supported Grey in asserting German guilt. He reported sympathetically on his breakfast meeting with Lichnowsky, but added damaging details: Lichnowsky 'thinks his Gov[ernmen]t mad'.[16]

Samuel then suggested a compromise based on his 'own conviction'. Britain must not contemplate war for 'the sake of our goodwill for France' nor for 'the balance of power'. If Britain went to war, it must be solely for British interests. Britain could wage war for two reasons only: 'for the protection of the northern coasts of France, which we could not afford to see bombarded by the German fleet and occupied by the German army, or for the maintenance of the independence of Belgium'.[17] This formula was attractive. For one thing, Samuel distinguished it from Grey's policy, which many characterised as war for the sake of the Entente. In addition, German action would appear to be the trigger.

At this point, Asquith read to the Cabinet the letter he had just received from the Conservative leaders Bonar Law and Lansdowne. The Tories stood firm for intervention, with no distinction between a war in the east and the west. There was no mention of Belgium. Masterman claimed the letter was 'hurriedly read and laid down without comment'.[18] But others carefully recorded its arrival. In Runciman's words, the letter meant that Law and Lansdowne 'promise that they will support us in going in with France'.[19] Harcourt scribbled down the Conservatives' cut-through line – 'fatal to the honour and security of the UK to hesitate'.[20]

What was the impact of the letter? Years later Asquith denied it had any bearing on the Liberals' decisions.[21] But taken together with Churchill's contacts with the Tories, and open talk of resignation, the letter threatened the insubordinate ministers. Some were fully seized of the heightened danger – of a coalition. Many observers noticed this. For example, Chirol told Hardinge that Asquith had been trying to 'parry' the Radicals' resignation threats with the threat of 'the formation of a coalition government'.[22] It was a fair assessment.

Quite apart from Tory pressure, the high political stakes that day were dramatised by Asquith's own talk of resignation. In the afternoon Asquith wrote to Venetia Stanley that Cabinet had been 'on the brink of a split'. Grey might go, he added, and 'I shall not separate myself from him.'[23] It is very likely the ministers appreciated this. According to Samuel, Asquith told him directly after lunch that day, 'I shall stand by Grey in any event.'[24] Samuel offered the same assessment that evening: 'Had the matter come to an issue Asquith would have stood by Grey in any event, and three others would have remained. I think all the rest of us would have resigned.'[25] As Samuel did the numbers, this meant the solid block in favour of intervention comprised Asquith and Grey, plus the 'three others', Haldane, Churchill and probably McKenna. Five. Had the Radicals pressed them to the point of resignation, these five would have walked, ending the Liberal Cabinet.

Evidence from a decade later certainly underlines the importance of the threats of Grey and Asquith to resign – whether direct or implied. 'Personally I was aware of this all along', Crewe recalled, and he added that others were aware too.[26] By this time Samuel was no longer so sure, recalling that a direct threat was made only 'in the final stages' and never 'definitely discussed' in the Cabinet itself.[27] Runciman wrote later that he 'knew throughout that Grey would resign if we did not come down on the side of France'.[28]

In pursuit of unity, Asquith did read to the Cabinet a six-point statement of his own position. This Runciman recorded as a summary both of 'considerations to weigh with the Cabinet' and of what Grey 'proposed to say in Parl[iamen]t'.[29] The summary was undoubtedly the same list that Asquith despatched to Venetia Stanley later on the Sunday:

(1) We have no obligation of any kind either to France or Russia to give them military or naval help.

(2) The despatch of the Expeditionary force to help France at this moment is out of the question and w[oul]d serve no object.

(3) We mustn't forget the ties created by our long-standing and intimate friendship with France.

(4) It is against British interest that France s[houl]d be wiped out as a Great Power.

(5) We cannot allow Germany to use the Channel as a hostile base.

(6) We have obligations to Belgium to prevent her being utilised & absorbed by Germany.[30]

This clever summary appeared to make concessions to both wings of the Cabinet. The first point, Britain's 'free hand', was listed to calm the Radicals. The second point acknowledged the Radical victory of Saturday 1 August: no BEF 'at this moment'. But the next four points put the case for intervention in Samuel's moderate terms, that is, on the basis of British interests. The 'ties' with France were based on 'friendship' – not on controversial commitments such as 'military conversations' – again, to calm the Radicals. Only Asquith's reference to 'obligations' to Belgium broke with the Cabinet's decisions so far. Intervention in support of Belgium had been deemed a matter of 'policy' and not of 'obligation' earlier in the week.

The interventionist ministers employed one more subtle argument. They deliberately fostered the impression that Britain's intervention in any war would be restricted to naval action. As Churchill explained to Lloyd George, 'The naval war will be cheap – not more than 25 millions a year.'[31] Such was the assurance used to drape the crudities of war. Samuel's formula for British intervention, making it dependent on German naval action on the French coast, must have added to the impression of a naval war. Samuel himself highlighted Britain's naval preparations in a letter to his wife. 'Our great fleet is in the north; a second is waiting in port on the south coast; a third is being distributed along the trade routes.'[32]

So, the Cabinet debated British intervention on Samuel's formula. Grey wanted more, a straightforward commitment to defend France and Belgium. As Samuel put it, 'Grey expressed a view which was unacceptable to most of us.'[33] There were moments of high drama. The interventionists' threats to resign provoked answering threats. Churchill goaded the neutralists: 'If Germany violates Belgian neutrality I want to go to war – if you don't I must resign.' Morley interjected, 'If you *do* go to war I resign.' Morley was 'very angry' at the revelation of naval mobilisation overnight, which was 'contrary to Winston's promise to Cabinet'. Some ministers leaned one way, then the other. For example, Harcourt thought that 'Crewe from all he said this morning seems to be with "us".'[34] Probably ten Cabinet members were still leaning toward neutrality: Harcourt, Lloyd George, Morley, Pease, McKinnon Wood, Beauchamp, Simon, Runciman, Birrell, and possibly Crewe.

On the other side of the debate, Grey, Asquith and Churchill pushed hard for a pledge of naval assistance for the French, to make safe the Channel and the French coasts – Britain's 'doorstep'. In the final few minutes of this three-hour Cabinet came the historic break-through. A momentous decision was made. Grey got his pledge to France. By a slender margin, a majority was found for a form of words suggested by either Samuel or Crewe.[35] Grey was authorised to promise the French ambassador that, if France faced a German naval attack, then 'the British fleet will give all the protection in its power'.[36] Downing Street had decided on the first trigger for war.

From this point – before anything was known of the German threat to Belgium – it was certain that the British government would intervene in any war in which France was embroiled with Germany.

But the political damage was immediate. John Burns protested. He 'leant forward' and spoke 'with deep feeling'. He spoke of the pain of separating from 'a P. M. whom he loved'.[37] But he was adamant: this pledge to France was 'an act of hostility' that might provoke Germany to 'declare war on us'.[38] Burns was 'almost in tears', announcing that he 'must resign at once'.[39] Beauchamp recalled the reaction: 'Everybody joined in a chorus of dissuasion & the PM spoke forcibly on "deserting colleagues" etc. Eventually he promised to return for the evening Cabinet.'[40]

Why had the majority of Radicals accepted Grey's demand for a pledge of naval support to France? Both strategic and political cal-culations had come into play. Morley's friendly parting exchange with Burns after the Cabinet helps explain the strategic thinking. 'I think you are mistaken in going on this particular proposal', he told his friend. 'The door-step argument makes a warning to Germany defensible, apart from the French Entente.' Britain, Morley conceded, could not 'acquiesce in Franco-German naval conflict in the narrow seas, on our doorstep so to say'.[41] Thus, as Morley told Burns, he too would resign – not over the pledge to France, but rather in protest at the whole course of Grey's foreign policy.

From this exchange with Burns, it is clear Morley believed the 'doorstep argument' had swung the Cabinet. The majority had been prepared to back a naval pledge to France, 'as a warning to Germany'. Samuel also cited the 'doorstep', explaining in a private letter that the Cabinet knew Britain would not be able 'to tolerate great naval conflicts at our doors'.[42] Pease similarly thought that the dispositions of the French and British fleets since 1912 had created a sense of obligation upon Britain to protect France's northern coast, whatever had been said at the time. He hoped that Germany might accept the warning to her navy.[43] In this way the *naval* promise to France assuaged consciences – and still seemed less than war.

Then political scheming had been factored in. The pledge to France had prolonged the life of the Cabinet and repelled the Tories. As Samuel explained to his wife, 'The morning Cabinet almost resulted in a political crisis to be superimposed on the international and financial crisis.' The concession on the French coasts had avoided it. As Samuel argued, 'the division or resignation of the Government in a moment of utmost peril for the country would have been in every way lamentable'.[44]

The Pledge to France – and Radical Misgivings

As soon as Cabinet was over, Grey crossed hurriedly from Downing Street to the Foreign Office. At an interview in his study at about 2.20 p.m., Grey passed over an *aide-mémoire* to Cambon:

> I am authorised to give an assurance that if the German fleet comes into the Channel or through the North Sea to undertake hostile operations against French coasts or shipping the British fleet will give all the protection in its power.

This assurance is of course subject to the policy of His Majesty's Government receiving the support of Parliament and must not be taken as binding His Majesty's Government to take any action until the above contingency of action by the German fleet takes place.[45]

In his explanation to Cambon, Grey stressed that the declaration 'did not bind us to go to war with Germany unless the German fleet took the action indicated'.[46] In spite of this, and the carefully formulated second paragraph with its nod to parliament, there was little doubt left – *neutrality* for Britain was next to impossible. Grey himself had exposed this in Cabinet. When Grey's critics had urged that he should genuinely neutralise the Channel, that is, seek 'the neutrality of France in (our) home waters also', he had refused.[47] No such even-handed negotiation would be considered.

The reaction of the French leaders confirmed this. They immediately recognised what they could do with Grey's pledge – portray it as an ally's commitment. Early on the Sunday evening, Grey reminded Paris that the pledge was 'very confidential'.[48] But Prime Minister Viviani telegraphed to Cambon in London that he proposed to reveal the British pledge – 'a first assistance' – in the Chamber of Deputies, and to give it a wide interpretation. He proposed to describe it as a promise to give the French Navy all assistance, in the Atlantic as much as the Channel, and to deny the Germans access to English ports.[49] Thus, from the Sunday evening Paris pressed London for the right to exploit the pledge publicly, to reassure France – and, in so doing, to tether Britain to her promise.

The secrecy of the British Cabinet's pledge caused trouble on another front. Grey had insisted in Cabinet on absolute confidentiality until he had addressed the House of Commons on the afternoon of Monday 3 August.[50] The Germans were not to be told immediately. Why? This was a curious way of proceeding if the intention was to protect the French coasts and French shipping by issuing a 'warning to Germany' – as some ministers had depicted it. This secrecy of the pledge worried Grey's critics.

But in any case, within hours, the secret was out. Churchill clearly regarded the pledge as akin to war. He summoned the French Naval Attaché, the Comte de Saint-Seine, to the Admiralty. Churchill revealed the pledge. Both sides agreed that 'the possibility of an alliance' should be anticipated. Therefore, packages containing 'secret signal books' were to be opened; the 'allied ships' of each nation were to be granted access to each other's bases; and senior officers should begin communicating. 'The general direction of the naval war to rest with the British Admiralty', it was recorded. Saint-Seine was given authority to communicate all this to Paris – so much for Grey's secrecy.[51] Later Churchill sent a message to his senior commanders falsely reporting that because *both* the French and German ambassadors had been given a note conveying the British pledge to France at 2.20 p.m. that afternoon, all naval forces must be 'prepared to meet surprise attacks'.[52]

In Paris, too, the news leaked. In spite of assurances that only the very top echelon of the French decision-makers knew about the British pledge, telegrams from Paris revealed otherwise. Bertie reported on Monday 3 August from Paris that French deputies and newspaper journalists were boasting of Grey's pledge. The German Embassy in London as well was certainly made aware of it during the morning of Monday 3 August.[53] This leaking in every direction testified to the obvious: the pledge to France had wiped out the possibility of British neutrality.

In this context it was no surprise that a great cloud of misgiving settled upon the Radicals. As soon as the Cabinet broke up on the Sunday, a group made its way the short distance to Halkyn House, Earl Beauchamp's grand residence at 13 Belgrave Square. Morley accepted a lift with Simon and Lloyd George and on the way 'our talk was on the footing that we were all three for resignation'. Simon confided to Morley that 'he felt pretty sure of decisive influence over Lloyd George, and that he (Simon) looked to resignation as quite inevitable'.[54]

On arrival at Halkyn House, Beauchamp hosted a working luncheon. His guests were Morley, Simon, Samuel, Harcourt and, significantly, Lloyd George. By telephone, three more colleagues were summoned, Pease, McKinnon Wood and Runciman. Morley recalled a general consensus that 'Burns was right', and 'that we should not have passed Grey's proposed language to Cambon'. All resented that 'the Cabinet was being rather artfully drawn on step by step to war for the benefit of France and Russia'.[55] Harcourt also recorded a short summary of the rueful talk: 'Beauchamp feels we were "jockeyed" this morning over the German fleet; Simon agrees & thinks we ought to have resigned with Burns.' But his account included an important concession: 'I differ as I think the prevention of a German fleet attack & capture of French territory on [the] shore of [the] Channel *a British interest.*'[56] This revealed the beginnings of a shift in Harcourt's position. Samuel also was impatient, privately complaining that Morley was 'so old' and his views 'inconsistent'.[57]

Nevertheless, it was Samuel who guided discussion as the Radicals turned to the next great issue – Belgium. He supplied a formula, which all agreed to adopt for the coming evening Cabinet. Harcourt jotted it down: 'We agreed to refuse to go to war merely on a violation of Belgian *neutrality* by a traverse for invasion purposes of territory but to regard any permanent danger or threat to Belgian *independence* (such as occupation) as a vital British interest.'[58]

Would more ministers resign? Morley, Beauchamp and Simon favoured this as the only honourable course. Lloyd George, they believed, was with them. Indeed Morley thought Lloyd George and Simon were 'heading the schism'.[59] Harcourt and Samuel, on the other hand, were edging toward the safety of office.

The Evening Cabinet and the Belgian Trigger

The second meeting of the Cabinet was scheduled to begin at 6.30 p.m. Once again, the neutralists caucused at Lloyd George's home a half-hour earlier.[60] 'Nothing new at this meeting', wrote Harcourt. The Radicals would defend Samuel's formula on Belgium. Beauchamp wrote that 'we expected a great fight over Belgian neutrality wh[ich] w[ould] end in a great rupture'.[61]

But the rupture did not come. Grey was disarming. He began with news designed to mollify the Radicals. 'Cambon has taken his communication quietly & had not pressed for further assurances about Belgium and Grey does not press for a decision on this tonight.'[62] The pledge of naval support appeared to be enough.

Recriminations were then aired, against Churchill in particular. Churchill explained his meeting with Saint-Seine and the measures for close naval cooperation he had set in train. This was too much for Morley. Another shouting match began. Morley was 'very angry' and accused Churchill of making an 'attempt to create an alliance for war'. Again the Radicals pressed that the Germans should be informed of the pledge of naval assistance to France. Grey was resolute: 'she must learn this from the statement in the H[ouse] of C[ommons] tomorrow'. This provoked questions from the neutralists. These were cut short when Asquith revealed that, in any case, he had told Lichnowsky in the morning that Britain would regard any action by the German fleet in the Channel 'very seriously' – as good as demanding that the Germans not use naval forces against France. Simon interrogated Churchill. Had any orders been issued instructing the Navy 'to attack [the] German fleet if they came out tonight'? Churchill answered with a definite no. Harcourt declared for good measure that 'it would be monstrous to attack them if they were coming out not against us and without having been informed of our decision'.[63]

The Cabinet then turned to the next and thorniest issue – Belgium. During the day, confirmation had arrived at the Foreign Office of German troop movements inside Luxemburg.[64] Grey offered in addition the inflammatory detail that 'the Germans have crossed the French frontier thro[ugh] Luxemburg and probably at Nancy'. Notwithstanding the 'probably', the Foreign Secretary, *the* source of up-to-the-minute intelligence, was suggesting an imminent invasion of France. Was Belgium the immediate target? Was this to be the second trigger for war for Britain? In the discussion, Samuel's formula, nutted out at Beauchamp's luncheon table in the afternoon, found favour. Eventually the Cabinet resolved that only 'a substantial violation' of Belgian neutrality would provide the formal *casus belli* that would be used to justify Britain's intervention in the continental war.[65] Later Churchill told Blunt that this was decided by 'a single vote'.[66]

The decision was clearly a compromise. A second trigger for British entry into war had been set. Through Radical pressure, the bar had been set higher – not any German trespass upon Belgian territory but rather something 'substantial' would drive Britain to war. Samuel was relieved. As he reported, 'the situation was easier, the point of contention was not pressed, and with the exception of the two I have mentioned [Burns and Morley] we remain solid'.[67] In his account of the Cabinet, Beauchamp highlighted another very human factor that had come into play – 'we were all jaded and exhausted'.[68] Radical resistance was being slowly worn down.

In this way, the decision of the second Cabinet of the Sunday complemented that of the first: it was made to appear, on sea and land, that German action would provoke British intervention. Samuel comforted himself with this. If peace foundered, he wrote, 'it will be an action of Germany's and not of ours which will cause the failure, and my conscience will be easy in embarking on the war'.[69]

Did the setting of these two triggers to war signal that all hope of peace was lost? Some ministers did not think so. Perhaps Germany might agree to stay out of the Channel *and* Belgium? Samuel, Pease and Crewe flirted with such hopes. Samuel thought it might prove a 'brilliant stroke of policy' on Britain's part and 'the greatest of all services' to France if Britain could protect both the French coasts and France's Belgian frontier 'without firing a shot'.[70] On the same basis, Pease 'thought it still possible, even on Sunday last, that Peace could be preserved'.[71] Crewe believed that if Britain could persuade Germany to accept these two limits, then the situation 'would have been so advantageous to France as to offer almost complete payment of our debt to her'.[72] But it was a long shot. Germany was being asked to refrain from any use of her naval forces in a war with France – a huge concession.

Restless Radical Spirits

At the end of this historic day, Radical consciences were restless. Burns and Morley were determined to resign on principle – and so those closest to them, Simon, Beauchamp and Harcourt, were tormented with doubt. They had sought guidance from each other during the evening Cabinet. Simon slipped a note to Burns: 'Stay at any rate *for tomorrow's Cabinet*. I am disposed to think that 7 or 8 of us may be with you.' Burns replied firmly on the same piece of notepaper: '*It is then too late*.'[73] At some point in the discussion, Beauchamp passed a note to Harcourt: 'I still think Burns was right this morning.' Harcourt replied 'Perhaps – but we are holding together with a good hope of keeping out of war altogether.' 'I agree or I s[houl]d join him', shot back Beauchamp. 'We *must* keep him', replied Harcourt.[74]

But they could not keep Burns. As the Cabinet finished at about 8 p.m., 'Burns renewed his protest', Beauchamp wrote. He announced that 'nothing had occurred to change his decision and he must resign tonight'. He agreed to talk with Asquith later. But 'he was immoveable'.[75] Burns then returned home to tell his wife Pattie and son Edgar of his final decision. 'It was for me to decide', he wrote in his diary. 'A man must be Captain of his own soul, pilot of his own course when a vital decision like mine has been taken.'[76]

Burns's resignation also instantly revealed another side of the political management of this crisis – secrecy. When Burns declared his resignation, he was immediately assailed with advice to keep it secret. Secrecy regarding any Cabinet crisis, all were told, would strengthen the nation's hand, preserve a 'united front' – and, temptingly, perhaps help to deter war. In their private letters, Cabinet members urged their families to keep silent on Cabinet divisions.[77] This veiling of dissent inside the Cabinet would be an important factor in the days ahead.

Long into the evening, the crisis continued to chase down some Cabinet ministers. Harcourt's experiences point to the frenetic activity. He had an especially worrying night – which may help explain the crumbling of his resolve to resist war. Harcourt had fled from

the Cabinet to dinner at home alone – 'housemaid, chop'. But at
10 p.m. he received a special message from the Admiralty: a war
plan was up and running. The Admiralty suggested that the South
Africans should mount an attack on Walvis Bay in German South-
West Africa. It took Harcourt an hour to persuade Asquith and then
Churchill that the proposal 'was mad'.[78]

Back at home at 11 p.m., Harcourt found another visitor, Sir
Thomas Robinson, the Agent-General for Queensland, Australia.
He suggested that Britain should immediately buy up a consign-
ment of 2,000 tons of meat from Queensland, currently afloat en
route to the United States, which Austria was attempting to pur-
chase and divert. The visit was a reminder that throughout this
crisis the Dominions' enthusiastic response to the prospect of war
was an embarrassment to Harcourt. The prospect of lending assistance to the Mother Country excited the imperial enthusiasts in the
Dominions. That excitement led them to a flurry of public offers of
military assistance to Britain, including offers to mount expeditionary forces – from New Zealand on Friday 31 July, from Canada on
Sunday 2 August, and from Australia on Monday 3 August.[79] These
were flaunted in the Conservative press and added to Harcourt's
pressures.[80]

Finally, at 11.30 p.m. Arthur Ponsonby was at Harcourt's door.
Ponsonby was seeking the latest information on the Cabinet's decisions. He asked Harcourt 'how we (Peace) were getting on'. Harcourt
summarised events. Then he was startled by indications from
Ponsonby that perhaps his own group of Radicals from the LFAG
was 'already split', having been spooked by reports of the German
troops in Luxemburg. Harcourt was amazed as he confessed, 'Not
one memb[er] of Cabinet (not even Grey) attaches any importance
to this!!'[81] Ponsonby recorded the conversation too. He had been at
the National Liberal Club until 11 p.m. and had met more than
a dozen MPs from his group – 'some already wavering because of
Germany's entry into Luxemburg'. So, he had walked to Berkeley
Square to talk to Harcourt. According to Ponsonby, Harcourt had
said 'the Cabinet had not split yet but it might and then there would
be a coalition'.[82]

The Conservatives at Brooks's

Indeed, while the Liberal ministers agonised over war all day and into the night, the Conservative leaders had shadowed them. They were satisfied with their letter to Asquith of Sunday morning. As Lansdowne interpreted this in a private note to his wife, the point of the letter was to hammer home the message 'that in our opinion this country should support France and Russia, and that we will support H.M.G. in this policy'. The support was sweeping. It was for a war of Entente solidarity. There was no suggestion that the Conservatives would back war only to prevent the invasion of Belgium.[83]

The 'pogrom' kept up its agitation too on Sunday 2 August. General Wilson, Amery, George Lloyd, Leo Maxse and Panouse from the French Embassy were all in close touch with each other and the Tory leaders. As Wilson recorded in his diary, there was 'much telephoning to Bonar Law, Austen, and others'.[84] During the day, the Conservatives learned of the pledge to France. But this only prompted General Wilson to press for instant mobilisation of the army and the despatch of the BEF. He complained: 'Was ever anything heard like this? What is the difference between the French coast and the French frontier?'[85] Later that afternoon George Lloyd supplied the inflammatory claim from the French Embassy that German troops had crossed the frontier without any formal declaration of war.[86]

The Conservative leaders linked up again that evening at about 9.30 p.m. at Brooks's Club in St James's Street to take stock. Bonar Law, Carson, Chamberlain, Devonshire and Lansdowne mulled over reports from inside the Cabinet – supplied by Churchill. His secretary, Edward Marsh, who happened to be a member of Brooks's, had spent the day 'as an errand-boy' carrying messages from Churchill to the Tories gathered there.[87] They learned the latest on prospects for British intervention: 'Winston and Grey are believed to be in favour of it, and perhaps Asquith – Lloyd George against', wrote Lansdowne. 'Things may end in a split and in our being approached, but a change of government would be deplorable at such a moment.'[88] Chamberlain learned that 'probably a majority' of the Cabinet might still resign. Naturally, full reports of Churchill's role arrived. He had mobilised the fleet, 'acting on his own authority'. The 'eighteen miles of warships' he had directed in the dead of night to Scapa Flow, according to earlier stories, was inflated to 'twenty-five miles of ships'.[89]

All this was reassuring. But the Conservatives were disconcerted when Bonar Law read to his colleagues Asquith's formal reply to their letter of Sunday morning. Asquith clung to the official Cabinet line: 'We are under no obligation, express or implied, either to France or to Russia to render them naval or military help.' He summarised the Cabinet's view of Britain's 'duties'. But he did give the text of the pledge of naval support given to Cambon. This lifted Tory expectations. Even more hopefully, from the Conservative viewpoint, Asquith directed attention to Belgium: 'It is right, therefore, before deciding whether any and what action on our part is necessary to know what are the circumstances and conditions of any German interference with Belgian territory.'[90] At length, the Conservatives decided the Liberals were still 'wavering' and might be 'searching for excuses to do nothing'.[91] So, still more pressure was needed.

After leaving Brooks's very late, Chamberlain wrote again to Lansdowne. He jotted down the best phrases from the daily indignation meetings at the French Embassy. Cambon was raising his 'bitter cry' about Britain losing all sense of 'honneur' [honour]. He recorded Cambon's latest plea: 'There is no written agreement of any sort or kind. There isn't a scrap of paper. But there is more. Everything, every act of the last few years gave us the assurance of your support.' Chamberlain coached his leader: 'Compare what you said tonight: "An Entente is stronger than an alliance, because it is not defined".'[92] Clearly, the Tories were searching to discover tethers already binding that troublesome Liberal 'free hand'. Chamberlain urged Lansdowne to demand another interview with Asquith immediately, and convey this message of lost honour, hopes betrayed, and the tight shackles of Entente. Britain must go to war – for France.

Bonar Law complied. He wrote to Asquith.[93] The interview was fixed for the next morning, Monday 3 August.

EIGHTEEN

Fracture Lines
Sunday 2 and Monday 3 August

Note to a friend. Aug. 1914.

Honour, Duty, Humanity all unite in my protest against this wanton war. I have resigned and three others have followed, Simon, Morley, Beauchamp.[1]

John Burns, 2 August 1914

Miraculously, it seemed, the Cabinet had just avoided implosion, but only by a narrow margin, on Sunday 2 August. As Morley remembered, the 'dissolution of the Ministry was that afternoon in full view'.[2] But by the evening, only Burns had jumped ship immediately. How many more – if any – would follow?

Resignations did follow. Their timing, and the explanations that each minister gave, are most revealing. They confound the sneering assumption that lurks in many narratives of these events, namely, that the mutinous ministers were gun-shy 'appeasers' who simply refused to face the reality of German aggression in Belgium.

The Sunday Evening Resignations: Burns and Simon

John Burns had spoken 'with remarkable energy, force and grasp' at the first Sunday Cabinet. He regarded the pledge to France as 'tantamount to a declaration of war'.[3] Burns condemned it 'not only because it was practically a declaration of war on sea leading inevitably to a war on land, but mainly because it was the symbol of an alliance with France with whom no such understanding hitherto existed'.[4] The word 'alliance' carried great significance. It was the word that unmasked the Entente. It was the word the neutralists now complained *was* applicable, because Britain was behaving as if handcuffed to France and Russia. If other ministers agreed with Burns, more resignations would follow.

After the Sunday evening Cabinet, Burns had confirmed his decision to go.[5] He returned to his office at the Board of Trade at Whitehall Gardens and penned a simple letter to Asquith: 'The decision of the Cabinet to intervene in a European war is an act with which I profoundly disagree.'[6] The letter gained Burns another interview with Asquith, but he proved to be 'obdurate'.[7]

It is important to stress two aspects of this resignation. First, the issue of Belgium did not figure. Burns certainly never forgot this vital reality, in timing or principle. In various verbal jousts during the war, Burns would remind his critics – and those in particular who sought to skewer him on the matter of Belgium, such as Arthur Nicolson – that he had 'resigned for higher reasons, before the Germans invaded Belgium'.[8] On one occasion Burns 'sprang' angrily at Nicolson, asserting that he had tried to save Britain from 'the loss of half a million of men, a national debt of thousands of millions, to be followed by a stalemate, a revolution and the disruption of Empire'.[9]

Second, it is significant that Asquith sent no letter to Burns accepting his resignation. Delay was vital. For the next three days, invitations to Cabinet meetings were sent to Burns. Asquith was manoeuvring to suppress knowledge of the rebellion. Burns, of course, thought differently. He hoped his resignation would prompt others. 'Honour, Duty, Humanity all unite in my protest against this wanton war', he wrote. 'I have resigned and three others have followed, Simon, Morley, Beauchamp.'[10]

John Simon, the Attorney General, spent part of the evening of Sunday 2 August brooding over the events of the day at a dinner party given by Sir George Riddell, owner of the *News of the World*. According to Riddell's diary, the other guests were Lloyd George, Masterman and Ramsay MacDonald. Simon and Lloyd George had just come from the evening Cabinet. The ministers explained to Riddell that Burns had resigned, and Simon, Beauchamp, Morley and Mackinnon Wood were 'considering the advisability of doing so'. During the meal, Simon showed a draft of his resignation letter to Lloyd George 'who handed it back to him without comment'. While Lloyd George was temporising, he did side with Simon in discussion.

Lloyd George outlined the Cabinet's decisions of the day. He explained – not accurately – that the Cabinet had agreed to tell Germany that 'England would remain neutral' if Germany agreed not to attack the French coasts and French shipping, and agreed also to respect Belgian neutrality. (In fact, as narrated above, Grey had pleaded for Germany to restrain her forces in this way but had definitely *not* agreed that England's neutrality would follow.) Lloyd George spoke 'very strongly' about the importance of maintaining Belgian neutrality. But he dwelt also on 'the danger of aggrandising Russia'. Simon, 'who looked very gloomy', agreed with Lloyd George. 'We have always been wrong when we have intervened. Look at the Crimea. The Triple Entente was a terrible mistake. Why should we support a country like Russia?' Simon asked. Masterman disagreed, however, focusing upon 'German aggression' and stressing that 'the present danger is the annihilation of France by Germany'.[11]

Lloyd George's consternation was clear. He even suggested that the Cabinet was on the point of breaking up. He prefaced some remark to Riddell with the doleful qualification 'if we are governing the country tomorrow, which is very doubtful'. But Riddell preached intervention – and pointed to the overriding factor, Grey's threat to resign. If Grey and then Asquith departed, the country would be 'horror stricken'. When MacDonald wrote up these events in his diary later, he was unimpressed. He recorded that among the Liberal cabinet ministers 'excuses were being searched for'. He summarised the situation: 'Masterman jingo, George ruffled, Simon broken.'[12]

Simon sent in his resignation letter, dated 2 August, later on that same Sunday evening. It was in Asquith's hands on the Monday morning.[13] Simon objected both to the naval pledge just given to France, and to Grey's demand that this be hidden from Germany. He wrote:

> The statement which Grey made to Cambon this afternoon, and which he does not propose to reveal to Germany until the announcement is made in the House of Commons tomorrow, will, I think, be regarded as tantamount to a declaration that we take part in this quarrel with France and against Germany. I think we should not take part, and so I must resign my post.[14]

He urged Asquith to 'please find a new Attorney General'. But Simon also indicated in his letter a courteous willingness to ease Asquith's burdens. He offered to continue doing any 'purely legal business'. He promised to sit on his resignation until after Grey had addressed the House of Commons on Monday afternoon. He explained that 'if we are involved in war (though I cannot agree in the policy pursued) the last thing I wish is to accentuate divisions'. Affectionate to the end, he thanked Asquith for his 'constant kindness'.

Once again, Asquith sent no letter in reply accepting the resignation.

The Monday Morning Resignations: Morley and Beauchamp

John Morley, the Lord President, was next to go. His departure was the culmination of persistent opposition. As he told Burns in the afternoon, his objection was to 'the general policy of armed intervention, as against diplomatic energy and armed neutrality, to which Grey has *step by step* been drawing the Cabinet on'.[15] 'My decision', he wrote later, 'was due to no one particular conversation, telegram, despatch.' Rather, 'it was the result of a whole train of circumstance and reflection.' Morley had mentioned his decision to resign to Asquith when Cabinet ended on the Sunday evening. Asquith pleaded with him successfully to 'sleep on it.'[16]

Therefore, Morley did not compose his resignation letter until after breakfast on Monday 3 August. It was a polite leave-taking, written 'with heartfelt pain'. He muted his criticisms. He saw war as imminent. In such a war, Morley advised, Asquith must avoid the 'fatal' weakness of 'divided counsels'. The fundamental consideration was the great dispute over the entire direction of the government's foreign policy. 'Grey had pointed out the essential difference between two views of Neutrality in the present case', as Morley put it. He explained that he could not be in a Cabinet where he inclined one way and 'three or four of my leading colleagues incline the other way' – a reference, of course, to the interventionism being pursued by Asquith, Grey, Churchill and Haldane. 'I press you, therefore, to release me', wrote Morley. He would make the Cabinet of Monday morning his last.[17] Once again Asquith did not immediately accept the resignation.

Doubts, sharpened with anger, assailed Earl Beauchamp on Sunday night. In the morning, he penned a letter of resignation to Asquith. With his own copy of this letter, he filed a revealing private memorandum. He stressed the blistering rapidity of the crisis: 'It is very difficult to sit down calmly in the middle of a crisis & to record events as they fly by.' Then he turned to the pledge to France, the burning issue for him:

> But the decision which was taken at yesterday's Cabinet – in the morning – to promise France defence of her coast and shipping against Germany was so momentous that I wish to fix it.
>
> Grey proposed it as a definite step in favour of France. For that reason I & others objected. There was however the overwhelming argument that we had tacitly allowed France to concentrate in the Mediterranean in virtue of those unfortunate naval conversations wh[ich] were [meant] to pledge no one to anything.
>
> It was obviously unfair to leave her in such circumstances unprotected.[18]

This underlines the crucial argument to which Beauchamp had capitulated at the first Sunday Cabinet: the 'unprotected' French coast. This was painful. Beauchamp, and other Radicals, remembered well the promises of 1912 that Britain would not be subject to blackmail on the basis of the redistribution of the fleets. Long into the future Beauchamp would lament that the Cabinet had been, in his view, misled, left in the dark, and engineered into a false position. He ended his private memorandum with a heartfelt cry: 'I cannot but feel that our promise to France is a *casus belli* to Germany. Alas for this country.'[19]

Beauchamp announced his resignation at the Cabinet table the next morning, Monday 3 August. After Morley had spoken, he passed over his resignation letter to Asquith. Invited to state his position, Beauchamp spoke briefly, simply seconding Morley's explanation for his resignation.[20] The letter was probably written at Halkyn House early in the morning and dated Monday 3 August. 'By successive acts the Cabinet has passed to a position at wh[ich] war seems to me inevitable', Beauchamp complained. Perhaps he should have resigned at 'some earlier moment', he wrote. But he had felt 'a real anxiety to cooperate as long as possible with colleagues and a chief for whom I have the greatest admiration & respect'. In common with the other three dissenters, Beauchamp was polite, even indicating that he 'would gladly do anything I can to mitigate any inconveniences which this step may cause'.[21] Again, Asquith sent no immediate answer. Postponing schism, and bottling up any wider defiance, was an essential element of his survival strategy.

The Significance of the Radical Resignations

Sometimes it is imagined that the Radical ministers resigned in a general protest against Britain entering the war – while ignoring the plight of Belgium. This is to misunderstand the timing of the crisis. The four resignations from the Cabinet came in the course of Sunday night and early Monday morning, 2–3 August. Thus, the decisions were all made before the first reports of the German ultimatum to Belgium reached London – at 10.55 a.m. on Monday morning.[22]

Therefore, quite clearly all four resignations from the Cabinet were essentially protests against the foreign policy that was driving Britain toward war on the basis of solidarity with France and Russia. The Radicals were appalled that the Liberal Imperialist leadership had extorted from the Cabinet a pledge of naval assistance to France immediately after an *eastern* war had been declared. Their resignations were protests against an act of partisanship, which they believed had destroyed Britain's chance to mediate during the crisis.

In addition, these resignations were protests against the 'bouncing' of the Cabinet. The Radicals accused the men of the inner circle of making crucial decisions that had pre-empted the decisions of the Cabinet as a whole. They had used their key positions to hurry the nation toward war. This charge could be heard in Morley's recollection of the discussion at Halkyn House on Sunday that the Cabinet's leaders were 'artfully' nudging the neutralist ministers, one step at a time, to accept a war of Entente solidarity.[23] Similarly, Morley had explained to Burns too that his protest was against the persistent manipulation of the Cabinet.[24] The charge could be heard as well in Beauchamp's complaint that the Cabinet had been 'jockeyed' into war.[25]

What decisions had 'jockeyed' the Cabinet? The Radicals rankled over a string of incidents: the concentration of the fleets, the move to war stations, the dogmatic rejection of all German attempts to negotiate, the two telegrams to Paris and Berlin seeking guarantees on Belgian neutrality, and the final step in naval mobilisation. In every case, Cabinet had been faced with a *fait accompli*.

The decision to mobilise the British Army would be made in a similar fashion. According to Haldane, late in the evening of Sunday, he responded to a telegram warning that 'the German Army was about to invade Belgium' – he gave no details. Haldane, Grey and Crewe pressed for immediate mobilisation of the British Army. Again, they obtained Asquith's agreement. The dutiful trio sent word to the French ambassador immediately.[26] Once more, the Cabinet heard the news after the event, on the Monday morning. Asquith explained consolingly that it had become necessary purely for home defence.[27]

The pattern is unmistakeable. Asquith and his satellites, a small knot of interventionist ministers, had exploited their Cabinet positions to drive the Cabinet ineluctably toward war. It was a triumph of the inner Executive over both Cabinet and parliament.

NINETEEN

Hidden Schism
Monday 3 August

Asq[uith] then said 'Burns has resigned; Morley, Simon, Beauchamp also going; many others uneasy: the Cabinet with much shattered authority in [a] time of great stress.'[1]
'Loulou' Harcourt, Monday 3 August 1914

The British people awoke on bank holiday Monday 3 August quite unaware that their government was tottering, and quite unaware that on Sunday their government had made a historic policy choice for the nation – to join France in any major war that opened on the Continent. No newspaper gave details of what had happened at the two Cabinets of Sunday. Similarly, outside a small circle at the top of both major parties, nobody knew of the Cabinet resignations. The newspapers simply informed the nation that Britain's policy would be explained when Sir Edward Grey rose to speak in the House of Commons in the afternoon.

Baying for War – Raging for Peace

The newspapers of the morning presented a baffling array of news items. The German declaration of war against Russia on the previous

Saturday evening dominated the news pages. War in the east was at hand. But events in the west were reported very differently according to the political affiliation of the newspaper.

The Conservative press reported French *claims* of German incursions into France, and announced that war had already begun in Western Europe. The newspapers claimed that the German Army had ignobly launched an invasion of France, before the German ambassador had left Paris, and without even declaring war. The *Scotsman* reported 'the invasion of France' at two points; *The Times* alleged invasion had begun at four points.[2] These reports – now known to be mainly false – were presented as a critical part of the case against Germany.[3] *The Times* even supplied a map entitled 'THE GERMAN INVASION OF FRANCE'.[4]

The editorials of both Northcliffe dailies, *The Times* and the *Daily Mail*, urged Britain's instant intervention in response to this horror. If Liberal ministers were doubtful, they should step aside and allow Asquith to find 'fresh blood'.[5] Britain must order full mobilisation of all her forces, advised Repington in *The Times*, lamenting that Britain was 'already 24 hours behind France'.[6] Yet the letters page of *The Times* was divided, with Valentine Chirol demanding war for France while Jo King MP decried it. One unexpected letter came from Sir Guy Fleetwood Wilson, a high-ranking imperial civil servant. He blamed Russia for the coming war, and concluded, 'It is not worth the life of one single British grenadier.'[7]

But elsewhere in the Northcliffe press on this day, the very friendly treatment accorded Russia shone brightly. For example, Robert Wilton, *The Times* correspondent in St Petersburg, supplied a remarkable – and mischievous – report. He described the scene on Saturday night in St Petersburg when, he claimed, a surging crowd of 50,000 patriotic Russians had surrounded the British Embassy singing 'God Save the King' and 'Rule Britannia'. 'The articles of *The Times* have done much to inspire hope,' counselled Wilton (blessing his own articles), 'but if, contrary to reasonable expectation, the British parliament insists on neutrality, there will be a terrible revulsion of feeling here.'[8]

The Northcliffe press was not alone in baying for war. Others were casting around for a *casus belli*. For example, Lord Burnham's *Daily Telegraph* claimed to have found an 'outrage' in the reported seizure of two British ships in the Kiel Canal. Britain must reply with war. It would be greeted with relief by 'every Briton with the stuff of manhood in him'. 'Since Germany will have it, she shall have it, and that in full measure', spat the *Daily Telegraph*.[9]

In complete contrast, the editorials of the Liberal newspapers on Monday 3 August held their nerve for neutrality. For example, the *Manchester Guardian* still raged against the prospect of Britain lending assistance to the Russian cause. The German declaration of war against Russia was regrettable but entirely understandable, argued the editorial. Now that war had erupted in the east, Britain's neutrality was more important than ever. 'Let us be quite clear about this. If we are jockeyed into fighting it will be for a cause supremely disreputable.' Neither Serbia nor Russia had a good case. 'If it were physically possible for Serbia to be towed out to sea and sunk there, the air of Europe would at once seem cleaner'. Russia's record was 'inky' in its blackness. Therefore, Britain's 'war conspirators' had to be resisted. 'They say that we cannot see France crushed. But can we see Germany crushed and Russia straddling across Europe as well as Asia?'[10] On the letters page of the *Manchester Guardian* appeared two manifestos from the neutrality committees of Angell and Wallas, and letters from a glittering array of Liberal MPs, businessmen, and publicists all arguing trenchantly for neutrality.[11]

Tory Pressures – French Pressures

The day began for Asquith with a visit from the 'frighteners'. Bonar Law and Lansdowne saw Asquith at Downing Street at 9.30 a.m., just a half-hour before the morning Cabinet meeting. The ostensible purpose was to discuss Asquith's cautious reply to the Tory leaders' letter of Sunday morning. But once inside the Prime Minister's black door, the two Conservatives, as coached by Chamberlain, repeated Cambon's exhortations regarding 'honour'. They 'urged upon Asquith that it was inevitable that we should be drawn into the struggle sooner or later.' Britain, they implored Asquith, should 'take part in it with honour and in time instead of waiting till it was too late and we were dishonoured'.[12]

Asquith in turn revealed a still unconfirmed report that apparently Germany had made a request to Belgium overnight for passage of her troops.[13] The Conservatives interjected that this was a reason 'for acting at once'. Asquith replied that the government was waiting for confirmation. Much to their chagrin, Asquith also reaffirmed that the Cabinet was still opposed to the BEF being sent to the Continent. Chamberlain wrote later that Asquith was 'very tired and obviously anxious to get rid of them' – as well he might, for shortly he would face his Cabinet and a rising total of resignations.[14]

The Tory patricians Balfour, Salisbury, Devonshire, Bob Cecil, Chamberlain, Walter Long, Lansdowne and Bonar Law then met again at Lansdowne House to debate tactics. Again in the middle of this assembly came another note from Churchill, confirming the Sunday Cabinet's big decision, supposedly still secret, the naval pledge to France. All agreed that, in light of this leak, Asquith's non-committal stance probably 'did not represent his real state of mind'. They took heart that Asquith 'apparently was with Grey and Winston Churchill'.[15]

While Asquith was enduring his uncomfortable interview with the Conservatives at Downing Street, Grey's diplomacy faced renewed pressure at the Foreign Office. At a morning interview, Cambon put to Grey Viviani's plans to reveal Grey's pledge of support in Paris. In response, Grey very significantly widened the terms of the pledge. Just before noon, Cambon cabled to Viviani a new version of the 'declaration' of naval support that Grey had given to him:

> In case the German fleet came into the Channel or entered the North Sea in order to go round the British Isles with the object of attacking the French coasts or the French navy and of harassing French merchant shipping, the British fleet would intervene in order to give to French shipping its complete protection, *in such a way that from that moment Great Britain and Germany would be in a state of war.*[16]

This put the matter beyond doubt: not just a pledge of support to France but war itself had been chosen on Sunday 2 August. Any chance of British neutrality was gone – before the House of Commons had spent a minute in debate.

The Cabinet Considers Belgium – and Four Resignations

When the Conservatives left Asquith, he prepared for the next meeting of his Cabinet, set for 10 a.m. There was great tension. At the forefront of every minister's mind, and certainly Asquith's, was the continuing political fallout from Sunday. Could the Cabinet hold together?

As the ministers gathered, eyes scanned the Cabinet room, no doubt, to see how far the crumbling of the Cabinet had gone. Only one missing mutineer was noted. 'J. Burns gone', recorded Harcourt, 'Simon resigned but sitting here. J. Morley probably going.' Indeed, Simon, Morley and Beauchamp were all still at the Cabinet table. But Asquith swept past the resignations. According to Harcourt's notes, Asquith allowed Grey to begin with a review of the latest international intelligence.

Sensational news from Brussels was unveiled: 'Belgium received demand from Germany for neutrality and has categorically refused. Germans concentrating at Liege.' The Germans, the Cabinet was told, had 'offered Belgium neutrality afterwards if they allow passage of German troops'. It appears, therefore, that Grey used the same report about a German 'demand' upon Belgium that Asquith had used when meeting the Tory leaders. This was very fresh news. After all, the Belgian government did not confirm the German ultimatum, and its rejection, until 8 a.m. As noted previously, a cable from Villiers reporting this – but citing the French ambassador as the source – did not reach London until 10.55 a.m. Presumably Grey told the Cabinet he was awaiting confirmation.[17] In any case, what should Britain do? 'We must support Belgium & France', Grey begged his colleagues.[18]

Grey also reported that Lichnowsky had already reacted to Asquith's warnings on Sunday about the northern French coasts, and the rumours of Britain's pledge to France. Lichnowsky 'pledges his Gov[ernmen]t [will] not attack French coast with fleet'. But Harcourt also recorded Grey's astonishing response: 'Grey does not think Lichnowsky [is] authorised to say this.' There was no indication Grey had followed this up. He simply aired his doubts. Undoubtedly this reminded the Radicals of Sunday's Cabinet, when Grey turned aside suggestions he should seek a trilateral neutralisation of the Channel. Now the Germans were offering to safeguard the French coast, and Grey cast doubt on the offer.

The political complications were excruciating. An imminent German threat to Belgium was being dropped in the laps of at least three ministers – Simon, Morley and Beauchamp – who were toying with resignation at the Cabinet table. Harcourt shifted his position. In a spirit of Machiavellian calculation, doubtless shared by others, he told the Cabinet that it would be a 'g[rea]t advantage if Germany declared war *on us*'. Asquith pounced. Screwing up the pressure on his unruly ministers, Asquith referred to his morning interview with Lansdowne and Bonar Law: 'they agreed with Burns, [that the] fleet proclamation is a declaration of war. They attach great importance to our supporting Belgium.'[19] This, of course, was flourished to intimidate the Radicals. Two uncomfortable truths were being rammed home. First, war had been chosen on Sunday – all sides agreed. Second, the Conservatives were as threateningly united in support of war on the new ground, Belgium, as they had been on the old ground, loyalty to the Entente. It was a powerful threat. The government might fall – but Britain's ensnarement in war would not necessarily be avoided.

Asquith next announced certain further preparatory military measures. He estimated that, if it came to war, the Royal Navy would require an extra £4 million per month. In addition, Asquith explained that the British Army's mobilisation was 'now necessary'. He calmly announced he had already ordered this, overnight. But, he assured his ministers, it was 'not for Expeditionary force, but for home safety and defence'. A cost of £8 million would be incurred to achieve the army's mobilisation, Asquith observed.[20] How cheap Britain's war might prove to be – so it seemed.

The Belgian complication undoubtedly assisted Asquith in getting away with this fresh example of critical decision-making outside the Cabinet – for army mobilisation was simply presented to the ministers, after the event. In fact, as Asquith spoke, Haldane was already at the War Office implementing Asquith's decision. Before the Cabinet could debate it, and before parliament had heard Grey's speech of Monday afternoon, the machinery of army mobilisation was whirring into life.[21]

Why did the Radicals swallow this? A clue lies in a note that Harcourt filed with his usual Cabinet memorandum for Monday 3 August. It recorded a critically important snippet of conversation with Asquith:

'You don't contemplate sending an expeditionary force to France?'
    ('No, certainly not.' Asq[uith])[22]

Similarly, Samuel's usual letter to Beatrice predicted big land battles, on the French frontier, in four to seven days. Again he made no mention of British troops being involved. 'But a naval engagement may take place at any time', he wrote. 'Our fleet, which is at least twice as powerful as the German, is absolutely ready in every particular.'[23] In all these discussions the navy's possible role shone out. The army was somewhere in the middle distance. The BEF was nowhere. The phantom of a cheap naval war was being kept alive.

Then the Cabinet turned to its immediate business, to instruct Sir Edward Grey regarding his statement to the House of Commons that afternoon. The first objective of the speech plainly was to both reveal and defend the Cabinet's decision to offer a naval pledge to France on Sunday. Returning to that decision, the Cabinet decided to ask Grey to add an additional justification. He should explain that not only 'moral obligations' but also enduring British interests had dictated the pledge. This, of course, was much safer political territory, skirting the issue of Britain having compromised itself by raising expectations in France and Russia.[24]

Only after all this did Asquith introduce the matter weighing on every mind at the Cabinet table – resignations. Asquith surveyed the splintering of his government so far: he had two resignation letters written on the Sunday already to hand, from Burns and Simon, and he had received a third on the Monday morning from Morley. At this point, as we have seen, 'Beauchamp leant forward and asked to be included.' That made four. Asquith, 'whose eyes filled with tears', told his colleagues that it was the first time in his six years as leader he had faced anything like this dissent. He explained that 'the party was still hesitating'.[25] Masterman remembered him, possibly at this moment, 'looking down the table over his glasses and observing "Seems as if I shall have to go on alone".'[26] The Prime Minister had a captivating gift for self-dramatisation, even now. According to Harcourt's notes:

> Asq[uith] then said 'Burns has resigned; Morley, Simon, Beauchamp also going; many others uneasy: the Cabinet with much shattered authority in [a] time of great stress. Labour will be against us: Irish will act for Ireland. Under other circ[umstances] Asq[uith] would have resigned. But [there would be] no Gov[ernmen]t with a majority in H[ouse] of C[ommons]. Dislikes and abhors a coalition – experiment none would like to see repeated. Asq[uith] will not separate from Grey – remains in best interests of the country. Asq[uith] 'most thankless task to me to go on'.[27]

In this way Asquith represented the prospect of coalition as distasteful to himself and dangerous to the country. As he painted it, a coalition was something he was prepared to resist, heroically, on behalf of his party and nation. But it was *his* threat of resignation that hypnotised. He had repeated his threat to walk away in company with Grey. Could Britain be left rudderless? As everyone recognised, the departure of the Prime Minister and Foreign Secretary, followed up undoubtedly by Churchill and Haldane, would have wound up the government. The upper ranks of the Cabinet were threatening to take the rest down with them. Similarly, it was this threat of resignation that Morley recalled most vividly. He described Asquith as making it clear 'almost at the beginning of his appeal' and 'with some emphasis that nothing would induce him to separate from Grey'.[28]

The ministers lined up to reply. 'The Cabinet was very moving. Most of us could hardly speak at all for emotion', Samuel wrote shortly afterwards.[29] Morley made a speech on the 'two reasons' motivating his resignation – long term and immediate objections. Simon, whose resignation had been submitted on the Sunday, was the first to show that sustained pressure from the top echelon of the Cabinet might win the day. He clung to his decision, but Harcourt recorded him as blurting out, 'If [the] country [was] at war it was the duty of men like himself and the peace party to support the Gov[ernmen]t', before breaking down.[30] Morley remembered that Simon 'was under great emotion and tears were in his eyes'.[31] Then other ministers in turn addressed the Cabinet crisis. Haldane, Churchill and Lloyd George directed their appeal to the unhappy Radicals 'not to resign now or at least not to announce it today'.[32] Lloyd George's stance in this was vital. He was the only possible replacement as an anti-war leader for a new government. He was not stepping forward. Asquith described Lloyd George as arguing effectively for *delay*. Those resigning were urged to be loyal and strong, not to 'desert' and not to 'abandon' their colleagues.[33]

A Pretence of Unity

The argument for delay had some effect. Asquith pleaded that 'the country was in danger and unity of counsel was essential'.[34] Harcourt recalled that Simon and Morley eventually agreed to silence. 'No statement will be made by any of them today', he wrote. Only Beauchamp put up stout resistance to this. He complained that 'our party ought to be informed'.[35] Dissenters on the Liberal back-bench were being given the 'wrong impression', he argued, because the Cabinet's unity was 'apparent but not real'.[36] Beauchamp wanted them to know the truth: that at least four of the nineteen ministers were opposed to the pledge Grey was about to defend in the House of Commons. But he was isolated and eventually submitted to the request for silence.

In this way, Asquith won a valuable point. Defiance was to be hidden. As Samuel wrote just after the Cabinet ended, 'Burns, Morley, Simon, Beauchamp have resigned. No announcements to be made yet.'[37] Hobhouse noted that the dissenters had agreed to stay until the House of Commons 'had indicated its opinion' – 'not very brave conduct', he added.[38] Asquith was fully alive to the significance of this. 'In the end', he explained to Venetia Stanley, 'they all agreed to say nothing today and to sit in their accustomed places in the House'.[39]

The agreement was vital. Burns, who did not attend this Cabinet, saw both Asquith and Simon at Downing Street in the early afternoon, and he imposed the obligation of silence upon himself. So, during Grey's speech that afternoon in the Commons, both Burns and Simon would be seen seated with the other ministers.[40] Later that day in the House of Lords, Beauchamp and Morley stayed silent. Thus, all four resigning ministers maintained the charade of unity. Most important, when Grey actually stood to deliver his speech, the reality of a serious rift in the Cabinet was not discernible.[41]

In addition, both Asquith and Grey must have sensed the imminent possibility of political deliverance from a small nation in the firing line – Belgium. If the early news from Brussels was confirmed, then opinion inside the Liberal Party might slide in their favour. The confirmation came – and something better. Soon after the morning Cabinet, a copy of the famous personal telegram from Albert King of the Belgians to King George V reached Downing Street. The telegram referred to the King's personal friendship, and 'the friendly attitude of England in 1870', and then made 'a supreme appeal to the Diplomatic intervention of your Majesty's Government to safeguard the integrity of Belgium'.[42]

The telegram, of course, did not ask Britain to make war. A request to Britain to attempt the renewal of Gladstone's treaties of 1870 might be read into it. The Belgians themselves were on that day still declining an offer of French assistance and were prepared to resist *any* incursions.[43] But King Albert's telegram offered a strong chance of political salvation for Britain's Liberal leadership. Grey could reveal it in the course of his speech to the House of Commons. Therefore, he could focus on the dangers of German aggression in Western Europe;

and the war in Eastern Europe would be driven from the consciousness of his listeners. The mutineers and their sympathisers would
probably be confronted with a sea of Conservatives in front, and
perhaps a majority of Liberals behind, urging British intervention to
save Belgium. The Cabinet crisis might pass.

But if the split was known, as Asquith had put it, his Cabinet's
authority would be 'shattered'. The first news from Belgium had
not persuaded any resigning minister to withdraw his resignation.
Personal relations were very strained. For example, writing from
Lloyd George's house to Beatrice, just after the 'fateful Cabinet' was
over, Samuel let fly at those resigning. 'Those four men have no right
to abandon us at this crisis – it is a failure of courage.'[44] The situation
facing Asquith was certainly dire. 'That is 4 gone!' Asquith wrote to
Venetia Stanley later that afternoon.[45] Would Grey be able to win
over the House of Commons – and more especially, the Liberal Party?

TWENTY

Magical Theatre
Monday 3 August

There is but one way in which the Government could make
certain at the present moment of keeping outside this war, and
that would be that it should immediately issue a proclamation of
unconditional neutrality. We cannot do that. We have made the
commitment to France that I have read to the House which pre-
vents us from doing that.[1]

Sir Edward Grey, 3 August 1914

Soon after 3 p.m. on the afternoon of Monday 3 August, Sir
Edward Grey rose to address the House of Commons. The
speech is believed to have changed the mind of the nation.
Certainly Grey amazed some with the passion of his address. His
task was to reveal and explain the pledge of naval assistance to France
given on Sunday. But he went further. He put the case that Britain
should rush to the assistance of France and Belgium – he said little
about Russia – if it came to war on the Continent.

Was it already too late? Was war imminent in east and west? Let
us recall quickly the steps that had already been taken. In response
to the Russian general mobilisation, the German elite had decided –
disastrously – to send two poorly framed ultimata to Russia and
to France on the afternoon of Friday 31 July.[2] Then, French and

German general mobilisations had been ordered almost simultaneously, in the late afternoon of Saturday 1 August.[3] Berlin had then
compounded disaster, declaring war upon Russia in the evening of
Saturday 1 August.[4] But this was the only declaration of war among
the Great Powers for two days. Certainly, when Grey spoke in the
mid-afternoon of Monday 3 August, war in the east was declared
and real. War in the west was neither. The next fatal step, the
German declaration of war upon France, was not announced in
Berlin until 6.45 p.m. on the evening of Monday 3 August – that
is, *after* the conclusion of Grey's speech of the afternoon.[5] News of
it came to London *after* debates in the House of Commons were
concluded.

But did the facts matter? Rumours darted about Westminster
and Downing Street. The Cabinet ministers shared in these.
For example, as mentioned, Herbert Samuel had gone from the
Monday morning Cabinet to lunch with Lloyd George at Number
11 Downing Street. Here Samuel wrote to his wife, before Grey's
speech, and reported rumours as if they were facts: 'The Germans
have invaded Belgium and her King has appealed for our help. It is
said they have also invaded Holland and Switzerland – every neutral
state within reach! Our participation in the war is now inevitable.'[6]
In this catalogue of German sins, only the appeal of the King of the
Belgians was true. Nothing else. If a Cabinet minister closeted with
the Chancellor of the Exchequer could believe such false information, what chance did the typical MP, with *The Times* open on his lap,
have of divining the truth?

The Spirit of the House of Commons

What was it like in the House of Commons on the warm afternoon of Monday 3 August? Newspaper accounts and memoirs all
testify to an extraordinary atmosphere in the 'crowded and breathless
House'.[7] Liberal Members had been summoned by 'telegraphic whip'
to be present 'without fail' for 'the transaction of new and important business'. *The Times* speculated that a Vote of Credit to fund a

war might be presented immediately – and, feeding the mood, *The Times* added that 'no opposition is expected, except, possibly from a small group of extreme Radicals and from some of the Labour members'.[8]

All the galleries were crammed full. The peers had been allowed to take their places in the Peers' Gallery before prayers, 'a privilege which spared them the indignity of a rush-and-tumble invasion in common with the general public'.[9] Prominent among these notables were the Archbishop of Canterbury and leading Conservative peers, including Lord Lansdowne. Even more important, in the Distinguished Strangers' Gallery sat the Russian ambassador, Count Benckendorff.[10]

The mood in the House was tense. In the expectation of unprecedented numbers of MPs, extra chairs had been arranged on the floor of the House itself, and in rows of four down the gangway.[11] This had not been seen since Gladstone's speech introducing the first Home Rule Bill in April 1886.[12] There was also an undertone of menace – a danger that some Conservative MPs might attempt to stampede the House. Filling the Opposition benches were some who had treated the House to displays of hooliganism over recent years – most notoriously in July 1911.[13] Some of those same hotheads were caught up in Wilson's 'pogrom' against neutrality, for example, F. E. Smith. In a raucous House, there was the possibility of Grey being swept toward truculence, and of dissenters being howled down.

When Grey entered, 'he slipped into his place almost unnoticed'.[14] But soon came signs of the 'pogrom' spirit. Cheering began as some ministers appeared. 'Mr Lloyd George and Mr Winston Churchill entered together, and both were cheered from all quarters of the House', reported *The Times*. The *Manchester Guardian* saw it differently, noting that 'the part taken in their ovation by the Opposition was particularly marked'. The hushing-up of Radical resignations was important at this point. 'As Ministers came to their seats those whose names had been associated with rumours of resignation were greeted with general cheering', noted the *Guardian*.[15] Asquith arrived with 'grave and impassive face'. He ignored the cheers. Finally, there was 'great cheering' as Grey advanced to the despatch box. As Grey spoke, all the Cabinet ministers sat on the front bench – making a show of unity.[16]

The House then displayed its impatience. Questions were given up. Business was rushed through. The Commons seemed to be 'in a state of nerves not reassuring to the nation', as the *Manchester Guardian* reported later. The atmosphere was 'neurotic'. The House 'excitedly brushed its work aside in its hurry to hear Sir Edward Grey'.[17]

Grey's Incredible Shrinking 'Free Hand'

Grey gazed at a raked theatre of needy vanity. In his opening words he reported that the crisis, originating in the Austro-Serbian dispute, had unfortunately escalated rapidly.[18] Britain, he insisted, had tried hard to preserve peace. But, he lamented, 'it is clear that the peace of Europe cannot be preserved. Russia and Germany, at any rate, have declared war on each other.'

Then he flourished Britain's 'free hand'. He reminded the House of the many occasions when he and Asquith had affirmed that there was 'no secret engagement which we should spring upon the House' in any crisis, nor any 'obligation of honour' arising from such secrecy. Similarly, he declared, Britain was not a member of any alliance system, merely a member of 'a Diplomatic group'. In the present crisis, Grey asserted, the distinction was important, for no promise of anything more than diplomatic support to any friendly power had been made – 'till yesterday'.

With these ominous words dropped into the sea of surging voices, Grey turned to France. Reviewing Britain's relations with France since 1906, Grey explained that, during the whole course of France's quarrels with Germany over Morocco, Britain had steadfastly maintained that no promise of military assistance could be given to France unless it received 'the whole hearted support of public opinion'. Then, raising a tender issue for Liberals, Grey explained that early in 1906 the French had requested military conversations with Britain, so that the naval and military experts would be ready to cooperate if the need arose. 'There was force in that', reasoned Grey. As a result,

Grey explained, he had authorised military conversations, but 'on the distinct understanding that it left the hands of the government free whenever the crisis arose'.

Naturally, Grey chose not to remind his audience of the hot water into which he had fallen in 1911 when it emerged that he had hidden his authorisation of these military conversations from most of the Cabinet for almost six years. The scar tissue from this squabble was still too tender. Instead, Grey moved to the healing letters – the exchange of letters with the French ambassador in the autumn of 1912 that the Cabinet had carefully overseen.

He read from the letter he had addressed to Paul Cambon on 22 November 1912. This acknowledged the record of military consultation but reaffirmed that 'such consultation does not restrict the freedom of either Government to decide at any future time whether or not to assist the other by armed force'. The redistribution of the French and British fleets, which had begun in 1912, was specifically mentioned: 'The disposition, for instance, of the French and British fleets respectively at the present moment is not based upon any engagement to co-operate in war.' The letter then explained that the two governments had agreed upon consultation if any crisis blew up. Grey read the key paragraph:

> I agree that, if either Government had grave reason to expect an unprovoked attack by a third power, or something that threatened the general peace, it should immediately discuss with the other whether both governments should act together to prevent aggression and to preserve peace, and, if so, what measures they would be prepared to take in common.

At this point in Grey's speech, Admiral Lord Charles Beresford interrupted him. He asked for the date of the letter. Grey answered him. It was not to help Grey's reputation for trustworthiness that, for whatever reason, Grey did not go on to read the last sentence of his letter: 'If these measures involved action, the plans of the General Staff would at once be taken into consideration, and the governments would then decide what effect should be given to them.' Here the reference to joint General Staff planning was compromising and vital. Grey's failure to read the whole letter was an important error – but it passed unnoticed.[19]

Why had Grey read this letter at all? It appeared to commit the government to nothing more than discussion upon common action. Grey's purpose was plain: the letter proved that the 'free hand' had been preserved.

For almost everyone in the House, this was the first they had heard either of the Grey–Cambon letters of 1912 or of the decision of Britain and France to adopt a new 'disposition' for their fleets at that time. The Cabinet ministers had debated Churchill's concentration of British naval forces in home waters in the summer of 1912. But coordination with France had been strenuously denied. Most ministers knew nothing in detail of the decision to 'redistribute' the British and French fleets, nor of the subsequent deals dividing up naval responsibilities, with the British naval forces chiefly defending the North Sea, on the assumption that the French would chiefly defend the Mediterranean Sea. Precise details of the naval plans were, of course, secret.[20]

Having documented Britain's free hand, Grey returned to the Austro-Serbian quarrel. He asserted that France was most reluctant to be drawn into any such quarrel, but France had a certain 'obligation of honour' arising from her Franco-Russian alliance. Then, in a sentence giving a spume of hope to Radicals, Grey observed that 'that obligation of honour cannot apply in the same way to us. We are not parties to the Franco-Russian Alliance'. But the Radicals' hopes were soon disappointed.

'I come now to what we think the situation requires of us', said Grey. In the second half of his speech, Grey's confidence kindled as cheers punctuated his declarations of Britain's firmness. He retreated altogether from the prospect of detachment. No longer, it seemed, was Britain 'perfectly free'. Grey referred to Britain's maturing 'friendship' with France and immediately sought to conflate this with the 'obligation' he had denied only minutes before. There was even an oblique reference to God: it had struck him lately, he recalled, that 'some benign influence had been at work' to produce the firm friendship with France. Britain was spiritually leagued with France. Then, with obvious emotion, Grey declared:

> But how far that friendship entails obligation – it has been a friendship between the nations and ratified by the nations – how far that entails an obligation let every man look into his own heart and construe the extent of the obligation for himself. I construe it myself as I feel it, but I do not wish to urge upon anyone else more than their feelings dictate as to what they should feel about the obligation. The House, individually and collectively may judge for itself. I speak my personal view, and I have given the House my own feeling in the matter.[21]

This catching at the heart of every MP was memorable theatre.

Grey then turned back immediately to the French fleet. Loaded words abounded. The French fleet was in the Mediterranean, so that 'the Northern and Western coasts of France are absolutely unde-fended' – 'absolutely undefended', said Grey, repeating the phrase three times in the course of his explanation. If France had moved her fleet to the Mediterranean 'because of the feeling of confidence and friendship' between Britain and France – no deals were mentioned – then, asked Grey, could Britain do nothing to defend France? Grey answered his own question with an uncharacteristically passionate flourish:

> My own feeling is that if a foreign fleet engaged in a war which France had not sought, and in which she had not been the aggres-sor, came down the English Channel and bombarded and battered the undefended coasts of France, we could not stand aside and see this going on practically within sight of our eyes, with our arms folded, looking on dispassionately, doing nothing! I believe that would be the feeling of this country. There are times when one feels that if these circumstances did arise, it would be a feeling which would spread with irresistible force throughout the land.[22]

This brought forth a great wave of cheering from the Opposition benches. Britain had a 'free hand' – but, hey presto, 'public opinion' must see the moral obligations that constrained her.

Next, Grey promised to look at the issue 'without sentiment and from the point of view of British interests'. Indeed, from this point in Grey's rhetorical dance, moral obligations and national interest waltzed arm in arm. If Britain left the French coast 'at the mercy of a German fleet coming down the Channel to do as it pleases', then it was likely, argued Grey, that the French would withdraw their fleet from the Mediterranean. He summoned from the darkness of the future a whole series of perilous 'consequences unforeseen' if Britain were to 'stand aside in an attitude of neutrality'. It was possible that Italy might abandon her neutrality in this crisis and threaten trade routes 'vital to this country'. Indeed, Britain's navy would have an impossible task defending her Empire's trade routes everywhere. If Britain insisted on her 'negative attitude' of neutrality, she might suddenly have to send ships to the Mediterranean, thus exposing Britain to 'the most appalling risk'. In any case, France was 'entitled to know – and to know at once! – whether or not in the event of attack upon her unprotected Northern and Western Coasts she could depend upon British support'. So, Britain *was* boxed in by her naval arrangements with France, which only five minutes before Grey had insisted had left Britain entirely free! In this way, against all assurances given in 1912, Grey used the position of the fleets in 1914 as a lever to promote intervention.

All this frightening of the assembled MPs was a preliminary to explaining the Cabinet's decision of Sunday. Because of the 'emergency' and the 'compelling circumstances', Grey explained, a decision of great importance had been taken: on the previous afternoon, Sunday 2 August, he had given the French ambassador a pledge of naval support. He then read the statement. Tellingly, Grey immediately felt moved to explain to the cheering Opposition that he had read the note 'not as a declaration of war'.

Then, Grey acknowledged an inconvenient complication. The Germans, he revealed, had moved to reassure him on the tender point of France's 'unprotected' northern coast. The German government had just notified London that Germany was willing 'if we would pledge ourselves to neutrality, to agree that its fleet would not attack the Northern coast of France'.[23] This conditional German offer, Grey announced dramatically, he had received 'shortly before I came to the House'. But Grey brusquely dismissed the latest German offer. It would not save the peace – 'it is far too narrow an engagement for us', he asserted.[24] Why? Because, as Grey explained, instantly leaping to another argument altogether, 'there is the more serious considera-tion – becoming more serious every hour – there is the question of the neutrality of Belgium'.

Neutral Belgium and Gladstone's Ghost

Immediately, the Foreign Secretary turned to the Treaty of 1839. This, he proclaimed, was the 'governing factor' in determining Britain's attitude. He then dipped into history, offering a brief survey of Britain's diplomacy at the time of the Franco-Prussian War of 1870. He produced two political poltergeists from that era, Prime Minister Gladstone and his Foreign Secretary, Lord Granville. Just as he had done at the Cabinet the week before, Grey reviewed the former Liberal leaders' commitments to Belgium's neutrality. He borrowed from their parliamentary statements of 8 and 10 August 1870. He first quoted a passage from Granville's speech, the Foreign Secretary asserting that it was 'impossible' for the Gladstone govern-ment, 'with any due regard to the country's honour or to the country's interest', to deny Belgium's neutrality.[25] Next Grey quoted a passage from Gladstone. He had observed that whatever the legal obligations toward Belgium, the signatory nations had to take account of the most vital consideration that 'all feel most deeply', namely, their 'common interests against the unmeasured aggrandisement of any Power whatsoever'.[26]

Grey then reviewed his own diplomacy on the matter. He stressed the two telegrams he had despatched to France and Germany on Friday 31 July seeking assurances regarding Belgian neutrality. Grey read to the House the French commitment to both respect and defend that neutrality, and the non-committal reply from Germany. Crucially, he noted the Belgians' own assurances that they would defend their country from any violation.

Then came another breathtaking surprise. Grey revealed to the House that fresh news had arrived during the day: just how accurate was this news he could not say, but it appeared that Germany had indeed presented an ultimatum to Belgium, demanding the passage of German troops. He next revealed, but only in the most general terms, the hitherto unknown fact of a German offer to achieve Britain's neutrality. In Grey's words, Britain had been 'sounded in the course of last week as to whether if a guarantee were given that, after the war, Belgium [*sic*] integrity would be preserved that would content us. We replied that we could not bargain away whatever interests or obligations we had in Belgian neutrality.' This, of course, was inaccurate and incomplete. The date and details of the original offer were not given. The original German offer (of 29–30 July) to respect French as well as Belgian territorial integrity after any conflict in Europe was not mentioned. The second offer on the part of Lichnowsky (on 1 August), to respect both French continental and colonial territory, was not mentioned. Of course, the initiative that Grey himself had launched and pursued briefly on 1 August – the possibility of Britain and France remaining neutral – was also not revealed to the House.

Even more dramatically, Grey then shared the very latest twist. He read to the House a telegram that, as he explained, he had received within the last hour. This was the telegram addressed to King George V from Albert King of the Belgians, as noted above, entreating Britain's 'Diplomatic intervention' to 'safeguard the integrity of Belgium'. But, Grey told the House, Britain had tried diplomatic intervention. Moreover, Belgium's 'integrity' after conflict was not enough, for if she tolerated German troops making passage, then 'the independence will be gone'. Britain would wage war to defend Belgium's neutrality, Grey appeared to signal, whether or not the Belgians wanted it.

How should Britain react to the German threat to Belgium? Again Grey conjured Gladstone to give his opinion. Betraying the rush of his preparations, he confessed he had not had time to check the context of Gladstone's speech of 1870, but he did not think it mattered. It was pure gold:

> We have an interest in the independence of Belgium which is wider than that which we may have in the literal operation of the guarantee. It is found in the answer to the question whether under the circumstances of the case, this country, endowed as it is with influence and power, would quietly stand by and witness the perpetration of the direst crime that ever stained the pages of history, and thus become participators in the sin.[27]

Grey now openly advocated British military intervention on the Continent to prevent German domination. Grey summoned up a nightmare vision for his hearers. If Belgian independence went, then 'Holland will follow'. Therefore, explained Grey, 'I ask the House from the point of view of British interests, to consider what may be at stake.' France might be 'beaten to her knees'. Not just Holland, but then Denmark would fall under German influence. Then, asked Grey, 'would not Mr. Gladstone's words come true' and 'just opposite to us there would be a common interest against the unmeasured aggrandisement of any Power?'

Grey Rules Out Neutrality in a Continental War

Next, Grey reviewed the theoretical possibility of neutrality. Britain might 'stand aside', husbanding its strength, or perhaps intervene only at the end of the war. But, as Grey put it, if Britain were to 'run away from those obligations of honour and interest as regards the Belgian Treaty', then Britain's force would be at a discount 'in face of the respect that we should have lost'. No intervention at the end of the war, he continued, would have the power to 'undo what had happened in the course of the war, to prevent the whole of the west of Europe opposite to us – if that had been the result of the war – falling under the domination of a single Power'. For good measure,

Grey added, if Britain stood aside her 'moral position would be such as to have lost us all respect'.

Then, introducing remarks that would linger as his most grotesquely misleading, Grey minimised the likely cost of war. He hinted strongly that war for Britain would be a cheap naval war – Churchill's argument. 'For us, with a powerful Fleet, which we believe able to protect our commerce, to protect our shores, and to protect our interests', Grey argued, 'if we are engaged in war, we shall suffer but little more than we shall suffer even if we stand aside'. So powerful was Britain's navy, observed Grey, that the 'amount of harm that can be done by an enemy ship to our trade is infinitesimal, compared with the amount of harm that must be done by the economic condition that is caused [by war] on the Continent'.

Moreover, Grey appeared to dismiss the 'continental commitment' for the British Army. Both the fleet and the army were being mobilised, he noted, but 'we have taken no engagement yet with regard to sending an Expeditionary armed force out of the country'. Grey did his best to make this seem unlikely, alluding to Britain's 'enormous responsibilities' in guarding her Empire, and other 'unknown factors' to be weighed before 'sending an Expeditionary Force out of the country'.

Here then was the alluring vision: in supporting a British military intervention, MPs could indulge their patriotism, defend little Belgium, prevent German hegemony, keep the nation's commerce alive, save their nation's honour, and salve guilty consciences inflamed by the prospect of Germany falling upon France's 'absolutely undefended coasts' – and it might not cost very much at all. MPs could imagine the Royal Navy mounting a blockade, or perhaps winning a short sharp sea battle. There would be no protracted horror. And Russia seemed utterly irrelevant to the issues.

In his peroration, Grey recapitulated the heart of his case. Presenting the politician's favourite device, the false dilemma, he explained that the only alternative to Britain's intervention 'would be that it [the government] should immediately issue a proclamation of unconditional neutrality'. He continued in sentences that would draw the ire of Radicals:

> We cannot do that. We have made the commitment to France that I have read to the House which prevents us from doing that. We have got the consideration of Belgium which prevents us also from any unconditional neutrality, and without those conditions absolutely satisfied and satisfactory, we are bound not to shrink from proceeding to use all the forces in our power.

In a cruel irony, the unpublished letter addressed to Cambon in November 1912 – 'the commitment to France that I have read to the House' – the letter painstakingly devised with the assistance of the Radicals and designed to preserve Britain's freedom of action in any crisis, was interpreted by Grey as imposing an obligation of honour.

Interests and honour were carefully interleaved to the last. Grey appealed to all: could Britain act as if the Belgian Treaty, the redistribution of the French and British fleets, and the prospect of French defeat 'mattered nothing, were as nothing'? And if Britain was to say 'we would stand aside, [then] we should, I believe, sacrifice our respect and good name and reputation before the world, and should not escape the most serious and grave economic consequences'. It was too ignoble to contemplate.

There came one more telling moment. Grey wondered aloud if some people were not unfortunately 'still thinking of the quarrel between Austria and Serbia'. He explained that the House of Commons and the nation must focus instead on 'impending dangers in the west of Europe'. There was safer ground – politically speaking.

Frogmarching Events

One frontbencher sensed an immediate opportunity. When Grey's speech was over, Churchill left the Chamber. There followed a scene that caught many eyes in the lobby. According to the Radical Francis Neilson, Hugh Cecil, the independent-minded Tory who had long been suspicious of the Entente, collared Churchill and 'shook him violently, and cried, "You did it! You did it" … He cast Churchill off and turned back the way he had come – a broken man, his face wet with tears.'[28]

Unabashed, Churchill went immediately to the Admiralty. At 5 p.m. he penned a note to Asquith and Grey. 'In consequence of declarations in the House this afternoon,' he began, 'I must request authorisation immediately to put into force the combined Anglo-French dispositions for the defence of the Channel.' The French had 'taken station'; Britain must move too. He concluded: 'My naval colleagues and advisers desire me to press for this; and unless I am forbidden I shall act accordingly.'[29] In a sense, Churchill dared the civilians to defy the military. Clearly for Churchill, Grey's speech was a boon – as good as a declaration of war. Acting ahead of events, once again, he sought to shape them.

TWENTY-ONE

Inventing 'Unanimity'
Monday 3 August

Public opinion since Grey made his statement in the House today, that we should not allow Germany to pass through the English Channel & that we should not allow her troops to pass through Belgium, has entirely changed public opinion [*sic*], & now every-one is for war & our helping our friends.[1]

King George V Diary, 3 August 1914

S upposedly Grey's famous speech of Monday 3 August melted the hearts of all who heard it. King George V himself wrote in his diary in the evening of 3 August that Grey's speech 'has entirely changed public opinion, & now everyone is for war & helping our friends'. This strained belief, for only two days before the King had written that 'public opinion is dead against the war'.[2] No matter. *The Times* carried the message of an oratorical miracle to the nation, proclaiming that there was 'general unanimity' in the Commons in praise of Grey.[3] The other Tory newspapers hurried to agree. Grey's tremendous annunciation had provoked a national sinking to the knees. This, no doubt, is how many of those who chose war preferred to remember it. But it is a fable. A great tug-of-war for the approval of the parliament and the people was started by Grey's speech. Grey was indeed anchorman for the interventionists –

but his speech did not bring about an instant tumbling victory for his team.

What did happen? In the tense House of Commons on Monday afternoon, three short speeches followed Grey's in rapid succession, one from the Conservatives, one from the Irish, and one from Labour.

The Conservatives and the Irish Close Ranks

Compared with the backbenchers, the Tory leaders had appeared relatively calm as Grey spoke. It seemed, as the *Manchester Guardian* reported, that 'the Opposition leaders were already aware of what was coming'.[4] Then, in response to Grey, Bonar Law offered a short, deliberately low-key speech. He clearly realised that to enthuse too much over Grey's line would discredit the Foreign Secretary in some Liberal eyes. He did not wave the flag of Tory joy. He noted with pride that the Dominions of the Empire, in offering expeditionary forces, had shown already that they could be relied upon. On behalf of his party, Bonar Law promised to the government a blank cheque, the Conservatives' 'unhesitating support' for 'whatever steps they think it necessary to take for the honour and security of this country'.[5] No limits, no words of caution, and no mention of Belgium – for Britain's war did not depend upon Belgium in the Tory assessment. The Tories were genuinely thrilled by Grey's 'perfect' speech.[6]

Then both John Redmond, the leader of the Irish Parliamentary Party, and Ramsay MacDonald, the Labour Party leader, rose in their places together. There were cries of 'Redmond!' The Speaker called upon him.

Redmond dazzled the House. Spectacularly he supported Grey. The retreat from the precipice of civil war in Ireland had been mentioned by Grey as the 'one bright spot' in the European crisis. Redmond confirmed this truly wonderful event. He assured the Commons that all the people of Ireland would respond with 'sympathy' for Great Britain if it had to face the crisis of war. While the Irish favoured peace, 'if the dire necessity is forced upon this country' then all Irishmen would shoulder the challenge. The government, he said, could even 'take their troops away'. He prophesied that 'armed Nationalist Catholics in the South will be only too glad to join arms with the armed Protestant Ulstermen in the North'. Irishmen, united as one, were prepared to 'defend the coasts of our country'. At this prospect of a love-feast taking hold inside the fortress of Ireland, Nationalist handkerchiefs fluttered and there was a great eruption of cheering.[7] In fact, it was no surprise to Asquith. Redmond had fore-shadowed his stance to Asquith some days beforehand, and Margot had written to him also to shepherd him into the commitment.[8]

In helping to create a plausible sense of unanimity in the House and the nation, Redmond's speech was of immense significance. If the Irish could put away their antagonisms and rally around the flag, then surely – Radical and Labour MPs were encouraged to think – all should do so. Redmond's tactic was plain: he had chosen to embrace war in the hope of making Home Rule for Ireland safe. The aim was to repel any accusation of disloyalty against Irishmen in this crisis that might derail Home Rule. 'The battle for Home Rule is already won', wrote one journalist.[9]

Some might speculate whether Redmond's deputy, John Dillon, believed all this. He had been a fierce critic of Grey and 'the secrecy of the foreign policy of this country'.[10] But Dillon was in Ireland on Monday 3 August. Later Dillon confessed privately to Wilfrid Blunt that he still believed the war and Britain's entry to be 'the almost inevitable results of Grey's policy'. He might regret Redmond's over-the-top 'sentences', but 'his *policy* has my heartiest approval'. The outbreak of war changed everything, and neutrality became 'absolute nonsense'. If the Irish leaders had opposed war, 'the whole work of our life would have been undone'.[11] Such was the *realpolitik* behind the rapture of 'Ireland's war'.

A Dissenting Voice from Labour

But a speech of conviction then followed that threatened to punc-ture this fantastic newfound unity of the nation. Before Redmond had stopped speaking, Ramsay MacDonald, the Labour Party leader, was on his feet. 'A snarl of dislike from the Tories greeted him, for they scented his purpose and desired to intimidate him', wrote one Gallery Correspondent. Insults were flung at him and 'some outraged patriots left the House rather than have their ears polluted by his treasonous remarks'.[12] The noisy hostility showed an intention to intimidate dissent. But MacDonald stood waiting for quiet in this hubbub. 'In a moment or two the House was listening in hostile silence', reported Labour's own *Daily Citizen*. MacDonald, 'a grey-haired, black-eyed, straight-backed figure', delivered a short speech defying Grey and those shouting for war.[13]

While conceding the moving character of Grey's speech, MacDonald announced bluntly that he was unconvinced. 'I think he is wrong. I think the Government which he represents and for which he speaks is wrong. I think the verdict of history will be that they are wrong.' Labour, promised MacDonald, would support a war of defence to protect Britain were the nation in danger. 'But he has not persuaded me that it is.' When Grey's speech was read 'in cold print' tomorrow, 'a large section of the country' would not be persuaded. Honour had been invoked. But, MacDonald reminded the House, statesmen frequently appealed to honour to cover all manner of 'crime', as at the time of the Crimean War and the South African War.

Then MacDonald turned to the key issue of Belgium raised by Grey. The safety of Belgium, MacDonald argued, could not be considered a sufficient objective justifying Britain's entry into this war, because the conflict would hardly be confined to Belgium. MacDonald directed the attention of the House away from Belgium and back to the seat of the conflict, in Eastern Europe:

> What is the use of talking about coming to the aid of Belgium, when, as a matter of fact, you are engaging in a whole European war which is not going to leave the map of Europe in the position it is now. The right honourable Gentleman said nothing about Russia. We want to know about that. We want to try and find out what is going to happen, when it is all over, to the power of Russia in Europe, and we are not going to go blindly into this conflict

without having some sort of a rough idea as to what is going to happen.[14]

According to one observer, these remarks about Russia 'had an electric effect on the previously impassive Ambassador in the gallery, who regarded the Labour leader with unconcealed disfavour'.[15]

No doubt feeling the 'snarls' of his opponents, MacDonald confessed, 'I not only know but feel that the feeling of the House is against us.' But he and other opponents of the South African War had 'been through this before', only to be vindicated in the long run. Perhaps appealing to his Radical friends to stand firm, he noted that the Liberal victory of 1906 against the Tories had come as 'part recompense' for those who had resisted the tide of chauvinism in 1899. 'It will come again', he prophesied. He finished on a note of defiance:

> So far as we are concerned, whatever may happen, whatever may be said about us, whatever attacks may be made upon us, we will take the action that we will take of saying that this country ought to have remained neutral, because in the deepest parts of our hearts we believe that that was right and that that alone was consistent with the honour of the country and the traditions of the party that are now in office.[16]

The Times' unfriendly account recorded that there was 'some laughter' as MacDonald resumed his seat.[17] But, as the *Daily Citizen* noted, 'It was the speech of a brave man, for it was no light thing to be the first to say such words in a House that had worked itself into a fever of force.'[18] The assertion of absolute 'unanimity' in the House had been dented.

There can be no doubting MacDonald's sincerity. Next day he told Robertson Nicoll that Grey's speech was 'diabolical'. He was shattered to see Grey so suddenly and angrily 'outdoing Churchill' in barking for war.[19]

The Myth of Universal Acclaim in the Commons

Nevertheless, according to most observers, Grey had succeeded. Clearly he had won over a majority of MPs – but, just as clearly, this was a majority dominated by the enemies of the Liberal government.

This was evident to one of the most experienced observers of the mood of the Commons, Sir Courtenay Ilbert, Clerk of the House. In his diary, he expressed no doubt about the sharply different reactions of the major parties to Grey's speech.

> E. Grey rose to deliver the statement about our position. It lasted for about an hour and a half and was loudly applauded by the Opposition, but viewed by the Liberals with serious distance, welcomed only by a cheer or two now and then. Lewis Harcourt was among the very few Liberals who loudly cheered. Grey's speech was one of great ability, but it was the speech of an advocate.[20]

The reference to Harcourt applauding Grey was revealing. He was revising his views.

Later that evening, Radicals also asserted that the House had been sharply divided by Grey's speech. Sir William Byles remarked that all 'heard the shouts of exultation which came from the other side'.[21] Another Radical speaker, J. Annan Bryce, also made reference to the lopsided reaction of the Commons, as he had perceived it. He insisted that the majority of the people of Britain still favoured neutrality and argued that 'the striking evidence of that was that during the whole course of the speech of the Foreign Minister there was not one single cheer from this side of the House' – an exaggerated but still telling claim.[22]

The newspaper correspondents from the major dailies also detected the air of regret on the Liberal benches and the mood of celebration on the Conservative benches. The account of Grey's speech by the parliamentary correspondent of *The Times*, Michael MacDonagh, not surprisingly stressed the widespread support that Grey received. Grey 'had the Opposition with him from the start', and soon won over 'many wavering Ministerialists'. There was no holding back in the final interpretation: 'All remains of doubt and hesitation vanished', he concluded. But in his diary, MacDonagh was more honest: 'It was from the Conservatives, sitting opposite and led by Bonar Law and Balfour, that came such applause as Grey had so far received.'[23]

The Liberal papers challenged the myth of universal acclaim. They gave more precise detail and revealed the resentment in Liberal ranks. Hugh Spender, the Parliamentary Correspondent of the *Westminster Gazette*, was certain: 'The speech made a painful impression on the Liberal Party, which above all has sought to avoid a war with Germany.' At Grey's declaration that Britain would not shrink from using all the forces of the Crown, Spender observed that 'the enthusiasm of the Unionist Party knew no bounds'.[24] The *Daily News* account explained which passages had inspired cheering. It noted that Grey's references to Britain's 'free hand' were greeted with 'Ministerial cheers'.[25] The *Guardian*, too, noted 'faint applause' from the Liberal benches when Grey gave them 'some fitful gleam of hope' that peace might yet be saved. This contrasted with 'the fierce outbursts of acclamation with which the Unionists hailed every additional portent of the gathering storm'. Asquith's ministers 'sat through it all in the tense attitude of men oppressed by a sense of heavy and solemn responsibility'.[26]

The Labour newspapers also remarked on the intimidating atmosphere. According to the *Daily Citizen*, as Grey's speech slowly unfolded and he began to speak of the impossibility of Britain standing aside, 'again the fierce shouts went up and the frantic wave of handkerchiefs fluttered a wild accompaniment. And so it went on. The war fever had crept into men's blood.'[27] This paper also reported that, during Grey's speech, there were remarkable scenes in the outer lobby of the House of Commons. The lobby was 'packed with an eager throng unable to gain admission to the gallery'. When word was passed around that Grey had promised British action against the German fleet in the Channel, then 'twice the great hall rang with cheers' and 'several small Union Jacks were seen above the heads of the assembly'. Police cries of 'Silence!' were required to calm this embarrassingly festal throng.[28]

Radical activists observing the speech were far from being persuaded. They were appalled by the swaggering mood in the Commons, and by Grey's terrible inconsistency. Some had sat steaming in the public gallery as Grey spoke. 'The show of placing before the House "the cause and the choice" was a mere pretence,' Francis Hirst noted with disgust. In light of the pledge of naval support given to France on Sunday, the truth was that 'the government really had declared war before they came to tell the House of Commons it was free to decide'.[29] Jim Middleton was shaken by the frenzy in the chamber: 'The cries of applause from the Tory benches that met every point from Grey against Germany were like the roars of fiends – for the first time I heard the yelps of the dogs of war.'[30] Vernon Lee, the internationalist writer, reached for satire. Grey's seizing on the redistribution of the fleets with France to justify war – while still flaunting the 'free hand' – was contemptible:

> No promises! Oh no, no promises. Only we accepted our good friend's little kind offer of relieving us of Mediterranean policing – an offer made, pray understand, *senza impegno* [without obligation], as the Italian bric-a-brac dealers say, an offer leaving us *quite free*, and *therefore* constantly owing a debt of gratitude which we *cannot neglect*.[31]

The Masking of the Cabinet Crisis

Marginalising the rebels in the Cabinet and Liberal Party was the immediate political task of interventionists in the aftermath of Grey's speech. In this, the shielding of knowledge about the division in the Asquith Cabinet did good service. Few beyond the Cabinet were aware.

One Radical speaker in the debate on that Monday evening, the combative Radical MP Joe King, complained that the back bench was fog-bound. 'I want to know whether the policy on which we are embarking has the support of the united Cabinet. We hear rumours, both inside the House and outside, that there are divisions, and that even one Cabinet Minister has resigned.' If this was so, the parliament should be told. If there was 'a united Cabinet' ready for war,

King explained, then he would be 'very much relieved'. But nobody knew.[32]

Needless to say, Asquith was fully alive to this. The secret of the Cabinet crisis was to be preserved until overtaken by events. Asquith and his fellow interventionists could be confident that if the next event was a German attack upon Belgium, then the story of the resigning ministers would simply be eclipsed by the biggest story of all – German perfidy. And unanimity could be saved, retrospectively.

TWENTY-TWO

Dissent
Monday 3 August

There were chairs up the gangway and the place was packed. There was a horrible feeling of panic about the whole thing and the horrible raucous cheers which greeted the strongest anti-German passages in Grey's speech gave me a despairing feeling of utter hopelessness.[1]

Arthur Ponsonby, 4 August 1914

Some Radicals with bad consciences assisted in fostering the legend that Grey's speech changed everyone's mind. Christopher Addison, a Radical until the outbreak of war, wrote later that 'Grey's speech convinced the whole House, perhaps with two or three exceptions, that our pledges compelled us to participate.'[2] So too John Simon. In his memoirs he wrote that 'Ramsay MacDonald was almost the only one in the House of Commons who spoke in opposition to the war.'[3]

The legend is demonstrably false. A great many of the Radicals listening to Grey's speech were appalled. They had listened with intensifying disgust. They found it tendentious and emotionally overwrought. The anti-German tone of the speech was a shock. The Radicals rejected the central claim: that armed intervention in support of France in the event of any war was the only honourable alternative for the nation.

The Radicals Challenge Grey's Speech

The spirit in the House astounded the Radicals. 'There was a horrible feeling of panic about the whole thing', Ponsonby wrote home to his wife Dolly. He admitted he was plunged into 'a despairing feeling of utter hopelessness' by the tone of Grey's speech and the whooping of the Opposition. 'We are accustomed to cool well-balanced moderate speeches from him and to see him carried away by passion and presenting such an obviously biased view was most alarming.'[4] Ponsonby observed in his diary: 'This pent-up hatred of Germany and rancorous prejudice against the Germans burst suddenly out into the open when the Tories and many Liberals too roared with purple faces at the deliberate aggressive passages in Grey's speech. I never sat more gloomily silent. It was horrible.'[5] Ponsonby was humiliated by the exultant reactions of Tory members, a typical example of which he recorded: 'The Liberal Government is splendid. We never thought they would fight. Tories could not have behaved better. Of course everyone will vote for them now. It is simply magnificent that they should have plunged in like this.'[6]

Charles Trevelyan's reactions were very similar. He was struck by Grey's strident tone. Grey made it so 'obvious' that he 'disliked the idea of neutrality' as utterly dishonourable. His speech was a 'barefaced, deliberate appeal to passion'. The Radicals, who had 'trusted the government', had been fooled about the entanglements with France. Grey had revealed that 'he had all along been leading her to expect our support and appealed to us as bound in honour'. The House was in no way united. 'I only want to record here that the Liberals, very few of them, cheered at all, whatever they did later, while the Tories shouted with delight.'[7] Dozens on the Radical benches were yet to be persuaded.

Lest it be thought that only Radicals found fault with the speech, it is intriguing to find that Asquith regretted the incitement of anti-German feeling. In the evening, he privately conceded that 'the anti-German note in Grey's speech was the only adverse criticism [of] a great speech which could possibly be made'.[8] So too Herbert Samuel, by this time a fervent believer in intervention, did not think Grey had entirely succeeded in shifting attention away from what was owed to France and on to Belgium and Britain's own safety: 'too much France and not enough Belgium and Channel in it to please me'.[9]

One consequence of Grey's speech often overlooked is that it instantly produced a fifth resignation from the Asquith ministry, that of Charles Trevelyan. As will be recalled, Trevelyan had been in contact with the two Neutrality Committees in London over the weekend. He had gone to the House of Commons on Monday 3 August in the company of two vehement critics of intervention, his brother George and Edmund Morel. They were waiting in his room beneath the 'Noe' lobby of the House as Charles went upstairs to listen to Grey's speech, and he rushed down his notes on the speech. Trevelyan denounced Grey's performance: 'The speech of a French Jingo … It means war … I shall resign. Burns, Morley, Simon and Harcourt are all resigning.'[10]

Trevelyan returned to the chamber to seek out the opinions of some of the ministers he believed to be neutralists. Trevelyan went to Simon 'looking very miserable' on the front bench. Not knowing that Simon had already resigned, Trevelyan 'touched him on the shoulder'. Trevelyan confided to him, 'Unless there was a better explanation I felt I must resign.' Simon signalled that he could not come for a talk just yet. After Redmond's speech, Trevelyan spoke also to Herbert Samuel, who asked him to 'think before resigning'. Next he consulted Lord Bryce, who 'after hearing me said he would think me right to resign'. Then he encountered Harcourt and 'had a good talk with him'. But Trevelyan took little notice of Harcourt, considering him 'of the opportunist type in the long run', even though he had 'really struggled for peace and for a proper understanding with France'.

Simon's view mattered much more. When the major speeches were over, Simon and Trevelyan linked up for a private talk. Trevelyan described the encounter:

I told him in a few strong words what I thought. He stood silent. Then he said he absolutely agreed, and that he had resigned. We talked for a quarter of an hour. I left the room sorry for him beyond all words, but quite certain that he would resign.[11]

Trevelyan went back to his brother George and Morel in his room downstairs, explaining he must resign. 'He buried his face in his hands,' recalled Morel. George praised his brother for 'playing the part he thought right.'[12] Charles immediately composed his letter of resignation to Asquith. He was bold enough to cite Grey's speech as the immediate cause:

> I listened today to Grey's speech and after hearing it I am afraid that I cannot conscientiously remain any longer in the Government. I deeply regret having to ask you to accept my resignation … I have not felt justified in troubling you at such a time with an expression of my opinion. But the difference I am afraid is fundamental, and concerns our whole relations with France and Germany. I have made up my mind after full deliberation and after conversing at length with more than one Cabinet minister.[13]

Immediately after the set-piece speeches in the House, a special meeting of the Liberal Foreign Affairs Group was held to consider strategy. It was the second meeting of the day. Twenty-seven Radical MPs met in a committee room of the House of Commons. The mood of the meeting was a mixture of defiance and anxiety. A clear majority indicated that they were not swayed by Grey's speech. The nation, they believed, was being pitchforked into war. Twenty-two of the twenty-seven attending the meeting agreed to the following resolution for release to the press:

> After hearing Sir Edward Grey's statement [this meeting] is of opinion that no sufficient reason exists in present circumstances for Great Britain intervening in the War and most strongly urges His Majesty's Government to continue negotiations with Germany with a view to maintaining our neutrality.[14]

But there was a keen debate over an amendment proposing 'that the violation of Belgium was a *casus belli*' – a sign of the 'wedge' that was coming. The amendment was defeated, but by a slender margin.[15]

The Attempt to Stifle Parliamentary Debate

Incredibly, it took some manoeuvring to secure a debate on Grey's speech in the House of Commons, on the evening of Monday 3 August. Dramatically exposing the lack of genuine democratic spirit at the heart of the government, even this single opportunity for debate was almost strangled at birth. Asquith himself showed little respect for the right of parliament to debate the rights and wrongs of British intervention. Rather, he sought to quash all debate.

When MacDonald sat down at about 4.30 p.m., the Prime Minister attempted then and there to shut down the debate. The Radical MP Philip Morrell rose to follow MacDonald only to find a Conservative MP reminding the Speaker that there was no motion before the House. The Speaker asked if there was 'any disposition to discuss the situation'. Shouts of 'No, no!' were heard. 'Something more behind our backs!' Josiah Wedgwood, a LFAG member, cried out in response. Morrell, speaking for the Radicals, stood defiantly and demanded: 'We wish to have an opportunity – an early opportunity – of expressing ourselves with regard to the proposed intervention of this country in the European war.' Asquith assured him there would be 'an early opportunity' for debate. 'Today?' inquired a number of Radicals. 'No', replied Asquith, supported by members shouting, 'Sit down!' at Morrell. Morrell remained standing, and suggested that at the very least the matter should be debated later in the evening upon the formal 'Motion for Adjournment'.

Eventually, it was the Speaker who rather reluctantly granted this slender opportunity for debate. With some MPs shouting, 'Let us have it now!' the Speaker left the Chair and the sitting was suspended until 7 p.m. The debate would have to wait until then.[16] The House of Commons had been allowed so far just two hours to consider the matter of Britain's diving into a European war. This might have been all. As Edmund Harvey wrote, 'Morrell held the fort splendidly in insisting on a discussion that day in spite of Speaker and Prime Minister.'[17]

Therefore, thanks to the Radicals, a debate was scheduled. But shamefully, a decision of all-embracing significance, Britain's possible intervention in a European war, was to be debated under an adjournment motion. No specific motion, to endorse or reject the foreign policy statement made by Grey, or indeed to endorse or reject the idea of British intervention in the war, would be before the House.

In the House of Lords on that same evening, the Liberals and Conservatives cooperated to stamp upon all debate – with only a flicker of opposition. At the session beginning at 6 p.m., Lord Crewe, the Liberal leader in the Lords, explained that he had initially intended to make a statement on 'the grave situation' – indeed, the peers had been summoned for it and the House of Lords was crowded. But, Crewe explained, he had spoken to the Tory leader Lord Lansdowne and he had agreed that it would be better 'to abstain from making a statement'. Grey's speech would suffice. Any additional statement, Crewe pleaded, 'could only lead to a debate which at this particular moment of extreme crisis would not, I think, be helpful to any of the real interests of the country'. Lansdowne then spoke endorsing this, and sang the praises of Grey's speech, remarking on 'the great pleasure' it had given him to hear it. The whole country should rally around Grey's speech and show 'a united front to the nations of the world'.

Lord Courtney then rose 'amid murmurs of disapproval'. He said that he could not allow the situation to pass 'without one word of comment'. He asked what motion was before the House. Evidently not wishing to be embarrassed by a fellow Liberal, Crewe explained that the only motion before the Lords would be a motion for adjournment. Those peers wanting to close the debate immediately cried, 'Move! Move!' Crewe entered 'a strong personal appeal' to Courtney 'to refrain from speaking upon it'. Unconvinced, Courtney rounded on his fellow peers: 'My Lords, will you allow me to utter a sentence?' He further pleaded, 'I think one sentence must be uttered'. In the end he uttered just five sentences. He explained that he and others had come up from the country having read in the press that the government's leader in the Lords would be making a statement on the crisis. 'No statement has been made', he complained, 'and I rise to utter a protest against this House so far abdicating its duty and functions as to commit itself to be bound in any way without having a statement as to the reasons why it should be so bound.' To no avail. The session was promptly closed, after just forty minutes.[18]

Thus, in both the Commons and the Lords, the government sought to commit the British nation to a war soon to be described as a great crusade for freedom, democracy and liberal principles – while simultaneously seeking to shut the mouths of all parliamentarians.

Radical Defiance: The Evening Debate, 3 August

When members returned to the debating chamber of the House of Commons for the promised debate on the adjournment at 7 p.m. on that Monday evening, the House was still crowded. Many of the Radicals no doubt came in a mood to challenge the government. Asquith introduced the motion to adjourn, and then Grey was on his feet.

Grey was now in possession of the perfect 'wedge' to confound the insubordinate backbenchers at the very outset of the debate. He made a short statement. Since his speech, he reported, he had received a note from the Belgian Legation in London. It confirmed the rumours. Germany had delivered an ultimatum to Belgium on the previous evening, at 7 p.m. on Sunday 2 August. It demanded free passage of German troops through Belgium and extended only a twelve-hour time limit for a reply. The Belgians had rejected it as 'a flagrant violation of the rights of nations', and were 'firmly resolved to repel aggression by all possible means'. Grey offered just two sentences in reaction to the Belgian note. He announced that the British government would 'take into grave consideration' this message and that he would 'make no further comment upon it'.[19] Both Grey and Asquith then left the chamber. So too did Bonar Law.

Thus, as members rose in their places to react to Grey's speech of the afternoon, he had enormously strengthened his position: it was no longer to be a debate about the merits of the pledge to France of Sunday 2 August, but a debate about the appropriate British response to the German threat to Belgium.

Nonetheless, in the evening adjournment debate of almost three and a half hours that followed, the Radicals entirely dominated. Sixteen Radicals spoke in support of peace and non-intervention.[20] This was no bunch of dishevelled revolutionaries. They were a combative band, but with impressive credentials. They included rich and powerful men of business, such as Josiah Wedgwood, Richard Denman, Percy Molteno and Sir Albert Spicer. There were passionate internationalists such as Joe King and Annan Bryce, brother of James Bryce. The eminent jurist Sir John Jardine was among them, and the Bradford newspaper proprietor Sir William Byles. There were men who had long advocated international arbitration, such as the two Welsh Radicals, Llewelyn Williams and Aneurin Williams. Quakers were among them, men like Arnold Rowntree and Edmund Harvey. One Labour MP, Keir Hardie, supported them. Many of these MPs had warned for years of the danger of Britain being hurled into war upon the signal of Russia and France. Their vehemence was driven by no last-minute horror. Only one Conservative, Arthur Balfour, and two Liberals, Arthur Markham and William Pringle, argued for British intervention.

No Cabinet minister spoke up for Grey. No resigning minister addressed the House. Those who knew the inner mysteries of the Cabinet's quarrels were keeping silent. It was to be a backbench debate. Most assumed it was a mere dress rehearsal for the real debate that was still to come, before the nation was committed – or so the leaders had promised.

Four important themes emerged. First, the Radicals drew attention to the fact that the Germans were still attempting to negotiate with Britain. Their approaches should not have been so hastily dismissed. Second, the Radicals conceded that Belgian neutrality was important to Britain, but they insisted that war to preserve that neutrality was a giant step beyond the Treaty of 1839. Third, the Radicals emphasised the provocative and precipitate role that Russia had played in the crisis. Fourth, the Radicals accused interventionists of rushing into war, heedless of enormous costs.

Philip Morrell began for the Radicals. He pointed out that Grey had offered two reasons for intervention, the defence of France's undefended northern coasts and the defence of Belgium's neutrality. He reminded the House that Germany, through a press release from the London Embassy, had that very day undertaken not to attack the French coast if Britain remained neutral. Grey should pursue further negotiations. Then Morrell turned on the Conservatives. The real reason why the 'Gentlemen opposite' were pressing for war, Morrell asserted, was 'fear and jealousy of German ambition', which was 'fostered by large sections of the Press'. If Britain intervened, Morrell warned, she would be 'going to war just as much to preserve the despotism of Russia as to interfere with German ambition'. Finally, he highlighted Grey's 'unworthy' claim that Britain would scarcely suffer more if she entered the war than if she remained neutral.[21]

A number of speakers called on Grey to keep negotiating with Germany. Edmund Harvey, for example, spoke of the 'magnificent efforts that have been made by the Foreign Secretary' to keep the peace so far. He highlighted the latest German offer to muzzle the German Navy, which Grey had dismissed as 'too narrow an engagement'. Grey had also alluded vaguely to a previous German offer regarding Belgium, also turned aside. Harvey implored Grey to resume his active diplomacy and build on the concessions Germany had signalled.[22] Llewelyn Williams repeated the plea.[23]

Percy Molteno, a Radical MP with extensive South African agricultural interests, delivered a fiery speech. He raised the issue of Grey and Asquith's untrustworthiness. Seeking to nail his own party's leaders, Molteno quoted Asquith and Grey's answers to parliamentary questions on four occasions over the last two years. Each had assured the House there was nothing 'unpublished' that could drive Britain to war. These assurances could not be squared with Grey's revelations that afternoon. The Radicals, he complained, had been deliberately led into 'this state of false security'. Obligations had been allowed to blossom. Then Molteno turned to the key issue of

Belgium. The Treaty of 1839, he stressed, 'does not compel us in any sense to go to war'. This was why Granville and Gladstone had negotiated new treaties in 1870. Why was Grey so lead-footed in comparison? Molteno bitterly regretted the impression given by Grey that 'nothing would satisfy him short of war'.[24]

But the power of the Belgian factor to divide the Radicals was on display. The first Liberal to support Grey, Sir Arthur Markham, announced he was a critic of the Entente. But he repeated Grey's argument that Britain could not stand by and 'admit the right of a great power in Europe to over-ride and beat down a small nationality'. War for Belgium would have to be faced, and 'we ought not to shrink, whatever the cost of blood or treasure may be, from doing what is our duty'.[25] On similar grounds, William Pringle, a Radical and a LFAG member, intervened to break from his colleagues. He explained that Britain must respond to a German attack on Belgium, or it would be 'the extinction of public law in Europe'. Thus, he argued, Britain must not stand outside 'the conflict between the forces that represent blood and iron and forces which represent international morality'. This provoked taunts of 'Russia! Russia!' 'I hold that so far as we are concerned the Russian question does not arise', he replied, inexplicably.[26]

Grey's tactics in his afternoon speech, focusing upon France and obscuring Russia, had been much resented by the Radicals.[27] In deliberate response, they now dwelt upon the disgraceful image of Britain siding with Russia. Morrell chided Grey with being ashamed to mention Russia in his speech. Rowntree accused Russia of riding roughshod over the terms of its convention with Britain over Persia. If the government 'is going to increase the power of Russia at the expense of Germany', warned Rowntree, 'I think of the frontier of India, I think of Afghanistan, and I think of Persia.' Robert Outhwaite argued that if Britain was justified in fighting to save the small state of Belgium from Germany, why did she do nothing to save the small states of Finland and Persia from Russian depredations? 'I see a Germany crushed and an all-conquering Russia', predicted Outhwaite. Joe King reminded all that in Russia there were about 100,000 people in prison without trial, and there were

1,000 executions a year. If Britain were to enter the war she would be fighting to support Russia's 'atrocious tyrannical Government'. Reviewing the diplomacy of the crisis, Aneurin Williams argued that the Russians' heart-thumping sprint toward general mobilisation lay at the very heart of the explosion into war.[28]

Finally, the Radicals accused the government of capitulating to a fever whipped up by reactionaries and a war-flogging press. Jardine was horrified that people were embarking on war as an adventure, 'in somewhat the same spirit as we might take part in a gorgeous parade or in a magnificent picnic at somebody else's expense'.[29] Josiah Wedgwood was angry. He denounced Grey's speech as frankly 'a wonderful Jingo speech – can anybody deny that it was a Jingo speech?' He spoke sneeringly of Grey's patriotic flourishes, citing his boast that 'the Army and the Navy were ready, to the last trouser button, to do their duty'. He flashed at those so smugly contemplating a swift war, like 'one of the dear old-fashioned wars of the eighteenth century'. This war would be catastrophic. Credit would be smashed. Once starvation faced the people of Europe, then 'civilization will topple down'. In that situation, Wedgwood concluded dramatically, 'you will see something far more important than a European War – you will see a revolution'.[30] Similarly, Llewelyn Williams predicted that too many were dismissing the 'hideous carnage' that was coming. 'It is not only going to be a matter of £50,000,000 or £100,000,000 – thrown into the sea!' he prophesied. Rather, 'the whole fabric of our social reform' would be imperilled.[31]

Memorably too, Ponsonby mocked the exhibitions of false 'patriotism' he had witnessed in St James's Street about midnight on the previous evening:

> We are on the eve of a great war, and I hate to see people embarking on it with a light heart. The war fever has already begun. I saw it last night when I walked through the streets. I saw bands of half-drunken youths waving flags, and I saw a group outside a great club in St James's Street being encouraged by members of the club from the balcony. The war fever has begun, and that is what is called patriotism![32]

Parliament and the War Powers

Passionate as this debate was, there was no division. Indeed, it is worth highlighting the scandalous fact that there was to be no parliamentary decision for or against war prior to its declaration. In constitutional terms, of course, this was perfectly in order. In 1914 the British parliament did not possess the final power to decide between peace and war. The 'war powers' were part of the royal prerogative – and so in practice the Prime Minister could simply advise the King, one way or the other.[33]

Yet in its rhetoric the government had indicated that the House of Commons *would* play a role in the actual decision-making. Grey had indicated war would not come as a result of any act of arbitrary power. Twice in his speech on Monday 3 August, Grey had observed that he and Asquith had promised that the House 'was free to decide what the British attitude should be'.[34] Toward the end of his speech, Grey explained that the 'most awful responsibility is resting upon the Government in deciding what to advise the House of Commons to do'.[35]

MPs might reasonably have concluded that the House of Commons would choose between peace and war – certainly that, before any declaration of war, the House of Commons would be given the opportunity for a full debate, in which the leading ministers would rise to defend a choice for war. The debate on the evening of 3 August – as events turned out, the *only* debate *before* the declaration – was scarcely that kind of debate. It is no surprise, therefore, that no speaker in these debates appears to have realised that the Cabinet might declare war on the very next day. The government indeed treated the debate as a forgettable spectacle. As Joe King complained at the mid-point of the debate, in spite of the overwhelming majority claimed by those pressing for intervention, 'supporters of this policy have lost their voice'.[36]

No one realised how imminent a declaration might be. 'There is no declaration of war yet', reasoned Byles, 'and the House of Commons can stop it. There is still time.'[37] Denman, similarly, pleaded, 'There is no declaration of war, and the speech of the Foreign Secretary

did not imply that in the immediate future there would be a declaration of war.'[38] Indeed, the one speaker from the Conservative
benches who spoke, Balfour, seemed embarrassed. He twice insisted
that 'this is not a Debate on the great question before the country'.
Rather, he explained, it was a tiresome necessity, to allow the 'various
Gentlemen below the Gangway' to vent their feelings. Thus, he
lamented, they had listened to 'the very dregs and lees of the Debate'.
Asquith had promised a 'full opportunity for debating the policy of
the Government'. 'That will come', Balfour assured his listeners.[39]
Colonel John Seely, a former War Secretary, also indicated that at
'the proper time I hope we may have a debate on this subject, which
will raise the true issue'.[40] Then the House was adjourned at about
half-past ten.[41]

In fact, all were speaking in the last debate before the declaration
of war, then just twenty-four hours away. The House of Commons
had been allowed a little shadow puppetry, giving the mere appearance of a democratic decision for war. The parliament would never
debate the *prospect* of war again.

TWENTY-THREE

Midnight Seductions
Monday 3 and Tuesday 4 August

I am clearly of opinion that, at such a moment as this you have something that nearly approaches to a public duty for the time being at any rate, to remain.[1]

H. H. Asquith to John Simon, 3 August 1914

On Monday evening 3 August, while the House of Commons was locked in its debate over British intervention, Asquith worked behind the scenes to shepherd the Cabinet toward a choice for war – and to save his government.

The Monday Evening Cabinet and the German Ultimatum

Although the German ultimatum had been delivered in Brussels on Sunday evening, the Belgian government had kept the news secret overnight while it debated its response. Details arrived in London only on Monday. The Cabinet that met at 6 p.m. in the evening of Monday 3 August was the first to consider the German threat to Belgium as a live thing. 'We had the text of Germany's arrogant ultimatum to Belgium', wrote Samuel.[2] The exact terms were laid out before the Cabinet; they were 'very stiff', noted Harcourt.[3] The issue was pressing: the Germans' time limit of only twelve hours had already passed, at 7 a.m. that morning. How should Britain react?

The Cabinet, which lasted under an hour, was very cautious. No immediate counter-ultimatum to Germany emerged. Perhaps this caution arose from a desire to complete Britain's own military preparations. Churchill reported that the fleet would be 'absolutely ready by 4 a.m. tomorrow'. But Asquith told the Cabinet that the army's mobilisation needed '3 days more'. Harcourt recorded the Cabinet's decision that 'Grey will telegraph to Germany tomorrow morning as to their ultimatum … & demand an answer.' Jack Pease noted it as a decision to postpone until the morning 'what might be said to Germany as our reply might be used as a justification for a (surprise) invasion by Germany'.[4] Therefore, no precise warning was sent to Germany overnight that the military action she had threatened against Belgium would provoke a British ultimatum, or even a declaration of war.

No doubt this caution also followed from the Cabinet's fragility. For Asquith next reported that on top of the four resignations still before him, he had received a fifth – from Charles Trevelyan. However, he informed the Cabinet, fortunately one of these five was already reconsidering: John Simon. He had approached Simon in the afternoon, sometime after Grey's speech, and again put the case for Cabinet unity. He had made some progress. This tale, of course, was told to weaken the resolve of other doubtful ministers. Harcourt took the hint, noting that 'Asq[uith] thinks Simon *may* not resign after all.'[5] Samuel also recorded that 'Simon may possibly reconsider his position, but I don't know.' The tug of political opportunity was on display. Once again, all ministers were encouraged to maintain their silence on the Cabinet crisis – perhaps at this point to make it easier for resigning ministers to return. As Samuel told Beatrice, again, 'Please say nothing about these resignations until a public announcement.'[6]

When the Cabinet finished just before 7 p.m., Grey and Asquith made their way quickly to the House of Commons. Here, as we saw, Grey simply confirmed the fact of the German ultimatum to Belgium in a very short statement. He told the Commons precisely nothing about the government's response to this event at the Cabinet just ended.[7] Neither man stayed around to hear the debate.

Asquith returned to Downing Street where Jack Pease was among his guests to dinner. Later Pease joined Asquith, Bonham Carter and Margot for bridge 'to stay the strain'. When cards were over, Asquith entrusted to Pease some of his reflections on the inner meaning of the crisis – with an eye, no doubt, to shoring up Pease's inclination to stay in the Cabinet. Asquith told Pease that he 'believed in a German rapprochement'. Indeed, he 'had believed in Germany's friendship & played up for it'. However, he complained, the Germans had 'intended' and 'worked' for war. They had banked on Britain being preoccupied by the Irish crisis, but miraculously it had vanished. At Pease's leave-taking, Asquith nearly broke down, and muttered to the Quaker that 'God moves in a mysterious way his wonders to perform.'[8] Asquith was rehearsing the arguments he would soon deploy in winning back his wayward ministers.

The Wooing of Simon and Beauchamp

The rescuing of his Cabinet still demanded Asquith's attention until late on Monday evening. If Asquith could induce the four Cabinet ministers to reconsider their resignations, he was home and dry – politically. Confirmation of the German threat to Belgium was likely to stem the loss of any more ministers, as well as boosting backbench support for intervention.

Simon's tears at the Cabinet had shown him to be the most anxious. In fact, on the night of Monday 3 August he shared his doubts with Hugh Cecil. He told him he 'did not quite trust' Grey, 'saturated' as he was in the Entente, and he thought Churchill was animated by 'something worse'. Cecil was definite: Simon should stay in the Cabinet 'and not weaken it at such a moment'.[9]

Later Asquith sent 'a strong appeal' to Simon.[10] Duty was the big theme. But Asquith added just a hint of special favours in advancing Simon's career, and tender solicitude toward his 'strong convictions'. 'I think that I can fully safeguard you', he wrote. 'I am clearly of

opinion that, at such a moment as this you have something that
nearly approaches to a public duty for the time being at any rate,
to remain', Asquith concluded. He signed off with more butter
about 'most gratefully and affectionately' recognising his 'invaluable
service to the Government and your loyal and devoted attachment
to myself'.[11]

Significantly, Asquith did not seek to exploit the news from
Brussels. He did not suggest that the German ultimatum offered
Simon a credible line of retreat. For good reason: Simon's protest –
in common with those of other dissidents – was a protest against the
whole thrust of Grey's foreign policy. Asquith's assurance to safeguard
career and conscience was enough. Simon replied yieldingly: 'I feel in
view of the assurance in your letter that I must respond to the appeal
which it contains, and I am doing so with goodwill; though with
a heavy heart.'[12] A month later Simon told C. P. Scott that he had
returned to Cabinet without in any way retreating from his criticisms
of intervention and purely to assist the nation in a moment of historic peril.[13] It did not wash. For the past week Simon had paraded
his willingness to sacrifice his career to preserve Britain's neutrality.
His decision to stay wrecked his reputation in Radical circles.[14]

This breakthrough must have encouraged Asquith in his quest.
There is no record of a letter to Beauchamp that Monday evening but
there was certainly an interview. Asquith pleaded with Beauchamp
on the basis of loyalty, both to the Liberal Party and to himself.
Overnight, Beauchamp surrendered.

The agonising was painful. After all, Beauchamp had provided his
London home as a meeting point for all the Radicals on Sunday 2
August. He was close to Morley. They had lunched at Halkyn House
again after the Monday morning Cabinet. Here the two peers had
confirmed that each would stick to resignation. They had calmly
'gossiped' over who might replace Morley as Lord President of the
Council. Morley flattered Beauchamp by observing that he was the
only capable man. 'Oh, but how could I take your place,' Beauchamp
objected cheerily, 'sharing the opinions for which you have left it?'[15]
After this, returning to the Cabinet, *and* taking Morley's place as Lord
President, must have been acutely embarrassing for Beauchamp.

There may have been a curious element of mischance in these events. If so, luck was with Asquith. Beauchamp received the normal printed summons to the Cabinet of Tuesday morning 4 August – as did all ministers, resigning or not. Beauchamp then went to Cabinet. Why? Among his reasons was a surprising indication he received from George Cunningham, an official at the Privy Council Office, that Morley was returning to Cabinet. This must have struck home. But it was false. Cunningham apologised the same day, in a revealing note. Cunningham took comfort from Beauchamp's explanation that it was not just Cunningham's 'misleading statement' that prompted his return to Cabinet: 'I understood from you that you were being guided by assurances given to Sir J. Simon in your action.'[16] Either Simon or Asquith must have conveyed 'assurances' that Asquith would have an eye to Beauchamp's convictions and career if he returned to Cabinet.[17]

One letter kept in Beauchamp's files points to an additional factor. Lionel Holland, a wealthy friend, wrote on Tuesday 4 August. He predicted that 'if our cooperation is made to hinge upon Belgian neutrality – with a groan at our having committed ourselves by previous assurances – most will submit – certainly not blame the Government'. Holland advised Beauchamp to stay and 'keep the influence that you possess so as to use it towards securing peace in the future'. Holland was frank: 'Since war seems from today's news certain for us', then 'the most popular line for a statesman to take' would be that 'it is best we should go right in, and that speedily'.[18]

The great difficulty for Beauchamp was explaining his decision to Morley. He quickly penned his excuses: 'Little did I think when last we met', began Beauchamp, referring to their lunch on Monday, 'of the divided lines we should follow today. We had gone so far together. I followed your lead.' On that day, he conceded, 'I thought the struggle was ours.' Then he attributed his change of mind to 'passion', the disabling speed of the crisis 'as events fly by', and his sense of 'loyalty to the party'. But most of all, there was Asquith's seductive power: 'To me he is the chief figure of my political life. Always kind and considerate, how difficult to resist a personal appeal!'[19]

Morley was generous in reply. 'The pressure for remaining was, as I felt myself, so *intense*, and I have no word of reproach for those who hold on.'[20] The implication was soft but definite: Beauchamp ought to have withstood that intense pressure, as Morley had done. A year later, on the first anniversary of the outbreak of the war, Beauchamp clung to his explanation. He told Loreburn and Burns that Asquith had collared him – and he had come to regret his decision.[21]

Radical Desertions: Morley Goes – Harcourt Stays

Asquith next pursued Morley. He wrote to him at midnight on Monday, a letter marked 'Urgent'. He employed a mixture of high emotion and flattery. It was 'a most afflicting moment', Asquith wrote. He reminded Morley of 'nearly 30 years of close and most affectionate association'. For him to lose Morley 'in the stress of a great crisis' was 'a calamity which I shudder to contemplate'. Again, Asquith did not raise Belgium. He was abject: 'I therefore beg you, with all my heart, to think twice and thrice, and as many times more as arithmetic can number, before you take a step which impoverishes the Government, and leaves me stranded and almost alone.'[22]

On his breakfast table the next morning, Tuesday 4 August, Morley again found the usual printed summons to Cabinet. Then Asquith's letter arrived by special messenger. It rocked his 'complacency' and threw him into 'mental anguish'. He stalked up and down his library, then his garden. Then he drove toward Buckingham Palace for a Privy Council meeting. The journey cleared his head and cooled his temper. Reaching his office in Whitehall, he drew up another letter to Asquith. 'Your letter shakes me terribly', he wrote. He acknowledged the 'affectionate association'. But he repelled Asquith's plea. His essential complaint remained the same. 'To swear ourselves to France, is to bind ourselves to Russia, and to whatever demands may be made by Russia on France', he asserted again.[23] Again, the Belgian issue was not mentioned. Morley gave the King his final decision that same morning.[24]

The Radical leader in the Cabinet who most controversially never resigned was Lewis Harcourt. During the crisis, 'Loulou' had represented the Radicals in interviews with Asquith. 'That I must resign is more and more evident', he had jotted on a piece of paper slipped to Morley across the Cabinet table on one occasion.[25] But, as will be remembered, he had given some indication of a change of mind at Beauchamp's lunch on Sunday 2 August. Then, as Burns, Morley and Simon submitted resignation letters, Harcourt did not do so. At the Cabinet on Monday morning, when Beauchamp handed in his resignation letter, Harcourt had no letter. In the afternoon he had cheered Grey while others sat glumly. He continued to sit at the Prime Minister's right hand. He was naturally buoyed up by the unexpected appearance of Beauchamp at the Cabinet on Tuesday morning 4 August. This, and Simon's appearance, took the pressure off him. Searching for reassurance, no doubt, Harcourt passed a note across the Cabinet table to Beauchamp: 'I cannot say how much it means to me to have you still by my side.'[26] Like a man rescued from a bruising accident, he seemed grateful just for rescue – and apparently unconscious of his unsightly bruises.

In explaining his position to friends, Harcourt fixed upon British interests. For Harcourt it was vital to repel the suggestion that Britain was going to war essentially for the sake of 'obligations' contracted under the Entente – the Radical nightmare. He told Liberal allies that he had acted 'not from any obligation of Treaty or honour, for neither existed, and it has been part of my work for the last four years to make it perfectly plain that such was the fact'. But, he explained, there were 'three overwhelming British interests'. Britain could not let Germany control 'under our neutrality' the North Sea and English Channel, could not let Germany occupy north-western France 'opposite our shores', and could not let Germany 'violate the ultimate independence of Belgium' and occupy Antwerp 'as a standing menace to us'.[27] The old Elizabethan argument about the 'narrow seas' had swayed him.

On Thursday 6 August, Harcourt added lashings of emotion to this same essential explanation, in a letter to his Radical mentor and his father's close friend, Morley. 'I ought to be with *you* – for this

is the crash of everything I care for and have worked for', he confessed. In any case, he wrote, 'my political life is over' – which must
have made Morley wince, for in clinging to office clearly it was not
over. Again Harcourt paraded 'great British interests', and dismissed
talk of 'any obligation actual or implied to France and of national
honour'. He added problematically that he was 'fighting *with* France
but not *for* France'. He concluded with the plea, 'I hope you do not
think I have betrayed you. I can never again spend such a week of
misery as this has been to me.'[28]

The letter demonstrates once again how a war-making Cabinet
minister could blithely cast aside the official explanations given out
by Asquith's government to the public for Britain's entry into the
war – obligations to save Belgium, to keep faith with France, and
to save national honour. Liberal leaders were repeating these from
public platforms, hand on heart, up and down the country. Harcourt
treated them as tosh.

Morley's reply was characteristic. He claimed to feel 'no trace of a
wound' while feeling 'pain beyond measure'. He acknowledged 'the
huge responsibility of resignation'. But, he wrote, '*I believe that I
took that line for other people last Sunday.* Anyhow, one set of arguments overwhelmed the other in your mind, another in mine. I have
no right whatever to throw a stone, and I've no stone to throw.' Yet
Morley's profound sense of disappointment in Harcourt was visible.
He *was* wounded. He had shown the way – and been left almost
alone. 'What things you and I have been through together!! I find
this the most *lacerating* of them all.'[29]

By the time Morley was preparing his *Memorandum on Resignation*,
his bitterness was irrepressible. The handwritten version of his
Memorandum shows that he held a stone or two. He contemplated
reproducing both Beauchamp's and Harcourt's letters to him. 'The
hardest case was *Loulou*'s. He had been for several days the active
& implacable instigator of it all.' Harcourt's letter was so weak he
was 'half unwilling' to reproduce it.[30] Finally, he decided to suppress
both letters. In the published version of the *Memorandum* he simply
recorded that he 'could not comprehend' the response of all of his
Cabinet colleagues, 'and two of them I had no choice but to *judge*'.[31]

From Morley's viewpoint, Asquith had confronted the two Radicals with a terrible choice: to scramble aboard the bandwagon to war and political safety, or be shoved in a tumbrel to political oblivion. They had made their choice.

'Sticking to the Ship'

Returning to the narrative of events, it is clear that by a late hour on Monday 3 August Asquith must have been more confident than in the morning that he could save his Cabinet. He could not be certain until the morning of Tuesday, but the successful seduction of two of the four ministers, Simon and Beauchamp, must have boosted hope. If both appeared at the Cabinet table on Tuesday morning, all would be well. He had divided the rebels. Two losses could be explained away. And the schism was still hidden.

'You will be relieved to hear there is a slump in resignations', Asquith wrote to Venetia Stanley next day. He attributed the fact that Simon and Beauchamp had 'returned to the fold' to the letter he had written to 'the Impeccable [Simon]'.[32] As Margot heard the story from Asquith, his persuasive power had saved the day. 'He persuaded Simon and Beauchamp to stay', Margot concluded in her diary.[33] The relief for Asquith must have been immense. If the worst happened in Belgium, he must have calculated, any ministers still harbouring doubts would stifle them.

Why then did so few ministers depart? The explanations of two Radical Cabinet ministers who clung to office, Walter Runciman and Jack Pease, are revealing. To understand their viewpoint, we must glance forward briefly from Monday 3 August, for both wrote letters to Charles Trevelyan over the next days.

Runciman was a close ally of Trevelyan's. He was the Radicals' contact man in Cabinet. He wrote to Trevelyan, probably after the morning Cabinet on Tuesday 4 August. His purpose, he explained, was 'to tell you as I have always told you what I have done and why I have done it'. After 'ten days of anxiety and torturing thought', he wrote, he and Harcourt, Lloyd George and Pease, had all decided 'to

remain where we are' and go on with 'the terrible work of the organisation of industry and food supply, and of defence'. He pleaded with
Trevelyan to do nothing until he had read the government's White
Paper – the diplomatic cables it had just decided to issue. He rejected
'taking the easy course of washing our hands of the dreadful responsibilities and going to our farms'.[34]

Jack Pease also wrote a full letter, to his cousin and fellow Quaker
Jonathan Hodgkin, on Tuesday 4 August. He sent a copy to Trevelyan.
He reviewed the whole crisis. Germany's dodging the Ambassadors'
Conference proved 'that Germany has premeditated the war'.
Britain's pledge to France on Sunday 2 August was 'only fair' in light
of the redistribution of the fleets, and to counter German aggression.
Pease fixed upon Belgium. The Treaty of 1839 was 'open to only
one interpretation', he asserted. He believed 'that to repudiate our
undertaking to preserve Belgium's neutrality would be dishonourable and discreditable'.[35] Thus, Pease had upgraded his understanding
of the Treaty of 1839. Gone was the Cabinet's stress on 'policy not
obligation' – or perhaps the policy now was to find the obligation.

In Pease's accompanying letter to Trevelyan he struck a judgemen-
tal note. He scolded Trevelyan: 'I had hoped that you would have
waited until you knew all the facts, before you deserted your colleagues.' He pulled religious rank, reminding Trevelyan that he was
'a Quaker with more peace blood in my veins than any man in the
House'. He urged Trevelyan to join him and 'make some sacrifice
of your personal feelings too'. Relief work beckoned, argued Pease.
He pleaded with Trevelyan to withdraw his resignation, and 'pluck-
ily face with our great Prime Minister the responsibilities *forced* on
the Government'.[36] Trevelyan dismissed both letters: one was 'flabby'
and the other 'a sticking plaster for a broken leg'.[37]

In the days ahead, German aggression in Belgium was the only
immediate reason needed by most ministers to explain to the public
and to history why they had chosen to remain. But the issue of
Belgium had received no consideration in the exchanges of correspondence between the Prime Minister and those contemplating
resignation from Sunday 2 August to Tuesday 4 August, neither
among those who stayed nor those who departed. Only Pease had

mentioned it, to Hodgkin. Belgium did not win back the rebels – whatever they were to say after the event.

The exchanges of correspondence show that it was the Prime Minister's personal appeals that had turned the heads of two of the rebels. 'The power of Asquith and Grey', as Morley wrote later, 'would prove too hard for an isolated group to resist.' By contrast, the Radical faction lacked a charismatic leader. After the decisions of Lloyd George and Harcourt to remain in the Cabinet, and of Simon and Beauchamp to return, there was, wrote Morley, 'no standard-bearer' for the neutralist cause.[38]

Among political factors, dissident and doubtful ministers must also have weighed carefully the argument that it was their duty to keep the Tories out. For the menace of coalition grew large. With this spectre materialising, some members of the Cabinet had chosen to fortify the existing Cabinet. For example, Herbert Samuel told his wife on 2 August that in the last analysis the result of rebellion within the Cabinet 'would have been either a Coalition Government or a Unionist Government either of which would certainly have been a war ministry'.[39] Certainly, Radicals freely admitted the possibility of a coalition. Harcourt had told Ponsonby on Sunday 2 August that a coalition would follow a split.[40] Asquith had mentioned it as a possibility to the Cabinet on the morning of Monday 3 August.[41] Runciman too had scolded Trevelyan with the remark that, miserable as were the Cabinet's Radicals in going to war, 'that is not in itself sufficient to justify us in handing over our policy and control to the Tories'.[42] Similarly, Jack Pease chided Trevelyan. 'If we all chucked as you have done,' he wrote, 'the alternative government must be one much less anxious for a peace policy than ourselves.'[43] Trevelyan estimated that this factor had weighed heaviest with Beauchamp and Simon: 'The chief pressure on them was I think that Asquith would have to form a coalition ministry, if several of his Cabinet went.'[44] So the argument went – better a Liberal-led war, if war it had to be.

Radicals were convinced that the Liberal leaders had deliberately exploited fear of a coalition government to get the choice for war endorsed by their own Cabinet. In September, Morley told a number of his friends, including Ramsay MacDonald, Lord Eversley and

Bertrand Russell, that 'if the actual invasion of Belgium had been postponed 48 hours the Government would have broken up and a Coalition one formed'.[45] Similarly, Hirst learnt that 'Simon was persuaded to stay on by a letter [of Sunday 2 August] from Bonar Law to the PM (which Asquith showed him) offering to join the Government and see them through the war. So Simon stayed on to save the party – a queer reason.'[46]

Finally, there was the human dimension. In Anthony Trollope's Victorian political novels, jaded Radicals occasionally longed for release from moderate Cabinets. But Trollope's Radicals had to measure the freedom that resignation would grant against 'the glory of being a Minister' and against 'the advantage of Government pay, and the prestige of Government power'.[47] This was all part of 'the natural "cohesion of office"' mentioned by Morley in his account.[48] It was the consideration that Ethel Pease put to her rattled husband Jack on Tuesday 4 August, as he agonised over 'sticking to the ship': 'What do you mean by "sticking to the ship" – did you intend resigning? You could not do it now in a moment of difficulty and no business prospects to look forward to.'[49] In the same way, Margot Asquith reflected on Simon's decision to return to the Cabinet: 'what a fool he would have been to have left politics at *the* most wonderful time in history!'[50] Withdrawing his resignation was careerism, but perfectly rational. Such considerations were among the mix that had saved Asquith's Cabinet, and helped him take Britain to war.

TWENTY-FOUR

Seizing the Moment
Tuesday 4 August

His Majesty's Ambassador in Berlin has received his passports and His Majesty's Government have declared to the German Government that a state of war exists between Great Britain and Germany as from 11 p.m. on August 4.[1]

Foreign Office Statement, 4 August 1914

For Britain, Tuesday 4 August proved to be the last day of peace – although few knew it as the day dawned. On that morning, those urging Britain's immediate intervention in the war about to engulf the Continent must have scanned the newspapers with increasing alarm, for Grey's interventionist speech of Monday was receiving very choppy press. In Britain, on the very eve of the Great War, nothing even approaching unanimity was to be seen.

The Gulf in the Press on the Eve of War

In the Conservative press that Tuesday, men of power were waving their spears. The editors extolled Grey's speech of the previous day. They reconstructed their arguments for intervention in accord with his. Britain should intervene the moment Germany touched upon either of the 'triggers' to war that Grey had created – the coasts of France or the neutrality of Belgium. *The Times* accepted that Britain was 'bound' to fight, 'by treaty, by honour, and by regard for our own safety'.[2] Other Conservative newspapers beseeched support for Grey and war. Grey had spoken for the whole nation, they agreed. For example, the *Scotsman* accepted the argument that Britain must go to war to defend the French coastline as 'a debt of honour to France' as well as 'a plain obligation of duty to ourselves'. Refraining from war would be 'a deep stain on our honour'.[3]

But the members of Britain's Liberal government would naturally have been more interested in the views expressed by the important Liberal dailies, such as the *Manchester Guardian*, the *Daily News* and the *Westminster Gazette*. Were they persuaded?

In fact, the two leading Liberal newspapers that appeared on the morning of Tuesday 4 August were implacable. They denounced Grey's speech as dishonest. The *Manchester Guardian* had an angry swing at Grey. The speech was 'not fair' and 'showed that for years he has been keeping back the whole truth and telling just enough to lull [us] into a false sense of security.' Grey was guilty of undertaking a 'long course of disloyalty to popular rights'. To ask the House of Commons to decide 'at a moment's notice and in circumstances of great excitement' was 'a mockery'. True Liberals should 'refuse to give up hope that we shall yet succeed in maintaining our neutrality'.[4] The *Guardian* was also especially critical of one notorious argument in Grey's speech: his attempt to minimise the 'appalling catastrophe' of war by claiming that Britain would suffer but little more in war than in peace. This was a 'strange blunder'. It revealed his desperate wrong-headedness.[5]

Similarly, A. G. Gardiner's editorial in the *Daily News* announced that the paper was 'unconvinced'. Gardiner insisted again that Britain had no obligation to fight to preserve Belgian neutrality under the terms of the Treaty of 1839. It was not a matter of honour. Gardiner rejected Grey's case as illogical and inconsistent. His argument that all the northern neutrals would be absorbed by Germany in the wake of an attack on Belgium 'does not persuade'. The parallel possibility that much of Eastern Europe would be swallowed up by the Russian

Empire if Britain assisted the Tsarist cause had to be factored in, yet Grey had studiously ignored this. The *Daily News* did make one rueful admission, that Grey had probably 'carried the overwhelming majority of the House with him by the combination of argument and rhetoric'.[6]

Of the Liberal papers, only the *Westminster Gazette*, an afternoon paper, suddenly swung behind intervention. J. A. Spender announced in his editorial that 'Sir Edward Grey speaks for us when he explains the obligations of honour and interest that rest upon us at this moment.' Spender supported the pledge that had been given to France, and accepted Grey's argument that the violation of Belgian neutrality must be a *casus belli*. The nation could not embrace 'unconditional neutrality': 'Sir Edward Grey's arguments on this question seem to us conclusive.'[7]

Thus, notwithstanding Spender's late conversion, Wilfrid Blunt was not far from the mark when he declared in the privacy of his diary on 5 August: 'Nothing is more remarkable than the entire disregard paid by the Cabinet to the Liberal press which was solid for neutrality. The Whigs in the Cabinet have got it wholly their own way.'[8]

The First Telegram – and the Morning Cabinet

And so they did. On the morning of Tuesday 4 August, Grey and Asquith took a momentous decision – just the two of them, in a few wild minutes. Meeting at Downing Street before the Cabinet opened, they composed the first 'ultimatum' to Germany, although it was not yet called that.

This first telegram was sent to Berlin at 9.30 a.m. It was addressed to the British ambassador in Berlin, Sir Edward Goschen, but it was of course prepared for official delivery to the German Foreign Minister, Gottlieb von Jagow. The telegram noted the King of the Belgians' appeal for Britain's 'diplomatic intervention' and the Belgians' refusal of the German ultimatum on the preceding day. The telegram registered Britain's 'protest against this violation of a treaty' and requested 'an assurance that the demand made upon Belgium will not be proceeded with'. Goschen was directed to 'ask for an immediate reply'. There was no time limit mentioned – and in that sense it was not an ultimatum.[9]

It is important to stress also that this first telegram was not a response to the German invasion of Belgium. German armed forces had actually crossed the border into Belgium at about 8 a.m. on the morning of 4 August, eventually advancing on a forty-kilometre front between Gemmenich and Malmédy during the day.[10] Tyrrell informed Downing Street of this, but not until about noon, well after the first telegram was on its way.[11]

The last peacetime Cabinet began its deliberations at 11.30 a.m. Naturally there was intense interest in Simon and Beauchamp's presence. This told the essential story: Asquith had indeed split the Radicals. Samuel did the numbers, and as usual urged Beatrice to keep the matter hush-hush: 'The two Honest Johns will go [Burns and Morley] … Simon and Beauchamp will stay by us. Please say nothing about the previous resignations.'[12]

Immediately Belgium became the focus. At first, the Cabinet discussed the latest German diplomatic note to Belgium, of Tuesday morning. 'Germany has informed Belgium that her territory will be violated by force of arms' was the description Harcourt scribbled down in his notes. Now the Cabinet responded: 'We are sending an ultimatum to Germany & [are] to have the answer by midnight', Harcourt continued. What ultimatum? Harcourt recorded later in the discussion that 'Grey read us his telegram to Goschen.' It demanded by midnight an answer 'similar to that from France last week – as to the neutrality of Belgium'. These references make it clear that the telegram discussed in Cabinet was a proposed *second* telegram. This would add to the pressure upon Germany, by nominating a time limit.[13]

But the Cabinet was not of one mind on a resort to force. The Radical ministers still acted as a brake on those looking for an imperial explosion. Far horizons distracted some at the table. 'Discussed seizure of German colonies', Harcourt jotted down. 'No, better wait a bit.' He told Cabinet he was 'holding back [the] Dominion

Exped[itionary] forces for the present'. Indeed, he jokingly explained how he had just fended off Sir David de Villiers Graaff, a visiting South African politician. He had suggested that South Africa should grab German South-West Africa – if Harcourt wished it. 'Will you *not* if I ask for it?' Harcourt had replied, dramatizing the eagerness of the Dominions.[14] The Cabinet approved Harcourt's caution.

Then, at Churchill's insistence, attention moved to the Mediterranean. Here the German battleship *Goeben* was expected to threaten French troop transports from North Africa. But Britain was not yet at war. Asquith restrained Churchill's zest for combat on the basis of an enlarged pledge to France. 'Winston, who had got on all his war-paint, is longing for a sea-fight in the early hours of to-morrow morning, resulting in the sinking of the *Goeben*', Asquith wrote.[15] Asquith sided with the moderates this time. So, Churchill was 'compelled' to send orders to British ships that they should not fire on the *Goeben* 'till we have become at war with Germany'.[16]

According to Pease, the Cabinet then considered a stunning initiative in propaganda. Grey proposed a White Paper, as foreshadowed in his speech on Monday, releasing a slice of diplomatic documents from the past fortnight. This unprecedented release of diplomatic cables would require the Foreign Office staff to work at break-neck speed for the printer. But it was a political necessity. MPs had to be permitted to peer into the world of diplomacy to see British innocence and German guilt. The Cabinet was certainly preparing the political ground for war.[17] With these decisions made, the Cabinet rose.

Did the ministers accept that war with Germany was imminent? Harcourt's notes suggest they did. But if it was war, then the Royal Navy was in the limelight. There had been no discussion of the BEF. Saturday's startling decision against the BEF's deployment still stood, so ministers believed. For instance, Samuel made mention only of coming naval action: 'The first engagement is likely to be in the Mediterranean.'[18]

But had the *Cabinet* decided upon war – and a declaration of war immediately upon expiration of the ultimatum, at midnight? The records leave this fundamental point unclear. Asquith 'curiously'

failed to send his usual letter to the King summarising Cabinet's
decisions, which might have resolved this. But, as Spender noted,
'the recollection of the survivors is that the drafting of the ultimatum
was left to Asquith and Grey'.[19] Similarly, Churchill insisted in his
memoirs that *all* the 'supreme decisions' – to send an ultimatum, to
declare war on Germany, and to send the BEF to the Continent –
'were never taken at any Cabinet'. These decisions 'were compelled by
the force of events, and rest on the authority of the Prime Minister'.[20]

The ultimate decision for war certainly belonged to the inner
ring of the Cabinet. But had the rest consented on the morning of
Tuesday 4 August? Samuel thought so: 'We had another Cabinet
this morning. Unless Germany alters her whole course, which is
now impossible, we shall certainly be at war by tonight.'[21] Similarly,
as Harcourt recorded later, Grey had read an 'ultimatum' to the
Cabinet – a draft of the second telegram. But its final composition
had been left to Asquith and Grey. Therefore, there is no incontest-
able evidence that the Cabinet as a whole had been asked to vote
in advance for a declaration of war against Germany at midnight.
George Trevelyan, Grey's biographer, was correct: 'Apparently there
never was a formal decision taken in the Cabinet to go to war or to
send an ultimatum to Germany.'[22]

As Spender and Churchill had attested, Grey and Asquith took
the matter of the final composition of the ultimatum into their own
hands. When Cabinet concluded at 1.35 p.m., the two men stayed
behind and drew up a final version of the second telegram for immediate despatch.[23] Churchill had left ten minutes earlier, going straight
to Buckingham Palace to tell George V that an ultimatum had been
sent to Germany requiring an answer by midnight.[24]

The Second Telegram – and the Fate of Belgium

This brief second telegram, sent at 2 p.m., was again written in the
form of instructions from Grey to Goschen. It did not give the text
of any British 'ultimatum' to be delivered to Jagow or Bethmann
Hollweg.

The telegram directed Goschen to repeat his request for a German assurance regarding Belgian neutrality. Next came the 'ultimatum'. Goschen must 'ask that a satisfactory reply' to the two telegrams of that day 'be received here by 12 o'clock tonight'. The crucial details followed: 'If not, you are instructed to ask for your passports and to say that His Majesty's Government feel bound to take all steps in their power to uphold the neutrality of Belgium and the observance of a Treaty to which Germany is as much a party as ourselves.'[25]

But was the meaning plain – respect Belgian neutrality or face war at midnight? That is certainly one interpretation. But, in fact, the framers of the telegram had left themselves some wriggle room. The instruction to Goschen – 'ask for your passports' – indicated only one certainty, that Britain was breaking diplomatic relations. After all, Goschen had been given no text, addressed to the Germans, to announce a declaration of war.

Why? The British government certainly did not want to eliminate the possibility that Germany might act first. A German declaration of war was still preferable, in political terms. It would be much more palatable for a Liberal government and its supporters. Far better that Britain should be seen to be reacting both to a German invasion of Belgium and a German declaration of war upon Britain.

From mid-morning on Tuesday 4 August, the fact of the German invasion of neutral Belgium naturally began to dominate over all others. The fact was horrible – but it was also an event delivering enormous political gains to Asquith's government. Indeed, the Liberal politicians would have been strange specimens of the breed if they had not chosen to exploit the situation. Belgium allowed the government to transform the story of the crisis. No longer was war contemplated as a war of solidarity with the Entente, a war to save 'the balance of power' in Europe, or a war to save France – such as it had been depicted in the Tory press all week, and in the Conservative leaders' letter to Asquith. Now, miraculously, it was transformed into a war of moral imperatives, to save Belgium and the sanctity of treaties.

Asquith coolly explained to Venetia Stanley that the German action in Belgium 'simplifies matters'.[26] In fact it was a blessed turn.

The howls of indignation over the German move of 4 August were bound to drown out mutterings of Liberal resentment over the British pledge to France of 2 August. The pledge would be excused as prescient preparedness. Asquith and Grey must have speculated that *all* the resignations from the Cabinet might yet be withdrawn. Those holding out could be depicted as recalcitrant men, wilfully blind to German aggression, and the government's wider political base would be much more easily converted to war.

So great was the political boon that if the Germans had not actually invaded Belgium, it might have become necessary to invent the invasion. Certainly it was not beyond the capacity of some to pray for it. Frances Stevenson, Lloyd George's secretary and lover, had listened to her man describing the tortuous Cabinet debates during that last hectic week of peace. Later she would confess: 'In those days I was not addicted to prayer, but I think as far as I could I prayed that the Germans would invade Belgium.' Notably also, Stevenson wrote that the great Liberal lion's mind 'was really made up from the first, that he knew we would have to go in, and that the invasion of Belgium was, to be cynical, a heaven-sent excuse for supporting a declaration of war'.[27]

In a sense, the 'heaven-sent excuse' became an essential shield. Any errors that the government had made in its diplomacy – for example, its failure to restrain either Russia or France – could be forgiven in the outpouring of rage against the German action. The *faits accomplis* in naval preparations presented to Cabinet could be forgiven as necessary 'safety-first' measures against an unscrupulous aggressor. Any failures to keep the parliament fully informed could be forgiven as necessary secrecy to confound such a perfidious enemy. In Belgium, the Asquith government had an issue of such candlepower in its hands that people would be dazzled. They would certainly be distracted from the most obvious truth: that Germany's passage through Belgium was merely the occasion, not the cause, of the declaration of war. As Jerome K. Jerome expressed it later, 'Had she gone round the Cape of Good Hope the result would have been the same.'[28]

The Pretence of a Parliamentary Decision for War

If politically the German invasion of Belgium was the icing on the cake, the cake itself could now be made to fit the icing – that is, the story of the diplomatic crisis could now be retold to fit the tragic climax. The government's willingness to exploit the tragedy in Belgium was on display when the House of Commons met at 2.45 p.m. on the afternoon of Tuesday 4 August. It was pure Victorian music hall: heroes, villains – with big moustaches – and the innocent in distress.

The Cabinet had come straight from Downing Street, where Asquith and Grey had just composed the second telegram to Berlin. Belgium was kept front and centre. Asquith, who was greeted with cheers, told the Commons of the decisive diplomatic steps. He read to the House the text of the first 'telegram' to Germany on Belgium. This, according to *The Times*, 'called forth an answering roll of cheers from every quarter of the chamber'.[29] Then Asquith read from telegrams received that morning, reporting the Germans' renewed threats upon Belgium and the violation of her territory.[30] He read next the official German explanation of this, pleading for British understanding of the German attack, because it was 'a question of life or death to prevent [a] French advance'. The German note renewed the promise that no Belgian territory would be annexed. This provoked 'an outburst of incredulous laughter', reported *The Times*. Asquith dismissed the German note.[31]

Asquith then explained that the government had just sent a second 'telegram' to Berlin, but he did *not* give its text. Summarising it, he explained that it repeated the request for 'the same assurance in regard to Belgian neutrality' that France had given last week. This telegram requested 'a satisfactory answer' on the Belgian issue 'before midnight'. Immediately, and with strenuous solemnity, Asquith then walked up to the Speaker and presented him with a message from the King, which was in turn read to the House. It was a message calling out the Army Reserve on permanent service.[32] This completed the army's mobilisation.

The drama of this scene bewitched many. Margot Asquith sat in the Speaker's Gallery, 'breathless'. According to her record, everyone knew war was only hours away. 'Without *thinking* at all,' she wrote, 'this runs like the screams of the firemen through every artery and blood vessel of the heart and brain.'[33] Most MPs apparently understood that an 'ultimatum' had been presented to Germany. Even Hansard headlined the word the following day. So too did *The Times*.[34] But in fact, Asquith never used the term 'ultimatum' and never announced that war would be declared at midnight. He described each communication as a 'telegram'.[35] In addition, curiously untidy threads were left. Was the 'midnight' to be Central European Time or Greenwich Mean Time?[36] In not reading the text of the second telegram to Berlin, Asquith had avoided telling the Commons of the final instructions to Goschen – to ask for his passports.

The reaction of the House of Commons on this day testified to the political advantage flowing toward the men with the power to make war. No one replied. The House passed meekly to Orders of the Day. Remarkably, Grey did not speak. Nor did any other frontbencher approach the supreme issue. After just ninety minutes, the House adjourned.[37] *The Times* buoyantly observed that the session passed 'without the raising of a single note of controversy'.[38]

Indeed, the Radicals did not challenge Asquith. Why? Perhaps they still believed in the promised major debate before any declaration of war. But most likely, the Radicals chose to tread cautiously and wait for confirmation of the facts from Belgium. It is possible, too, that the sudden adjournment of the House, under a recent and controversial Speaker's ruling 'that was little understood', caught the Radicals off guard.[39]

If the Radicals simply lost their courage and chose silence on Tuesday 4 August, so too did the Cabinet ministers. Only one Liberal frontbencher, Grey, had been on his feet in the Commons defending intervention, on the previous day. The ornaments of British Liberalism, Asquith himself, Lloyd George, Samuel, Churchill and McKenna, had all said next to nothing on British policy. Britain prepared to go to war without her Prime Minister even arguing the case for it. He would do so only after the event.

The Rump of the Cabinet Decides for War

'There is a Cabinet meeting at midnight to consider the German reply to our ultimatum, and it is morally certain that we shall declare war', Hankey proudly told his wife that night.[40] Not so. There was no Cabinet meeting at midnight. Characteristically for the Asquith government, the ultimate step was taken not by Cabinet, but rather by a small clique bunkered down in the Cabinet room. A mere coffee-table's worth of the Cabinet gathered there on the night of Tuesday 4 August: Asquith, Grey and Haldane, joined later by Lloyd George and McKenna. This little assembly made the final choice for war. In this sense, as Keith Wilson argues, 'the Cabinet, as such, never did make a decision for war'.[41]

How, then, was the final decision made? Just after 9 p.m., the five men gathered in the Cabinet room learned from an intercepted phone message from Berlin to the German Embassy in London that, soon after 7 p.m., Goschen had demanded his passports, 'declaring war'. On the strength of this intercepted message, the five men considered the choice: peace or war? Sometime around 10 p.m. they made their decision: Britain must formally declare war upon Germany, and do so immediately upon the expiration of the 'midnight' deadline. Then the ministers suddenly chose to advance this to 11 p.m., London time, just in case the Germans should make a great raid on British shipping or coasts. 'We resolved to wait until eleven', as Lloyd George wrote. Significantly, no request for military assistance from Belgium had arrived when the ministers made their decision – although it was on its way.[42]

At the Foreign Office on that same evening there was some confusion. According to Harold Nicolson, the great Foreign Office building on Whitehall was filled with staff and stiflingly warm. In this atmosphere, dozens of draft telegrams were prepared to inform all parts of the Empire of the outbreak of war, with spaces left blank to meet either of the two eventualities, a British or a German declaration. Also drafted was a simple letter to accompany passports for Lichnowsky, reflecting the more likely event, a British declaration of war.[43]

But hope still lingered during the evening at the Foreign Office – as at 10 Downing Street – that Germany might leap first. Thus, when the Admiralty intercepted a wireless message to all German shipping about imminent war, it was interpreted as meaning that *Germany* had declared war. The Foreign Office had this information at 9.40 p.m. Work began immediately with rubber stamps to finalise the dozens of telegrams prepared for the Empire. So too a fresh letter was prepared for Lichnowsky on the basis of a fortuitous German declaration. A Foreign Office man delivered this letter to Lichnowsky at the German Embassy at 9 Carlton House Terrace about 10 p.m.[44] When the Foreign Office discovered that the Germans had made no such declaration, there was panic. It was decided the incorrect letter delivered to Lichnowsky had to be retrieved.

The young Harold Nicolson was ordered to undertake 'this invidious mission'. He returned to the darkened Embassy soon after 11 p.m., gaining admission at a small door on the Duke of York steps. A footman explained that the ambassador was now asleep. Pleading the importance of his mission, Nicolson was shown upstairs to a lamp-lit bedroom. He politely explained to Lichnowsky, who was 'reclining in pyjamas' on a brass bedstead, that 'there had been a slight error in the document previously delivered'. A new letter was slipped into a torn envelope containing the passports, and a receipt signed.[45]

The blunder serves to underline the politics in this story right through to the denouement: a German declaration of war suited the men at the Foreign Office, so they had jumped at the shadow of it.

The Women's Last Defiance of War

While all this was happening, just one mile away at the Kingsway Hall in Holborn, a protest meeting against war had begun at 8 p.m. The new hall seated 2,000 people. They had come in numbers, responding to calls from the international women's movement and women's trade unions.[46]

The hall was 'crowded to overflowing' and the speeches were rousing. Millicent Garrett Fawcett, presiding for the IWSA, opened the rally in a pessimistic tone, noting that war had already broken out. When she denounced the 'insensate devilry of war', there was a burst of applause.[47] Louise Creighton, widow of the late Bishop of London, also spoke moderately as she presented a first resolution, urging arbitration.[48] But the next speaker, Eleanor Barton of the Women's Cooperative Guild, struck a rebellious note. 'No enmity', she argued, 'exists between the work-people of England and the work-people of Germany.' To illustrate this, she told of an incident that took place as her train had left Sheffield, when an older British sailor in uniform and two young Germans had greeted each other and denounced their governments. This speech got 'a great reception'. Two speakers, Helena Swanwick and Mabel St Clair Stobart, then pleaded the case that female suffrage was essential to build peace.

The international speakers, with their accents, brought emotional punch. Madame Gellrich of Germany 'received a great welcome'. She urged the reconciliation of Britain and Germany, led by women, who would defy men with the message 'there must be no war'. Rosika Schwimmer spoke of her homeland, Hungary, already disrupted by war. The Hungarian parliament had closed, because the Speaker and many members 'had gone into the firing-line' – a remark that prompted ironic cheers from those suspicious of Britain's gallant politicians. Next Madame Malmberg, representing Finland, raised the tender issue of Russia. 'The Jingo Press', she claimed, 'was ashamed to mention Russia as Britain's friend and ally. Britain was really being asked to fight to keep the Czar upon his throne and enable him to beat down the free people of her native land.' Finally, speaking for Switzerland, Madame Lucy Thoumaian mocked the social-Darwinist assumptions and pseudo-religiosity that lurked behind war. War was not 'a dispensation from the Almighty', nor was it 'something like measles, that we cannot avoid', she argued. 'It is not from God this war. It is a man made war, and it is for woman to unmake it.' The first resolution passed in a storm of applause.

A second resolution followed, urging women's societies everywhere to assist 'the sufferers' in war. Two British women labour activists made this a radical rallying cry. First, Mary Macarthur challenged those urging war for Britain's 'honour'. 'Was it to the honour of England that millions of women should be toiling for starvation wages and little children should be suffering?' Genuine honour should prompt a 'war against poverty'. The speech of Marion Phillips, a young Australian, was prophetic. Phillips called for 'a real sisterhood, working for common needs, which no Government and no wars could ever break again'. The second resolution was carried by acclamation.

What was the significance of the rally? Only the Liberal and Labour papers covered it. The *Daily News* called it 'a last rally of peace forces and common sense'.[49] *The Times* ignored it completely. A sense of defeat weighed upon some of the women even as they left the Kingsway Hall. Margaret Bondfield, for example, noted in her diary that she swiftly came upon the 'Guards on [their] way to Dover'.[50] Many historians ignore the rally, as if it were a forgettable exercise in sentimentalism. But the meeting was one for the ages. Representing about twelve million women, the IWSA had denounced war on its very eve.[51] As Evelyn Sharp noted, it was unprecedented that so many had spoken out 'on behalf of womanhood and childhood and the home'. The rally was 'a protest, passionate, sane, and practical, of the civilised against the barbaric'.[52] Similarly, as Maude Royden argued, the rally exhibited the real mood of vast numbers of people. Women 'had come to protest with all the strength that was in them against war'. Royden stressed that the speakers that night who spoke only of social work to relieve distress were 'coldly received', but speakers 'who denounced the war' provoked a great response. 'To many,' she concluded, 'the tone of this meeting, gathered together in so haphazard a way, was a revelation of the force of anti-war feeling amongst women of the working class.'[53]

The King, the Privy Council, and the Declaration of War

Over those same two hours, the men choosing war considered the means. How exactly was Great Britain to declare war? British constitutional procedures and international law had to be respected. Under the terms of the Hague Convention III of 1907, a formal declaration of war was required prior to hostilities.

But there was no requirement for anything so transparent as a Cabinet minute recording a choice for war – and nothing so dangerously democratic as a parliamentary decision. Of course, the Liberal leaders claimed to believe in the supremacy of the House of Commons. But they slid away from this. When it came to making war, all the respected legal authorities, from Blackstone to Dicey, declared grandly that the Crown held the power, as a part of the Royal Prerogative.[54] So too Lord Halsbury's new Edwardian masterpiece, the *Laws of England*, confirmed it: 'declarations of war and peace, are intrusted solely to him [the monarch] and his ministers'.[55]

What body, then, could authorise war? The King's Privy Council – the instrument of the Royal Prerogative – was near at hand. Again, the eminent constitutional authorities offered no suggestion that the Privy Council was subject to democratic procedures. Halsbury noted that there were almost 300 Privy Councillors by the time George V ascended the throne, but no quorum was required for meetings.[56] A tiny fragment of this body was sufficient to rubberstamp the decision for war.

Sir Almeric FitzRoy, the Clerk of the Privy Council, worked closely with Asquith to secure exactly this outcome. FitzRoy, a believer in intervention, had been carefully monitoring the Cabinet's debates. By 4 August, he had organised a timetable of the movements of two compliant Liberal Privy Councillors at court, Viscount Allendale, Lord-in-Waiting, and the Earl of Granard, Master of the Horse. Both agreed to be near a telephone and to dash to a Privy Council when required.[57]

The Privy Council was busy on Tuesday 4 August. At Buckingham Palace in the afternoon came a kind of dress rehearsal for the big moment. Morley saw the King, explained his resignation, and then presided over his last Council. It was a small gathering. Five proclamations, connected with army mobilisation, were approved.[58] Soon after, the Archbishop of Canterbury and the Bishop of London joined another small Council. It commissioned the Archbishop to compose a 'Special Form of Intercession with Almighty God' on behalf of Britain's fighting men.[59] The nation prepared to lean on the arm of God – or the tribal deity that passed for God in these circles.

Late in the evening of Tuesday came the next dramatic summons. After Asquith's closest satellites had agreed upon war at Downing Street, at 10.15 p.m. the Prime Minister contacted FitzRoy. He instructed him to call a Privy Council at Buckingham Palace as soon as possible. 'In a quarter of an hour I had my men on the spot', FitzRoy recorded proudly.[60] King George V wrote in his diary that Asquith himself had telephoned Buckingham Palace at 10.30 p.m. 'to say that Goschen had been given his passports at 7.0[0] this evening'.[61] War it was to be. It was Asquith's choice. At exactly this time, soon after 10 p.m., when the Kingsway Hall rally ended, Fawcett and several other speakers, forming a small deputation, brought a copy of the two resolutions around to 10 Downing Street. An envelope containing the resolutions was posted through the door.[62] This must have landed in the hall at about the time Asquith was telephoning FitzRoy and the King with his request for a Privy Council to declare war.

In an excruciating twist for Beauchamp – remembering how recently he had withdrawn his resignation – he was asked to represent the government at this Privy Council. Beauchamp agreed. He was the only Cabinet minister present and was listed as 'Acting for the Lord President of the Council'.[63] Seated with the King were just three men: Earl Beauchamp, Lord Allendale and Earl Granard. This tiny Privy Council opened at 10.35 p.m.[64]

The Privy Council had one vital task, to confer formal approval upon the actual declaration of war. Two detailed proclamations on shipping and contraband did the trick.[65] There was no clarion call to a war for freedom, democracy or civilisation. Rather, the proclamations simply referred to an existing state of war.[66] It took almost no time. As FitzRoy wrote, 'at a few minutes after 10.30 the order indicative of a state of war was approved'.[67] Thus, all immediate legalities were complete. The King, acting on the advice of his Prime Minister, and assisted by just three Privy Councillors, had 'declared war'. The King recorded the fact: 'I held a Council at 10.45 to declare war with Germany, it is a terrible catastrophy [sic], but it is not our fault.'[68] Faithfully reflecting the pre-democratic order, four men had launched Britain's war. There was not one elected man among them.

While the Privy Council was swiftly approving the war, the sounds of a large crowd in front of Buckingham Palace could be heard. People had been gathering since sunset, until 'the Victoria Memorial was black with people', singing, clapping and hooting.[69] Appearances by the King and Queen, with David, the Prince of Wales (the future Edward VIII), and Princess Mary, excited the 'enormous crowd'. The Royal Family had made the first of a series of appearances on the new palace balcony at about 7 p.m., provoking a 'mighty cheer' from the crowd, which then sang the national anthem 'with the utmost fervour'.[70] After dinner, at about 9.30 p.m. the Royal Family had appeared again. Then, according to one newspaper, around the time of the Privy Council's meeting, the crowds were hushed by the Bobbies: 'the police passed the word around that silence was necessary as the King was holding a meeting in the Palace'.[71] But soon after 11 p.m., with the Council concluded, the Royal Family came back onto the balcony. The sea of people gave them a rapturous reception. The King recorded the event: 'When they heard that War had been declared the excitement increased & it was a never to be forgotten sight when May & I with David went on to the balcony, the cheering was terrific. Please God it may soon be over & that he will protect dear Bertie's life [Albert, the future George VI].'[72]

According to *The Times*, the crowd in front of Buckingham Palace grew silent at midnight, believing the chimes from Big Ben marked the onset of war. Then they cheered 'for nearly twenty minutes' and sang the national anthem.[73] The small group of Asquith's courtiers still gathered at 10 Downing Street at midnight knew better – by their decree Britain's war was in fact already an hour old.

At the Foreign Office, the last formality in the drama took place just after midnight. An official single-sentence statement was issued to the press, announcing that it was war – war for Belgium:

Owing to the summary rejection by the German Government of the request made by His Majesty's Government for assurances that the neutrality of Belgium will be respected, His Majesty's Ambassador in Berlin has received his passports and His Majesty's Government have declared to the German Government that a state of war exists between Great Britain and Germany as from 11 p.m. on August 4.[74]

It is worth stressing that among the major powers Great Britain was the only one to resort to a declaration of war at the very instant her own ultimatum expired. Goschen passed on the ultimatum to Jagow in Berlin at about 7 p.m. Berlin time on the Tuesday.[75] Thus, the British declaration of war came just five hours later, at midnight, Berlin time. Comparisons with other ultimata and declarations of war are instructive. Austria-Hungary declared war on Serbia at about noon on Tuesday 28 July, three days after the expiration of the Austro-Hungarians' forty-eight-hour ultimatum. Germany's ambassador in St Petersburg passed over the declaration of war on Russia at 7 p.m. on Saturday 1 August, seven hours after the expiration of the Germans' twelve-hour ultimatum. In the case of France, the Germans waited much longer. Germany's ambassador in Paris passed over the declaration of war on France at about 6.45 p.m. on Monday 3 August, more than two days after the expiration of the Germans' twelve-hour ultimatum.[76] London waited least.

Of course, a German declaration of war would have been in every way more acceptable. So acceptable that rumours of it were still spreading, in spite of the facts. They reached high places. For example, at 11.30 p.m. that night Amery and General Wilson telephoned Milner with the happy news. 'Germany has declared war on us', wrote Milner in his diary, adding, 'It is *better* to have *an end* to the uncertainty.'[77] There were no long faces in these circles.

Swift decisions by handfuls of men took Britain to war in a great leap. In the face of war itself, the politicians could invoke the safety of the nation, and undoubtedly gain the benefit of the doubt. By Asquith's rapid decision, both the full Cabinet and the Parliament were to be confronted, yet again, not with a choice but with a hugely powerful *fait accompli*. A great majority in favour of war, essential for the survival of the government itself, could be bumped into being by one last rushed act – the declaration of war itself.

From War for Belgium to War for Empire

In the aftermath of the declaration there were rough lessons – starting at Downing Street. At about midnight, Churchill and Harcourt joined the men keeping vigil there as the lamps of peace were snuffed out. Churchill shocked the little company by announcing it was time to block Amsterdam and the mouth of the Rhine, violating Dutch neutrality. His amazed colleagues reminded him, 'Our defence of small nationalities [is] our greatest asset. We insisted on this.' Then Harcourt was appalled as some at the table pressed for the immediate despatch of the BEF to the Continent. Shocked, Harcourt stood firm. He pleaded that this would endanger India. Moreover, he warned, troops might soon be vital in England to deal with 'possible revolution in [the] North'.[78] After all, this was a class society embarking upon war.

In any case, within hours the much-heralded defensive war for the sake of Belgium began to escalate into a war of imperial spoils. The very next morning, Wednesday 5 August, Harcourt chaired a joint committee to make recommendations to Cabinet on expeditions to capture various German colonies – German East Africa, German South-West Africa, Togoland, the Cameroons, German New Guinea, Nauru and Samoa.[79] In the same spirit, the full Cabinet that met at 11.30 a.m. discussed widening the war. 'Can we buy Italy?' Harcourt speculated in his notes: 'Tell them if they go in with us they can have our help on the Adriatic coast against Austria.'[80] But would British troops be used in Europe? Still Asquith hedged on this. He told the Cabinet that he was meeting with the military men in the afternoon 'to examine use, *if any*, of troops'.[81]

In the aftermath of the declaration of war, many Radicals still cherished the hope that if war itself could not be resisted, the despatch of the BEF might still be refused and Britain spared immersion in total war.[82] The War Council that gathered in the afternoon at 10 Downing Street had other ideas. Only the interventionist ministers, Asquith, Haldane, Churchill and Grey, sat down with the military chiefs, Lord Kitchener, Lord Roberts, John French, Douglas Haig, Henry Wilson and others. Various sworn enemies of the government were now advising it. For example, Roberts was the incorrigible President of the National Service League, and Wilson's diary for the last month was peppered with denunciations of Asquith's 'pestilent government', 'Squiff and his filthy Cabinet' and the 'cursed Cabinet' of pacifists.[83] Since the morning of Tuesday 4 August Wilson had been colluding with leading Tories to twist arms and get Asquith to 'send the "Expeditionary Force" *at once*'.[84] Wilson had his way. The War Council recommended that the BEF should be sent to the Continent immediately.[85]

The next morning, Thursday 6 August, the Cabinet would crumple. With Kitchener at the table as War Secretary – an appointment pressed hard by the Tories[86] – the Cabinet doffed its cap. The bulk of the BEF was to go to the Continent.[87] Kitchener told the Liberal ministers that Britain must 'put armies of millions in the field' and prepare for 'great battles on the Continent'. This was met with 'silent assent', so Churchill recalled.[88] It was a complete victory for the continentalists. Schemes for the seizure of German colonies and radio stations were swiftly approved. Harcourt, the former Radical, warmed to his new tasks: 'German colonies: I shall take most of them.'[89] Asquith made light of this. In the evening he shared with Venetia Stanley the joke he had offered his Cabinet colleagues that 'we looked more like a gang of Elizabethan buccaneers than a meek collection of black-coated Liberal Ministers.'[90]

While all this was being planned, the parliament was easily bounced. On the previous afternoon, Wednesday 5 August, Asquith had told the Commons nothing about the military plans already contemplated by the government. He read the text of the Belgian appeal for military assistance – and clearly Belgian resistance was even more important in building support for Britain's war than was the invasion of Belgium itself.[91] He explained gravely that he could tell the House nothing more.[92] Next day, Thursday 6 August, Asquith would introduce in the House of Commons the War Credit of £100 million. But again, where would British forces fight? In his speech Asquith did not reveal the plan to send the BEF to the Continent.[93] In deciding on the War Credit, MPs still imagined a naval war.

But the deceptions were to pass unnoticed. Asquith's focus

upon Belgium, echoing Grey, succeeded fabulously. Even the Radicals, faced with war as a declared fact, did not oppose the War Credit. But they found their voices. The first Radical to speak was Arthur Ponsonby. Amid jeers and shouts of 'Sit Down!' he stood his ground. 'The war was not made from the correspondence on the White Paper,' he asserted. 'The causes of the war are far back beyond that, and I profoundly disagree with the policy that has been pursued and that has culminated in this war.' He shouted that the war was 'a diplomatists' war and not a peoples' war'. Boldly he prophesied that facts beyond the White Paper would eventually be discovered. Then people would see 'that we were committed to a friendship with France long ago, though declarations to the contrary were made to us. I regret very much that we were deceived on that point.'[94]

That speech, in Asquith's face, testified to Radical passion. Ponsonby's colleagues Willoughby Dickinson, Josiah Wedgwood, Wilfrid Lawson, Arnold Rowntree, Aneurin Williams, and Allen Baker made similar speeches. Most announced immediately that they would support the Vote of Credit – because war had arrived as the ultimate *fait accompli*. Beginning his speech, Wedgwood declared, 'As I do not want my country to be beaten, I shall certainly vote for this Vote of Credit.'[95] 'I believe we all agree that we must vote this money, and that we must see our country through this crisis,' Aneurin Williams announced.[96] But speaker after speaker from the Radical benches, amid interruptions and calls for an instant division, blamed the 'policy of the Entente' for producing the catastrophe. 'I do believe that if we had had a different policy in the past, we might have prevented this war,' said Allen Baker.[97] In short, the Radicals in the parliament acknowledged that Britain must now be defended – but they refused to leave uncriticised the foreign policy that, they believed, had tumbled Britain into the European cataclysm.

The majority of MPs accepted the case for war as unanswerable. As various journalists later recalled, Britain's governors had 'poetised the smash'. One wrote, 'It's the same kind of sureness you'd have about what to do when a kiddy falls into the river. Not reason and proof and all that. Simply sureness.'[98] War for 'a moral purpose' was insisted upon. 'Men couldn't do this thing unless they persuaded themselves out of their minds.'[99] Britain's little army was off to Europe, to save Belgium. 'The long, unendurable nightmare had begun. And the reign of Cant, Delusion, and Delirium.'[100]

TWENTY-FIVE

Radical Recriminations

All has turned out as I expected. The violation of Belgium gives only a very convenient excuse – and most valuable to the war section of the Cabinet – to solidify the Party and the Country. I never had any doubt that Grey's policy would end in a great European war. And that whenever it suited Russia to advance – then we would sink and would inevitably go in.[1]

John Dillon, 12 August 1914

In his grand speech of Thursday 6 August 1914, Asquith told the House of Commons that his government had 'made every effort any government could possibly make for peace'. Could anyone doubt, he asked, that Grey had pursued peace and had 'persisted to the very last moment of the last hour in that beneficent but unhappily frustrated purpose?'[2]

But some did doubt it. Some highly placed Britons with rare insights into these events doubted it. Recriminations bubbled away.

Recrimination I: The 'Redistribution of the Fleets'

One source of recrimination was Grey's appeal at the height of the crisis to a British obligation to fight for France on the basis of the so-called 'redistribution' of the French and British fleets.[3] The coasts of France were undefended, he had pleaded, on Monday 3 August. Thus, Britain had a moral obligation to stand with France. The assurances given the Cabinet in 1912 – that there was no obligation – were as nothing.[4] As Cabinet looked on, Grey had wrung hearts over moral obligation. Loreburn, the retired minister, was incensed at this. Britain's war, he wrote, had resulted from 'the insensate engagement we made with France in secret'.[5]

Radical MPs and journalists were enraged too. In Percy Molteno's opinion, Britain had been set up for moral blackmail – and her own leaders had then blackmailed the parliament. He protested on 5 August that the government had swallowed French intimidation, making Britain's plunge into war 'automatic'.[6] A week later, surveying the course of the crisis, Charles Montague wrote to C. P. Scott that clearly 'the Mediterranean naval arrangement with France, years ago, was a deadly piece of self-committal, without the nation's knowledge'.[7]

Insiders knew it. Lord Beauchamp, although he had rejoined the Cabinet in August 1914, nursed deep resentments. In 1922 he wrote publicly that Grey's appeal to the 'redistribution of the fleets' on the eve of the war had only exposed how Britain's freedom of action had been compromised in 1912.[8] He agreed with Molteno that Churchill's naval deal was 'the worst feature of pre-war activities'.[9] In 1930 he told G. P. Gooch, co-editor of the official *British Documents on the Origins of the War*, that the details of Churchill's pre-war naval deals were 'never communicated to the British Cabinet'. The pledge to France, extorted from the Cabinet on Sunday 2 August 1914, had shredded all hope of neutrality.[10] The Germans, he lamented, must have regarded all Britain's professions of peace before the war as 'hypocritical'.[11]

Radicals were not alone in telling this tale of last-minute revelations of compromising military deals. In February 1922, Austen

Chamberlain spoke candidly to the Commons about the events of Monday 3 August 1914. 'We found ourselves on a certain Monday', he recalled, 'listening to a speech by Lord Grey at this box.' It was 'the first public notification to the country' of these 'obligations'. As a result of 'the closest negotiations and arrangements', Britain and France were bound together. 'There was not a word on paper binding this country,' Chamberlain conceded, 'but in honour it was bound as it had never been bound before.'[12] As an interventionist in 1914 he approved, of course – but he admitted the secrecy, and the consequences of the secrecy.

Recrimination II: 'Document 123'

Very late in the evening of Wednesday 5 August, the Foreign Office published the White Paper entitled *Correspondence Respecting the European Crisis*. Suddenly more than 150 selected diplomatic exchanges were in the hands of the parliamentarians and the press.[13] The purpose was to persuade MPs of the justice of Britain's cause when Asquith requested the War Credit on Thursday 6 August.

When Asquith addressed the House, most MPs had barely had time to read the White Paper. So rushed was the production that, unbelievably, someone forgot to distribute it to the House of Lords.[14] Asquith distilled it for the bewildered MPs. Following the example of *The Times*, he highlighted just two documents, 'Document 85' and 'Document 101'.[15] Stoking forensic indignation, Asquith explained that these showed the Germans' 'infamous proposal' designed to seduce Britain into neutrality, and Grey's heroic rejection of that barefaced bribery. Clearly Britain had striven for peace; Germany had driven straight for war. Britain was fighting, he declared, 'to fulfil a solemn international obligation' and 'to vindicate the principle that small nations are not to be crushed'.[16] After a short debate, the £100 million Vote of Credit to prosecute the war was passed – without a division.[17]

Naturally the Conservative press hailed Asquith's self-righteous speech on the White Paper.[18] Opinion-makers on all sides were bowled over by the disgorging of diplomatic secrets. Lo and behold! There was not a single spider in the Foreign Office cupboard. For example, the historian Hugh Seton-Watson told Hirst that in his opinion 'democracy with a big D has never yet made such a triumphant raid into diplomacy before'.[19]

Then Grey's Radical critics saw 'Document 123'. This telegram from Grey to Goschen, dated Saturday 1 August 1914, gave a summary of a conversation with Lichnowsky. It recorded the German ambassador asking whether 'if Germany gave a promise not to violate Belgium [*sic*] neutrality we [Britain] would engage to remain neutral'. Grey had declined: 'I replied that I could not say that; our hands were still free, and we were considering what our attitude should be.' Lichnowsky then asked whether Grey could not 'formulate conditions' under which Britain might 'engage to remain neutral'. Lichnowsky had 'even suggested that the integrity of France and her colonies might be guaranteed'. The exchange revealed Germany's willingness to increase her offer to achieve safety in the west. At the very least, it was an invitation to negotiate. And Grey had replied that he 'felt obliged to refuse definitely any promise to remain neutral on similar terms, and I could only say that we must keep our hands free'.[20]

Radicals were aghast at this. It appeared that Germany *had* offered to respect Belgian neutrality – and had been told it would gain her nothing. In Radical eyes, the real agenda was exposed: Britain wished to fight for France, irrespective of Belgium. Moreover, neither Grey nor Asquith had mentioned this German approach in their major war speeches of Monday 3, Tuesday 4 and Thursday 6 August.

Some recalled the speech by Llewelyn Williams on this very issue in the Commons debate on Monday 3 August. Grey had insisted on two special concerns for Britain, Williams had noted – the French coastline and Belgian neutrality. Germany had then offered not to use her fleet against that coastline if Britain was neutral. Surely Grey should continue negotiating, Williams had pleaded. Even on the very night of the debate, Williams had entreated Grey to ask Germany the question: 'If we remain neutral, are you willing not to bombard the towns of France with your fleet, *and* to respect the neutrality of

Belgium?'[21] After Williams finished, Lloyd George had waved him down to the front bench for a private word: this was 'the very thing' he had pressed on the Cabinet, said Lloyd George, 'and carried by a 2/3 rds majority'. But he blamed Germany for not taking up the offer. 'If Germany had accepted, we should be kept out of war', said Lloyd George.[22] Lloyd George, and even Haldane, had toyed with such an offer being made to Germany.[23] But 'Document 123' demonstrated there was never such an offer to Germany. It was 'the very thing' Grey would *not* do: he would not offer British neutrality to Germany on any conditions – even when Germany offered to respect Belgian neutrality.

Grey's critics were appalled at his failure to pursue the German offer. Grey should have sought its authorisation at the very least, Eversley remarked to Hirst.[24] Hirst believed the document proved 'that the British Government could probably have secured not only the neutrality of Great Britain but the neutrality of Belgium and the neutrality of the Channel'.[25] James Anson Farrer, a Radical barrister, cousin of the Liberal peer Lord Farrer, concluded that Germany was clearly willing to negotiate to get 'our neutrality at almost any price'. 'If I read aright document no. 123 in the White Paper,' he explained, 'she was prepared to offer not only the neutrality of Belgium but the integrity both of France and her colonies.' The offer of Saturday 1 August was 'a great extension' on the first. Why then, Farrer asked, had Grey 'broken off' negotiations on Thursday 30 July, 'four days before Germany actually threatened Belgium'?[26] The Radical MPs were quick off the mark. Meeting on the morning of Friday 7 August, seventeen Radical MPs considered Morrell's argument for releasing a fiery statement to the press on 'Document 123'. Assured that Norman Angell was still preparing material on the matter, they opted for delay.[27]

But the Radical peer Lord Courtney harried his colleagues. He alerted Scott to the 'terrible document'.[28] He threatened Crewe on Sunday 9 August that he would make 'a brief plain statement' in the Lords, complaining that Grey, Asquith and Crewe himself had failed to mention 'Document 123' in their parliamentary speeches pressing the case for war.[29] Over the weekend, Lady Courtney challenged her neighbour in Chelsea, Eleanor Acland, wife of Francis Acland, Under-Secretary for Foreign Affairs. Acland was in awe of Grey, and shared his scorn for all German attempts to 'bargain'.[30] Acland sent his wife Eleanor next door on Sunday evening with the Foreign Office explanation: Grey had 'rightly refused to say anything' in response to Lichnowsky on 1 August 'because that *same day* Germany had *officially* refused to guarantee to respect the neutralization of Belgium' – a reference to Germany's reply to Grey's telegram of Friday 31 July. This 'made no impression' on the Courtneys. Grey had hidden the German offer, they protested. 'Lady Courtney marched up and down the room wringing her hands and saying, "We might have done more!"'[31] After agonising for three days, Courtney let the matter drop in the Lords, believing 'at this hour [it] would be futile for good'.[32]

Most Radicals believed the document had exposed Grey's premature commitment to war. In Courtney's words, Grey had spurned Lichnowsky because he realised 'that all conditions were futile since he was irreclaimably committed to active co-operation in war'.[33] Llewelyn Williams concluded in his diary that 'Document 123' exposed a hard truth: 'Grey did his level best to prevent the outbreak of war, but he did not lift a finger to keep us out of it after it had become inevitable. He felt that he *must* go in support of France.'[34] This percolated down into the Liberal Party as *the* interpretation. For example, William Clark, a Liberal celebrity, conceded that the White Paper showed Grey had 'worked hard for peace' until war broke out in the east, 'but after that he seems to have determined that we must go into it'.[35] Loreburn agreed that 'Grey and the others did earnestly desire to avoid war but they had tied themselves up with France.'[36]

In this controversy, one more nagging question arose. Did Grey tell the key Cabinet of Sunday morning – the Cabinet that agreed to the naval pledge – about Lichnowsky's offers as exposed in 'Document 123'? When Burns learned of the document, he told Courtney he was 'furious', complaining 'that 123 had never been communicated to him'.[37] None of the detailed accounts of that Sunday morning Cabinet make any mention of Grey revealing Lichnowsky's offer.[38] Morley simply recorded his disappointment at Grey's 'wooden *non possumus* [we cannot]' attitude. Grey had discounted Lichnowsky's 'ideas and suggestions' as 'merely personal and unauthorized by instructions'.[39] Morley gave no detail. It is almost certain, therefore, that Grey did not tell the critical Sunday Cabinet about the specifics of Lichnowsky's renewed attempts to negotiate.

However, Harcourt did record that on Monday 3 August Grey told the morning Cabinet about Lichnowsky's new pledge, that Germany would not attack the French coast – because Grey and Asquith had made this a red line. But again Grey threw cold water on the offer. 'Grey does not think Lichnowsky is authorized to say this', wrote Harcourt in his Cabinet notes.[40] In fact, that same day the German Embassy made the offer official.[41] The pattern was repeated: Germany produced offers, and Grey threw up his hands.

The Radical press took up 'Document 123' during August. C. P. Scott wrote that he would 'not shrink' from chasing the truth.[42] The *Manchester Guardian* invited an explanation for 'Document 123'.[43] None came. In the *Nation* Bertrand Russell provided one: 'It thus appears that the neutrality of Belgium, the integrity of France and her colonies, and the naval defence of the northern and western coasts of France, were all mere pretexts. If Germany had agreed to our demands in all these respects, we should still not have promised neutrality.'[44]

In late August the Germans revived the issue, publishing Lichnowsky's cables that showed Grey's own 'kite-flying' regarding neutrality on Saturday 1 August. The government had to respond. In an inspired article, *The Times* blamed Lichnowsky for misunderstanding Grey.[45] This prompted Keir Hardie to quiz Grey regarding 'Document 123' in the House of Commons on 27 August. Grey responded with the Foreign Office 'line': Lichnowsky's proposals were mere 'personal suggestions' that could not be taken to Cabinet. As Hardie persisted on the matter, the shout 'Coward' was heard.[46]

But the controversy rattled on, for years. Why, Radicals asked, was 'Document 123' included in the White Paper if Lichnowsky's offers were valueless?[47] Ramsay MacDonald fiercely assailed the Grey myth. The documents showed Grey had brusquely spurned all German offers, MacDonald alleged, and 'no attempt was made to negotiate diplomatically to improve them'. Then, in speeches committing the nation to war, both Grey and Asquith had 'withheld the full truth from us'.[48] It was the conclusion that best fitted the evidence.

Recrimination III: The Half-Truth of a War for Belgium

As the nation learned on the outbreak of war, the reason for British intervention was Germany's failure to respect Belgian neutrality. On Thursday 6 August, in his first major speech on the war, Asquith fixed upon Belgium – only Belgium – as the reason for Britain's war. Germany had tried to bribe Britain to desert Belgium and France, with her 'infamous proposal' of July 30 on neutrality. But, as Asquith explained, Britain could not abandon Belgium – so she had dashed into war on her behalf.[49]

This, at best, was a shiny half-truth. Few at the centre of power doubted that Britain would have entered the war to assist France, even if Belgium had been left free – or indeed if France had invaded Belgium pleading defensive purposes, as Joffre had planned.[50] Belgium fireproofed the Liberal Cabinet. Of course, Belgium made a difference, a huge difference, to the nation's reaction, once war arrived as a fact. Even for some Radical MPs, it changed their whole outlook. For example, Josiah Wedgwood volunteered for military service, declaring he couldn't leave France 'in the lurch'.[51] Some peace celebrities flipped over, Andrew Carnegie for one, who sent an open letter to *The Times* acknowledging that Britain 'was in honour bound to protect Belgium'.[52]

But seasoned critics of Grey were full of contempt for this explanation. For example, just one week into the war, John Dillon, deputy leader of the Irish Parliamentary Party, wrote to C. P. Scott:

> All has turned out as I expected. The violation of Belgium gives only a very convenient excuse – and most valuable to the war section of the Cabinet – to solidify the Party and the Country. I never had any doubt that Grey's policy would end in a great European war. And that whenever it suited Russia to advance –

then we would sink and would inevitably go in … The Blame is hard to apportion – no doubt – the German war party must bear a good share. But I cannot resist the conviction the greater share of the guilt lies with the new English foreign policy identified with Rosebery and Grey.[53]

Much early Radical recrimination was necessarily private – British soldiers and sailors were putting their lives on the line. 'If Germany had attacked us,' Ponsonby wrote to his wife Dolly on 5 August, 'I should be in the street myself waving a flag, but to plunge us into a war because of the technical interpretation of a treaty made in 1839 is criminal folly.'[54] Ponsonby began a personal 'war diary' with a series of angry rhetorical questions: 'Do we stand purely for the protection of Small Countries – did we go to war only to protect little Belgium [?] – if little Belgium was at the further end of Europe should we have lifted a finger to help her [?] – look at Persia.'[55] Ponsonby recorded the true causes: 'We are not fighting to protect a weak and small nation. We are not fighting to preserve Belgian neutrality. We are fighting because we are jealous of the power of Germany.' The government, he asserted, had foolishly joined with Germany's continental rivals and had 'plotted and prepared to frustrate her and to take whatever pretext was handy when the most favourable moment came to shatter her. "We" being the Government – not the people.'[56]

Llewelyn Williams recorded in his diary the typical Radical's conclusion. Asquith and Grey, he alleged, were speaking endlessly about Belgium to distract from their own 'insincere declarations of non-entanglement' with France. Talk of the rights of small nations was all 'fudge and fustian', and 'is used to salve the conscience of Lloyd George'.[57] Anti-war Radicals pressed this case upon pro-war Radicals. For example, Vernon Lee put it to H. G. Wells that Belgium was 'a mere excuse' for British entry, and that Britain had been 'bullying' Belgium to resist, fatally 'embroiling her as chief battlefield'.[58] Later Morley preserved this same complaint in his memorandum. It was clear, he wrote, that 'the precipitate and peremptory blaze about Belgium was due less to indignation at the violation of a Treaty than to natural perception of the plea that it would furnish for intervention on behalf of France, for expeditionary force, and all the rest of it'.[59]

The Radicals also perceived that Conservative pressure, and the Liberal leaders' resignation threats, had driven the Cabinet's choice for war, on Sunday 2 August, *before* the Belgian complication. Morley regaled his fellow dissenters with his memories on this point. Threats of resignation came early, possibly as early as Wednesday 29 July. According to MacDonald this proved 'the subordination of Belgium in the cause of the war'. He concluded, 'Belgium had nothing whatever to do with the Cabinet decisions. Without it there would have been more resignations but there still would have been a war.'[60] Similarly, Radical MPs heard from Cabinet insiders that Belgian neutrality 'did weigh with four or five of the Cabinet – in any case it would have been war – only war, with a Coalition ministry owing to resignations.'[61]

Many suspected that the rage about Belgium was also being exploited to blur the timing of the British commitment to war. The issue of timing was crucial. For Radicals perceived that Belgium was in a very real sense a victim of *both* the rival alliance systems. Britain had committed herself to war for the Entente on Sunday 2 August, as war dawned in the east – and the invasion of Belgium on the morning of Tuesday 4 August was as much as a consequence of that commitment as the cause of Britain's own declaration of war in the evening.

Most provocatively, in the House of Commons debate of Monday 3 August, Llewelyn Williams had pointed to the possible connection between the British pledge to France of Sunday 2 August and the crisis over Belgium on Monday 3 August. The German ultimatum to Belgium had followed the British pledge to France – although prepared beforehand. The Germans, as Williams put it, could scarcely conceal from themselves the signals that Britain had already given by Sunday 2 August that she was firmly in the Entente camp.[62] Williams was close to the truth. The Germans' decision during the afternoon of Sunday 2 August to deliver the ultimatum to Belgium that evening had indeed come after hope in British neutrality had expired in Berlin, and Moltke had eclipsed the civilians – following the collapse of Grey's 'kite-flying' (the 'misunderstanding') on Saturday 1 August.[63]

Percy Molteno was correct also that British efforts to safeguard Belgian neutrality – the telegrams to Paris and Berlin of Friday 31 July – were mere gestures. As Molteno argued after the outbreak of war:

> When Sir Edward Grey spoke [on Monday 3 August] there had been no violation of Belgian neutrality, but we had on the previous day [Sunday] given France the assurance of our help to protect her coast and ports, thus we had taken the part of one of the belligerents before the question of Belgian neutrality had arisen. We therefore did not go with clean hands to Germany to ask them to maintain Belgian neutrality, so that the question of Belgian neutrality is not the one which has plunged us into war.[64]

Molteno remained fervent on this subject. It was the Liberal government's diplomacy that had failed to save Belgium. Gladstone's diplomacy had worked; Grey's had been disastrous. Grey's telegrams of Friday 31 July were 'an empty enquiry with nothing in return'. The pledge to France on Sunday 2 August was a 'unilateral engagement' that marked 'our real entry into the war'. Molteno's conclusion was provocative:

> The fact is, that the invasion of Belgium was not a cause but a consequence of our entry into the war, it became a most convenient *causa suasoria* [persuasive cause] in the hands of those who supported our entry into the war on the grounds of our Entente with France, and in reconciling the conscience of the country to going to war with Germany.[65]

Recrimination IV: The Role of Russia

Radicals writhed to think that Britain had rushed into war at the side of the Tsar. For example, Israel Zangwill, the Radical playwright, denounced Britain's sudden blindness to Russia's 'medievalism'. He fulminated against Liberals who refused to see the dangers of Russian despotism and anti-Semitism – both of which quickly produced atrocities in Russian-occupied Austrian Galicia in 1914 and 1915.[66] Late in the war, Vernon Lee still railed against 'the grim farce of girding against autocracy in Germany when we had allied ourselves with, indeed were indirectly drawn into war by the deeds of, the incomparably worse autocracy of Russia'.[67]

The reluctance of Asquith's Cabinet to focus on Russia during the crisis had infuriated Morley. He denounced the winking at Russian aggrandisement: ' "Have you ever thought," I put to them, "what will happen if Russia wins? If Germany is beaten and Austria is beaten, it is not England and France who will emerge pre-eminent in Europe. It will be Russia. Will that be good for Western Civilisation?" '[68] MacDonald had raised this in his speech on Monday 3 August, and so also had several Radicals in the evening debate.[69]

But for political reasons, during 'war week' in London, Tsarist Russia virtually disappeared. In Asquith's address to the House of Commons on 6 August, he referred to Russia only in passing. Her contribution to the crisis, apparently, was nil.[70] In his reply for the Opposition, Bonar Law referred to Russia only once, gloating over the Germans' miscalculation in gambling that Russia was not in a condition to go to war.[71] In the House of Lords, Crewe absolved Russia of any blame, when he cited Germany's failure to restrain Austria as 'the original cause of the Russian partial mobilisation'.[72] In his reply, Lansdowne made no mention of Russia whatsoever.[73] In its editorial columns, the Conservative press trod the same safe path. *The Times* was typical: in its major editorial of 5 August in support of war, *The Times* simply eliminated Russia from the story altogether.[74]

On this same day the government made one effort to show that Britain had tried to restrain Russia. *The Times* was authorised to publish the interchange of telegrams between King George and Tsar Nicholas, which Asquith had initiated in the early hours of Saturday 1 August. The headline 'KING AND TSAR: ROYAL EFFORTS TO AVERT WAR' offered the essential interpretation.[75] It was scarcely arresting proof that Britain had worked hard to restrain

Russia. Indeed, critics pointed to reports showing that Buchanan in St Petersburg had hardly shown restraint. Late on Monday 3 August he had addressed 'crowds of thousands of people' surrounding the British Embassy. As *The Times* reported,

> Sir George Buchanan, the Ambassador, appeared at the window and addressed the crowd. Amid frantic cheering he declared England's perfect sympathy with Russia. The Secretary of the Embassy, standing beside the Ambassador, then raised cheers for Russia.[76]

Such embarrassing reports indicated that documents showing contacts between Russia and Britain during the crisis would need some special cleansing. The White Paper was the major effort to put Russian diplomacy in the best light. In preparing it, the Foreign Office was induced to act as Britain's moral laundry – so all the stains had to go.

But in sanitising the record of Anglo-Russian diplomacy during the crisis, the White Paper was a very dodgy dossier indeed. Key documents from St Petersburg were surreptitiously trimmed or tidied up. Among the total of 159 documents in the White Paper, there were eleven from Buchanan. Of these eleven documents, ten were paraphrased and cut. Nothing was acknowledged. All the documents were simply labelled 'Telegraphic', as if original. The cuts swept away evidence that Russian Foreign Minister Sazonov, hand in glove with French Ambassador Paléologue, had squeezed Britain hard to show 'solidarity'.[77]

A few examples of the doctoring must suffice. A telegram of Saturday 25 July was shorn of the fact that Russia had decided to mobilise 1,100,000 men – something Grey told the Commons only on Thursday 30 July. In the published version Sazonov declared that Russia was ready to resist Austria, remarking that '*if* she feels secure of the support of France, she will face all risks of war' – the 'if' was added. Expunged was Paléologue's promise that 'France placed herself unreservedly on Russia's side.' Removed too were his pointed remarks to Buchanan that the 'French Government would want to know at once whether our [British] fleet was prepared to play [the] part assigned to it by [the] Anglo-French Naval Convention. He could not believe that England would not stand by her two friends, who were acting as one on this matter.'[78] Entirely suppressed was Buchanan's personal advice to London that we 'shall have to choose between giving Russia our active support or renouncing her friendship'.[79]

Other cables were eliminated that showed Buchanan barracking for instant intervention.[80] Gone was a significant 'Private' telegram of Sunday 26 July. In this, Buchanan coached Grey to enlighten the parliament and the newspapers that 'it is not Russia but Austria who is at fault'. Another 'mutilated telegram' of Sunday 2 August was omitted. It recorded the Tsar's appeal for Britain to join the war, and Buchanan's supporting argument that, if Britain chose peace, we would 'find ourselves without a friend in Europe, while our Indian Empire will no longer be secure from attack by Russia'.[81] In this way, the fact that Buchanan had urged war on the basis of safeguarding India – from Russia – was suppressed.

One other significant document was cut, at the last moment. This was a telegram from Grey to Buchanan on Saturday 25 July. It exposed the reluctance of Ambassador Benckendorff to agree to Grey's proposed Ambassadors' Conference. Benckendorff had complained that a gathering of disinterested powers would give Germany the impression that France and Britain were 'detached' from Russia. Considering the pox the British cast upon the Germans for rejecting the conference, this telegram was especially embarrassing. It was dropped, on Grey's command, supposedly to spare Benckendorff's feelings.[82] So late was the decision that under the heading 'No. 28' in the White Paper there appeared, embarrassingly, the word 'Nil'.[83]

Thus did Britain's war-makers seek to minimise Russia's contribution to the disaster. And well they might. It was most significant. It is clear that under pressure from her French ally, Russia had moved after 1912 from a strategic defensive to an offensive war plan, guaranteeing the invasion of East Prussia by the fifteenth day of mobilisation. The decisions of the Russian Council of Ministers on Friday 24 and Saturday 25 July to introduce the 'Period Preparatory to War' – on both the German and Austrian fronts – was regarded by Russia's military elite 'as a green light to war'.[84] In the days that followed, the Russian generals paralleled the German in harrying the monarch to embrace war. But in the German record there is nothing to top the story of Sazonov's phone call to General Yanushkevich on the afternoon of 30 July, telling him to issue his orders for general mobilisation, then to 'disappear for the rest of the day' and 'smash the telephone' – lest the Tsar should countermand the order.[85]

What was the effect of this attempt to shield Russia from criticism by falsifying the record in the White Paper? Britain's parliament, which endorsed the £100 million War Credit, was deliberately misled. Not only MPs, but also ordinary Britons looked trustingly to the White Paper, reprinted cheaply as a Blue Book.[86] Everywhere, earnest young men contemplating enlistment consulted it. One fifteen-year-old schoolboy may speak for thousands:

> On finishing the Blue Book I was convinced of the righteousness of Britain's cause – and joined the O.T.C. [Officer Training Corps]. But I very well remember saying to myself – 'It's perfectly clear – if only they've told me everything and haven't left anything out.' They had not told me everything, and they left some things out.[87]

If the men in the Cabinet and Foreign Office shared misgivings about Russia's role in the crisis, they could not say so. Not after Tuesday 4 August. Their candid views on the low calibre of leading Russian figures were buried. But clues survive. For example, in 1912 Crewe had met Sazonov, on whom so much would depend in 1914. He described him as 'capable' – but also 'either tired or below par', with 'too little vitality to care as much as a foreign minister ought how events shape themselves'.[88] Only later were further insights let slip. For example, in his autobiography Hardinge lowered his guard. So critical was he of Russia's abandonment of war in late 1917 that he wrote: 'It is curious to recall that it was in defence of Russia that the Allies went to war, and that it was Russia that put the Allies "into the cart".'[89]

TWENTY-SIX

Conclusion

We still hold with Morley and Burns that the policy of strict neutrality was the proper policy to adopt.[1]

Francis Hirst, 18 August 1914

How utterly improbable it was! Six weeks into the Great War, Norman Angell told a gathering of supporters from his old Neutrality League that, in the last days of peace, 'not a bus full of people' could have been found in Britain to back 'an agreement to place on the Continent a million people in support of France because of an outbreak of war in some remote corner such as Serbia'.[2] And yet Britain was doing it.

A hundred years later, British historians of the 'dire necessity' school still assert that Britain's Great War should be remembered simply as a harsh reality that had to be faced. They insist that nothing other than a righteous war against German militarism was conceivable in 1914. They plead for the old sugary verities to be reasserted – that Britain was in the right, that Germany was in the wrong, that the cause was just, and that it was a stand-tall moment – imagining this is loyalty to the dead.[3] Conscious of the magnitude of the disaster, can we be consoled by such simplicities?

Britain's Road to War

Let us begin with a swift retelling of the feel-good story of Britain's decision for war as told by believers in 'dire necessity'. According to this tale, Britain did her very best to avoid war. All her leaders wanted diplomatic mediation to resolve the crisis. But Germany would not have it. Luckily Britain had long prepared against the possibility of German aggression and so she clung to her Ententes with France and Russia. Only when Germany invaded Belgium on Tuesday 4 August did Britain finally decide upon intervention. Britain went to war for high moral purposes – essentially to protect Belgium. The process of choosing war shows how a robust parliamentary democracy made the difficult decision to face down German militarism. Happily, the British people were practically unanimous in support of the politicians' decision for war. So, they saw it through. We should all be proud.

Naturally, there is a parallel tale regarding the role of Britain's dissenters that is unremittingly hostile toward them. According to this tale, only a contemptible rump of 'pacifists' indulged themselves in a futile advocacy of Britain's neutrality in 1914. They simply refused to look facts in the face. In a self-indulgent gesture, two Cabinet ministers resigned. If these Radicals had been successful in urging Britain's neutrality, the inevitable outcome would have been the triumph of German aggression. They should be ashamed.

This book has sought to demonstrate that this fairy tale, parading Britain's moral superiority and scolding the Radicals' futility, is simplistic, unfair, lacking in nuance, and often flatly contradicted by the documentary evidence.

What really happened? The Liberal government was deeply divided over how to handle the crisis of 1914. There were significant forces at work on the Right of British politics eager for war with Germany – for they believed it was a favourable moment. Sections of the Conservative press whirled their bull-roarers for intervention from an early date. The Liberal Cabinet's response to the crisis was cautious. Grey hoped that a policy of 'apparent indecision' would be sufficient to deter both sides from rash action. He attempted mediation. But in the last analysis, Britain failed to mediate effectively as a genuinely neutral Power. Under pressure to show solidarity with the Entente, Britain did very little to restrain either France or Russia. Instead, the pro-Entente interventionists in the Cabinet leapt forward to make early preparations for war that boosted the confidence of the hard-liners in Russia and France willing to risk war. When war in Eastern Europe was declared late on Saturday 1 August, Britain's leaders ceased efforts to keep Britain out of a wider war. The minority of Cabinet interventionists eventually 'jockeyed' the neutralist majority into a rushed choice for war on Sunday 2 August, in the shape of a pledge of naval assistance to France. The pledge locked Britain into any war *before* news of the German ultimatum to Belgium. It very nearly wrecked the government, initially provoking four Cabinet resignations. Grey then preached debts of honour and fear of abandonment by allies – and the Cabinet clique rushed to a declaration of war. Throughout the crisis, the Cabinet's pro-Entente leaders were manipulative and deceptive. They made crucial decisions outside the Cabinet, which steered the neutralist majority toward war. There was no democratic decision for war.

On the other side of the question, the Radicals and peace activists tried hard to prevent the catastrophe. In the Liberal Party, they probably commanded the support of the majority. They argued against early military steps that would incite Russia and France. They pressed for a credible, active diplomacy of mediation – strengthened by a commitment to strict neutrality and genuinely even-handed negotiation – which was not tried. The great bulk of the Liberal and Labour press stood solidly for this neutral diplomacy when the crisis broke, and fiercely maintained a demand for neutrality to the end. The Radicals were blindsided for the first week of the crisis, misled by assurances that Britain was avoiding all provocation and pursuing a strictly neutral diplomacy. She did neither.

Only at the last gasp, over the weekend of 1–2 August, did the forces of internationalism in Britain – Radical, Labour, pacifist and feminist – come out loudly and openly. They began to rally public opinion, mounting significant demonstrations. There was deep resentment and recrimination when the decision came so rapidly to declare war on Tuesday 4 August. The speed of the crisis had defeated attempts to rouse a great public campaign, but a promising start had been made. Given more time, it might have grown to be formidable. But public opinion had scarcely had time to make up its mind when war was declared. Certainly there was no overwhelming public pressure for war.

And what of the Radical critique of the government's handling of the crisis? The Radicals were essentially correct when they accused the Liberal Imperialist minority of 'bouncing' the Cabinet and parliament. They were correct in denouncing the government's dishonesty in trumpeting the war as a war of necessity forced upon Britain by German action in Belgium on Tuesday 4 August. They saw that the government had determined upon war by Sunday 2 August in solidarity with France, and that Belgium came later as a gift to propagandists. They correctly interpreted Britain's decision for war as a triumph for Grey and the policy of the Entente. Ultimately, Grey had steered his colleagues and the nation to war, in line with his own endlessly repeated conviction that fidelity to the Entente was indispensable. For instance, way back in 1907, Grey had expressed this, almost as a vow, to his astonished ambassador Frank Lascelles in Berlin – no 'wavering by a hair's breadth from our loyalty to the Entente'.[4]

Did the British Radicals Embolden the German Militarists?

Crusaders for Britain's righteous war will reject this Radical critique. They reply that those pursuing neutrality for Britain in July–August 1914 were playing into the hands of the German militarist aggressors, and ironically making war more likely. According to one long-running argument, Grey had to adopt a stance of 'apparent indecision' for fear of the Radicals. He was unable to give a clear warning to Germany, because the Radicals prevented him. The neutralists hobbled deterrence and, therefore, Britain failed to deter war.[5]

The case for this is weak. First, Grey did repeatedly issue loud warnings to Germany, through Lichnowsky, who passed them on, backing them up with his own.[6] Berlin, scene of both panic and braggadocio by turns as the crisis deepened, was not emboldened in a choice for war by any lack of warnings from London. Second, Grey embraced the policy of 'apparent indecision' as his very own, not something forced upon him. It was after all in keeping with his long-established belief that the 'policy of the Entente' could restrain Russia and France by the very nature of its ambiguity.[7] Third, there was no high-profile Radical campaign for neutrality in the House of Commons that might have fortified the wild men in Berlin. Not a single question was asked, not a single speech was delivered, urging neutrality during the week beginning Monday 27 July – because Grey had pleaded successfully for silence from the Radical backbench. Fourth, there is no trail of evidence in the German documents that confidence in the power of British Radicals to keep Britain neutral encouraged the German militarists to risk war. A very few samples of the British press reached the Kaiser, but the opinions were in different directions. His marginal notes recorded a 'Bravo' for Radical opinion early in the crisis, but he complained later that it was having no impact upon Grey's initially cautious but increasingly hostile stance.[8] Fifth, if one factor above others is to be detected in the German documents sustaining hope in British neutrality during the crisis, it was the Kaiser's faith in George V's consoling words to Prince Heinrich on Sunday 26 July indicating his desire for neutrality.[9]

Keeping both sides in Europe guessing, by citing enigmatic British public opinion as the final arbiter, was Grey's preferred diplomatic tactic – not something forced upon him. After the commencement of the war, when mixing with friends, Grey readily conceded that during the crisis he had felt he had no choice but to be inscrutable and to rely on public opinion. He did not indict the Radicals for foisting this upon him. For example, in May 1915, Grey told Francis and Eleanor Acland that

one of his strongest feelings in the days just before the war was that he himself had no power to decide policy, and was only the mouthpiece of England. Lichnowsky on the one hand and Sazonov and Cambon on the other were always saying – will you stay out? On what terms will you stay out? And on the other hand, will you definitely come in? But all he could say was 'I don't know. I'm not England.'[10]

What Might Have Happened

Contemporary believers in the absolute necessity of Britain's war point to what might have happened to clinch their case. If Britain had maintained her neutrality on Tuesday 4 August, they insist, a disaster for France, Belgium and Europe would have ensued: the German armies would have reached Paris, European democracy would have been destroyed, and German hegemony established in Europe. Historians in the correct manly tradition that celebrates military endeavour claim to know that *only* war could have repelled the nightmare of German domination.

What would have happened if Britain had remained neutral in 1914? The only truthful answer to the question is that we do *not* know. We simply cannot know. Those who insist they *do* are trading on our credulity – and our tendency to be spooked by ghost stories. We can debate what is conceivable, but we cannot prove things about paths not taken. It is time Britain's choice for war in 1914 lost the sheen given it by many historians who fraudulently claim that they *know* there was no other conceivable outcome – and no better outcome. They know no such thing.

Against the fatalistic view of an irresistible war against German aggression, let us simply take account of three famous 'bumps' along the way to war. First, on the evening of Wednesday 29 July a single telegram from William II to Tsar Nicholas caused him to rebel against his military advisers and seek a delay in general mobilisation.[11] Second, early in the morning of Thursday 30 July, Viviani and Poincaré sent a telegram to St Petersburg that leant toward caution. It urged Russia to avoid 'any measure which might offer Germany a pretext for a total or partial mobilisation of her forces'. But, sadly, it also included the usual assurances that 'France is resolved to fulfil all the obligations of the alliance'.[12] The Russian leaders briefly paused

in their preparations. Then they chose to trust the assurances –
and decided upon general mobilisation that afternoon. Third,
on the evening of Saturday 1 August, when Lichnowsky's famous
cables arrived in Berlin, briefly reviving hope of British neutrality,
the Kaiser also challenged his military advisers. As we saw, he can-
celled orders for the occupation of Luxembourg, and sought to limit
the scope of the impending war.[13] Was war really inevitable? Perhaps
war was entirely avoidable. The facts jostle. What slowing of the
'march of events' might have been achieved by other interventions?
None can say.

Most of those who had struggled against war in July–August 1914
fiercely maintained their faith in neutrality for Britain as the better
option. Francis Hirst wrote to his American friends at the Carnegie
Endowment in mid-August:

> A great many of us, with the support of Bryce and Loreburn,
> worked very hard in the short week we had to keep Britain at
> peace. We still hold with Morley and Burns that the policy of
> strict neutrality was the proper policy to adopt. [We believe] that
> the British Government could probably have secured not only the
> neutrality of Great Britain but the neutrality of Belgium and the
> neutrality of the Channel.[14]

Was he right? We shall never know. But certainly Britain's leaders
might have done a great many things differently during the crisis if
they had steadfastly pursued a neutral diplomacy. They might have
refused Churchill's demands for early naval movements – as Harcourt
had pleaded – because of the risk of inciting Russia. They might have
put the Russian and French ambassadors in London under real pressure on the matter of Russia's early mobilisation. Their diplomacy
might have focused directly upon reversing this dangerous step. They
might have delayed sending their own 'Warning Telegram' to the
Empire. The leadership clique might have presented each crucial
diplomatic and military step to the Cabinet beforehand – rather
than pre-empting its decisions. Would all of this only have served to
incite Germany, or might it have slowed the rush down the slope to

catastrophe? We cannot tell. But often in history, the unforeseen – and even the unimagined – can intervene and carry the day.

The Essential Shield of German Perfidy

The fatalistic insistence that Britain's war was unavoidable is often rooted in a belief that the Germans' drive toward aggression was inexorable, and therefore any moderation on Britain's part would have only encouraged war. Believers point to what did happen in 1914: German aggression in Belgium and France, followed by top-level planning for annexation in east and west – Bethmann Hollweg's 'September Memorandum' most memorably.[15] But this is a dangerous argument. The Germans could also point to what *did* happen in 1914: the Russians *did* invade East Prussia, the British *did* seize German colonies, and the British *did* strangle Germany's seaborne commerce and starve the nation. The German Right pointed to all this as evidence of the Entente's hunger for aggression. No one can afford to confuse the results of war with causes.

The British certainly planned for the aggrandisement of Empire and the commercial ruin of Germany. Harcourt himself drew up in March 1915 a secret memorandum for the Cabinet, 'The Spoils', outlining sweeping plans for the newly inflated British Empire in Africa, Asia, the Middle East and the Pacific.[16] Many more plans followed. Any objective study of the war aims of all the Great Powers during the Great War reveals that all sides had shopping lists.[17] Germany was never uniquely in thrall to believers in the old law of grab – the 'simple plan', as Wordsworth had put it,

> That they should take who have the power,
> And they should keep who can.

The easy way out of all this is to reassert German perfidy as the complete explanation for the *outbreak* of war. To find the cause in the adversary comforts the conscience. If one can indict the Germans, one can absolve the war. Grey fed the hysteria on this throughout the

war. He told the House of Commons in January 1916 that the war
was 'a war forced upon Europe after every effort had been made to
find a settlement without war, which could perfectly easily have been
found (cheers) … by conference, as we suggested. Prussian militarism would not have any other settlement but war.'[18] Evils certainly
flowed from 'Prussian militarism' – and they could be diabolical. But
German militarism was never a singular evil in militarised Europe
before or during the Great War.[19] The insistence upon German
perfidy as a complete explanation for the cataclysm of 1914 has
always served a reactionary purpose. It was indispensable in obscuring the great realities exposed by the resort to war.

First, the descent into war revealed the ignominious collapse of
essential elements of the old order. The New Imperialism, the great
cheap labour scam run to enrich fragments of the economy at the
expense of the rest, had landed everyone in a bloodbath. The 'old
diplomacy' – under which men from a half-dozen public schools
presumed to manage competitive imperialism against a combustible
backdrop of vast armaments and rival alliances – had failed to safeguard peace. The scramble for Dreadnoughts had failed to deter war.
None of this could be admitted, so German evil was depicted as a
new immoral element that had upset the good old system.

Second, depicting Britain's war as a battle against German perfidy
in Belgium helped blur diplomatic realities – that Britain's choice
for war was an absolute triumph for Russian and French diplomacy,
and a diplomatic disaster for Britain. After nine years of exquisite
difficulty for Liberal ministers as they tap-danced around the slip-
pery claim that Britain was merely the 'partner' of Russia and France,
every string was pulled by the Entente in July–August 1914 and
Britain had dashed off to war like an ally. The war of solidarity with
the Entente – always a hard sell – had to be repackaged, at the last
moment, as a war for moral righteousness in Belgium.

Third, German perfidy could be relied upon to eclipse reactionary
Russia. With all eyes focused on the battles to throw back German
militarism in the west, Liberals could ignore the east. Germany's
scarlet sins, so near and so visible, outshone all. Liberals could suppress their gnawing doubts that Russia's leaders – reactionaries, such

as Nicholas II, Goremykin, Sazonov, Izvolsky, and Sukhomlinov – were fit partners in a crusade for the rights of small nations against despotism.

Fourth, German perfidy enabled at least half the Cabinet ministers to stifle their knowledge that the sad-eyed and sensitive Grey – a man without languages or drive or imagination – had been hopelessly ineffectual. For years past, Lloyd George had told friends in confidence that Grey was just putty in the hands of his advisers: 'He simply carries out Harding[e]'s instructions.' Grey was 'immoveable', 'stolid, unimaginative', with only 'the appearance of weight and wisdom'.[20] The struggle against lying Germans transformed him into the very button of British moral superiority – that inexhaustible, self-approving moral force that was so 'adorably irresponsible' for the war, as critics satirised it.[21]

In a sense, those in London who chose war in August 1914 could count themselves lucky that the first months of fighting did not expose their gambles as utterly reckless. Nobody knew for certain what kind of a nightmare was avoided – or unleashed – by Britain's choice for war. In choosing to back Russia and France, no one knew how the battles would play out in the first months. The Russian armies might have been victorious in East Prussia. German cities such as Allenstein, Königsberg and Breslau might have fallen to the advancing Russians – as they would have done if the Russian armies had advanced 300 kilometres into Germany, as they did into Austrian Galicia. As events turned out, the fortuitous 'war map' produced by late 1914, with great chunks of France and Belgium in German hands while the Russians were tossed out of East Prussia, helped the British claim to have intervened against aggression. But how would the British decision to back France and Russia have looked if the French armies invading Alsace and Lorraine had got to Freiburg, and the Russians had reached Breslau? Let no one imagine that those who support war are always realists, and those who oppose it are always sentimentalists. Hatred is also a sentiment.

'Cosmic Murder'

Once the choice was made in Britain, the sentimentalism of war – Thomas Hardy's 'faith and fire within us' and Cecil Spring-Rice's 'love that asks no question' – swept through the political leadership and was carried to the people. All the usual justifications for war did good service – self-defence, last resort, safety first, 'dire necessity', and no alternative. If only it were so.

This book is very much a top-down study – necessarily so, because those at the top launch wars. But let us pause briefly to recall the savagery that was unleashed on ordinary people when the industrialised kill-chain whirred into action in 1914. The impressions preserved in the diary of Caroline Playne, an observant friend of both Quakers and military men in London during the Great War, must suffice to give us glimpses into the charnel house. In July 1916 she spoke to a friend nursing at King George's Hospital in London, 'full of men with part of [their] face blown away … not able to take solid food. What will these men's further lives be?' Playne's friend 'hoped the worst cases would not survive.' Playne spoke with a woman who saw each soldier's death as 'a splendid sacrifice like the death of Christ' – 'it was so fine, so glorious, it was better than if they had lived'. She attended sermons repudiating the idea that one should love one's enemies, because 'if we had been more ready to kill Germans and to kill more of them – we might have saved Belgian women from outrage.' A lady from the right-wing Navy League told Playne it would be best for humanity if the Germans 'could all be killed'. She heard a Russian officer dismissing the Belgian atrocities in light of the wholesale massacres he had witnessed in Hungarian villages during the Russian retreat of 1915. ' "What about the inhabitants?" he was asked. "Oh they all went to the devil." ' Playne soon learned that the daily atrocities of normal military operations dwarfed these horrific incidents behind the lines. A British officer told her his soldiers routinely 'killed the wounded Germans'. The men heard their Colonel's complaints, and then 'as soon as the Colonel was gone they said they would do as they had done'. Playne listened to British officers describing the 'horrible heaped-up slaughter', and sights in the stinking ooze that would make a butcher retch. She marvelled at 'the coolness and the calmness of it, all told in a pretty drawing room under a reproduction of Botticelli's Venus – this was the nightmare.' Eventually she grew inured to tales of 'slaughtered youth'. Then her own young nephew, Leslie Playne, asked her just before being sent to France, 'What was Armageddon?'[22]

On the British side, the commitment to this ever-widening imperial conflict in August 1914 eventually cost the lives of approximately three-quarters of a million British servicemen – or closer to a million if military and civilian deaths across the Empire are added.[23] The war began a frantic pillaging of the public coffers, present and future. Only two weeks into the fighting, Lloyd George told the Cabinet he was 'much distressed as to expenditure'. 'We may have to borrow one thousand millions before the war is over', Churchill replied. As some ministers laughed, Churchill declared, 'It is time we got something out of posterity.'[24] And so they did. By July 1916, Britain's average daily spending on the war exceeded £6 million; by May 1917 it reached £7.9 million per day. When it was over, British war expenditure had reached the staggering total of £9,593 million, and the national debt stood at £8,000 million. These figures take on real meaning when it is recalled that the last peacetime British budget of May 1914 proposed a total annual expenditure of only £207 million.[25] The choice for war in 1914 was a choice for mechanised slaughter at stupendous cost – in the words of one soldier-novelist, a 'crowning imbecility', a 'cosmic murder', a war of 'lunatic waste'.[26] Its prolongation incubated the future horrors of Fascism and Communism.

Nations going to war are very like each other. Britain's descent into war was marked, as elsewhere, by panic, manipulation, deception, recklessness, high-handedness, and low political calculation – and decisions made at a tearing pace. The Radical MP Percy Molteno captured it neatly in the first, the last, and the only House of Commons debate granted on the choice for war, on the evening Monday 3 August. The people and the parliament were being stampeded, Molteno alleged. 'I feel very strongly on this subject', he explained, fighting hard to contain his emotions. The parliamentarians should have been granted 'a fair and straight opportunity of considering, discussing, and deciding on this question'. It was vital, he argued, that we 'should give the people of this country a chance to decide'. Instead, the nation was witnessing 'a continuation of that old and disastrous system where a few men in charge of the State, wielding the whole force of the State, make secret engagements and secret arrangements, carefully veiled from the knowledge of the people, who are as dumb driven cattle without a voice on the question'.[27]

How should Britain's Great War be remembered after a century? In a 'national spirit'? Perhaps the idea that for Britain there was no alternative to war, no error in her handling of the crisis, and no deed left undone in pursuit of peace is an essential consolation. But it is fairy dust. There is really only one story worth telling about the Great War: it was a common European tragedy – a filthy, disgusting and hideous episode of industrialised killing. Not the first, and not the last. It was unredeemed by victory. The uplifting element of the story lies in the struggle to avert it.

Notes

Introduction

1 Representative of the genre are Gary Sheffield, *Forgotten Victory: The First World War: Myths and Realities* (London, 2002), and Gordon Corrigan, *Mud, Blood and Poppycock: Britain and the First World War* (London, 2003).

2 Among many military studies, see Shelford Bidwell and Dominick Graham, *Fire-Power: British Army Weapons and Theories of War, 1904–1945* (Boston, 1982), Robin Prior and Trevor Wilson, *Command on the Western Front* (Oxford, 1992), Paddy Griffith, *Battle Tactics of the Western Front: The British Army's Art of Attack, 1916–1918* (New Haven, 1994), P. H. Liddle, ed., *Passchendaele in Perspective: The Third Battle of Ypres* (London, 1997), Brian Bond and Nigel Cave, eds., *Haig: A Reappraisal 70 Years On* (London, 1999), Gary Sheffield, *The Somme* (London, 2003), Robin Prior and Trevor Wilson, *Passchendaele: The Untold Story* (Melbourne, 2003), Peter Simkins, *The Western Front 1914–1916* (Oxford, 2003), Gary Sheffield and Dan Todman, eds., *Command and Control of the Western Front 1914–1918: The British Experience* (Staplehurst, 2004), Gary Sheffield and John Bourne, eds., *Douglas Haig: War Diaries and Letters, 1914–1918* (London, 2005), Andrew A. Wiest, *Haig: The Evolution of a Commander* (Dulles, 2005), Robin Prior and Trevor Wilson, *The Somme* (Sydney, 2006), J. P. Harris, *Douglas Haig and the First World War* (Cambridge, 2008), William Philpott, *Bloody Victory: The Sacrifice on the Somme and the Making of the Twentieth Century* (London, 2009).

3 Corrigan, *Mud, Blood and Poppycock*, 50.

4 Sheffield, *Forgotten Victory*, 48–9.

5 Brian Bond, *The Unquiet Western Front: Britain's Role in Literature and History* (Cambridge, 2002), 5.

6 Niall Ferguson, 'The Kaiser's European Union: What if Britain had "Stood Aside" in August 1914?', in Niall Ferguson, ed., *Virtual History: Alternatives and Counterfactuals* (London, 1997), 228–80, and Niall Ferguson, *The Pity of War* (London, 1998), especially ch. 6.

7   Keith Wilson's many fine research articles have been collected in three works: *The Policy of the Entente: Essays on the Determinants of British Foreign Policy, 1904–1914* (Cambridge, 1985), *Empire and Continent: Studies in British Foreign Policy from the 1880s to the First World War* (London, 1987), and *The Limits of Eurocentricity: Imperial British Foreign and Defence Policy in the Early Twentieth Century* (Istanbul, 2006). An overview of his arguments about British foreign policy across the nineteenth and in the early twentieth century is offered in Keith Wilson, *Problems and Possibilities: Exercises in Statesmanship, 1814–1918* (Stroud, 2003). A summary of his view of the British choice for war is given in his chapter 'Britain', in Keith Wilson, ed., *Decisions for War, 1914* (New York, 1995), 175–208.

8   Raymond Poincaré, the French President, and René Viviani, his new Prime Minister, made their state visit to Russia on the battleship *France* in mid-July 1914, that is, on the very eve of the international crisis. See Eugenia C. Kiesling, 'France', in Richard F. Hamilton and Holger H. Herwig, eds., *The Origins of World War I* (Cambridge, 2001), 247, Sean McMeekin, *The Russian Origins of the First World War* (Cambridge, MA, 2011), 45–6, and Gerd Krumeich, *Armaments and Politics in France on the Eve of the First World War* (Leamington Spa, 1984), 215–6.

9   M. B. Hayne, *The French Foreign Office and the Origins of the First World War, 1898–1914* (Oxford, 1993), 299, fn. 138. Two bundles of Paléologue's telegrams were returned to the French Foreign Office archives only after an interval of many years. Poincaré tampered with his diary. See Christopher Clark, *The Sleepwalkers: How Europe Went To War in 1914* (New York, 2012), 504.

10 Keith Robbins, *Sir Edward Grey: A Biography of Lord Grey of Fallodon* (London, 1971), vii, Stephen Valone, ' "There must be some misunderstanding": Sir Edward Grey's Diplomacy of August 1, 1914', *Journal of British Studies*, XXVII (1988), 406, fn. 6, and Konrad Jarausch, *The Enigmatic Chancellor: Bethmann Hollweg and the Hubris of Imperial Germany* (New Haven, 1973), x.

11 Nicholas D'Ombrain, *War Machinery and High Policy: Defence Administration in Peacetime Britain, 1902–1914* (Oxford, 1973), xiii.

12 Holger Herwig, 'Clio Deceived: Patriotic Self-Censorship in Germany After the Great War', in Keith M. Wilson, ed., *Forging the Collective Memory: Government and International Historians Through Two World Wars* (Providence, 1996), 97.

13 See especially Stefan Schmidt, *Frankreichs Aussenpolitik in der Julikrise 1914: Ein Beitrag zur Geschichte des Ausbruchs des Ersten Weltkrieges* (Munich, 2009). The evidence from Schmidt is summarised in Marc Trachtenberg, 'French Foreign Policy in the July Crisis, 1914: A Review Article', H-Diplo/ISSF, 26 Nov. 2010, available at www.h-net.org.

14 Irwin Halfond, *Maurice Paléologue: The Diplomat, The Writer, The Man and the Third French Republic* (Lanham, 2007), 89. Halfond concludes: 'All that can be said with any certainty is that Paléologue made the Russian option for general mobilisation a more feasible one and that he made it more difficult – if not impossible – for France to impose effective restraints upon Russia' (96). On Paléologue's role in 1914, see also critical accounts in Hayne, *French Foreign Office*, 294–301, and Glenn H. Snyder, *Alliance Politics* (Ithaca, 2007), 302.

15 Kiesling, 'France', in Hamilton and Herwig, *Origins of World War I*, 251.

16 William Mulligan, *The Origins of the First World War* (Cambridge, 2010), 219.

17 McMeekin, *Russian Origins of the First World War*, 233. See also Sean McMeekin, *July 1914: Countdown to War* (New York, 2013).

18 This vast field can be explored through elegant summaries that appear in various articles in Holger Afflerbach and David Stevenson, eds., *An Improbable War: The Outbreak of World War I and European Political Culture before 1914* (New York, 2007), and in Alan Kramer, *Dynamic of Destruction: Culture and Mass Killing in the First World War* (Oxford, 2007), David Stevenson, *Armaments and the Coming of War, Europe 1904–1914* (Oxford, 1996), and David G. Herrmann, *The Arming of Europe and the Making of the First World War* (Princeton, 1996).

19 Fritz Fischer, *Germany's Aims in the First World War* (London, 1967), 87.

20 To list only the landmark works in this huge field, we may include Karl Kautsky, Walther Schücking and Max Montgelas, eds., *German Documents on the Outbreak of the War* (New York, 1924), cited hereafter as *GD*, Fischer, *Germany's Aims in the First World War*, Imanuel Geiss, ed., *July 1914: The Outbreak of the First World War: Selected Documents* (London, 1967), Fritz Fischer, *War of Illusions: German Policies from 1911 to 1914* (London, 1975), John Moses, *The Politics of Illusion: The Fischer Controversy in German Historiography* (London, 1975), Gerhard Ritter, *The Sword and the Scepter: The Problem of Militarism in Germany*, 4 vols. (Coral Gables, Florida, 1973), Jarausch, *The Enigmatic Chancellor*, Volker Berghahn, *Germany and the Approach of War in 1914* (London, 1973), John Röhl, *1914: Delusion or Design? The Testimony of Two German Diplomats* (London, 1973), Isabel V. Hull, *The Entourage of Kaiser Wilhelm II, 1888–1918* (Cambridge, 1982), John Röhl, *The Kaiser and His Court: Wilhelm II and the Government of Germany* (Cambridge, 1994), Manfred F. Boemke, Roger Chickering and Stig Förster, eds., *Anticipating Total War: The German and American Experiences, 1871–1914* (Cambridge, 1999), 343–76, Annika Mombauer, *Helmuth von Moltke and the Origins of the First World War* (New York, 2001), Terence Zuber, *Inventing the Schlieffen Plan: German War Planning, 1871–1914* (Oxford, 2002), Annika Mombauer and Wilhelm Deist, eds., *The Kaiser: New Research on Wilhelm II's Role in Imperial Germany* (Cambridge, 2003), and Mark Hewitson, *Germany and the Causes of the First World War* (Oxford, 2004).

21 To cite only summaries of the huge research effort that has explored the German elite's role in the July–August crisis, one might note Mombauer, *Moltke*, ch. 4, Holger Herwig, 'Germany', in Hamilton and Herwig, eds., *Origins of World War I*, and John Röhl, 'The Curious Case of the Kaiser's Disappearing War Guilt: William II in July 1914', in Afflerbach and Stevenson, eds., *An Improbable War?* Among older but essential contributions see John Röhl, 'Germany', in Wilson, ed., *Decisions for War*, and Hartmut Pogge von Strandmann, 'Germany and the Coming of War', in R. J. W. Evans and Hartmut Pogge von Strandmann, eds., *The Coming of the First World War* (Oxford, 1990).

22 See the judicious articles assembled in the 'Special Issue: The Fischer Controversy after Fifty Years' of the *Journal of Contemporary History*, 48, 2 (Apr., 2013), which estimate the merits and deficiencies of the 'Fischer Thesis'. Annika Mombauer, 'The Fischer Controversy Fifty Years On', *German Historical Institute London Bulletin*, 34, 1 (2012), 173, concludes that, to

advance our understanding of *why* the crisis happened, 'the focus must now also be on the actions of the other Great Powers'.

23 Herwig, 'Germany', in Hamilton and Herwig, eds., *Origins of World War I*, 183.

24 See for example the Kaiser's notes, on The Ambassador at Petersburg to the Foreign Office, 30 July 1914, *GD*, Doc. 401. Similarly, confronted with evidence that Austrian diplomats were betraying German assurances that Austria would seek no annexations in Serbia, Bethmann Hollweg exploded: 'This duplicity of Austria's is intolerable.' See his notes on The Ambassador at Vienna to the Imperial Chancellor, 27 July 1914, *GD*, Doc. 302.

25 McMeekin, *July 1914*, 405.

Prelude, 2 August 1914

1 'Our London Correspondence', *Manchester Guardian*, 3 Aug. 1914.

2 'ENGLAND STAND CLEAR', handbill advertising the Trafalgar Square demonstration, Rosika Schwimmer Papers, Box 1 (Hoover Institution Archives, Stanford – hereafter Hoover).

3 *Parliamentary Debates*, Commons, 5th series, vol. 65, 1787 (31 July 1914).

4 'The War of Wars', *Observer*, 2 Aug. 1914.

5 The *aide-mémoire* to Cambon is reproduced in Grey to Bertie, 2 Aug. 1914, in G. P. Gooch and Harold Temperley, eds., *British Documents on the Origins of the War, 1898–1914*, vol. XI: *The Outbreak of War: Foreign Office Documents June 28th–August 4th, 1914* (London, 1926), Doc. 487. Henceforth, all vols. cited as *BD*.

6 This account of the Cabinet of Sunday 2 August is based on an untitled, undated (but from internal evidence 3 Aug. 1914) private memorandum, on '13 Belgrave Square' notepaper, filed with Beauchamp's resignation letter to Asquith 3 Aug. 1914, Beauchamp Papers; Harcourt, Cabinet Memorandum, 2 Aug. 1914, Harcourt Papers (Bodleian Library); John Viscount Morley, *Memorandum on Resignation, August 1914* (London, 1928); and J. A. Pease Diary, 2 Aug. 1914, in Keith Wilson, 'The Cabinet Diary of J. A. Pease, 24 July–5 August 1914', *Leeds Philosophical and Literary Society*, XIX, III, (1983), [47] 9.

7 'Our London Correspondence', *Manchester Guardian*, 3 Aug. 1914.

8 Accounts of the demonstration in Trafalgar Square are given in 'Protest Meeting', *The Times*, 3 Aug. 1914, 'Against the War', *Daily News*, 3 Aug. 1914, 'Peace Demonstration in London', *Scotsman*, 3 Aug. 1914, 'Anti-War Demonstration in London' and 'Our London Correspondence', *Manchester Guardian*, 3 Aug. 1914, 'Britain Must Be Neutral', *Daily Citizen*, 3 Aug. 1914, 'The Workers' War on War', *Daily Herald*, 3 Aug. 1914, and 'Labour's War on War', *Labour Leader*, 6 Aug. 1914.

1 The Myth of an Irresistible War

1 Goldsworthy Lowes Dickinson, *The Autobiography of G. Lowes Dickinson*, edited by Dennis Proctor (London, 1973), 189.
2 Walter Hines Page to President Woodrow Wilson, 9 Aug. 1914, in Arthur S. Link, ed., *The Papers of Woodrow Wilson, Vol. 30* (Princeton, 1979), 370.
3 Untitled speech notes, n.d. (but because of references to President Wilson's 'Peace Without Victory' speech, probably early 1917), Edwin Montagu Papers, MONT 6/10/33 (Trinity College Library, Cambridge).
4 Charles Hobhouse Diary, 27 July 1914, in Charles Hobhouse, *Inside Asquith's Cabinet: From the Diaries of Charles Hobhouse*, edited by Edward David (London 1977), 177.
5 'The Cabinet which decided that war with Germany was inevitable.' See note by Runciman on his official summons (dated Saturday 1 August), Runciman Papers, WR 135/92 (Robinson Library, Special Collections, Newcastle University).
6 Burns to Asquith, 2 Aug. 1914 [handwritten copy], Burns Papers, Add. MSS. 46282/158 (British Library).
7 Simon to Asquith, 2 Aug. 1914, in a journal marked 'Diary #5', MS. Simon 2, Simon Papers (Bodleian Library).
8 Morley to Asquith, 3 Aug. 1914, in Morley, *Memorandum*, 22.
9 Beauchamp to Asquith, 3 Aug. 1914, Beauchamp Papers.
10 Charles Hobhouse Diary, Aug. [n.d.] 1914, in Hobhouse, *Inside Asquith's Cabinet*, 180.
11 Lucy Masterman, *C. F. G. Masterman: A Biography* (London, 1968), 265.
12 Cabinet Memorandum, 3 Aug. 1914, Harcourt Papers.
13 Herbert Samuel to Beatrice Samuel, 2 [but should be 3] Aug. 1914, Herbert Samuel Papers, SAM/A/157 (Parliamentary Archives).
14 Asquith to Stanley, 3 Aug. 1914, in Michael and Eleanor Brock, eds., *H. H. Asquith Letters to Venetia Stanley* (Oxford, 1985), 148. On this affair, see the introduction, 'Master of the Commons', in *Letters to Venetia Stanley*, and Naomi B. Levine, *Politics, Religion and Love: The Story of H. H. Asquith, Venetia Stanley and Edwin Montagu, Based on the Life and Letters of Edwin Samuel Montagu* (New York, 1991).
15 On Mon. 27 July, Harcourt had listed eleven ministers in the 'Peace Party': Lewis Harcourt (Colonial Office); John Morley (Lord President); Walter Runciman (Board of Agriculture); T. McKinnon Wood (Scotland); 'Jack' Pease (Board of Education); Reginald McKenna (Home Office); Lord Beauchamp (First Commissioner of Works); John Burns (Board of Trade); John Simon (Attorney General); Charles Hobhouse (Postmaster-General); and Augustine Birrell (Ireland). He added two more names as 'probably' inside his camp, Herbert Samuel (Local Government Board), and Charles Masterman (Duchy of Lancaster), making a total of thirteen. See Cabinet Memorandum, 27 July 1914, Harcourt Papers.
16 Charles Trevelyan to Asquith, 3 Aug. 1914 (Draft), Charles Trevelyan Papers, CPT 59 (Robinson Library, Special Collections, Newcastle University). See A. J. A. Morris, *C. P. Trevelyan, 1870–1958: Portrait of a Radical* (New York, 1977).

17 The most important history of the Radical dissenters is A. J. A. Morris, *Radicalism Against War, 1906–1914* (London, 1972).

18 At about 10.15 p.m. Asquith contacted Sir Almeric FitzRoy, the Clerk of the Privy Council. He in turn requested King George V to preside at a meeting of the Privy Council at Buckingham Palace as soon as possible. It gathered at the palace at 10.30 p.m. within fifteen minutes of Asquith's direction. Sir Almeric FitzRoy, *Memoirs* (London, 1922), vol. II, 561, and Typescript headed 'AT THE COURT OF BUCKINGHAM PALACE, THE 4TH DAY OF AUGUST 1914 (AT 10.35 P.M.)' listing only the King, Granard, Beauchamp, and Allendale as 'Present', appended to Almeric FitzRoy to Beauchamp, 30 Oct. 1918, in Beauchamp Papers.

19 Cabinet Memorandum, 3 Aug. 1914, Harcourt Papers; H. Samuel to B. Samuel, 2 [but should be 3] Aug. 1914, Samuel Papers.

20 For example, in David Fromkin's popular *Europe's Last Summer*, there is no mention of any of the five resignations. Describing the Cabinet meeting of Mon. 3 August, Fromkin writes, 'Opinion in the cabinet was practically unanimous.' See David Fromkin, *Europe's Last Summer: Who Started the Great War in 1914?* (New York, 2004), 248. Similarly, Hew Strachan, in his magisterial history of 1914, seems impatient to remove these troublesome men. 'By the morning of 3 August the cabinet and the country were at last effectively united.' See Hew Strachan, *The First World War. Volume I: To Arms* (Oxford, 2001), 97.

21 The anti-fascist historian Emil Ludwig was one: 'These [Morley and Burns] were the only two men in Europe who, being in possession of power, refused to subscribe to a decision, the unrighteousness of which men in every cabinet recognised but preferred not to notice.' See Emil Ludwig, *July 1914* (London, 1929), 180–1.

22 *Parliamentary Debates*, Commons, 5th series, vol. 65, 2080 (6 Aug. 1914). The same phrase was used by the editorial of the *Daily Telegraph*, 3 Aug. 1914.

23 C. E. Montague, *Disenchantment* (London, 1922), 3.

24 Lieutenant-Colonel Charles à Court Repington, *The First World War, 1914–1918: Personal Experiences* (London, 1920), I, 18–19.

25 'Proceedings in Parliament', *The Times*, 4 Aug. 1914.

26 'The Nation and the Government', editorial, *The Times*, 4 Aug. 1914 (written by John Woulfe Flanagan).

27 'Prime Minister's Eloquent Speech', *The Times*, 7 Aug. 1914.

28 Editorial, *Scotsman*, 29 Aug. 1914.

29 A. D. Harvey, *Collision of Empires: Britain in Three World Wars, 1793–1945* (London, 1994), 255.

30 Ponsonby to Asquith, 30 July 1914, Ponsonby Papers, MS. Eng. hist. c. 660 (Bodleian Library). On the formation of the Liberal Foreign Affairs Group, see Marvin Swartz, 'A Study in Futility: The British Radicals at the Outbreak of the First World War', in A. J. A. Morris, ed., *Edwardian Radicalism 1900–1914* (London, 1974), 249, Morris, *Radicalism Against War*, 408, and Cameron Hazlehurst, *Politicians at War, July 1914 to May 1915: A Prologue to the Triumph of Lloyd George* (London, 1971), 35.

31 'England's Duty in a European War: Neutrality the One Policy: The Crime and Folly of Joining In', *Manchester Guardian*, 1 Aug. 1914.

32 Asquith to Stanley, 2 Aug. 1914, in *Letters to Venetia Stanley*, 146.

33 For example, Morley to Andrew Carnegie, 28 Aug. 1914, Morley-Carnegie Correspondence, Morley Papers, MS Film 569 (Bodleian Library), and Morley to C. P. Trevelyan, 6 Oct. 1914, Trevelyan Papers, CPT 73. Emphasis in original.

34 For example, Ramsay MacDonald Diary, 6 Oct. 1914, MacDonald Papers, TNA: PRO 30/69/1753/1. (The National Archives, Kew).

35 John Morley to C. P. Scott, 13 Aug. 1914, Manchester Guardian Archive, 333/124 (University of Manchester Library).

36 See the remarks on Harcourt and Beauchamp in the handwritten version of 'Memo on Resignation', Morley Papers, MS. Eng d. 3585.

37 Morley to Carnegie, 13 Nov. 1914, Morley-Carnegie Correspondence, Morley Papers, MS Film 569.

38 W. R. Nicoll, 'Luncheon with Lord Morley at Wimbledon, 8 July 1915', in William Robertson Nicoll Papers, MS. 3518/26/6 (Aberdeen University).

39 Morley, *Memorandum*, 14.

40 The Reminiscences of Norman Angell (May 1951), 124, in the Columbia Center for Oral History Collection (hereafter referenced as CCOHC).

41 John Burns Diary, 5 Aug. and 10 Dec. 1915, Burns Papers, Add. MSS. 46337.

42 J. C. Beaglehole to his mother, 23 Dec. 1928, Beaglehole Papers, New Zealand Electronic Text Centre, Victoria University of Wellington, New Zealand, available at www.nzetc.org. For similar instances, see William Kent, *John Burns: Labour's Lost Leader: A Biography* (London, 1950), 238, 240, 249, 379.

43 John Burns Diary, 5 Aug. 1915, Burns Papers, Add. MSS. 46337.

44 See Beauchamp's letter to the editor, 'Questions of Peace', *Economist*, 17 June 1916.

45 Simon had played a prominent role in Cabinet revolts in 1911 and 1912 against commitments to the Ententes. For example, see Simon to Harcourt, 15 July 1912, filed with Harcourt Cabinet Memoranda, 1912, Harcourt Papers.

46 Simon to Asquith, 2 Aug. 1914, 'Diary #5', MS. Simon 2, Simon Papers (Bodleian Library).

47 Ibid., Simon to Asquith, 4 Aug. 1914.

48 C. P. Scott interview with Simon, 4 Sept. 1914, Scott Papers 50901, fol. 159 (British Library), as cited in James Edwin Lindsay, 'The Failure of Liberal Opposition to British Entry into World War I', unpublished PhD. thesis, Columbia University, 1969, 159.

49 Simon to Trevelyan, 29 July 1915, Trevelyan Papers, CPT 74.

50 Trevelyan to Ponsonby, 24 July 1915, Ponsonby Papers, MS. Eng. hist. c. 662.

51 Charles Trevelyan, 'Mr C. P. Trevelyan's Resignation', *Manchester Guardian*, 7 Aug. 1914, and 'Why I Left the Government', *Daily Citizen*, 7 Aug. 1914.

52 Trevelyan to Morel, 5 Aug. 1914, Morel Papers, F 6/1 (London School of Economics Archives).

53 The Reminiscences of Norman Angell (May 1951), 122–3, CCOHC.

54 By the time the UDC General Council had its first annual meeting in October 1915, there were sixty-four branches of the UDC across the United Kingdom, and twenty more in London. 'Secretary's Report. First Annual Meeting of the General Council of the Union of Democratic Control', in Minute Book of

General Council, 17 Nov. 1914 to 8 Mar. 1919, UDC Archives, UDDC/1/1 (Hull History Centre).

55 For the history of the UDC, see Marvin Swartz, *The Union of Democratic Control in British Politics During the First World War* (Oxford, 1971), and Sally Harris, *Out of Control: British Foreign Policy and the Union of Democratic Control* (Hull, 1996).

56 John Burns Diary, 1 Nov. 1911, Burns Papers, Add. MSS. 46333.

57 For example, Loreburn to Harcourt, 1 Aug. 1914, MS. Harcourt 444.

58 For example, Loreburn to Scott, 14 Oct. 1914, Manchester Guardian Archive, 333/154, or Loreburn to Hirst, 23 Dec. 1914, Francis Hirst Papers (Bodleian Library), or Loreburn to Morley 3 Nov. 1915, Morley Papers, MS. Eng. d. 3581.

59 Lord Loreburn to F. Hirst, 8 and 15 Sept. 1914, Hirst Papers.

60 Earl Loreburn's speech, *Parliamentary Debates*, Lords, 5th series, vol. xx, 181–6 (8 Nov. 1915).

61 Earl Loreburn, *How the War Came* (London, 1919), 17 and 107.

62 *Parliamentary Debates*, Commons, 5th series, vol. 65, 1833–84 (3 Aug. 1914).

63 See the minute book of the group, showing meetings on 6, 7, 10, 25, 26, 27, 28, and 31 Aug. and 9 Sept. 1914, and a roll call of leading Radicals, in Denman Papers, Box 7, Folder 4/28 (Bodleian Library).

64 P. A. Molteno to J. X. Merriman, 14 Aug. 1914, Hirst Papers.

65 R. D. Denman, 'England and the War', *Carlisle Journal*, 4 Aug. 1914, letter dated 'London, Sunday Evening.' Clippings in Denman Papers, Folder K.

66 R. D. Denman, 'Parliamentary Notes', *Carlisle Journal*, 6 (?) Aug. 1914, article dated 'House of Commons, Wednesday Evening [5 Aug. 1914]'. Clippings in Denman Papers, Folder K.

67 Trevelyan, 'Mr C. P. Trevelyan's Resignation', and 'Why I Left the Government'.

68 L. T. Hobhouse to Emily Hobhouse, 8 Aug. 1914, quoted in Jennifer Balme, *To Love One's Enemies: The Work and Life of Emily Hobhouse* (Cobble Hill, 1994), 543–4.

69 C. P. Scott to Lord Newton, 27 Aug. 1914, Manchester Guardian Archive, 333/131, 333/132.

70 F. Hirst to M. Hirst, 1 Nov. 1914, Hirst Papers.

71 Dillon to T. P. O'Connor, 5 Aug. 1914, Dillon Papers, TCD MS 6740/224 (Trinity College Dublin).

72 Ibid., Dillon to C. P. Scott, 6 Aug. 1914, TCD MS 6843/30.

73 For example, Dillon to Blunt, 1 May 1915, Wilfrid Scawen Blunt Papers, MS 131–1975 (Fitzwilliam Museum).

74 Dillon to Ellery Sedgwick, 29 Aug. 1914, Dillon file, Ellery Sedgwick Papers (Massachusetts Historical Society, Boston).

75 'Mr MacDonald and the Party', *Daily Citizen*, 7 Aug. 1914, and Christopher Howard, 'MacDonald, Henderson, and the Outbreak of War, 1914', *Historical Journal*, 20, 4 (1977), 871–91.

76 'Mr MacDonald and the War – Explanation to his Constituents', *Daily Citizen*, 8 Aug. 1914.

77 Ramsay MacDonald, 'Why We Are At War – A Reply to Sir Edward Grey', *Labour Leader*, 13 Aug. 1914.

78 Ramsay MacDonald Diary, 1 October 1914, MacDonald Papers, TNA: PRO 30/69/1753/1.

79 See Robert E. Dowse, *Left in the Centre: The Independent Labour Party, 1893–1940* (London, 1966), ch. 2. Membership of the ILP in 1909 was about 22,000.

80 NUWSS, Minutes of the Executive Committee, 18 Feb., 4 Mar., 18 Mar., and 15 Apr. 1915, showing the resignations of Royden, Courtney, Marshall, Swanwick, Ashton, Clark, Ford, Harley, Leaf, Schuster, Stansbury, and Tanner, National Union of Women's Suffrage Societies (NUWSS) Archives, 2 NWS/A1/7. See also Marshall to Fawcett, 28 Nov. 1914, Catherine Marshall Papers, D MAR 3/39 (Cumbria Record Office).

81 Eversley to Burns, 5 Aug. 1914, Burns Papers, Add. MSS. 46303.

82 George W. Russell to Edmund Barton, 6 Dec. 1914, Barton Papers NLA MS51/1/1470a/S2 (National Library of Australia).

83 W. S. Blunt Diary, 5 Aug. 1914, MS13–1975, Wilfrid Scawen Blunt Papers.

84 Bryce to Charles Trevelyan, 11 Aug. 1914, Trevelyan Papers, CPT 73.

85 Arthur Ponsonby Diary, 13 Aug. 1914 [describing 12 Aug.], Ponsonby Papers (Shulbrede Priory).

86 Dickinson, *Autobiography*, 189.

2 Mixing Signals, 23 to 26 July

1 Asquith to Stanley, 24 July 1914, in *Letters to Venetia Stanley*, 122–3.

2 Harold Nicolson, *Sir Arthur Nicolson, Bart., First Lord Carnock: A Study in the Old Diplomacy* (London, 1930), 410–11. According to Nicolson, at the Foreign Office 'everybody expected Austria to take strong action', and only Vienna's delay in launching a 'punitive expedition' against Serbia 'upset the optimistic calculations of Downing Street and the Wilhelmstrasse'.

3 This is the view of Herbert Butterfield, 'Sir Edward Grey in July 1914', *Historical Studies* [Ireland], 5 (1965), 8–11.

4 Grey to Rumbold, 6 July 1914, *BD*, vol. XI, Doc. 32.

5 Lichnowsky to Bethmann Hollweg, 6 July 1914, in Prince Lichnowsky, *Heading for the Abyss: Reminiscences* (London, 1928), 370.

6 Grey to Bertie, 8 July 1914, *BD*, vol. XI, Doc. 38.

7 Ibid., Grey to Rumbold, 9 July 1914, Doc. 41.

8 Lichnowksy to Bethmann Hollweg, 9 July 1914, and Lichnowsky to the Foreign Office, 15 July 1914.

9 J. F. V. Keiger, *Raymond Poincaré* (Cambridge, 1997), 165–9.

10 Grey to de Bunsen, 23 July 1914, *BD*, vol. XI, Doc. 86.

11 Ibid., Grey to de Bunsen, Doc. 91.

12 Michael Ekstein, 'Some Notes on Sir Edward Grey's Policy in July 1914', *Historical Journal*, XV, 2 (1972), 321–4.

13 Masterman, *Masterman*, 265–6.

14 Charles Hobhouse Diary, 27 July 1914, in Hobhouse, *Inside Asquith's Cabinet*, 176–7.

15 Asquith to Stanley, 24 July 1914, in *Letters to Venetia Stanley*, 122–3.

16 See Keith Wilson, 'The Question of Anti-Germanism at the Foreign Office Before the First World War', in Wilson, *Empire and Continent*, 50–72.

17 Buchanan to Grey, 24 July 1914, *BD*, vol. XI, Doc. 101. Emphasis added.
18 Asquith to Stanley, 26 July 1914, in *Letters to Venetia Stanley*, 125.
19 Foreign Office Telegram no. 166, Buchanan to Grey, 24 July 1914, in Montagu Papers, MONT 6/10/4. Among lines underlined in red are: 'His Majesty's Government would proclaim their solidarity with France and Russia'; '...we could not efface ourselves'; 'If war did break out, we would sooner or later be dragged into it'; and 'should not have played a "beau rôle"'.
20 Buchanan to Grey, 26 July 1914, *BD*, vol. XI, Doc. 153.
21 Ibid., Buchanan to Grey, 28 July 1914, Doc. 247.
22 Ibid., Minute of Eyre Crowe (dated 25 July) on Buchanan to Grey, 24 July 1914, and see Crowe to Grey, 31 July 1914, Doc. 101, 369. Emphasis added.
23 Ibid., minute of Eyre Crowe on Bertie to Grey, 30 July 1914, Doc. 318.
24 Ibid., Grey to Bertie, 26 July 1914, and repeated to Vienna, St Petersburg, Nish, Berlin and Rome, Doc. 140.
25 Ibid., Lichnowsky to Grey, 26 July 1914, Doc. 145.
26 For example, Grey's speech of 26 Jan. 1916, reproduced as *Great Britain's Measures Against German Trade* (London, 1916), 30.
27 Viscount Grey of Fallodon, *Twenty-Five Years, 1892–1916* (London, 1925), I, 321.
28 Grey to Buchanan, 20 July 1914, *BD*, vol. XI, Doc. 67. 'It would be very desirable that Austria and Russia should discuss things together if they become difficult.'
29 Ibid., Buchanan to Grey, 22 July 1914, Doc. 76.
30 Ibid., Grey to Buchanan, 22 July 1914, Doc. 79.
31 For example, ibid., Grey to Rumbold, 24 July 1914, Grey to Buchanan, 25 July 1914, Grey to Rumbold, 25 July 1914, and Grey to Buchanan, 25 July 1914, Doc. 99, 112, 116, 132.
32 Ibid., Grey to Buchanan, 25 July 1914, Doc. 132.
33 The quotation here is from Harold Nicolson, *King George V: His Life and Reign* (London, 1952), 244. A different version of the quotation from George V's Diary, 25 July 1914, is quoted in Catrine Clay, *King, Kaiser, Tsar: Three Royal Cousins Who Led the World to War* (New York, 2007), 305: 'It looks as though we were on the verge of a European War caused by sending an ultimatum to Serbia by Austria.'
34 Nicolson to Grey (n.d. – July 26), Grey to Resident Clerk, Foreign Office, 26 July 1914, and Nicolson to Grey, 26 July 1914, *BD*, vol. XI, Doc. 139 (a) and (b), 144.
35 On Nicolson's life and foreign policy outlook, see Zara Steiner, *The Foreign Office and Foreign Policy, 1898–1914* (Cambridge, 1969), 121–53, Keith Neilson, '"My Beloved Russians": Sir Arthur Nicolson and Russia, 1906–1916', *The International History Review*, 9, 4 (Nov. 1987), 521–54, and Nicolson, *Sir Arthur Nicolson*.
36 What King George V actually said to Prince Heinrich remains controversial. According to a record drawn up later by the King, clearly designed to minimise its significance, the discussion was brief: 'He then asked what England would do if there was a European war. I said "I don't know what we shall do, we have no quarrel with anyone & I hope we shall remain neutral. But if Germany declared war on Russia, & France joins Russia, then I am afraid we shall be dragged into it. But you can be sure that I & my Government will do all we

can to prevent a European war!" Undated note in Royal Archives, R.A.Q. 1167 (15), quoted in Nicolson, *King George V*, 245–6.

37 Nicolson to Grey, 26 July 1914, *BD*, vol. XI, Doc. 144.

38 Ottoline Morrell Journal, reporting upon 25 July 1914, reproduced in Robert Gathorne-Hardy, ed., *The Early Memoirs of Lady Ottoline Morrell* (London, 1963), 258.

39 Levine, *Politics, Religion and Love*, 177.

40 *Early Memoirs of Lady Morrell*, 258.

41 Harcourt Memorandum, 26 July 1914, Harcourt Papers.

42 'Policy of Great Britain: Speeches by Sir J. Simon and Mr. Acland', *The Times*, 27 July 1914. Emphasis added.

43 For example, 'British Troops Fire on Irish Nationalists', *Daily Citizen*, 27 July 1914.

44 Julian S. Corbett, *History of the Great War, Based on Official Documents: Naval Operations, vol. 1. To the Battle of the Falkland Islands, December 1914* (London, 1920), 22–3.

45 Admiralty to C. in C. Home Fleets, 26 July 1914, Churchill Papers, CHAR 13/36/33, 'Admiralty note on the significant dates of the mobilisation of the Fleet in July–August 1914', Churchill Papers, CHAR 13/27B/2–3 (Churchill Archives Centre), Martin Gilbert, *Winston S. Churchill, Volume III: 1914–1916* (London, 1971), 6, and Corbett, *Naval Operations*, 24–5. According to Corbett, 'Quietly, too, the Admiralty proceeded to take other precautionary actions which had been left open to it.'

46 Winston Churchill, *The World Crisis 1911–1918* (London, 1938), I, 160.

47 Masterman, *Masterman*, 265.

48 'British Naval Measures', *The Times*, 27 July 1914.

49 Grey to Buchanan, 27 July 1914, *BD*, vol. XI, Doc. 177, marked 'Repeated to Paris', and Grey to Bertie, 28 July 1914, *BD*, vol. XI, Doc. 238.

50 'Sea Forces of the Powers', *The Times*, 28 July 1914.

51 McMeekin, *Russian Origins of the First World War*, 59. Emphasis in original.

52 Kiesling, 'France', in Hamilton and Herwig, eds., *The Origins of World War I*, 229–30, and see Krumeich, *Armaments and Politics*, 216.

53 See Schmidt, *Frankreichs Aussenpolitik in der Julikrise 1914*, reviewed in Trachtenberg, 'French Foreign Policy in the July Crisis', 6.

54 Poincaré Diary, 25 July 1914, quoted in Krumeich, *Armaments and Politics*, 220.

55 Ibid., 27 July 1914, quoted ibid., 221. The telegram was probably Cambon's report of his first interview with Grey on the ultimatum on Friday 24 July. See also Grey to Bertie, 24 July 1914, summarising this Cambon interview, *BD*, vol. XI, Doc. 98.

56 Poincaré Diary, 27 July 1914, quoted in Keiger, *Poincaré*, 170, and Krumeich, *Armaments and Politics*, 221.

57 Quoted in Krumeich, *Armaments and Politics*, 221. Emphasis added.

58 Keiger, *Poincaré*, 170.

3 'Apparent Indecision', 27 July

1 Charles Hobhouse Diary, 27 July 1914, in Hobhouse, *Inside Asquith's Cabinet*, 177.
2 Henry Massingham, 'Events of the Week', *Nation*, 8 Aug. 1914.
3 Compare the different assessments of the leanings of the ministers in the Cabinet made by historians who have studied these events most closely. See 'Parties in the Cabinet', a document drawn up by H. W. Temperley in 1928, when, with the assistance of J. A. Spender, he investigated the position of the surviving Cabinet ministers. See Temperley to Spender, 1 Jan. 1928, Spender Papers, Add. MSS. 46386 (British Library). See also varying judgements made by Lindsay, 'The Failure of Liberal Opposition to British Entry into World War I', 61, fns. 4, 5, Cameron Hazlehurst, *Politicians at War, July 1914 to May 1915: A Prologue to the Triumph of Lloyd George* (London, 1971), ch. 5., Michael Brock, 'Britain Enters the War', in Evans and von Strandmann, eds., *The Coming of the First World War*, 145–178, Keith Wilson, 'Britain', in Wilson, ed., *Decisions for War*, 175–208, and J. Paul Harris, 'Britain', in Hamilton and Herwig, eds., *Origins of World War I*, 282.
4 Runciman to Harcourt, 24 Aug. 1911, Harcourt Cabinet Memoranda, 1911, Harcourt Papers.
5 John W. Coogan and Peter F. Coogan, 'The British Cabinet and the Anglo-French Staff Talks, 1905–1914: Who Knew What and When Did He Know It?', *Journal of British Studies*, 24, 1 (1985), 110–31, Hew Strachan, 'The British Army, Its General Staff and the Continental Commitment, 1904–1914', in David French and Brian Holden Reid, eds, *The British General Staff: Reform and Innovation, 1890–1939* (London, 2002), 75–94. For the documents on the beginnings of this process, both Anglo-French and Anglo-Belgian conversations, see also *BD*, vol. III, ch. XX.
6 Morley to Harcourt, 8 Sept. 1911, Cabinet Memoranda, 1911, Harcourt Papers.
7 Cabinet Memorandum, 15 Nov. 1911, Harcourt Papers.
8 'Decision of the Cabinet, 15 Nov. 1911', and separate notes giving consent from Loreburn and Morley to Harcourt filed with Cabinet Memorandum, 15 Nov. 1911, Harcourt Papers.
9 Quoted in Samuel R. Williamson, *The Politics of Grand Strategy: Britain and France Prepare for War, 1904-1914* (Cambridge, MA, 1969), 287.
10 Minute from Churchill to Asquith and Grey, 23 Aug. 1912, Churchill Papers, CHAR 13/10/40–42.
11 Cabinet Memorandum, 15 July 1912, Harcourt Papers. Emphasis in original.
12 J. A. Simon to Harcourt, 15 July 1912, filed with Harcourt Cabinet Memoranda, 1912, Harcourt Papers.
13 Ibid., Morley to Harcourt, 15 July 1912.
14 Ibid., Cartoon with caption, filed between Cabinet Memoranda dated 22 and 30 Oct. 1912.
15 Cabinet Memorandum, 30 Oct. 1912 and 1 Nov. 1912, Harcourt Papers. Emphasis in original.
16 Grey to Cambon, 22 Nov. 1912, *BD*, vol. X, pt. 2, Doc. 416.

17 Cabinet Memorandum, 30 Oct. 1912, Harcourt Papers.

18 H. Asquith to M. Asquith, 5 Jan. 1914, Margot Asquith Papers, MS. Eng. c. 6691. (Bodleian Library).

19 F. W. Wiemann, 'Lloyd George and the Struggle for the Navy Estimates of 1914', in A. J. P. Taylor, ed., *Lloyd George: Twelve Essays* (London, 1971), 79, and John Grigg, *Lloyd George: From Peace to War 1912–1916* (London, 1997), 134–6.

20 George Riddell Diary, 14 Dec. 1913, in John McEwen, ed., *The Riddell Diaries: A Selection* (London, 1986), 73.

21 H. Asquith to M. Asquith, 20 Jan. 1914, M. Asquith Papers, MS. Eng. c. 6691.

22 Ibid., H. Asquith to M. Asquith, 20 and 27 Jan. 1914.

23 Asquith to Churchill, 1 Feb. 1914, in Randolph S. Churchill, ed., *Winston Spencer Churchill: Companion Volume*, II, 3 (Boston, 1969), 1860–1.

24 H. Asquith to M. Asquith, 20 Jan. 1914, M. Asquith Papers, MS. Eng. c. 6691.

25 Useful introductions to this vast field are Avner Offer, *The First World War: An Agrarian Interpretation* (Oxford, 1989), 'Part Three: the Atlantic Orientation', and Bernard Semmel, *Liberalism and Naval Strategy: Ideology, Interest and Sea Power during the Pax Britannica* (Boston, 1986), esp. chs. 6–9.

26 For example, see Hazlehurst, *Politicians at War*, ch. 6, Bentley B. Gilbert, 'Pacifist to Interventionist: David Lloyd George in 1911 and 1914. Was Belgium an Issue?', *Historical Journal*, 28, 4 (1985), 863–85, Keith Wilson, 'The War Office, Churchill, and the Belgian Option – August to December 1911', in Wilson, *Empire and Continent*, 126–40, and 'The Military Entente with France', in Wilson, *Policy of the Entente*, 121–34.

27 The case that Grey and Asquith were not exactly alike in their enthusiasm for the Entente, and that Asquith's intense friendship with Grey was the crucial factor, is put in George Cassar, *Asquith as War Leader* (London, 1994), 22.

28 Asquith to Stanley, 3 Aug. 1914, in *Letters to Venetia Stanley*, 148.

29 Ibid., Asquith to Stanley, 1 Aug. 1914, 140.

30 Martin Farr, *Reginald McKenna: Financier Among Statesmen, 1863–1916* (New York, 2008), 207–22.

31 McKenna to Spender, 8 May 1929, Spender Papers, Add. MSS. 46386. Farr quotes a slightly different, but equally fatalistic, formulation: 'I never had the slightest doubt during the cabinet discussions that we should be fully engaged in the war.' See McKenna to J. A. Spender, 6 Feb. 1929, quoted in Farr, *Reginald McKenna*, 259.

32 Margot Asquith Diary, 2 Sept. 1912, 'Snap Division Dinner', Nov. 1912, and 'The Enchantress Tour, May 1913', M. Asquith Papers, MS. Eng. c. 3210.

33 Cabinet Memorandum, 9 Apr. 1913, Harcourt Papers.

34 Ibid.

35 Churchill note to Morley, 29 Apr. 1914, Churchill Papers, CHAR 21/36.

36 W. Runciman to C. P. Trevelyan, 4 Jan. 1914, Trevelyan Papers, CPT 33.

37 John Morley to Reginald McKenna, 3 July 1912, McKenna Papers, MCKN 4/4 (Churchill Archives Centre).

38 Churchill, *World Crisis*, I, 161.

39 Grey, *Twenty-Five Years*, I, 334.

40 Morley, *Memorandum*, 4.

41 Cabinet Memorandum, 27 July 1914, Harcourt Papers.

42 Ibid., 29 July 1914. He dropped Birrell, Masterman, Pease and McKenna from the list.

43 Runciman, untitled document in response to Harold Temperley questionnaire, 4 Nov. 1929, Spender Papers, Add. MS. 46386.

44 Herbert Samuel to Clara Samuel, 26 July 1914, Samuel Papers, SAM/A/156. He told his wife Beatrice the same thing. H. Samuel to B. Samuel, 2 Aug. 1914, Samuel Papers, SAM/A/157, recalling his conversation of 'Last Sunday'.

45 H. Samuel to C. Samuel, 26 July 1914, Samuel Papers, SAM/A/156.

46 Northcliffe to Dawson, 8 Aug. 1912, Northcliffe Papers, Add. MS. 62244 (British Library). Geoffrey Robinson changed his surname to Dawson in 1918 to fulfil the terms of a legacy. The name Dawson is employed hereafter to avoid confusion.

47 Later, in the leader-writer diary of *The Times*, the editorial was attributed to Flanagan, but if Steed's account is accurate the thrust of it was Steed's. See Henry Wickham Steed, 'Across the Years' (1951), unpublished autobiography in typescript, 287–9, in Henry Wickham Steed Papers, Add. MS. 74199 (British Library), and 'Times Editorial Diary for 1914', 27 July 1914, Times Newspapers Limited Archive, hereafter TNLA (News International Record Office, Enfield). On Steed's significance at this time, see *The History of the Times*, vol. IV: *The 150th Anniversary and Beyond, 1912–1948*, pt. I (London, 1952), 207, and Evelyn Wrench, *Geoffrey Dawson and Our Times* (London, 1955), 103–4.

48 Steed, 'Across the Years', 287–8, Steed Papers, Add. MS. 74199.

49 'Europe and the Crisis', editorial, *The Times*, 27 July 1914.

50 Scott Diary, 27 July 1914, in Trevor Wilson, ed., *The Political Diaries of C. P. Scott, 1911–1928* (London, 1970), 91.

51 Edmund Harvey to his father, 30 July 1914, Thomas Edmund Harvey Papers.

52 Asquith to Stanley, 27 July 1914, in *Letters to Venetia Stanley*, 127.

53 *Parliamentary Debates*, Commons, 5th series, vol. 65, 936–8 (27 July 1914).

54 H. Samuel to B. Samuel, 27 July 1914, Samuel Papers, SAM/A/157, and Cabinet Memorandum, 27 July 1914, Harcourt Papers.

55 In his post-war *Memorandum*, Morley recalled Grey pressing the Cabinet, even at this early stage, to 'make up its mind plainly whether we were to take an active part with the other two Powers of the Entente, or to stand aside in the general European question, and preserve an absolute neutrality'. See Morley, *Memorandum*, 1, fn. 1. But Morley in preparing his manuscript first dated this to 26 July, then substituted 'On or about July 24–27'.

56 Grey, *Twenty-Five Years*, I, 334, 338.

57 Pease Diary, 27 July 1914, in Wilson, 'Diary of Pease', [43] 5.

58 Morley, *Memorandum*, 1.

59 Charles Hobhouse Diary, 27 July 1914, in Hobhouse, *Inside Asquith's Cabinet*, 177.

60 H. Samuel to B. Samuel, 27 July 1914, Samuel Papers.

61 Cabinet Memorandum, 27 July 1914, Harcourt Papers.

62 The Director General of the Hapag [Ballin] to the Secretary of State for Foreign Affairs, 24 July 1914, Kautsky, *GD*, Doc. 254. On Grey's dissembling over the Anglo-Russian naval conversations, see Grey, *Twenty-Five Years*, I, 284.

63 Cabinet Memorandum, 27 July 1914, Harcourt Papers.

64 On the discrepancies in the surviving German sources and British sources on Ballin's mission, see Lamar Cecil, *Albert Ballin: Business and Politics in Imperial Germany, 1888–1918* (Princeton, 1967), 205–10. Churchill later turned aside requests from the American historian Bernadotte Schmitt to resolve the issues. See Bernadotte Schmitt to Churchill, 12 Mar. 1928, Churchill Papers, CHAR 2/157/59, and Edward Marsh to Schmitt, 14 Mar. 1928, Churchill Papers, CHAR 2/157/57.

65 Asquith to the King, 28 July 1914, reproduced in J. A. Spender and C. Asquith, *Life of H. H. Asquith, Lord Oxford and Asquith* (London, 1932), II, 81.

66 Ibid.

4 Manoeuvring in the Dark, 27 and 28 July

1 Cabinet Memorandum, 27 July 1914, Harcourt Papers.

2 Ibid.

3 Ibid.

4 Diary entry for 28 July 1914, in FitzRoy, *Memoirs*, II, 557.

5 Scott Diary, 27 July 1914, in Wilson, *Political Diaries of C. P. Scott*, 92–3.

6 Cabinet Memorandum, 27 July 1914, Harcourt Papers.

7 Grey to Rumbold, 6 July 1914, *BD*, vol. XI, Doc. 32.

8 Ibid., minute on Buchanan to Grey, 27 July 1914, Doc. 179.

9 Ibid., Goschen to Grey, 27 July 1914 (received at 9 p.m.), Doc. 185.

10 Ibid., Grey to Goschen, 28 July 1914, Doc. 218.

11 See ibid., Goschen to Grey, 28 July 1914 (received Wednesday 29 July, 8 a.m.), Doc. 249.

12 Ibid., Grey to Goschen, 29 July 1914, Doc. 263.

13 Partial mobilisation, under the guise of 'preparatory measures', was in fact decided upon by the Tsar and his Ministerial Council on Saturday 25 July. See David Allan Rich, 'Russia', in Hamilton and Herwig, eds., *Origins of World War I*, 221. This was known about at the Foreign Office in London late in the evening of 25 July, when Buchanan's cable arrived; see Buchanan to Grey, 25 July 1914, *BD*, vol. XI, Doc. 125. See also L. C. F. Turner, 'The Russian Mobilisation in 1914', *Journal of Contemporary History*, III (1968), 65–88.

14 Bertie to Grey, 27 July 1914, *BD*, vol. XI, Doc. 183.

15 Ibid., Doc. 192.

16 Ibid., Doc. 184. The minutes attached show that Crowe advised Grey against any such action.

17 Fischer, *War of Illusions*, 484–8.

18 S. B. Fay, *The Origins of the World War* (Toronto, 1966), II, 386, and compare Bernadotte Schmitt, *The Coming of the War, 1914* (New York, 1966), II, 49–51.

19 For documents from the Russian Embassy in London on the Anglo-Russian naval conversations in May–June 1914, and the Grey–Benckendorff discussions on how Grey might evade parliamentary questions on the matter, see B. de Siebert, *Entente Diplomacy and the World War*, edited by George Abel Schreiner (New York, 1921), 724–34, Docs. 850–8.

20 Kurt Riezler Diary, 7 July 1914, quoted in Wayne C. Thompson, *In the Eye of the Storm: Kurt Riezler and the Crisis of Modern Germany* (Iowa City, 1980), 74.

21 Zara Steiner and Keith Neilson, *Britain and the Origins of the First World War* (London, 2003), 132.

22 Grey to Buchanan, 25 July 1914, *BD*, vol. XI, Doc. 132.

23 Ibid., Crowe minute, 28 July, on Goschen to Grey, 27 July 1914, Doc. 185.

24 Hobhouse Diary, 14 Aug. 1914, in Hobhouse, *Inside Asquith's Cabinet*, 182.

25 As early as 22 July Crowe advised that Britain could not address 'admonitions' to Russia, as such a policy would be a capitulation to German designs, and 'the much desired breach between England and Russia would be brought one step nearer realisation'. See H. Rumbold to Sir Edward Grey, 22 July 1914, minute by Eyre Crowe, in *BD*, vol. XI, Doc. 77. Similarly Nicolson advised Grey on 25 July that 'Our attitude during the crisis will be regarded by Russia as a test and we must be careful not to alienate her.' See George Buchanan to Sir Edward Grey, 24 July, and minutes by Crowe and Nicolson, in *BD*, vol. XI, Doc. 101.

26 See ibid., Buchanan to Grey, 25 July 1914, Doc. 124.

27 These lines are underlined in Harcourt's copy of Telegram no. 169, Buchanan to Grey, 25 July 1914, in Foreign Office Telegrams, May–Aug. 1914, MS Harcourt 552.

28 On Bertie's reservations about Russia, see Bertie to Grey, 27 July 1914, *BD*, vol. XI, Doc. 192. See also Wilson, 'Britain', in his *Decisions for War*, 184–6, 200.

29 See Lichnowsky to the Foreign Office [in Berlin], 24 July and 25 July 1914, Lichnowsky, *Heading for the Abyss*, 389 and 393.

30 Ibid., Lichnowsky to the Foreign Office [in Berlin], 25 July 1914, 394.

31 Ibid., 395.

32 Ibid., Lichnowsky to the Foreign Office [in Berlin], 27 July 1914 [two cablegrams], 398–401, and see Harry Young, *Prince Lichnowsky and the Great War* (Athens, Georgia, 1977), 110.

33 Grey had given instructions, following Radical complaints, that the phrase 'Triple Entente' – constantly used by *The Times* – was not to be used in official documents because it wrongly suggested that England was a member of a formal alliance system comparable with 'Triple Alliance'. See Harcourt to Grey, 8, 9 and 14 Jan. 1914, and Grey to Harcourt, 10 and 11 Jan. 1914, filed with Harcourt Cabinet Memoranda, 1914, Harcourt Papers, and see Wilson, 'Grey', in Keith Wilson, ed., *British Foreign Secretaries and Foreign Policy: From Crimean War to First World War* (London, 1987), 189.

34 Admiralty to all Cs in C. abroad, 27 July 1914, Churchill Papers, CHAR 13/37/59, and, for example, Admiralty to S.N.O. Gibraltar, S.N.O. New Zealand, 27 July 1914, ADM 137/7/11, and see Churchill, *World Crisis*, I, 166. Emphasis in original.

35 Churchill, *World Crisis*, I, 171.

36 Admiralty to C. in C. Home Fleets, 28 July 1914, Churchill Papers, CHAR 13/36/35.

37 Churchill, *World Crisis*, I, 171.

38 Corbett, *Naval Operations*, 26.

39 Churchill to Clementine, 28 July 1914, in Churchill, ed., *Churchill: Companion Volume*, II, 3, 1989.

40 Churchill, *World Crisis*, I, 171.
41 Bunsen to Grey, *BD*, vol. XI, Doc. 226.
42 Churchill to Lloyd George, Cabinet note, undated (possibly 1 Aug. 1914), Lloyd George Papers, LG/C/13B, number 8 (Parliamentary Archives).
43 Henry Wilson Diary, 26, 27, 28 July 1914, reproduced in C. E. Callwell, ed., *Field-Marshal Sir Henry Wilson* (London, 1927), I, 151–2.
44 Churchill, *World Crisis*, I, 161. Emphasis in original.
45 'Measures at Home and Abroad', *The Times*, 30 July 1914.
46 'England and the War Menace', *Manchester Guardian*, 30 July 1914, including an extract from the editorial of the *Daily Chronicle*.
47 Corbett, *Naval Operations*, 26–7.
48 Reuter's Correspondent, 'Russia: War Excitement', dated 'St Petersburg, Thursday', *Manchester Guardian*, 31 July 1914.
49 The report was widely circulated. For example, see 'The War Fever: Russia's Determination', dated 'St Petersburg, 31 July 1914', *Sydney Morning Herald*, 1 Aug. 1914. For a similar report, see Harold Williams, 'War Fever in St Petersburg', *Irish Times*, 31 July 1914.
50 Churchill, 'Winston Churchill. Fleet.', 26 Nov. 1914, Asquith Papers, MS Asquith 26.
51 Corbett, *Naval Operations*, 31.
52 Fisher to Churchill, 31 July 1914, Churchill Papers, CHAR 13/28/21–2.

5 Facing Both Ways, 29 July

 1 H. Samuel to B. Samuel, 29 July 1914, Samuel Papers. The letter is quoted also in Hazlehurst, *Politicians at War*, 78–9.
 2 For example, Buchanan to Grey, 25 July 1914, specified the Tsar's decision to sanction the drafting of an Imperial Ukase which ordered the mobilisation of more than a million soldiers, and Buchanan noted that preliminary preparations for mobilisation would 'be begun at once'; *BD*, vol. XI, Doc. 125. See also ibid., 'Communication from the French Embassy', 27 July 1914, Buchanan to Grey, 28 July 1914, and Consul-General Roberts to Grey, 29 July 1914, Docs. 173, 234, 260. Confirmation of the partial mobilisation came in M. de Bunsen to Grey, 29 July 1914 (received London, 30 July, 11 a.m.), *BD*, vol. XI, Doc. 295.
 3 Cabinet Memorandum, 29 July 1914, Harcourt Papers. Emphasis in original.
 4 Ibid.
 5 See the terms of the treaty, *Parliamentary Debates*, Commons, 3rd series, vol. 203, 1776 (10 Aug. 1870).
 6 Cabinet Memorandum, 29 July 1914, Harcourt Papers.
 7 Ibid.
 8 Pease Diary, 29 July 1914, in Wilson, 'Diary of Pease', [44] 6.
 9 See Gladstone's announcement of the terms of the treaties and the subsequent debate, *Parliamentary Debates*, Commons, 3rd series, vol. 203, 1699–1706, 1776–92 (8 and 10 Aug. 1870).
10 Cabinet Memorandum, 29 July 1914, Harcourt Papers.

11 Ibid.
12 Asquith to the King, 30 July 1914, reproduced in Spender, *Life of Asquith*, II, 81.
13 Cabinet Memorandum, 29 July 1914, Harcourt Papers. Emphasis in original.
14 Ibid.
15 Pease Diary, 29 July 1914, in Wilson, 'Diary of Pease', [44] 6–[45] 7.
16 Ibid.
17 Cabinet Memorandum, 29 July 1914, Harcourt Papers. Emphasis in original.
18 H. Samuel to B. Samuel, 29 July 1914, Samuel Papers.
19 Cabinet Memorandum, 29 July 1914, Harcourt Papers. Although he did not record Lloyd George in this list, he did note that the Chancellor was 'less bellicose' in this Cabinet meeting.
20 Pease Diary, 29 July 1914, in Wilson, 'Diary of Pease', [44] 6–[45] 7.
21 Ramsay MacDonald Diary, 6 Oct. 1914, MacDonald Papers, TNA: PRO 30/69/1753/1.
22 Morley, *Memorandum*, 2.
23 Cabinet Memorandum, 29 July 1914, Harcourt Papers.
24 Pease Diary, 29 July 1914, in Wilson, 'Diary of Pease', [44] 6–[45] 7.
25 Asquith to the King, 30 July 1914, reproduced in Spender, *Life of Asquith*, II, 81.
26 M. Crackanthorpe to Grey, *BD*, vol. XI, Doc. 269, and 'Belgrade Fighting', *Manchester Guardian*, 30 July 1914.
27 Luigi Albertini, *The Origins of the War of 1914*, vol. III (New York, 2005), 38.
28 Henry Wilson Diary, 29 July 1914, reproduced in Callwell, *Wilson*, I, 151–2.
29 Grey to Bertie, 29 July 1914, *BD*, vol. XI, Doc. 283 and see Wilson, 'Britain', in *Decisions for War*, 190.
30 Lichnowsky to Foreign Office [Berlin], 29 July 1914, Lichnowsky, *Heading for the Abyss*, 405–6. Emphasis in the original. See also Grey to Goschen, 29 July 1914, *BD*, vol. XI, Docs. 284, 285 (both marked 'Not sent – War'), and see Young, *Lichnowsky*, 111.
31 Maurice Hankey, *The Supreme Command 1914-1918* (London, 1961), I, 154–5.
32 Hankey to Adeline, 29 July 1914, Hankey Papers, HNKY 3/19 (Churchill Archives Centre).
33 Ibid.
34 'Measures at Home and Abroad', *The Times*, 30 July 1914.
35 Asquith to Stanley, 29 July 1914, in *Letters to Venetia Stanley*, 132.
36 Margot Asquith Diary, 29 July 1914, M. Asquith Papers, Ms. Eng. d. 3210.
37 Ibid.
38 Cabinet Memorandum, 29 July 1914, Harcourt Papers.
39 Cabinet Memorandum, 29 and 30 July 1914, Harcourt Papers.
40 Cabinet Memorandum, 30 July 1914, Harcourt Papers.
41 Harcourt lists his source as 'Lambert of Admiralty', which means that his source was either Captain Lambert, the Fourth Sea Lord, or possibly George Lambert MP, the Civil Lord of the Admiralty at this time.
42 Cabinet Memorandum, 29 and 30 July 1914, Harcourt Papers.

6 Drum-Taps, 27 to 31 July

1 'Interests and Duty of Great Britain', editorial, *The Times*, 31 July 1914 (written by Henry Wickham Steed).

2 *The History of the Times*, vol. IV, pt. I, 197.

3 'The Powers and Mediation', editorial, *The Times*, 28 July 1914 (written by John Woulfe Flanagan).

4 Charles Repington, 'The Great Powers and the War', *The Times*, 30 July 1914.

5 'The Efforts for Peace', editorial, *The Times*, 29 July 1914 (written by John Woulfe Flanagan).

6 'The Efforts for Peace', editorial, and Parliamentary Correspondent, 'Sir Edward Grey's Proposals', *The Times*, 29 July 1914.

7 'Lowering Clouds', editorial, *The Times*, 30 July 1914 (written by John Woulfe Flanagan).

8 For example, 'A Cruel Suspense', editorial, *Daily Telegraph*, 30 July 1914. Confirmation reached the Foreign Office in London during the morning of 30 July; Sir M. de Bunsen to Grey, 29 July 1914 (received at 11 a.m., 30 July), *BD*, vol. XI, Doc. 295. Grey confirmed this in a reply to Bonar Law in the Commons on 30 July; see *Parliamentary Debates*, Commons, 5th series, vol. 65, 1574 (30 July 1914).

9 'Interests and Duty of Great Britain', editorial, *The Times*, 31 July 1914.

10 For example, see the editorials, *Daily Mail*, 25 and 26 July 1914.

11 For example, see 'A United Front', editorial, *Daily Mail*, 31 July 1914.

12 See J. Lee Thompson, *A Wider Patriotism: Alfred Milner and the British Empire* (London, 2008), and John Kendle, *The Round Table Movement and Imperial Union* (Toronto, 1975).

13 Chirol to Hardinge, 4 Aug. 1914, Hardinge Papers, 93 Part I (Cambridge University Library). See also his editorial, 'The Responsibilities', *The Times*, 5 Aug. 1914.

14 The official *History of the Times* claimed that 'at Northcliffe's wish, Steed was in charge of the paper from the morning of the 26th until the night of July 31–August 1'. See *The History of the Times*, vol. IV, pt. I, 207. According to his wife Molly, Northcliffe himself had masterfully stepped in to administer close control over the editorial line of *The Times* when the paper's normal chief editor Geoffrey Dawson 'had broken down'. See Alan Clark, ed., *A Good Innings: The Private Papers of Viscount Lee of Fareham* (London, 1974), 133.

15 Geoffrey Dawson Diary, 24 July 1914, MSS. Dawson 20, Geoffrey Dawson Papers (Bodleian Library). See 'Child Killed on the Embankment', *The Times*, 29 July 1914. The child was Hector McAdam, aged ten.

16 Dawson Diary, 26 July 1914, MSS. Dawson 20.

17 'Times Editorial Diary for 1914', 27 July 1914, TNLA.

18 Dawson Diary, 27 July 1914, MSS. Dawson 20.

19 Ibid., 28 July 1914.

20 'Times Editorial Diary for 1914', 28 July 1914, TNLA.

21 He acknowledged many years later that he was in command only for the weekend 24-27 July. See Steed, 'Across the Years', 287–8, Steed Papers, Add. MSS. 74199.

22 Dawson Diary, 29 July 1914, MSS. Dawson 20.

23 'Times Editorial Diary for 1914', 30 and 31 July 1914, TNLA.
24 Dawson Diary, 31 July 1914, MSS. Dawson 20.
25 'War', editorial, *Daily Telegraph*, 29 July 1914.
26 Leo Amery Diary, 1 Aug. 1914, in John Barnes and David Nicholson, eds., *The Leo Amery Diaries: Volume One: 1896–1929* (London, 1980), 105.
27 'A Cruel Suspense', editorial, *Daily Telegraph*, 30 July 1914.
28 'A Gloomy Prospect', editorial, *Daily Telegraph*, 31 July 1914.
29 *Morning Post*, 27 July 1914.
30 *Pall Mall Gazette*, 29 July 1914, quoted in Jonathan French Scott, *Five Weeks: The Surge of Public Opinion on the Eve of the Great War* (New York, 1927), 236.
31 William Tyrrell to Ponsonby, 31 July 1914, Ponsonby Papers, MS. Eng. hist. c. 660, f. 56.
32 T. G. Otte, 'Détente 1914: Sir William Tyrrell's Secret Mission to Germany', *Historical Journal*, 56, 1 (2013), 175–204.
33 Charles Trevelyan, 'C. P. T's personal record of the days that led up to the War of 1914 and to his resignation', twelve-page typescript, Trevelyan Papers, CPT 59.

7 Hope and Dread, 27 to 31 July

1 'Russia and the War', editorial, *Daily News*, 29 July 1914.
2 'Storm Clouds', editorial, *Westminster Gazette*, 25 July 1914.
3 'A Duty For All Parties', editorial, *Westminster Gazette*, 27 July 1914.
4 'A "Clean Cut" – of Law-Breaking', editorial, *Westminster Gazette*, 28 July 1914.
5 'Hopes and Fears', editorial, *Westminster Gazette*, 29 July 1914, and 'Extreme Gravity', editorial, *Westminster Gazette*, 30 July 1914.
6 'Extreme Gravity', editorial, *Westminster Gazette*, 30 July 1914.
7 'Between Fear and Hope', editorial, *Westminster Gazette*, 31 July 1914.
8 David Ayerst, *The Manchester Guardian: Biography of a Newspaper* (Ithaca, 1971), 372–3, and H. D. Nichols, 'Scott's Lieutenants', in William Haley, et al., *C. P. Scott, 1846–1932: The Making of the Manchester Guardian* (London, 1946), 119–20. Scott himself was visiting Jena in Germany during July 1914, for medical assistance with his eyes, and he did not return until Mon. 27 July. In the writing of editorials during the week of diplomatic crisis, therefore, Scott probably shared the task with Sidebotham. L. T. Hobhouse turned aside praise for the editorials for that week; see L. T. Hobhouse to Lord Courtney, 4 Aug. 1914, Leonard and Kate Courtney Papers, vol. XI (London School of Economics Archive).
9 'The European Crisis', editorial, *Manchester Guardian*, 25 July 1914.
10 For example, 'A Terrible Danger', editorial, *Manchester Guardian*, 27 July 1914, and 'England and the European Crisis', editorial, *Manchester Guardian*, 28 July 1914.
11 'England and the European Crisis', *Manchester Guardian*.
12 'Peace or War', editorial, *Manchester Guardian*, 29 July 1914.
13 'England's Danger', editorial, *Manchester Guardian*, 30 July 1914.
14 Ibid.

15 'Parliament and the Crisis', editorial, *Manchester Guardian*, 31 July 1914.
16 'On the Brink of War', editorial, *Daily News*, 27 July 1914.
17 'A Day of Hope', editorial, *Daily News*, 28 July 1914.
18 'Russia and the War', editorial, *Daily News*, 29 July 1914.
19 'Hopes and Fears', editorial, *Daily News*, 30 July 1914.
20 For example, *Daily News*, letters to the editor, 'England and the Crisis – Why We Should Not Be Drawn In', with letters from Lord Lamington, John Jardine MP, Joseph King MP, and Francis Hirst, 31 July 1914. Many more letters to the editor were to appear under the title 'England and the Crisis', *Daily News*, 3 Aug. 1914.
21 'Our Duty', editorial, *Daily News*, 31 July 1914. The editorial was perhaps the model for the very similar angry editorial which appeared the following day in the *Manchester Guardian*, also devoted to denouncing the evil influence of *The Times*.
22 See extracts from the *Daily Chronicle* in Scott, *Five Weeks*, 222, 224, 226-7, 230-1, 238, 240.
23 On the foundation of the *Daily Citizen*, see Deian Hopkin, 'The Labour Party Press', in K. D. Brown, ed., *The First Labour Party, 1906–1914* (London, 1985), 119. Ramsay MacDonald was a prominent adviser on the board of the paper, working closely with the editor Frank Dilnot.
24 'A War Cloud', editorial, *Daily Citizen*, 22 July 1914.
25 'The Russian Strikes', editorial, *Daily Citizen*, 23 July 1914.
26 'Is It War?', editorial, *Daily Citizen*, 25 July 1914.
27 'Austria Declares War on Serbia', *Daily Citizen*, 27 July 1914.
28 'Europe or Bedlam?', *Daily Citizen*, 30 July 1914.
29 'Catastrophe It Is Impossible to Measure', *Daily Citizen*, 31 July 1914.
30 W. C. Anderson, 'Socialists and European War', *Labour Leader*, 30 July 1914.

8 Smearing Neutrality, 30 and 31 July

1 Grey to Goschen, 30 July 1914, *BD*, vol. XI, Doc. 303.
2 Various narratives explore how the German approach arose. Most agree that the decision to test the possibility of British neutrality arose out of Moltke's demands for immediate German mobilisation at a meeting of the Crown Council at Potsdam on the afternoon of Wednesday 29 July. Fischer argues that Bethmann Hollweg made his approach to Britain after the Crown Council at Potsdam on 29 July 'probably because the military were pressing for the military time-table to be preserved'. See Fischer, *War of Illusions*, 492–4. See different assessments in Jarausch, *The Enigmatic Chancellor*, 169–70, and Mombaucr, *Moltke*, 203.
3 Goschen to Grey, 29 July 1914, *BD*, vol. XI, Doc. 293.
4 For the ongoing historical controversy surrounding German war planning, see Annika Mombauer, 'German War Plans', in Richard F. Hamilton and Holger H. Herwig, eds., *War Planning 1914* (Cambridge, 2010), 48–78, and Terence Zuber, *The Real German War Plan, 1904–14* (Stroud, 2011).
5 Grey, *Twenty-Five Years*, I, 325–9.
6 Grey to Goschen, 30 July 1914, *BD*, vol. XI, Doc. 303.

7 Asquith to Stanley, 30 July 1914, in *Letters to Venetia Stanley*, 136.
8 Francis Neilson, *How Diplomats Make War* (New York, 1915), 268.
9 The cable in question was The Ambassador at London to the Foreign Office, 29 July 1914, *GD*, Doc. 368, conveying Grey's warnings, and Goschen to Grey, 30 July 1914, reporting the apologetic words of Foreign Minister von Jagow, *BD*, vol. XI, Doc. 305.
10 Neilson, *How Diplomats Make War*, 264.
11 Herwig remarks: 'When news confirming Russian partial mobilisation of the military districts of Moscow, Kazan, Odessa and Kiev arrived in Berlin on 29 July, panic ensued.' See Herwig, 'Germany', in Hamilton and Herwig, eds., *Origins of World War I*, 179.
12 Notes on 10 Downing Street notepaper, Harcourt to Pease, Pease to Harcourt, Harcourt to Simon, and Simon to Harcourt, all dated '?30 July 1914', filed with Cabinet Memoranda 1914, Harcourt Papers. Emphasis in original.
13 *Parliamentary Debates*, Commons, 5th series, vol. 65, 1601–2 (30 July 1914).
14 Cabinet Memorandum, 30 July 1914, 1914, Harcourt Papers.
15 Margot Asquith Diary, 29 July 1914 [misdated – should be 30 July], M. Asquith Papers, Ms. Eng. d. 3210.
16 Cabinet Memorandum, 30 July 1914, Harcourt Papers.
17 Ibid. Emphasis in original.
18 Ibid.
19 Ibid.
20 Ibid.
21 Mary Ruth Brooke to Violet Asquith, 28 Apr. 1915, in Mark Pottle, *Champion Redoubtable: The Diaries and Letters of Violet Bonham Carter, 1914–1945* (London, 1999), 44.
22 Margot Asquith Diary, 31 July 1914, M. Asquith Papers, Ms Eng. d. 3210.
23 'Stock Exchange: Continued Paralysis of Markets', *The Times*, 31 July 1914.
24 Cabinet Memorandum, 31 July 1914, Harcourt Papers.
25 Grey's embarrassment over his pre-empting the Cabinet may explain the misleading account in his memoirs. He claimed that his reply to the German approach of Thursday 30 July was read to the Cabinet and approved 'in the afternoon' of that day, before it was sent. It could not have been. There was no Cabinet on the afternoon of Thursday 30 July. See Grey, *Twenty-Five Years*, I, 329.
26 Cabinet Memorandum, 31 July 1914, Harcourt Papers. Emphasis in original. Harcourt, but no one else, records that Lloyd George was shown the German cable and approved Grey's rejection of it: 'Grey refused this at once in an admirable telegram (approved before sent by Asq[uith] & Ll[oyd] Geo[rge]).'
27 H. Samuel to B. Samuel, 29 and 31 July 1914, Samuel Papers.
28 Ibid., 31 July 1914. In the evening, Samuel told his wife that 'Nothing untoward happened at the Cabinet to-day.'
29 Morley, *Memorandum*, 5, and see Lindsay, 'Failure of Liberal Opposition', 101, for the dating of Lloyd George's remarks.
30 Cabinet Memorandum, 31 July 1914, Harcourt Papers.
31 Ibid. Emphasis in original.
32 Pease Diary, 31 July 1914, in Wilson, 'Diary of Pease', [45] 7. Emphasis in original.

33 Harcourt to Pease and Pease to Harcourt, undated, and Simon to Harcourt and Harcourt to Simon, dated 31 July 1914, on 10 Downing Street notepaper, both filed with Cabinet Memorandum, 31 July 1914, Harcourt Papers.

34 Cabinet Memorandum, 31 July 1914, Harcourt Papers. Emphasis in original.

35 Grey to Bertie, 31 July 1914, *BD*, vol. XI, Doc. 348, marked as sent also to Berlin.

36 There is no reference to this as a Cabinet decision in Asquith's letter to Venetia Stanley, in Samuel's letters, in Pease's diary, or in Harcourt's Cabinet Memoranda. As Asquith saw the King face-to-face in the afternoon, he appears not to have written the usual summary of proceedings in the Cabinet for him. See Spender, *Life of Asquith*, II, 81. Only Herbert Samuel, *Memoirs* (London, 1945), 101, claims that the Cabinet approved this. Hazlehurst concludes that 'there is no contemporary evidence that the Cabinet was even consulted in advance'. See Hazlehurst, *Politicians at War*, 85, n. 3.

37 Grey, *Twenty-Five Years*, I, 329.

38 Grey to Bertie, 31 July 1914, *BD*, vol. XI, Doc. 367.

39 See special note attached to Buchanan to Grey, 31 July 1914, *BD*, vol. XI, Doc. 347.

40 *Parliamentary Debates*, Commons, 5th series, vol. 65, 1787 (31 July 1914).

41 Buchanan to Grey, 31 July 1914, *BD*, vol. XI, Doc. 347, marked as received at 5.20 p.m., but the editors believe this telegram to be misdated, and much more likely to have been sent the previous day.

42 Grey, *Twenty-Five Years*, I, 330.

43 Margot Asquith Diary, 31 July 1914, M. Asquith Papers, Ms. Eng. d. 3210. Emphasis in original.

9 The Internationalists Awake, 28 to 31 July

1 Resolution included with Ponsonby to Grey, 29 July 1914, Ponsonby Papers, MS. Eng. hist. c. 660. f. 49.

2 Charles Trevelyan, 'C. P. T's personal record', Trevelyan Papers, CPT 59.

3 R. D. Denman, 'War and the Private MP', a manuscript memoir, Denman Papers, Box 9.

4 The definitive biography is Raymond A. Jones, *Arthur Ponsonby: The Politics of Life* (London, 1989).

5 Arthur Ponsonby to Dolly Ponsonby, 10 July 1914, Ponsonby Papers (Shulbrede).

6 Ibid., A. Ponsonby to D. Ponsonby, 27 July 1914.

7 For detail on the agitation of the Liberal Foreign Affairs Group against British intervention see Jones, *Ponsonby*, 82–3, Morris, *Radicalism Against War*, 408–10, Swartz, 'Study in Futility', 252–3, and Hazlehurst, *Politicians at War*, 35–7.

8 The resolution was included with the letter Ponsonby to Grey, 29 July 1914, Ponsonby Papers, MS. Eng. hist. c. 660, ff. 47–9. It is also reproduced in Hazlehurst, *Politicians at War*, 36–7. It was signed by Ponsonby, W. H. Dickinson, Thomas Lough, C. N. Nicholson, Percy Molteno, Philip Morrell, Noel Buxton, Arnold Rowntree, Harry Nuttall, David Mason and G. J. Bentham.

9 Ponsonby to Grey, 29 July 1914, Ponsonby Papers, MS. Eng. hist. c. 660, ff. 47–8.

10 Ibid., Ponsonby, 'Notes of Grey's Statement to me on July 29, [19]14', f. 43.

11 Edmund Harvey to his father, 30 July 1914, Thomas Edmund Harvey Papers.

12 Ponsonby to Churchill, 31 July 1914, and Churchill to Ponsonby, 31 July 1914, in Churchill, ed., *Churchill: Companion Volume*, II, 3, 1990–1, and Churchill to Ponsonby, 31 July 1914, Ponsonby Papers, MS. Eng. hist. c. 660, f. 58.

13 See E. B. Baker and P. J. Noel Baker, *J. Allen Baker* (London, 1927), 221–6.

14 Randall Davidson Diary, 31 July 1914, in G. K. A. Bell, *Randall Davidson: Archbishop of Canterbury* (London, 1935), II, 733–4. This was the manifesto, published in the *Daily News* on 5 August 1914 and signed by a score of mainly non-conformist church leaders, calling on British Christians to seize a 'wonderful opportunity of acting as peace-makers' and to press for 'a just and a peaceful solution' to the war in the Near East. See 'Appeal to Nation in Cause of Peace', *Daily News*, 5 Aug. 1914.

15 *Parliamentary Debates*, Commons, 5th series, vol. 65, 1574 (30 July 1914).

16 Ponsonby to Asquith, 30 July 1914, Ponsonby Papers, MS. Eng. hist. c. 660, f. 50.

17 Cabinet Memorandum, 31 July 1914, Harcourt Papers.

18 Tyrrell to Ponsonby, 31 July 1914, Ponsonby Papers, MS. Eng. hist. c. 660, f. 56, and see Jones, *Ponsonby*, 83.

19 Cabinet Memorandum, 31 July 1914, Harcourt Papers.

20 Asquith to Ponsonby, 31 July 1914, Ponsonby Papers, MS. Eng. hist. c. 660, f. 52.

21 On Runciman, see Charles Trevelyan, 'C. P. T's personal record', Trevelyan Papers, CPT 59.

22 Cabinet Memorandum, 30 July 1914, Harcourt Papers.

23 Christopher Addison, *Politics from Within, 1911–1918* (London, 1924), I, 37.

24 M. Philips Price to Hirst, 31 July 1914, Hirst Papers.

25 Charles Trevelyan, 'C. P. T's personal record', Trevelyan Papers, CPT 59.

26 See Martin Ceadel, *Living the Great Illusion: Sir Norman Angell, 1879-1962* (Oxford, 2009).

27 The Reminiscences of Norman Angell (May 1951), 117–8, CCOHC. Emphasis by author.

28 Dennis Robertson to Norman Angell, 15 Sept. 1950, Angell–Robertson correspondence, Angell Papers (Ball State University), and see Norman Angell, *After All* (London, 1951), 182.

29 Charles Trevelyan, 'C. P. T's personal record', Trevelyan Papers, CPT 59.

30 Angell, 'The Menace of War', *The Times*, 1 Aug. 1914.

31 Wallas to Ellery Sedgwick, 21 Nov. 1914, Wallas file, Ellery Sedgwick Papers.

32 Charles Trevelyan, 'C. P. T's personal record', Trevelyan Papers, CPT 59.

33 J. A. Hobson, *Confessions of an Economic Heretic* (Sussex, 1976), 103, and Swartz, 'Study in Futility', 255.

34 The Reminiscences of Normal Angell (May 1951), 120–1, CCOHC.

35 'Neutrality League Announcement No. 2', Rosika Schwimmer Papers, Box A38 (New York Public Library – hereafter NYPL). See also *Manchester Guardian*, 4 Aug. 1914, under the title 'Britons, Do Your Duty'.

36 The International Council of Women had been launched in 1888, and the

IWSA in 1904. See Leila J. Rupp, 'Constructing Internationalism: The Case of Transnational Women's Organisations, 1888–1945', *American Historical Review*, 99, 5 (Dec. 1994), 1571–600.

37 See Frances S. Hallowes, 'Woman and War', *Jus Suffragii*, 1 Sept. 1914.

38 On arrangements for the IWSA visit to London, see Marshall Papers, D MAR 3/31. The Board included Annie Furuhjelm, (Finland), Marguerite de Witt-Schlumberger (France), Anna Lindemann and Marie Stritt (Germany), Dr Aletta Jacobs (Netherlands), and Anna Wicksell and Signe Bergman (Sweden).

39 Mary Sheepshanks, 'The Long Day Ended', Sheepshanks Papers, 7/MSH (Women's Library); Francesca Wilson, 'Kathleen Courtney', Courtney Papers, KDC/K12/13 (Women's Library); Agnes Maude Royden, draft autobiography, ch. VIII, Royden Papers, 7/AMR/1/46 (Women's Library), The Guildhouse Fellowship, *In Memoriam: Maude Royden* (London, 1956), Royden Papers, 7/AMR/2/09, Sheila Fletcher, *Maude Royden: A Life* (Oxford, 1989), 109, Jo Vellacott, *From Liberal to Labour with Women's Suffrage: The Story of Catherine Marshall* (Montreal 1993), 16, and Johanna Alberti, *Beyond Suffrage: Feminists in War and Peace, 1914–1928* (London, 1989), 11–15.

40 Sheepshanks was editor of the IWSA's journal, *Jus Suffragii*, Courtney was Secretary of the NUWSS, Royden was editor of the NUWSS journal *Common Cause* in 1914, Swanwick had been editor before her, and Marshall was the Parliamentary Secretary of the NUWSS.

41 'The Meeting of the International Board of Officers', *Jus Suffragii*, 1 Aug. 1914.

42 Carrie Chapman Catt to Rosika Schwimmer, 25 July 1914, Schwimmer Papers, Box A38 (NYPL).

43 Ibid., Schwimmer, Diary fragment, 9 July 1914.

44 Ibid., M. Talmadge to Schwimmer, 16 July 1914; printed invitation to attend an 'At Home' at the home of Sir John and Lady Barlow to meet Norman Angell, 16 July 1914; circular from the Organising Committee of the Interparliamentary Union, 13 July 1914; cutting from *Daily Chronicle*, 29 July 1914.

45 Anne Wiltsher, *Most Dangerous Women: Feminist Peace Campaigners of the Great War* (London, 1985), 13–14. Wiltsher cites Schwimmer's unpublished memoir, Schwimmer Papers, Box B20 (NYPL).

46 Alberti, *Beyond Suffrage*, 8–11, 18–20, and Wiltsher, *Most Dangerous Women*, 11–12.

47 'International Manifesto of Women', *Jus Suffragii*, 1 Sept. 1914.

48 Rosika Schwimmer, Diary notes, 31 July 1914, 'Peace Manifesto', 'Appeal to Queen Wilhelmina', and 'Appeal to the Governments of Europe', in Schwimmer Papers, Box A38 (NYPL).

49 'Women and War: An International Protest', *Manchester Guardian*, 1 Aug. 1914, and 'Women and Peace', *Sunday Times*, 2 Aug. 1914.

50 Rosika Schwimmer, 'Appeal to Queen Wilhelmina', Schwimmer Papers, Box A38, 'Women's Appeal to Queen Wilhelmina', *Observer*, 2 Aug. 1914, and David S. Patterson, *The Search for Negotiated Peace: Women's Activism and Citizen Diplomacy in World War I* (New York, 2008), 31.

51 Wiltsher notes enquiries from Frida Perlen in Germany, Elna Munch in Denmark, Madame Marguerite de Witt-Schlumberger in France, and Anita Dobelli-Zampetti in Italy, urging the IWSA to act. See Wiltsher, *Most Dangerous Women*, 20–1.

52 Alberti, *Beyond Suffrage*, 20.
53 'Notes and Comments – Women's Meeting', *Common Cause*, 7 Aug. 1914.

10 Doing Diplomacy in a Dressing Gown, 31 July and 1 August

 1 Grey to Rumbold, 24 July 1914, reporting on a meeting with Lichnowsky, *BD*, vol. XI, Doc. 99.
 2 Turner, 'The Russian Mobilisation in 1914', 86, and McMeekin, *Russian Origins of the First World War*, 74.
 3 Turner, 'The Russian Mobilisation in 1914', 86.
 4 Buchanan reported to Grey that notices announcing a general mobilisation were pasted up at 4 a.m. on 31 July. Buchanan to Grey, 31 July 1914 (received 1 Aug.), *BD*, vol. XI, Doc. 410.
 5 Ibid., Grey to Bertie, 31 July 1914, Doc. 367.
 6 Ibid., Communicated by German Embassy, midnight, 31 July. Grey to Bertie, 31 July 1914, Doc. 372.
 7 Clay, *King, Kaiser, Tsar*, 309.
 8 King George V Diary, 1 Aug. 1914, quoted in Robert Lacey, '1914 – The Diary of King George V', BBC Radio 4, July 2004, also available at Imperial War Museum, Audio Recording, 20866.
 9 Grey to Buchanan, 1 Aug. 1914, *BD*, vol. XI, Doc. 384.
10 Asquith to Stanley, 1 Aug. 1914, in *Letters to Venetia Stanley*, 140. Asquith says the meeting was at 'about 1.30 a.m.' and that he got back to Downing Street at about 2 a.m.
11 *Parliamentary Debates*, Commons, 5th series, vol. 65, 1872 (3 Aug. 1914).
12 Neilson, *How Diplomats Make War*, 282.
13 Jennifer Siegel, *Endgame: Britain, Russia and the Final Struggle for Central Asia* (London, 2002), 182–96.
14 Lichnowsky to the Foreign Office [Berlin], 15 July 1914, Lichnowsky, *Heading for the Abyss*, 375.
15 Grey to Bertie, 24 July 1914, *BD*, vol. XI, Doc. 98.
16 Ibid., Grey to Rumbold, 24 July 1914, reporting on a meeting with Lichnowsky, Doc. 99. Similarly, the next day, Grey wrote as if a Russian mobilisation was inevitable. 'We should now apparently soon be confronted by a moment at which both Austria and Russia would have mobilised.' See Grey to Rumbold, 25 July 1914, reporting on a meeting with Lichnowsky, *BD*, vol. XI, Doc. 116. Buchanan at least pleaded for a delay in Russian mobilisation. Buchanan reported his conversation with Sazonov on 27 July: 'If, however, we were to succeed, his Excellency must do nothing to precipitate a conflict, and I therefore trusted that [the] mobilisation ukase would be deferred as long as possible, and that when it was issued troops would not be allowed to cross the frontier.' See Buchanan to Grey, 27 July 1914, *BD*, vol. XI, Doc. 170.
17 Ibid., Grey to Buchanan, 27 July 1914, Doc. 177.
18 Ibid., Bertie to Grey, 27 July 1914, Doc. 192.

19 Lichnowsky to the Foreign Office [Berlin], 29 July 1914, Lichnowsky, *Heading for the Abyss*, 404.

20 Benckendorff to Sazonov, 5–18 May 1914, in Siebert, *Entente Diplomacy and the World* War, 719–20, Doc. 846. See also Fiona K. Tomaszewski, *A Great Russia: Russia and the Triple Entente, 1905–1914* (Westport, 2002), especially ch. 6.

21 Benckendorff to Grey, 1 Aug. 1914, *BD*, vol. XI, Doc. 409. He did send to Arthur Nicolson, the pro-Russian Permanent Under-Secretary, four communications.

22 Ibid., Docs. 132, 177 and 309.

23 Grey to Gilbert Murray, April 1918, quoted in George Trevelyan, *Grey of Fallodon* (London, 1937), 249.

24 Notes by Mr G. P. Gooch of a conversation with Lord Grey, 14 Feb. 1929, quoted in Trevelyan, *Grey of Fallodon*, 253.

25 Grey, *Twenty-Five Years*, I, 330.

26 Grey to Buchanan, 1 Aug. 1914, *BD*, vol. XI, Doc. 384 (including the text of the German Memorandum, Doc. 372). See also George Buchanan, *My Mission to Russia and Other Diplomatic Memories* (London, 1923), vol. I, 204–206, Asquith to Stanley, 1 Aug. 1914, in *Letters to Venetia Stanley*, 140, Valone, 'Sir Edward Grey's Diplomacy', 422, and Schmitt, *Coming of the War*, I, 328.

27 Grey to Buchanan, 1 Aug. 1914, *BD*, vol. XI, Doc. 422.

28 Grey, *Twenty-Five Years*, I, 302–3.

29 For example, see Bertie to Grey, 30 July 1914, *BD*, vol. XI, Doc. 318.

30 The letter is reproduced in full in Raymond Poincaré, *The Memoirs of Raymond Poincaré (1913–1914)* (London, 1928), 245–6. See also Nicolson, *George V*, 247, and Keiger, *Poincaré*, 179. Emphasis added.

31 Paul Cambon to Viviani, 31 July 1914, Geiss, ed., *July 1914*, 327–8.

32 *Parliamentary Debates*, Commons, 5th series, vol. 65, 1815 (3 Aug. 1914). 'We are not parties to the Franco-Russian Alliance. We do not even know the terms of that alliance.'

33 See Annan Bryce, *Parliamentary Debates*, Commons, 5th series, vol. 65, 1875 (3 Aug. 1914).

34 H. Samuel to B. Samuel, 28 July 1914, Samuel Papers.

35 Ibid., 29 July 1914.

36 Ibid., 30 July 1914.

37 Ibid., 31 July 1914.

38 Ibid., 1 Aug. 1914.

39 Morley, *Memorandum*, 6–7.

40 Crewe, 'Replies to Questions', 8 May 1929, in Spender Papers, Add. MS. 46386.

41 Samuel, untitled document in reply to Harold Temperley's questionnaire, 1928, Spender Papers, Add. MS. 46386.

42 Runciman, untitled document, in reply to Temperley's questionnaire, 4 Nov. 1929, Spender Papers, Add. MS. 46386.

43 Butterfield, 'Sir Edward Grey in July 1914', 14.

11 The Russian Jolt, 1 August

1 A. Gardiner, 'Why We Must Not Fight', *Daily News*, 1 Aug. 1914.
2 Wilton to Steed, 17 Feb. 1914, 26 Mar. 1914, 1 April 1914, 2 April 1914, 13 May 1914, Steed Papers, Wilton File, TT/ED/HWS/1, TNLA.
3 Ibid., Wilton to Steed, 24 Dec. 1913.
4 Ibid., Wilton to Steed, 20 Feb./5 Mar. 1914.
5 Ibid., Steed to Wilton, 5 Mar. 1914.
6 Ibid., Wilton to Steed, 2 April 1914.
7 Ibid., Wilton to Steed, 24 Dec. 1913.
8 Ibid., Wilton to Steed, 27 Aug. 1914.
9 Dawson Diary, 31 July 1914, MSS. Dawson 20, Geoffrey Dawson Papers.
10 'Europe in Arms' (written by Lovat Fraser), editorial, *The Times*, 1 Aug. 1914.
11 'The Empire and The Crisis – A Democratic Duty' (written by Edward Grigg), editorial, *The Times*, 1 Aug. 1914.
12 Steed, 'Across the Years', 311, Steed Papers, Add. MS. 74199, and *The History of the Times*, vol. IV, pt I, 207.
13 Steed, 'Across the Years', 304–5, Steed Papers, Add. MS. 74199, H. W. Steed, *Through Thirty Years* (New York, 1924), vol. II, 8, and *The History of the Times*, vol. IV, pt I, 208.
14 Chisholm, 'The Blow to Markets', *The Times*, 27 July 1914.
15 Steed, 'Across the Years', 304–5, Steed Papers, Add. MS. 74199, Steed, *Through Thirty Years*, II, 8–9, and *The History of the Times*, vol. IV, pt. I, 208.
16 Steed, 'Across the Years', 305–7, Steed Papers, Add MS. 74199.
17 Dawson Diary, 1 Aug. 1914, MSS. Dawson 20, Geoffrey Dawson Papers.
18 Steed, 'Across the Years', 307–8, Steed Papers, Add. MS. 74199.
19 Reginald Pound and Geoffrey Harmsworth, *Northcliffe* (London, 1959), 463, and J. Lee Thompson, *Politicians, the Press, and Propaganda: Lord Northcliffe and the Great War, 1914–1919* (Kent, Ohio, 1999), 24.
20 John Charmley, *Lord Lloyd and the Decline of the British Empire* (London, 1987), 33–4.
21 Steed, 'Across the Years', 301–2, Steed Papers, Add. MS. 74199.
22 Dawson Diary, 1 Aug. 1914, MSS. Dawson 20, Geoffrey Dawson Papers.
23 Steed, *Through Thirty Years*, II, 10–11, Pound, *Northcliffe*, 463, and *The History of the Times*, vol. IV, pt. I, 210.
24 Steed, 'Across the Years', 300, Steed Papers, Add. MS. 74199.
25 Ibid., 312.
26 Steed, *Through Thirty Years*, II, 12.
27 Steed, 'Across the Years', 313, Steed Papers, Add. MS. 74199.
28 'The Need for Guidance', editorial, *Morning Post*, 1 Aug. 1914.
29 Gwynne to Tyrrell, 1 Aug. 1914, in Keith M. Wilson, ed., *The Rasp of War: The Letters of H. A. Gwynne and the Countess Bathurst, 1914–1918* (London, 1988), 18–19.
30 'Britain's Duty', editorial, *Spectator*, 1 Aug. 1914.
31 L. T. Hobhouse to Emily Hobhouse, 2 Aug. 1914, quoted in J. Hobhouse Balme, *To Love One's Enemies*, 543.
32 'England's Duty', editorial, *Manchester Guardian*, 1 Aug. 1914.

33 'England's Duty: Neutrality the One Policy: The Crime and Folly of Joining In', *Manchester Guardian*, 1 Aug. 1914.

34 'Liberal Members and the Cabinet', *Manchester Guardian*, 1 Aug. 1914.

35 See 'More Views of Correspondents', *Manchester Guardian*, 1 Aug. 1914, for letters from Harry Nuttall MP, Graham Wallas, John Barlow MP, Charles Buxton, Henry W. Nevinson, Professor E. G. Browne and eight academic colleagues, Leyton Richards, and others.

36 Alfred Gardiner, 'Why We Must Not Fight', *Daily News*, 1 Aug. 1914.

37 'Keep the Peace', editorial, *Daily News*, 1 Aug. 1914.

38 The senior journalist J. L. Hammond produced the issue of the *Nation* for Saturday 1 August because the usual editor, H. W. Massingham, had been ill for the preceding ten days. See A. Manson to Norman Angell, 28 July 1914, Angell Papers, *Nation* correspondence, and Alfred F. Havighurst, *Radical Journalist: H. W. Massingham (1860–1924)*, (Oxford, 1974), 228.

39 'The Part of England', editorial, *Nation*, 1 Aug. 1914.

40 'Events of the Week', *Nation*, 1 Aug. 1914. See the Reuter's report, 'Russia: War Excitement', dated 'St Petersburg, Thursday', *Manchester Guardian*, 31 July 1914.

41 'On the Brink', editorial, *Westminster Gazette*, 1 Aug. 1914.

42 Ibid.

43 J. A. Spender, *Life, Journalism and Politics* (London, 1927), II, 15. The original cable is The Imperial Chancellor to the Ambassador at Vienna, 30 July 1914, *GD*, Doc. 396.

44 For example, see H. Asquith to M. Asquith, 7 Feb. 1912, M. Asquith Papers, MS. Eng. c. 6991.

45 Margot Asquith Diary, 1 Aug. 1914, M. Asquith Papers, MS. Eng. d. 3210.

12 'Pogrom', 31 July and 1 August

1 Edmund Harvey to his father, 30 July 1914, Edmund Harvey Papers. Harvey recognised only Lord Henry Cavendish Bentinck, sister of Ottoline Morrell, and 'a few others' in the Conservative Party as eager for peace, but he observed that 'I am afraid they would be swept away by the rest of the party if they tried to protest.'

2 See Leo Maxse, 'An Aide-Mémoire to the Historian', *National Review*, July 1919, 659–79, and ch. VI, 'When War Came', in Austen Chamberlain, *Down the Years* (Edinburgh, 1935), 92–106. For a secondary account, see Nigel Keohane, *The Party of Patriotism: the Conservative Party and the First World War* (Farnham, 2010), ch. 1.

3 Leo Maxse to Ludovic Naudeau, 14 May 1914, Maxse Papers, 469 (West Sussex Record Office, Chichester).

4 George Adam to Steed, 16 Aug. 1914, Steed Papers, George Adam File, TT/ED/HWS/1, TNLA.

5 For example, see the tables on the educational origins of diplomats, showing the small number of schools drawn upon, in R. A. Jones, *The British Diplomatic Service 1815–1914* (Gerrards Cross, 1983), ch. VIII.

6 Keith Jeffery, *Field Marshal Sir Henry Wilson: A Political Soldier* (Oxford, 2008), 88, and Callwell, *Wilson*, I, 120.

7 Keith M. Wilson, *A Study in the History and Politics of the Morning Post, 1905–1926* (Lewiston, 1990), 179.

8 Wilson, ed., *Rasp of War*, 223.

9 Henry Wilson Diary, 12 Oct. 1913, in Callwell, *Wilson*, I, 128.

10 Ibid., 30 July 1914, in ibid., 152.

11 Cited in Jeffery, *Wilson*, 128.

12 Henry Wilson Diary, 31 July 1914, in Callwell, *Wilson*, I, 152.

13 Ibid., 153.

14 Leo Amery Diary, 4 Aug. 1914, in Barnes and Nicholson, eds., *Leo Amery Diaries*, I, 107, and the editors' explanatory footnote regarding a 'pogrom'.

15 Crowe to Grey, Memorandum, 31 July 1914, *BD*, vol. XI, Doc. 369.

16 R. J. Q. Adams and Philip P. Poirier, *The Conscription Controversy in Great Britain, 1900–18* (London, 1987), 10, 34.

17 'Court Circular', *The Times*, 3 Aug. 1914.

18 Henry Wilson Diary, 31 July 1914, in Callwell, *Wilson*, I, 152–3.

19 Schmitt, *Coming of the War*, II, 288.

20 Huguet to Wilson, 26 July 1914, quoted by Jeffery, *Wilson*, 129.

21 Charmley, *Lord Lloyd*, 33.

22 Ibid., 33–4.

23 Steed, 'Across the Years', 301–2, Steed Papers, Add. MS. 74199. Steed dates this visit to 30 July, but from the context Friday 31 July is probably more likely.

24 Lloyd to Austen Chamberlain, 31 July 1914, quoted by Charmley, *Lord Lloyd*, 34.

25 Leo Amery Diary, 31 July 1914, in Barnes and Nicholson, eds., *Leo Amery Diaries*, I, 103.

26 Leo Amery Diary, 1 Aug. 1914, in Barnes and Nicholson, eds., *Leo Amery Diaries*, I, 103.

27 Ibid., 105.

28 Chirol to Hardinge, 4 Aug. 1914, Hardinge Papers, 93 Part I.

29 Charmley, *Lord Lloyd*, 33–4, R. J. Q. Adams, *Bonar Law* (London, 1999), 169, Chamberlain, 'Memorandum', Saturday 1 August, in Chamberlain, *Down the Years*, 94, and Leo Amery Diary, 1 Aug. 1914, in Barnes and Nicholson, eds., *Leo Amery Diaries*, I, 104.

30 Leo Amery Diary, 31 July and 1 Aug. 1914, in Barnes and Nicholson, eds., *Leo Amery Diaries*, I, 103–5.

31 Charmley, *Lord Lloyd*, 34.

32 See Steiner, *Foreign Office*, 104.

33 Devonshire Mss., Chatsworth, Diaries of Victor Cavendish, 9th Duke of Devonshire Diary, 31 July 1914 (Chatsworth) and Stephen Gwynn, ed., *The Letters and Friendships of Sir Cecil Spring-Rice: A Record* (London, 1929), II, 210.

34 Louis Mallet to Maxse, 1 Aug. and 15 Oct. 1914, Maxse Papers, 469.

35 Hardinge to Nicolson, 8 Oct. 1914, Hardinge Papers, 93 pt. II.

36 Adams, *Bonar Law*, 169.

37 F. E. Smith to Churchill, 31 July 1914, Churchill Papers, CHAR 13/26/148, and Churchill to F. E. Smith, 1 Aug. 1914, in Second Earl of Birkenhead, *F. E.: The Life of F. E. Smith, First Earl of Birkenhead* (London, 1960), 241.

38 Devonshire Mss., Chatsworth, Diaries of Victor Cavendish, 9th Duke of Devonshire Diary, 1 Aug. 1914.
39 Lord Lansdowne to Lady Lansdowne, 2 Aug. 1914, Lansdowne Papers, LANS (5) 85/7.
40 Lloyd, cited by Charmley, *Lord Lloyd*, 35.
41 Lord Lansdowne to Lady Lansdowne, 2 Aug. 1914, Lansdowne Papers, LANS (5) 85/7.
42 Devonshire Mss., Chatsworth, Diaries of Victor Cavendish, 9th Duke of Devonshire Diary, 1 Aug. 1914.
43 Ibid.
44 Lloyd, cited by Charmley, *Lord Lloyd*, 35.
45 Chamberlain, 'Memorandum', Saturday 1 August, in Chamberlain, *Down the Years*, 945–5.

13 The High Tide of Neutralist Hope, 1 August

1 Grey to Bertie, 1 Aug. 1914, *BD*, vol. XI, Doc. 426.
2 Hankey to Adeline, 1 Aug. 1914, Hankey Papers, HNKY 3/19.
3 Bertie to Grey, 31 July 1914, and Goschen to Grey, 31 July 1914, *BD*, vol. XI, Documents 382 and 383.
4 Ibid., Grey to Villiers, 31 July 1914, Doc. 351.
5 Later, King Albert complained to Howard Whitehouse, the Radical MP, that Grey had 'practically given Belgium instructions to defend herself.' He and his Cabinet felt 'almost resentment'. He said that 'Belgium would probably have permitted the Germans to go through upon guarantee that Belgian integrity would subsequently be respected.' See Irene Cooper Willis to Vernon Lee, 5 Oct. 1914, Violet Paget Papers (Colby College, Waterville).
6 Villiers to Grey, 1 Aug. 1914, *BD*, vol. XI, Doc. 395.
7 Ibid., Villiers to Grey, 31 July 1914, Doc. 377.
8 Cabinet Memorandum, 1 Aug. 1914, Harcourt Papers.
9 F. E. Smith to Churchill, 31 July 1914, Churchill Papers, CHAR 13/26/148.
10 Churchill to F. E. Smith, 1 Aug. 1914, in Birkenhead, *F. E.*, 241.
11 Harcourt to Beauchamp and Beauchamp to Harcourt, 1 Aug. 1914, on 10 Downing Street notepaper, filed with Cabinet Memorandum, 1 Aug. 1914, Harcourt Papers. Emphasis in original.
12 Asquith to Stanley, 1 Aug. 1914, in *Letters to Venetia Stanley*, 140, and see Wilson, 'Britain', in *Decisions for War*, 192.
13 Cabinet Memorandum, 1 Aug. 1914, Harcourt Papers.
14 Lichnowsky to Foreign Office [Berlin], 1 Aug. 1914, Lichnowsky, *Heading for the Abyss*, 415, and see Wilson, 'Britain', in *Decisions for War*, 191–2.
15 Churchill to Naval Secretary and First Sea Lord, 1 Aug. 1914, Churchill Papers, CHAR 13/29/98.
16 Cabinet Memorandum, 1 Aug. 1914, Harcourt Papers.
17 Asquith to Stanley, 1 Aug. 1914, in *Letters to Venetia Stanley*, 140.
18 Cabinet Memorandum, 1 Aug. 1914, Harcourt Papers.
19 Churchill, *World Crisis*, I, 174–5.

20 Cabinet Memorandum, 1 Aug. 1914, Harcourt Papers. See George Riddell to W. R. Nicoll, 13 Aug. 1914, Nicoll Papers, MS. 3518/26/1.
21 See the discussion on the significance of this decision in Hazlehurst, *Politicians at War*, 86–91 and Wilson, *Policy of the Entente*, 137.
22 Charles Trevelyan, 'C. P. T's personal record', Trevelyan Papers, CPT 59.
23 Charles Trevelyan to Molly Trevelyan, 2 Aug. 1914, Trevelyan Papers, CPT EX 106.
24 Francis Neilson, *My Life in Two Worlds* (Appleton, 1952), I, 331–2.
25 FitzRoy, *Memoirs*, II, 559.
26 Asquith to Stanley, 2 Aug. 1914, in *Letters to Venetia Stanley*, 146.
27 Chamberlain, 'Memorandum', in Chamberlain, *Down the Years*, 103.
28 Crewe to the King, 2 Aug. 1914, Spender, *Life of Asquith*, II, 82. Emphasis added.
29 *Daily Chronicle*, reported in 'Special Morning Express', *Manchester Guardian*, 3 Aug. 1914, and 'England's Day of Suspense', *New York Times*, 3 Aug. 1914.
30 *Daily Chronicle*, 3 Aug. 1914.
31 Bertie to Grey, 3 Aug. 1914, *BD*, vol. XI, Doc. 566.
32 Northcliffe to Repington, 31 July 1914, in Northcliffe Papers, Add. MSS. 62253 (British Library).
33 Tom Clarke, *My Northcliffe Diary* (London, 1931), 65, and Pound, *Northcliffe*, 464.
34 Loreburn to Harcourt, 1 Aug. 1914, MS. Harcourt 444.
35 Lichnowsky to Jagow, 1 Aug. 1914, in Geiss, ed., *July 1914*, Doc. 174, 345–6, and see Young, *Lichnowsky*, 117–18, and Sir Edward Grey to Sir Edward Goschen, 1 Aug. 1914, *BD*, vol. XI, Doc. 448.
36 The Ambassador at London to the Foreign Office, 1 Aug. 1914, *GD*, Doc. 596.
37 Grey to Bertie, 1 Aug. 1914, *BD*, vol. XI, Doc. 426.
38 Ibid., but on Cambon's version of the interview see also Wilson, 'Britain', in *Decisions for War*, 192–3.
39 Nicolson, *Sir Arthur Nicolson*, 419.
40 Henry Wilson Diary, 1 Aug. 1914, in Callwell, *Wilson*, I, 154.

14 Kite-Flying, 1 August

1 Grey to Bertie, 1 Aug. 1914, *BD*, vol. XI, Doc. 419.
2 Haldane to his mother, Mary E. Haldane, 27 July 1914, Haldane Papers, MSS 5991, and Elizabeth Haldane Diary, 8 Aug. 1914, Elizabeth Haldane Papers, MSS 20240 (National Library of Scotland).
3 Haldane to Mary Haldane, 28 July, 31 July 1914, Haldane Papers, MSS 5991, and see Stephen E. Koss, *Lord Haldane: Scapegoat for Liberalism* (New York, 1969), 115.
4 Elizabeth Haldane Diary, 8 Aug. 1914, E. Haldane Papers, MSS 20240.
5 For full accounts of this controversial episode from the British perspective, see especially Keith Wilson, 'Understanding the "Misunderstanding" of 1 August 1914', *Historical Journal*, 37, 4 (1994), 885–9, which builds on

Harry Young, 'The Misunderstanding of August 1, 1914', *Journal of Modern History*, XLVIII (1976), 644–65, and Valone, 'Sir Edward Grey's Diplomacy', 405–24.

6 Lichnowsky to the Foreign Office [Berlin], 1 Aug. 1914, Lichnowsky, *Heading for the Abyss*, 413–4. The wording is slightly different in the translation of Kautsky's collection of German Documents; see The Ambassador at London to the Foreign Office, 1 Aug. 1914, *GD*, Doc. 562.

7 Valone, 'Sir Edward Grey's Diplomacy', 414. See Cabinet Memorandum, 1 Aug. 1914, Harcourt Papers. 'Grey not committed to Cambon' and 'Grey two alternatives (no obligation)' were all that Harcourt recorded.

8 The Ambassador at London to the Foreign Office, 1 Aug. 1914, *GD*, Doc. 570. Emphasis in original.

9 Ibid., Doc. 596. Emphasis in original.

10 Grey had been told the previous day that French neutrality in the event of a Russo-German war was out of the question. See Grey to Bertie, 30 July 1914, and Grey to Bertie, 1 Aug. 1914, *BD*, vol. XI, Docs. 319, 426.

11 Ibid., Grey to Bertie, 1 Aug. 1914, Doc. 426.

12 Ibid., Doc. 419.

13 Ibid., Doc. 426.

14 Ibid., Bertie to Grey, Doc. 453, and Lord Bertie Diary, 1 and 2 Aug. 1914, in Lady Algernon Lennox, ed. *The Diary of Lord Bertie, 1914–1918* (London, 1924), I, 7–8. 'Asquith's Government is a house divided against itself, and they change their attitude day by day … It will not be long now before it is "Perfide Albion"… I have been feeling sick at heart, and ashamed, that "Perfide Albion" should really be applicable.'

15 Arthur C. Murray Diary, 1 Aug. 1914, Elibank Papers, MSS. 8814 (National Library of Scotland).

16 Arthur C. Murray, *Master and Brother: Murrays of Elibank* (London, 1945), 119.

17 Steed, 'Across the Years', 296, Steed Papers, Add. MS. 74199.

18 The visit is recorded in 'Court Circular', *The Times*, 3 Aug. 1914. Valone estimates that Grey was at the Palace between 8.30 p.m. and 9.30 p.m. See Valone, 'Sir Edward Grey's Diplomacy', 422.

19 The Ambassador at London to the Foreign Office, 1 Aug. 1914, *GD*, Docs. 562, 570.

20 The Emperor to the King of England, 1 Aug. 1914, *GD*, Doc. 575.

21 See 'Notes of a Conversation between Burnham and the King', 21 Aug. 1917, Burnham Papers, HLWL/10 (Imperial War Museum).

22 The King of England to the Emperor, 1 Aug. 1914, *GD*, Doc. 612.

23 At 10.50 a.m. Grey sent this brief cable instructing Bertie to disregard his former suggestions to explore the possibility of neutrality. Presumably this was after reading Bertie's reply to his proposals of Saturday. Grey to Bertie, 2 Aug. 1914, *BD*, vol. XI, Doc. 460.

24 The Ambassador at London to the Foreign Office, 1 Aug. 1914, *GD*, Docs. 562, 570.

25 Quoted in Mombauer, *Moltke*, 219.

26 Falkenhayn Diary, quoted in Albertini, *The Origins of the War*, III, 173.

27 On these events, see Albertini, *Origins of the War*, III, 171–8, Geiss, ed., *July 1914*, 336–7, Herwig, 'Germany', in Hamilton and Herwig, eds., *Origins of*

World War I, 182–3, Mombauer, *Moltke*, 219–24, and McMeekin, *July 1914*, 339–49.

28 For example, John Röhl, 'The Curious Case of the Kaiser's Disappearing War Guilt', in Afflerbach and Stevenson, eds., *An Improbable War?*, 88.

29 See Holger Afflerbach, 'William II as Supreme Warlord in the First World War', in Mombauer and Deist, eds., *Kaiser*, 200.

30 News of the German declaration was confirmed in a telegram from Buchanan received at the Foreign Office at 11.15 p.m. Buchanan to Grey, *BD*, vol. XI, Doc. 445. But Churchill had news of it 9.30 p.m. See Valone, 'Sir Edward Grey's Diplomacy', 423.

31 Gilbert Murray to Francis Neilson, 9 Oct. 1952, Neilson Papers, Murray File (the John Rylands Library, University of Manchester).

32 Elizabeth Haldane Diary, 8 Aug. 1914, Elizabeth H. Papers, MSS 20240.

33 Ibid.

34 Cambon to his son, 2 Aug. 1916, quoted by Valone, 'Sir Edward Grey's Diplomacy', 423. Emphasis in original. See Valone's fn. 74 for a full discussion of the French sources.

35 Cambon to Viviani, 31 July 1914, *Documents diplomatiques français, 1871–1914*, 3rd Series, XI, no. 445, quoted in Wilson, 'Britain', in *Decisions for War*, 193, and Schmitt, *Coming of the War*, II, 288.

36 *Observer*, 2 Aug. 1914, 9.

37 Churchill, *World Crisis*, I, 175, and Lord Beaverbrook, *Politicians and the War, 1914–1916* (London, 1928), 35–6.

38 Corbett, *Naval Operations*, 29.

39 Ibid, 31. The naval documents show the orders to the Naval Reserves were issued at 2 a.m. on Sun. 2 Aug. See 'Admiralty note on the significant dates of the mobilisation of the Fleet in July–August 1914', Churchill Papers, CHAR 13/27B/2–3.

40 Lichnowsky to Grey, 'Saturday', reproduced in Grey, *Twenty-Five Years*, II, 232.

41 Charles Dickens, *Hard Times* (London, 2003, first published 1854), 99.

42 'Grey's efforts to keep the peace thus ended on the evening of 1 August.' See Valone, 'Sir Edward Grey's Diplomacy', 423.

15 Tightening the Screws, 2 August

1 Chamberlain, 'Memorandum', Sun. 2 August, in Chamberlain, *Down the Years*, 96.

2 Amery Diary, 1 Aug. 1914, in Barnes and Nicholson, eds., *Leo Amery Diaries*, I, 104.

3 'The War of Wars', editorial, *Observer*, 2 Aug. 1914.

4 Burns Diary, 2 Aug. 1914, Burns Papers, Add. MSS. 46336.

5 Chamberlain, 'Memorandum', Sun. 2 Aug. 1914, in Chamberlain, *Down the Years*, 96.

6 Amery Diary, 2 Aug. 1914, Barnes and Nicholson, eds., *Leo Amery Diaries*, I, 105.

7 Bonar Law to Asquith, 2. Aug. 1914, signed, on Bonar Law's personal note-paper of 'Pembroke Lodge, Edwardes Square', LG/C/6/11/20, Lloyd George Papers (Parliamentary Archives). This was also the version read by Bonar Law to a Unionist meeting on 14 Dec. 1914. See 'A Page of Secret History', *The Times*, 15 Dec. 1914. Chamberlain recorded in his *Down the Years* that the version originally in his 'Memorandum' was incorrect and he inserted 'the actual text' (99). This is a rather more pointed version than that in Lloyd George's papers, ending with an 'assurance of the united support of the Opposition *in all measures required by England's intervention in the war.*' (Emphasis added) Adams, *Bonar Law*, 170, reproduces this version. See also Lord Newton, *Lord Lansdowne* (London, 1929), 440, and the copy in Lansdowne's papers, Bonar Law to Asquith, 2 Aug. 1914, Lansdowne Papers, LANS (5) 85/7.

8 Chamberlain, 'Memorandum', Sun. 2 August, in Chamberlain, *Down the Years*, 99; and Newton, *Lansdowne*, 439.

9 Newton, *Lansdowne*, 439.

10 Grey, *Twenty-Five Years*, I, 337. In a footnote, Grey insisted that Law never told him his opinion, and he assumed he was in favour of supporting France, but Grey's impression was that some beyond the Conservative Party front bench were reserving judgement.

11 Chirol to Hardinge, 4 Aug. 1914, Hardinge Papers, 93 Part I.

12 Ibid.

13 Chamberlain, 'Memorandum', Sun. 2 Aug., in Chamberlain, *Down the Years*, 98.

14 Lord Robert Cecil to Winston Churchill, 1 Aug. 1914, and Churchill to Robert Cecil, 1 Aug. 1914, in Churchill, ed., *Churchill: Companion Volume*, II, 3, 1995–6.

15 Lord Lansdowne to Lady Lansdowne, 2 Aug. 1914, Lansdowne Papers, LANS (5) 85/7.

16 Chamberlain, 'Memorandum', Sun. 2 Aug., in Chamberlain, *Down the Years*, 98.

17 'British Policy', *The Times*, 3 Aug. 1914.

18 Devonshire Mss., Chatsworth, Diaries of Victor Cavendish, 9th Duke of Devonshire Diary, 2 Aug. 1914.

19 Simon to Asquith, 2 Aug. 1914, in journal marked 'Diary #5', MS. Simon 2, Simon Papers (Bodleian Library), and see also Wilson, 'Britain', in *Decisions for War*, 199.

20 See Leo Maxse, 'Retrospect and Reminiscence', *National Review* (August 1918), 726–52.

21 Devonshire Mss., Chatsworth, Papers of Victor Cavendish, 9th Duke of Devonshire, 'His Grace's Views on the European War, 1914', enclosed with Albert Beveridge to Devonshire, 11 Mar. 1915.

22 Devonshire Mss., Chatsworth, Diaries of Victor Cavendish, 9th Duke of Devonshire Diary, 2 Aug. 1914.

23 Carson to Churchill, 4 Aug. 1914, Churchill Papers, CHAR 2/64/14.

24 Dawson to his aunts, 3 Aug. 1914, quoted in Wrench, *Geoffrey Dawson and Our Times*, 105.

25 Dawson to Maurice Headlam, 6 Aug. 1914, Dawson Papers, Headlam File, TT/ED/GGD/2, TNLA. The editorial 'The Nation and the Government', *The Times*, 4 Aug. 1914, made the same point.

26 Chirol to Hardinge, 4 Aug. 1914, Hardinge Papers, 93 Part I.
27 Ibid., Nicolson to Hardinge, 5 Sept. 1914.
28 Francis Hirst to Margaret Hirst, 17 Aug. 1914, Hirst Papers.

16 'To the Square!', Sunday 2 August

1 'STAND CLEAR, ENGLAND!', handbill, Schwimmer Papers, Box 1 (Hoover).
2 Bruce Glasier Diary, 27 and 28 July, Glasier Papers, GP/2/1/21 (University of Liverpool).
3 International Socialist Bureau, Official Record, 29 July 1914, reproduced in Georges Haupt, *Socialism and the Great War: The Collapse of the Second International* (Oxford, 1972), appendix, 251–9.
4 Glasier, 'The Last Watch of the International', *Labour Leader*, 6 Aug. 1914.
5 International Socialist Bureau, Official Record, 30 July 1914, in Haupt, *Socialism and the Great War*, 263.
6 Bruce Glasier Diary, 29 and 30 July 1914, Glasier Papers, GP/2/1/21, and Glasier, 'The Last Watch of the International', *Labour Leader*, 6 Aug. 1914.
7 'Workers Must Stop the War!', *Daily Herald*, 31 July 1914.
8 'The War Must Be Stopped', *Labour Leader*, 30 July 1914.
9 'War Against War', editorial, *Daily Citizen*, 31 July 1914.
10 Bruce Glasier Diary, 31 July 1914, Glasier Papers, GP/2/1/21. Emphasis in original.
11 'Stop the War', editorial, *Daily Herald*, 1 Aug. 1914.
12 On planning for the rally within the British National Committee, the British Section of the ISB, see Douglas Newton, *British Labour, European Socialism and the Struggle for Peace* (Oxford, 1985), 324–5. On the ILP's meetings, see 'The ILP Leads the Campaign', *Labour Leader*, 6 Aug. 1914.
13 'Down with the Horror of War', *Daily Citizen*, 1 Aug. 1914.
14 'To the British People: Manifesto of the British Section of the International: Down with the War' was issued under the signatures of Hardie and Arthur Henderson, as Chair and Secretary of the British Section, in the *Daily Herald*, 1 Aug. 1914. It appeared as 'An Appeal to the British Working Class', in the *Labour Leader*, 6 Aug. 1914.
15 'WAR AGAINST WAR', advertisement, *The Times*, and *Daily News*, 1 Aug. 1914.
16 'Stop the War!', editorial, *Daily Herald*, 1 Aug. 1914.
17 'The Shadow of a Great Crime', *Daily Herald*, 1 Aug. 1914.
18 'Protest Against War', advertisement, *Daily Herald*, 1 Aug. 1914.
19 'Workers to the Square Tomorrow', *Daily Herald*, 1 Aug. 1914.
20 'ENGLAND STAND CLEAR!', handbill of the Civil Union, Schwimmer Papers, Box 1 (Hoover).
21 Ibid., 'STAND CLEAR, ENGLAND!', handbill.
22 Bruce Glasier Diary, 31 July 1914, Glasier Papers, GP/2/1/21. Emphasis in original.
23 'Labour's War on War', *Labour Leader*, 6 Aug. 1914.

24 'The Workers' War on the War', *Daily Herald*, 3 Aug. 1914.

25 'Peace Demonstration in London', *Scotsman*, 3 Aug. 1914.

26 'Against the War', *Daily News*, 3 Aug. 1914.

27 'Our London Correspondence', *Manchester Guardian*, 3 Aug. 1914.

28 'Britain Must Be Neutral', *Daily Citizen*, 3 Aug. 1914.

29 See image HU056172, Hulton-Deutsch Collection/CORBIS or image 2-378-081, Stapleton Historical Collection, or image 2642377, Hulton Archive/Getty Images.

30 'Britain Must Be Neutral', *Daily Citizen*, 3 Aug. 1914.

31 'Labour's War on War', *Labour Leader*, 6 Aug. 1914.

32 Ibid.

33 'The Workers' War on the War', *Daily Herald*, 3 Aug. 1914.

34 'Anti-War Demonstration in London', *Manchester Guardian*, 3 Aug. 1914, and 'The Workers' War on the War', *Daily Herald*, 3 Aug. 1914.

35 'Our London Correspondence', *Manchester Guardian*, 3 Aug. 1914.

36 'Britain Must Be Neutral', *Daily Citizen*, 3 Aug. 1914.

37 Cyril Pearce, *Comrades in Conscience: The Story of an English Community's Opposition to the Great War* (London, 2001), 56–69, and 'Big Protest from Huddersfield', *Labour Leader*, 6 Aug. 1914.

38 Pearce, *Comrades in Conscience*, 65–8, and 'Big Protest from Huddersfield', *Labour Leader*, 6 Aug. 1914.

39 'Britain's Position. Strong Peace Agitation', and 'Peace Meeting in Carlisle', *Carlisle Journal*, 4 Aug. 1914. News-cuttings from the *Carlisle Journal* are in the Denman Papers, Box 1, Folder K.

40 'Britain's Position: Central Edinburgh Radicals Declare for British Neutrality', 'North Berwick Congregation's Resolution', 'Roxburghshire Radicals and the Crisis' and 'An Edinburgh UF Minister on the Crisis', *Scotsman*, 3 Aug. 1914.

41 'The ILP Leads the Campaign Against War – Vast Audiences Carry Strong Resolutions', *Labour Leader*, 6 Aug. 1914.

42 Gerry J. Bryant, 'Bolton and the Outbreak of the First World War', *Transactions of the Historic Society of Lancashire and Cheshire*, 138 (1989), 182–9, cited by Stephen Roberts, 'Did the British People Welcome the Declaration of War in August 1914?', *History Review*, 52 (Sept. 2005), 48.

43 'Voices Crying Out For Peace', *Daily Herald*, 4 Aug. 1914.

44 The most significant trade union opposition was that of the South Wales Miners Federation. Meeting in Cardiff on Saturday 1 August, the miners declared for neutrality and refused to scrap a scheduled holiday to ensure extra coal for the navy. See 'South Wales Miners Against War', *Daily Herald*, 3 Aug. 1914.

45 James Maxton and William Stewart, 'A Letter to the Press', *Labour Leader*, 6 Aug. 1914.

46 For example, Ian Beckett, *Home Front 1914–1918: How Britain Survived the Great War* (Kew, Richmond, 2006), 11.

47 'Protest Meeting', *The Times*, 3 Aug. 1914. The *Scotsman* similarly suggested that 'a large proportion of the crowd consisted of foreigners, as evidenced by the babel [sic] of tongues'. See 'Peace Demonstration in London', *Scotsman*, 3 Aug. 1914.

48 For example, 'Anti-War Demonstration in London', *Manchester Guardian*, 3 Aug. 1914, and 'The Workers' War on the War', *Daily Herald*, 3 Aug. 1914.

49 Harold Frederick Bing, interview (1974), Department of Sound Records, Imperial War Museum, Cat. No. 358.

50 Beatrice Webb Diary, 5 Aug. 1914, in Norman and Jeanne MacKenzie, eds., *The Diary of Beatrice Webb: Volume Three, 1905–1924: 'The Power to Alter Things'* (London, 1984), 212. This was written after the Belgian factor had come in to play.

51 'The ILP Leads the Campaign Against War – Vast Audiences Carry Strong Resolutions', *Labour Leader*, 6 Aug. 1914.

52 'Our London Correspondence', *Manchester Guardian*, 3 Aug. 1914.

53 'Notes of the Day', *Daily Herald*, 4 Aug. 1914.

54 'London and the Coming of War', *The Times*, 5 Aug. 1914, and King George V Diary, 3 Aug. 1914, quoted in Clay, *King, Kaiser, Tsar*, 313, and Miranda Carter, *The Three Emperors: Three Cousins, Three Empires and the Road to World War One* (London, 2010), 443.

55 Elizabeth Cadbury Family Journal, 6 Aug. 1914 (describing Tues. 4 Aug. 1914), Elizabeth Cadbury Papers, MSS 466/205/21 (Birmingham Central Library).

56 For example, 'Scenes in London: The Demeanour of the Crowd: Excitement But No War Fever', *Manchester Guardian*, 3 Aug. 1914, 'A Strange Holiday in London: Scenes in the Streets and Still No War Fever', *Manchester Guardian*, 4 Aug. 1914, 'British Interest in the War: Eager Crowds in London', *Illustrated London News*, 8 Aug. 1914, 'England Must Keep Out Of It!', *Daily Herald*, 3 Aug. 1914.

57 Chirol to Hardinge, 4 Aug. 1914, Hardinge Papers, 93 Part I.

58 James Middleton to his parents, 8 Aug. 1914, Middleton Papers, MID 12.

59 Beatrice Webb Diary, 5 and 6 Aug. 1914, MacKenzie, eds., *Diary of Beatrice Webb*, vol. III, 212, 214.

60 Arthur H. D. Acland to Morley, 6 Aug. 1914, Morley Papers, MS. Eng. d. 3585.

61 Elizabeth Haldane Diary, 8 Aug. 1914, E. Haldane Papers, MSS 20240.

62 Algernon Firth to Harcourt, 9 Aug. 1914, MS. Harcourt 444.

63 See Roger Chickering, ' "War Enthusiasm?" Public Opinion and the Outbreak of War in 1914', in Afflerbach and Stevenson, eds., *An Improbable War?*, 200–212. For discussion of the British evidence, see Adrian Gregory, 'British "War Enthusiasm" in 1914: A Reassessment', in Gail Braybon, ed., *Evidence, History and the Great War* (London, 2003), Adrian Gregory, *The Last Great War: British Society and the First World War* (Cambridge, 2008), ch. 1, 'Going to War', and Catriona Pennell, *A Kingdom United: Popular Responses to the Outbreak of the First World War in Britain and Ireland* (Oxford, 2012).

17 'Jockeyed', 2 August

1 Cabinet Memorandum, 2 Aug. 1914, Harcourt Papers.

2 Asquith to Pamela McKenna, 1 Aug. 1915, McKenna Papers, MCKN 9/3.

3 The Ambassador at London to the Foreign Office, 2 Aug. 1914, *GD*, 676.

4 Ibid.

5 Margot Asquith Diary, 2 Aug. 1914, M. Asquith Papers, Ms. Eng. d. 3210. Emphasis in original.

6 O. H. L. Baynes to Harcourt, 2 Aug. 1914, filed with Cabinet Memorandum, 2 Aug. 1914, Harcourt Papers.

7 Cabinet Memorandum, 2 Aug. 1914, Harcourt Papers.

8 Note by Runciman on his official summons (dated Saturday 1 August) to the Cabinet of Sun. morning 2 Aug. 1914, Runciman Papers, WR 135/92.

9 H. Samuel to B. Samuel, 31 July 1914, Samuel Papers.

10 News that a German force had entered Luxembourg was first received in London at 11.45 a.m. on Sunday. See F. Villiers to Grey, 2 Aug. 1914, *BD*, vol. XI, Doc. 465.

11 Cabinet Memorandum, 2 Aug. 1914, Harcourt Papers. Emphasis in original.

12 Ibid.

13 Pease Diary, 2 Aug. 1914, in Wilson, 'Diary of Pease', [46] 8–[47] 9, and Asquith to Stanley, 2 Aug. 1914, in *Letters to Venetia Stanley*, 146.

14 Runciman's Cabinet Memorandum, 2 Aug. 1914, Runciman Papers, WR 135.

15 H. Samuel to B. Samuel, 2 Aug. 1914, Samuel Papers.

16 Cabinet Memorandum, 2 Aug. 1914, Harcourt Papers.

17 H. Samuel to B. Samuel, 2 Aug. 1914, Samuel Papers.

18 Masterman, *Masterman*, 265.

19 Runciman's Cabinet Memorandum, 2 Aug. 1914, Runciman Papers, WR 135. Grey also says that the letter was read out at the morning Cabinet. See Grey, *Twenty-Five Years*, II, 11. Lindsay argues, on the strength of Leo Maxse's testimony, that the Conservatives' letter reached Asquith 'shortly after midday' on 2 August. See Lindsay, 'Failure of Liberal Opposition', 118–19 and fn. 10.

20 Cabinet Memorandum, 2 Aug. 1914, Harcourt Papers. The importance of the letter was not lost on Burns. In his diary entry for that day he added a note to himself: 'See B. L.'s letter to P. M.', Burns Diary, 2 Aug. 1914, Burns Papers, Add. MSS. 46336.

21 Leo Maxse's *National Review* argued in 1918–19 that the Conservatives' pressure had pushed the Liberals into war. Asquith claimed not to remember the details of the Conservatives' letter, nor whether he had read it to the Cabinet. He did note its arrival 'on the Sunday morning' in a letter to Crewe, but mocked the idea that the Liberals 'were persuaded to take an active line by the letter which I received from Lansdowne and B. Law'. Finding a classical parallel, he quipped, 'It was said that Aspasia's dog was the real author of the Peloponnesian War'. See Asquith to Crewe, 11 Aug. 1918, MS. Asquith 46 (Bodleian Library) and Asquith to Lewis Harcourt, 4 July 1919, MS. Harcourt 421.

22 Chirol to Hardinge, 4 Aug. 1914, Hardinge Papers, 93 Part I.

23 Asquith to Stanley, 2 Aug. 1914, in *Letters to Venetia Stanley*, 146.

24 Samuel, answer to question 6, in untitled document, in reply to Harold Temperley's questionnaire, 1928, Spender Papers, Add. MS. 46386.

25 H. Samuel to B. Samuel, 2 Aug. 1914, Samuel Papers.

26 Crewe, 'Replies to Questions', 8 May 1929, Spender Papers, Add. MS. 46386.

27 Samuel, untitled document, in reply to Temperley's questionnaire, 1928, Spender Papers.

28 Runciman, untitled document, in reply to Temperley's questionnaire, 4 Nov. 1929, Spender Papers. Surprisingly (because most Radicals considered

Runciman a determined neutralist before July 1914), Runciman also claimed in his submission to Temperley that 'I would have acted with him [Grey], and Asquith always knew that I would.'

29 Runciman's Cabinet Memorandum, 2 Aug. 1914, Runciman Papers, WR 135.
30 Asquith to Stanley, 2 Aug. 1914, in *Letters to Venetia Stanley*, 146.
31 Churchill to Lloyd George, undated Cabinet note, in Churchill, ed., *Churchill: Companion Volume*, II, 3, 1997.
32 H. Samuel to B. Samuel, 2 Aug. 1914, Samuel Papers.
33 Ibid.
34 Cabinet Memorandum, 2 Aug. 1914, Harcourt Papers. Emphasis in original. Crewe would have been a surprising addition for, as remarked above, he had accompanied Grey and Haldane to 10 Downing Street only the night before and, according to Elizabeth Haldane, had agreed to Grey sending the note to Cambon outlining the pledge of naval support.
35 Who originally put forward the idea that France should be promised naval assistance is not clear. Grey argued in *Twenty-Five Years* that the 'anti-war party' put the idea forward. Wasserstein argues that Samuel first proposed it; see Bernard Wasserstein, *Herbert Samuel: A Political Life* (Oxford, 1992), 162–3. But in Samuel's answers to Harold Temperley's questionnaire of 1928, he responded that he did not know who first raised this. See Samuel, untitled document in reply to Temperley, 1928, Spender Papers, Add. MS. 46386. Crewe suggests that he proposed it. See Crewe, 'Replies to Questions', 8 May 1929, in Spender Papers, Add. MS. 46386.
36 Reproduced in Grey to Bertie, 2 Aug. 1914, *BD*, vol. XI, Doc. 487.
37 Hobhouse Diary, Aug. [undated] 1914, in Hobhouse, *Inside Asquith's Cabinet*, 180.
38 H. Samuel to B. Samuel, 2 Aug. 1914, Samuel Papers.
39 Cabinet Memorandum, 2 Aug. 1914, Harcourt Papers.
40 Untitled, undated [3 Aug. 1914] private memorandum, Beauchamp Papers.
41 Morley, *Memorandum*, 12.
42 H. Samuel to B. Samuel, 2 Aug. 1914, Samuel Papers.
43 Pease to J. B. Hodgkin, 4 Aug. 1914, copy, with Pease to Trevelyan, 5 Aug. 1914, Trevelyan Papers, CPT 59.
44 H. Samuel to B. Samuel, 2 Aug. 1914, Samuel Papers.
45 Reproduced in Grey to Bertie, 2 Aug. 1914, *BD*, vol. XI, Doc. 487.
46 Ibid.
47 Pease Diary, 2 Aug. 1914, in Wilson, 'Diary of Pease', [46] 8–[47] 9.
48 Grey to Bertie, 2 Aug. 1914, *BD*, vol. XI, Doc. 495.
49 Viviani to Cambon, 2 Aug. 1914, in *French Yellow Book*, No. 138, in *Documents Regarding the European War, Series V: The French Yellow Book* (New York, 1915). In the event, French parliamentarians were not summoned to meet until the afternoon of Tuesday 4 August, by which time the Germans had declared war on France. Here Viviani revealed for the first time the Grey–Cambon letters of 1912 and the British pledge of naval support conveyed on Sunday 2 August. See Frederick L. Schuman, *War and Diplomacy in the French Republic: An Inquiry into Political Motivations and the Control of Foreign Policy* (New York, 1969), 245, 249.
50 Bertie to Grey, 3 Aug. 1914, *BD*, vol. XI, Doc. 536.
51 'Précis of a Conversation between WSC, First Lord of the Admiralty and

the French Naval Attaché' [2 Aug. 1914], Churchill Papers, CHAR 13/29/231–2.

52 Admiralty to C. in C. Home Fleet, C. in C. Home Ports, Vice-Admiral 2nd and 3rd Fleet, 2 Aug. 1914, Churchill Papers, CHAR13/36/37.

53 Grey to Cambon, 2 Aug. 1914, and two telegrams, Bertie to Grey, 3 Aug. 1914, *BD*, vol. XI, Doc. 488, 536, 566. See the explanation in Grey's minute attached to Doc. 536 conceding that Asquith had given Lichnowsky information about the pledge on Monday morning.

54 Morley, *Memorandum*, 14–15.

55 Ibid., 15.

56 Cabinet Memorandum, 2 Aug. 1914, Harcourt Papers. Emphasis in original.

57 H. Samuel to B. Samuel, 2 Aug. 1914, Samuel Papers.

58 Cabinet Memorandum, 2 Aug. 1914, Harcourt Papers. Emphasis in original.

59 Morley, *Memorandum*, 15.

60 H. Samuel to B. Samuel, 2 Aug. 1914, Samuel Papers.

61 Untitled, undated [3 Aug. 1914] private memorandum, Beauchamp Papers.

62 Cabinet Memorandum, 2 Aug. 1914, Harcourt Papers.

63 Ibid.

64 See documents unfortunately not stamped with the time of receipt, Consul Le Gallais to Grey, 2 Aug. 1914, *BD*, vol. XI, Doc. 468, and an undated 'Communication from German Embassy', received 2 Aug. 1914, Doc. 472.

65 Cabinet Memorandum, 2 Aug. 1914, Harcourt Papers.

66 See the notation at Blunt Diary, 5 Aug. 1914, Blunt Papers, MS 13–1975.

67 H. Samuel to B. Samuel, 2 Aug. 1914, Samuel Papers.

68 Untitled, undated [3 Aug. 1914] private memorandum, Beauchamp Papers.

69 H. Samuel to B. Samuel, 2 Aug. 1914, Samuel Papers.

70 Ibid.

71 Pease to J. B. Hodgkin, 4 Aug. 1914, copy, with Pease to Trevelyan, 5 Aug. 1914, Trevelyan Papers, CPT 59.

72 Crewe to Hardinge, n.d., quoted in James Pope-Hennessy, *Lord Crewe: The Likeness of a Liberal* (London, 1955), 145.

73 Simon to Burns, and Burns to Simon, 2 Aug. 1914, MS. Simon 50, Simon Papers, emphasis in original, and see David Dutton, *Simon: A Political Biography of Sir John Simon* (London, 1992), 29.

74 Untitled notes on 10 Downing Street card, Beauchamp Papers. Emphasis in original.

75 Cabinet Memorandum, 2 Aug. 1914, Harcourt Papers, and Untitled, undated [3 Aug. 1914] private memorandum, Beauchamp Papers.

76 Burns Diary, 2 Aug. 1914, Burns Papers, Add. MSS. 46336.

77 H. Samuel to B. Samuel, 2 Aug. 1914, Samuel Papers.

78 Cabinet Memorandum, 2 Aug. 1914, Harcourt Papers.

79 See Prime Minister Massey in the New Zealand Parliament, 31 July 1914, quoted in Telegram of The Governor of New Zealand to the Secretary of State for the Colonies (received Colonial Office 4.24 p.m., 1 Aug. 1914); 'Paraphrase of Telegram from Gov. General Canada (received 9 a.m., 2 Aug. 1914), ADM 137/3/8; The Governor-General [of Australia] to the Secretary of State [Harcourt] (received 6.20 p.m., 3 Aug. 1914), in The Parliament of

the Commonwealth of Australia, *Papers Presented to Parliament, vol. V, Session 1914–17*, 1434.
80 For example, 'Dominions Rally', and 'On the Brink of War', *The Times*, 31 July 1914, 'Awaiting Britain's Call', *Scotsman*, 1 Aug. 1914, 'The Empire Ready: Canadian Expeditionary Force', and 'Offer of Men from New Zealand', *The Times*, 1 Aug. 1914, 'Australia: Help for the Motherland: To Our Last Man and Our Last Shilling', *Scotsman*, 3 Aug. 1914, and 'The Empire and the War', editorial, *The Times*, 3 Aug. 1914.
81 Cabinet Memorandum, 2 Aug. 1914, Harcourt Papers.
82 A. Ponsonby to D. Ponsonby, 3 Aug. 1914, Ponsonby Papers (Shulbrede).
83 Lansdowne to Lady Lansdowne, 2 Aug. 1914, Lansdowne Papers, LANS (5) 85/7.
84 Henry Wilson Diary, 2 Aug. 1914, in Callwell, *Wilson*, I, 155.
85 Ibid.
86 Chamberlain, *Down The Years*, 99–100.
87 Edward Marsh, *A Number of People: A Book of Reminiscences* (London, 1939), 245.
88 Lansdowne to Lady Lansdowne, 2 Aug. 1914, Lansdowne Papers, LANS (5) 85/7.
89 Chamberlain, *Down The Years*, 100.
90 Asquith to Law, 2 Aug. 1914, Lansdowne Papers, LANS (5) 85/7.
91 Chamberlain, *Down The Years*, 101.
92 Austen Chamberlain to Lansdowne, 2 Aug. 1914, Lansdowne Papers, LANS (5) 85/7.
93 Law to Asquith, 2 Aug. 1914, Lansdowne Papers, LANS (5) 85/7.

18 Fracture Lines, 2 and 3 August

1 Handwritten note on his resignation letter, Burns to Asquith, 2 Aug. 1914, Burns Papers, Add. MSS. 46282/158.
2 Morley, *Memorandum*, 17.
3 Ibid., 12.
4 These words are written in Burns's hand on Morley's manuscript of his 'Memorandum on Resignation', typescript version, Morley Papers, Ms Eng. d. 3585 (Bodleian Library). The position Burns had come to is dated in Morley's narrative to the Saturday evening. See also Kent, *Burns*, 237.
5 Asquith to Stanley, 3 Aug. 1914, *Letters to Venetia Stanley*, 147–8.
6 Burns to Asquith, 2 Aug. 1914 [handwritten copy], Burns Papers, Add. MSS. 46282/158, also reproduced in Kent, *Burns*, 237–8.
7 Cabinet Memorandum, 2 Aug. 1914, Harcourt Papers.
8 Burns Diary, 7 Nov. 1916, Burns Papers, Add. MSS. 46338.
9 Baron Carnock [Arthur Nicolson] to Ronald Munro Ferguson, 30 Nov. 1916, Novar Papers, Box 9 (National Library of Australia). I am grateful to Bruce Hunt for this reference.
10 Handwritten note on his resignation letter, Burns to Asquith, 2 Aug. 1914, Burns Papers, Add. MSS. 46282/158.

11 George Riddell, *Lord Riddell's War Diary* (London, 1933), 4–5, and McEwen, ed., *Riddell Diaries*, 87. Beaverbrook also maintained that Masterman was a key influence on Lloyd George at this time. Beaverbrook recalled him 'arguing for war', and 'his whole interest was concentrated on the effect his remarks were having on Lloyd George'; see Beaverbrook, *Sunday Express*, [n.d.] 1926, quoted in Masterman, *Masterman*, 267.

12 Ramsay MacDonald Diary, 23 Sept. 1914, MacDonald Papers, TNA: PRO 30/69/1753/1.

13 Asquith to Stanley, 3 Aug. 1914, *Letters to Venetia Stanley*, 148.

14 Simon to Asquith, 2 Aug. 1914, 'Diary #5', MS. Simon 2, Simon Papers, and see Dutton, *Simon*, 30.

15 Morley, *Memorandum*, 13.

16 Ibid.

17 Morley to Asquith, 3 Aug. 1914, in Morley, *Memorandum*, 22.

18 Untitled, undated [3 Aug. 1914] private memorandum, Beauchamp Papers.

19 Ibid.

20 Charles Hobhouse Diary, August [undated, 1914], in Hobhouse, *Inside Asquith's Cabinet*, 180, Asquith to Stanley, 3 Aug. 1914, *Letters to Venetia Stanley*, 148, and Cassar, *Asquith*, 25–6.

21 Beauchamp to Asquith, 3 Aug. 1914, Beauchamp Papers. It is noteworthy that this letter referred to Beauchamp's desire to 'confirm' his resignation, so, in common with Morley, Beauchamp must have given Asquith some indication of his intention to resign on the Sunday.

22 Villiers to Grey, 3 Aug. 1914 (received at 10.55 a.m.), *BD*, vol. XI, Doc. 521. In response to this Grey made a request for 'full facts'. See ibid., Grey to Villiers, 3 Aug. 1914 (despatched at 12.45 p.m.), Doc. 525. Two earlier documents in the series, reporting the German ultimatum to Belgium, Docs. 514 and 515, give no time of receipt in London.

23 Morley, *Memorandum*, 15.

24 Ibid., 13.

25 Cabinet Memorandum, 2 Aug. 1914, Harcourt Papers.

26 Richard Burdon Haldane, *An Autobiography* (London 1929), 275.

27 Harcourt Cabinet Memorandum, 3 Aug. 1914, Harcourt Papers.

19 Hidden Schism, 3 August

1 Cabinet Memorandum, 3 Aug. 1914, Harcourt Papers.

2 *Scotsman*, editorial, 3 Aug. 1914. *The Times*, quoting 'French semi-official sources', alleged German incursions near Lunéville, Mulhouse, Longwy and at one unspecified location. See 'Five Nations at War' and 'France Invaded', *The Times*, 3 Aug. 1914. This added to the reports in the special Sunday edition of *The Times*, which had reproduced information supplied by the French Embassy in London, giving details of alleged frontier violations by Germany at Cirey; 'German Invasion: Statement by the French Embassy', *The Times*, 2 Aug. 1914. See also 'Surprise Invasion of France', *Times of India*, 3 Aug. 1914.

3 There was no German invasion of France on Sunday 2 August. Rather, there

was an incursion at Joncherey, near Belfort. One German and one Frenchmen were killed. The first major fighting in the west came with the German invasion of Belgium on 4 August and the French advance against Mulhouse on 7 August 1914. See Holger H. Herwig, *The Marne, 1914: The Opening of the World War I and the Battle that Changed the World* (New York, 2009), xi, 76, 110.

4 'France Invaded', *The Times*, 3 Aug. 1914.

5 For example, 'The Mailed Fist Strikes', editorial, *Daily Mail*, 3 Aug. 1914, 'The German Invasion' and 'Britain's Part in the Crisis', editorials, *The Times*, 3 Aug. 1914.

6 Repington, 'The War Day by Day', *The Times*, 3 Aug. 1914.

7 Ibid., 'Public Opinion and the Crisis'.

8 Ibid., 'War Declared: Russian Rejection of German Demands'. The report of a crowd of 50,000 is fanciful. See Buchanan, *My Mission*, I, 207, where he refers merely to finding 'the door blocked by an enthusiastic crowd'.

9 *Daily Telegraph*, editorial, 3 Aug. 1914.

10 'On the Brink' and 'A Shameless Argument', editorials, *Manchester Guardian*, 3 Aug. 1914.

11 For example, ibid., 'Public Opinion and the War: England's Duty' and 'England's Duty – Neutrality the One Policy'.

12 See Chamberlain, 'Memorandum', Mon. 3 Aug., Chamberlain, *Down the Years*, 102.

13 See ibid., 103. See 'Germany's Ultimatum to Belgium, Exchange Company's special Telegram', dated 3 Aug. 1914, *BD*, vol. XI, Doc. 514, with no time of receipt.

14 Chamberlain, 'Memorandum', Mon. 3 Aug., in Chamberlain, *Down the Years*, 102.

15 Ibid., 102–103.

16 Paul Cambon to Viviani, 3 Aug. 1914, *French Yellow Book*, No. 143, reproduced in Geiss, ed., *July 1914*, 356, emphasis added.

17 Sir Francis Villiers to Grey, 3 Aug. 1914, *BD*, vol. XI, Doc. 521, and for Grey's request to Villiers to confirm the details from the Belgian government directly, see ibid., Grey to Villiers, 3 Aug. 1914 (despatched at 12.45 p.m.), Doc. 525.

18 Harcourt did not actually use the word 'ultimatum' in his notes, but rather 'demand'. See Cabinet Memorandum, 3 Aug. 1914, Harcourt Papers.

19 Ibid. Emphasis in original.

20 Ibid.

21 Haldane, *Autobiography*, 274–6, and for discussion see Albertini, *Origins of the World War*, III, 508–10.

22 Note in Harcourt's handwriting, 3 Aug. 1914, filed with Cabinet Memorandum, 3 Aug. 1914, Harcourt Papers.

23 H. Samuel to B. Samuel, 3 Aug. 1914 (section of the letter headed '5.30 p.m.'), Samuel Papers.

24 Pease Diary, 3 Aug. 1914, Wilson, 'Diary of Pease', [48] 10.

25 Charles Hobhouse Diary, August [n.d.] 1914, in Hobhouse, *Inside Asquith's Cabinet*, 180.

26 Masterman, *Masterman*, 265.

27 Cabinet Memorandum, 3 Aug. 1914, Harcourt Papers.

28 Morley, *Memorandum*, 26–7.

29 H. Samuel to B. Samuel, 2 [but should be 3] Aug. 1914, Samuel Papers. The letter is dated 2 August, but from internal evidence, the reference to the resignations and the King of the Belgians' appeal to Britain, as well as the envelope dated '3 Aug. 1914, 7.45 p.m.' this letter is almost certainly misdated and should be 3. Aug. 1914.
30 Cabinet Memorandum, 3 Aug. 1914, Harcourt Papers.
31 Ramsay MacDonald Diary, 6 Oct. 1914, MacDonald Papers, TNA: PRO 30/69/1753/1.
32 Cabinet Memorandum, 3 Aug. 1914, Harcourt Papers.
33 Asquith to Stanley, 3 Aug. 1914, *Letters to Venetia Stanley*, 148.
34 Hobhouse Diary, Aug. [n.d.] 1914, in Hobhouse, *Inside Asquith's Cabinet*, 180.
35 Cabinet Memorandum, 3 Aug. 1914, Harcourt Papers.
36 Pease Diary, 3 Aug. 1914, in Wilson, 'Diary of Pease', 10 [48].
37 H. Samuel to B. Samuel, 2 [but should be 3] Aug. 1914, Samuel Papers.
38 Hobhouse Diary, Aug. [undated] 1914, in Hobhouse, *Inside Asquith's Cabinet*, 180.
39 Asquith to Stanley, 3 Aug. 1914, *Letters to Venetia Stanley*, 148.
40 In his diary, Burns mentioned the visit to Downing Street, and did not record shifting to the backbench in the House of Commons; see Burns Diary, 3 Aug. 1914, Burns Papers, Add. MSS. 46336.
41 The eventual resignations of Burns and Morley were not announced until the morning edition of *The Times*, 5 Aug. 1914.
42 His Majesty the King of the Belgians to His Majesty King George, 3 Aug. 1914 (telegram), in *The Belgian Grey Book: Diplomatic Correspondence Respecting the War* (London, 1914), Doc. 25, and 'The Belgian Appeal', *The Times*, 4 Aug. 1914.
43 Albertini, *Origins of the War*, III, 467.
44 H. Samuel to B. Samuel, 2 [but should be 3] Aug. 1914, Samuel Papers.
45 Asquith to Stanley, 3 Aug. 1914, *Letters to Venetia Stanley*, 148.

20 Magical Theatre, 3 August

1 Grey in *Parliamentary Debates*, Commons, 5th series, vol. 65, 1825 (3 Aug. 1914).
2 Schoen, the German Ambassador in Paris, handed his ultimatum over to Viviani, French Premier and Foreign Minister, at 7 p.m. on Friday 31 July; Pourtalès, the German Ambassador in St Petersburg, handed his ultimatum over to Sazonov at about midnight on Friday 31 July. Schmitt, *Coming of the War*, II, 267–8, Fay, *Origins of the World War*, II, 528, and Schuman, *War and Diplomacy*, 236–7. See *GD*, Docs. 490 and 491, sent at 3.30 p.m.
3 Herwig, *Marne*, 14, and Albertini, *Origins of the War*, III, 102–3.
4 Albertini, *Origins of the War*, III, 183.
5 Schmitt, *Coming of the War*, II, 374.
6 H. Samuel to B. Samuel, 2 [misdated, should be 3] Aug. 1914, Samuel Papers.
7 Edmund Harvey to his father, 4 Aug. 1914, Harvey Papers.

8 'Today's Meeting of Parliament', *The Times*, 3 Aug. 1914.

9 'A Fateful Sitting of the Commons', *Manchester Guardian*, 4 Aug. 1914.

10 Ibid.

11 'The Proceedings in Parliament', *The Times*, 5 Aug. 1914.

12 'A Memorable Day in the Commons', *The Times*, 4 Aug. 1914. See references to the 'unprecedented appearance' of the House, with chairs on the floor and in gangways, in 'Parliamentary Intelligence', *The Times*, 9 Apr. 1886. The *Manchester Guardian* reported that chairs had been similarly placed on the presentation of the Second Home Rule Bill in 1893; 'A Fateful Sitting of the Commons', *Manchester Guardian*, 4 Aug. 1914.

13 *Parliamentary Debates*, Commons, 5th series, vol. 28, 1467–84 (24 July 1911).

14 'The Policy of Britain – Sir Edward Grey's Statement', *Daily Citizen*, 4 Aug. 1914.

15 'A Fateful Sitting of the Commons', *Manchester Guardian*, 4 Aug. 1914.

16 'Defining Great Britain's Policy', *Illustrated London News*, 8 Aug. 1914.

17 'The Nerves of Parliament', *Manchester Guardian*, 4 Aug. 1914.

18 Grey's speech can be found in *Parliamentary Debates*, 5th series, Commons, vol. 65, 1809–27 (3 Aug. 1914).

19 Hermann Lutz, *Lord Grey and the World War* (New York, 1928), 100. The full text of the letter was given when the Government published its White Paper on 6 August. See Grey to Cambon, 22 Nov. 1912, and Cambon to Grey, 23 Nov. 1912, reproduced in *Great Britain and the European Crisis* (White Paper, Miscellaneous No. 6, Cd. 7467, London, 1914), encls. No. 1 and No. 2 with Doc. 105, 56–7. Grey also failed to read the reply of Paul Cambon of 23 November 1912 with its reference to the two governments considering 'the plans of their general staffs'.

20 The redistribution of British fleets (but without any reference to any proposed deal with France) had been explained in general terms in Churchill's speech to the House of Commons on Naval Estimates in March 1912. See *Parliamentary Debates*, Commons, 5th series, vol. 35, 1563–4. The later Anglo-French naval arrangements, promoted chiefly by Churchill and Cambon in 1912, had been finalised verbally during Churchill's visit to Toulon and Battenberg's secret visit to Paris, both in March 1913. See Battenberg to Churchill, 5 Mar. 1913, Churchill Papers, CHAR 13/9/38.

21 *Parliamentary Debates*, Commons, 5th series, vol. 65, 1815 (3 Aug. 1914).

22 Ibid. This was a point familiar in conversation with Grey's friend, J. A. Spender. See Spender, *Life, Journalism and Politics*, II, 12.

23 The German offer was made by Lichnowsky in the morning and confirmed in the afternoon by Herr von Wesendonk, Secretary at the Embassy. See Lichnowsky to the Foreign Office [Berlin], 3 Aug. 1914, Lichnowsky, *Heading for the Abyss*, 423–4, and Communication from the German Embassy, 3 Aug. 1914, *BD*, vol. XI, Doc. 531. The German offer was formally released to the press in the morning of 3 August by Baron von Kühlmann, Councillor of the German Embassy: 'Germany would be disposed to give an undertaking that she will not attack France by sea in the North, or make any warlike use of the coast of Belgium or Holland, if it appeared that Great Britain would make this undertaking on condition of her neutrality *for the time being*.' Emphasis added. See 'Germany's Offer', *Westminster Gazette* [late city extra edition], 3 Aug. 1914.

24 *Parliamentary Debates*, Commons, 5th series, vol. 65, 1818 (3 Aug. 1914).
25 The original reference is *Parliamentary Debates*, Lords, 3rd series, vol. 203, 1672 (8 Aug. 1870).
26 The original reference is *Parliamentary Debates*, Commons, 3rd series, vol. 203, 1787 (10 Aug. 1870). Ibid., 5th series, vol. 65, 1819 (3 Aug. 1914).
27 The original reference is *Parliamentary Debates*, Commons, 3rd series, vol. 203, 1788 (10 Aug. 1870).
28 Neilson, *My Life in Two Worlds*, I, 325.
29 Churchill to Asquith and Grey, 3 Aug. 1914 (marked '5 p.m.') Churchill Papers, CHAR 13/27/B4.

21 Inventing 'Unanimity', 3 August

1 King George V Diary, 3 Aug. 1914, quoted by Clay, *King, Kaiser, Tsar*, 314.
2 Ibid., 1 Aug. 1914, quoted in ibid., 311, 314.
3 'The Nation and the Government', editorial, *The Times*, 4 Aug. 1914.
4 'A Fateful Sitting of the Commons', *Manchester Guardian*, 4 Aug. 1914.
5 *Parliamentary Debates*, Commons, 5th series, vol. 65, 1827–8 (3 Aug. 1914).
6 See Balfour's remarks in W. R. Nicoll, 'Dinner at Sir George Riddell's to meet Balfour, 10 Sept. 1914', Nicoll Papers, MS. 3518/26/6.
7 *Parliamentary Debates*, Commons, 5th series, vol. 65, 1828–9 (3 Aug. 1914).
8 Margot Asquith Diary, 29 July and 1 Aug. 1914, M. Asquith Papers, Ms. Eng. d. 3210.
9 'Britain Only Waits for German Ships to Fire on France', *New York Times*, 4 Aug. 1914.
10 *Parliamentary Debates*, Commons, 5th series, vol. 32, 81 (27 Nov. 1911).
11 Dillon to Blunt, 21 Mar. 1915, MS 129–1975, and Dillon to Blunt, 22 Apr. 1915, MS 130–1975, Blunt Papers, emphasis in original, and see F. S. L. Lyons, *John Dillon: A Biography* (London, 1968), 354–5.
12 Gallery Correspondent, 'Labour's Protest in Parliament', *Labour Leader*, 6 Aug. 1914.
13 'The Policy of Britain – Sir Edward Grey's Statement', *Daily Citizen*, 4 Aug. 1914.
14 *Parliamentary Debates*, Commons, 5th series, vol. 65, 1829–31 (3 Aug. 1914).
15 Gallery Correspondent, 'Labour's Protest in Parliament', *Labour Leader*, 6 Aug. 1914.
16 *Parliamentary Debates*, Commons, 5th series, vol. 65, 1831 (3 Aug. 1914).
17 'British Plans', *The Times*, 4 Aug. 1914.
18 'The Policy of Britain – Sir Edward Grey's Statement', *Daily Citizen*, 4 Aug. 1914.
19 MacDonald to W. R. Nicoll, 4 Aug. 1914, Nicoll Papers, MS. 3518/27/1.
20 Courtenay Ilbert Diary, 3 Aug. 1914, Courtenay Ilbert Papers, ILB/2/12 (Parliamentary Archives).
21 *Parliamentary Debates*, Commons, 5th series, vol. 65, 1873 (3 Aug. 1914).
22 Ibid. and the parliamentary report in 'British Plans', *The Times*, 4 Aug. 1914.

23 'Proceedings in Parliament', *The Times*, 4 Aug. 1914, and Michael MacDonagh, *In London During the Great War: The Diary of a Journalist* (London, 1935), 5.

24 Hugh Spender, 'A Dramatic Scene', *Westminster Gazette*, 4 Aug. 1914.

25 'House of Commons', *Daily News*, 4 Aug. 1914.

26 'A Fateful Sitting of the Commons', *Manchester Guardian*, 4 Aug. 1914.

27 'The Policy of Britain – Sir Edward Grey's Statement', *Daily Citizen*, 4 Aug. 1914, and see Keir Hardie, 'The Government's Crime', *Labour Leader*, 6 Aug. 1914.

28 'In the Outer Lobby', *Daily Citizen*, 4 Aug. 1914.

29 Hirst Notes 'Grey's speech Aug. 3' [1914], Hirst Papers.

30 James Middleton to his parents, 8 Aug. 1914, Middleton Papers, MID 12.

31 Vernon Lee to Ottoline Morrell, 4 Aug. 1914, Ottoline Morrell Papers, 17/2 (Harry Ransom Centre, University of Texas). Emphasis in original.

32 *Parliamentary Debates*, Commons, 5th series, vol. 65, 1864–5 (3 Aug. 1914).

22 Dissent, 3 August

1 A. Ponsonby to D. Ponsonby, 4 Aug. 1914, [incorrectly dated 4–VII–14], Ponsonby Papers (Shulbrede).

2 Addison, *Politics from Within*, I, 37.

3 John Simon, *Retrospect* (London, 1952), 95, 97.

4 A. Ponsonby to D. Ponsonby, 4 Aug. 1914, [incorrectly dated '4–VII–14'].

5 Arthur Ponsonby, entry for n.d. August 1914, 'War Diary', Ponsonby Papers (Shulbrede).

6 Ibid.

7 Charles Trevelyan, 'C. P. T's personal record', Trevelyan Papers, CPT 59.

8 Pease Diary, 3 Aug. 1914, in Wilson, 'Diary of Pease', [49] 11.

9 H. Samuel to B. Samuel, 3 Aug. 1914 (section of the letter headed '5.30 p.m.'), Samuel Papers.

10 Morel Diary (written 18 Aug. 1914) describing events of 3–4 Aug. 1914, E. D. Morel Papers, F 1/1/14.

11 Charles Trevelyan, 'C. P. T's personal record', Trevelyan Papers, CPT 59.

12 Morel Diary, 18 Aug. 1914, Morel Papers, F 1/1/14.

13 Charles Trevelyan to Asquith, 3 Aug. 1914 (Draft), Trevelyan Papers, CPT 59 and see Morris, *Trevelyan*, 99.

14 See notes on meetings, resolution, and list of signatures attending the second of two LFAG meetings, headed 'Aug. 3', Ponsonby Papers, MS. Eng. hist. c. 660, f. 64–7. This shows that two voted against the resolution, George Scott Robertson and Christopher Addison, while three others abstained.

15 See 'Liberal Meeting', *Daily News*, 4 Aug. 1914, and 'Liberal Members and Neutrality', *Manchester Guardian*, 4 Aug. 1914.

16 *Parliamentary Debates*, Commons, 5th series, vol. 65, 1831–2 (3 Aug. 1914) and 'British Plans', *The Times*, 4 Aug. 1914.

17 Edmund Harvey to his father, 4 Aug. 1914, Harvey Papers.

18 *Parliamentary Debates*, Lords, 5th series, vol. xvii, 318–20 (3 Aug. 1914), and 'House of Lords', *The Times*, 4 Aug. 1914.

19 *Parliamentary Debates*, Commons, 5th series, vol. 65, 1834 (3 Aug. 1914).
20 The sixteen Radicals who spoke against intervention were Philip Morrell, Josiah Wedgwood, Edmund Harvey, Arthur Ponsonby, Albert Spicer, Arnold Rowntree, Percy Molteno, Llewelyn Williams, Robert Outhwaite, Joseph King, John Jardine, Aneurin Williams, William Byles, Annan Bryce, Richard Denman and Ellis Davies.
21 *Parliamentary Debates*, Commons, 5th series, vol. 65, 1833–7 (3 Aug. 1914).
22 For example, Edmund Harvey's speech, *Parliamentary Debates*, Commons, 5th series, vol. 65, 1838–41 (3 Aug. 1914).
23 *Parliamentary Debates*, Commons, 5th series, vol. 65, 1859 (3 Aug. 1914).
24 Ibid., 1848–53.
25 Ibid., 1842–4.
26 Ibid., 1880.
27 Edmund Harvey to his father, 4 Aug. 1914, Harvey Papers.
28 *Parliamentary Debates*, Commons, 5th series, vol. 65, 1836, 1846, 1861–2, 1867, 1872 (3 Aug. 1914).
29 Ibid., 1870.
30 Ibid., 1837–8.
31 Ibid., 1860.
32 Ibid., 1841.
33 On the King's ultimate and formal responsibility to control foreign policy and to make a declaration of war, unfettered by Parliament, see Lord Halsbury, ed., *The Laws of England*, 1st ed., vol. VI (London, 1909), 375, 386, 427–8, 440–1, 442, 444.
34 *Parliamentary Debates*, Commons, 5th series, vol. 65, 1810, 1814 (3 Aug. 1914).
35 Ibid., 1826.
36 Ibid., 1864.
37 Ibid., 1874.
38 Ibid., 1876–7.
39 Ibid., 1881–2.
40 Ibid., 1884.
41 Ibid. Hansard incorrectly records the time as 'Thirty-seven minutes before Ten o'clock' but this is clearly an error, as '10.0 p.m.' is noted during Bryce's speech. The parliamentary report in 'British Plans', *The Times*, 4 Aug. 1914, records that the debate ended and the House rose 'shortly after half-past 10 o'clock'.

23 Midnight Seductions, 3 and 4 August

1 Asquith to J. A. Simon, 3 Aug. 1914, 'Diary #5', MS. Simon 2, Simon Papers.
2 H. Samuel to B. Samuel, 3 Aug. 1914 (section of the letter headed '10 p.m.'), Samuel Papers.
3 Cabinet Memorandum, 3 Aug. 1914, Harcourt Papers.
4 Pease Diary, 3 Aug. 1914, in Wilson, 'Diary of Pease', [48] 10–[49] 11.
5 Cabinet Memorandum, 3 Aug. 1914, Harcourt Papers. Emphasis in original.
6 H. Samuel to B. Samuel, 3 Aug. 1914 (section of the letter headed '10 p.m.'), Samuel Papers.

7 *Parliamentary Debates*, Commons, 5th series, vol. 65, 1834 (3 Aug. 1914).

8 Pease Diary, 3 Aug. 1914, in Wilson, 'Diary of Pease', [48] 10–[49] 11.

9 Lord Hugh Cecil, Note, 4 Aug. 1914, quoted in Kenneth Rose, *The Later Cecils* (London, 1975), 257.

10 Asquith to Stanley, 4 Aug. 1914, *Letters to Venetia Stanley*, 150.

11 Asquith to J. A. Simon, 3 Aug. 1914, 'Diary #5', MS. Simon 2, Simon Papers.

12 Ibid., Simon to Asquith, 4 Aug. 1914.

13 C. P. Scott interview with Simon, 4 Sept. 1914, Scott Papers (British Library) Add. MSS. 50901, fol. 159, as cited in Lindsay, 'Failure of Liberal Opposition', 159.

14 Francis Hirst to Helena Hirst, 4 Jan. 1918, Hirst Papers.

15 Morley, *Memorandum*, 27.

16 George Cunningham to Beauchamp, 4 Aug. 1914, Beauchamp Papers.

17 There is a copy of Asquith's letter to Simon in Beauchamp's files. Asquith to Simon, 3 Aug. 1914, typed copy, filed with Beauchamp's resignation letter to Asquith 3 Aug. 1914, Beauchamp Papers.

18 Lionel Holland to Beauchamp, 4 Aug. 1914, Beauchamp Papers.

19 Beauchamp to Morley, 4 Aug. 1914, copy, Beauchamp Papers. There is a copy in the original manuscript of 'Memorandum on Resignation', Morley Papers, MS. Eng. d. 3585.

20 Morley to Beauchamp, 5 Aug. 1914, Beauchamp Papers. Emphasis in original.

21 Burns Diary, 5 Aug. 1915, Burns Papers, Add. MSS. 46337.

22 Asquith to Morley, 3 Aug. 1914, reproduced in Morley, *Memorandum*, 29–30.

23 Morley to Asquith, 4 Aug. 1914, reproduced ibid., 30–1.

24 Morley, *Memorandum*, 31. Morley attended his last Privy Council meeting as Lord President on the morning of Wednesday 5 August. See 'Court Circular', *The Times*, 6 Aug. 1914.

25 Morley, *Memorandum*, 4.

26 Harcourt untitled note, on 10 Downing Street notepaper, undated but probably 4 Aug. 1914, Beauchamp Papers.

27 Harcourt to F. G. Thomas, 5 Aug. 1914, quoted by Lindsay, 'Failure of the Liberal Opposition', 160. Thomas was a leading member of the Liberal-aligned Eighty Club.

28 Harcourt to Morley, 6 Aug. 1914, Morley Papers, MS. Eng d. 3585. Emphasis in original.

29 Morley to Harcourt, 6 Aug. 1914, Harcourt Papers, 427. Emphasis in original.

30 Handwritten version of 'Memo on Resignation', Morley Papers, MS. Eng d. 3585. Emphasis in original.

31 Morley, *Memorandum*, 32. Emphasis in original.

32 Asquith to Stanley, 4 Aug. 1914, *Letters to Venetia Stanley*, 150.

33 Margot Asquith Diary, 4 Aug. 1914, M. Asquith Papers, Ms. Eng. d. 3210.

34 Runciman to Trevelyan, 4 Aug. 1914, Trevelyan Papers, CPT 33.

35 Pease to J. B. Hodgkin, 4 Aug. 1914, copy, with Pease to Trevelyan, 5 Aug. 1914, Trevelyan Papers, CPT 59.

36 Ibid., Pease to Trevelyan, 5 Aug. 1914. Emphasis in original.

37 Ibid., Charles Trevelyan, 'C. P. T's personal record'.

39 H. Samuel to B. Samuel, 2 Aug. 1914, Samuel Papers.

40 A. Ponsonby to D. Ponsonby, 3 Aug. 1914 [describing events of 2 Aug.], Ponsonby Papers.

41 Morley, *Memorandum*, 25.
42 W. Runciman to C. Trevelyan, 4 Aug. 1914, Trevelyan Papers, CPT 59.
43 Ibid., J. A. Pease to C. Trevelyan, 5 Aug. 1914.
44 Ibid., Charles Trevelyan, 'C. P. T's personal record'.
45 F. W. Hirst to Margaret Hirst, 29 Sept. 1914, Hirst Papers. For other examples, see Lord Eversley to Burns, 1 Oct. 1914, Burns Papers, 46303, and Bertrand Russell to Ottoline Morrell, 24 Nov. 1914, Morrell Papers, 25/2.
46 F. W. Hirst to M. Hirst, 'Sunday Night' (filed as November 1914), Hirst Papers.
47 Anthony Trollope, *Phineas Finn* (Oxford, 2008), vol. I, 130, 258, and vol. II, 54.
48 Morley, *Memorandum*, 20.
49 Ethel Pease to Jack Pease, 4 Aug. 1914, quoted in Wilson, *Policy of the Entente*, 147.
50 Margot Asquith to Harcourt, 14 Aug. 1914, MS Harcourt 421. Emphasis in original.

24 Seizing the Moment, 4 August

1 Foreign Office Statement, 4 Aug. 1914, reproduced in 'War Declared', *The Times*, 5 Aug. 1914 and 'Why There is War', *Daily Mirror*, 5 Aug. 1914.
2 'The Nation and the Government', editorial, *The Times*, 4 Aug. 1914.
3 Editorial, *Scotsman*, 4 Aug. 1914.
4 'Peace or War?', editorial, *Manchester Guardian*, 4 Aug. 1914.
5 'Sir Edward Grey's Strange Blunder', editorial, *Manchester Guardian*, 4 Aug. 1914.
6 'Sir Edward Grey's Statement', editorial, *Daily News*, 4 Aug. 1914.
7 'Here We Stand', editorial, *Westminster Gazette*, 4 Aug. 1914.
8 W. S. Blunt Diary, 5 Aug. 1914, MS13–1975, Wilfrid Scawen Blunt Papers.
9 Grey to Goschen, 4 Aug. 1914, *BD*, vol. XI, Doc. 573.
10 John H. Horne and Alan Kramer, *German Atrocities, 1914: A History of Denial* (New Haven, 2001), 10, and Jeff Lipkes, *The German Army in Belgium, August 1914* (Leuven, 2007), 39.
11 'In Downing Street', *The Times*, 5 Aug. 1914. See also Asquith to Stanley, 4 Aug. 1914, *Letters to Venetia Stanley*, 150. Villiers to Grey, 4 Aug. 1914 (received 6.30 p.m.), *BD*, vol. XI, Doc. 621.
12 H. Samuel to B. Samuel, 4 Aug. 1914, Samuel Papers.
13 Cabinet Memorandum, 4 Aug. 1914, Harcourt Papers.
14 Ibid., 3 Aug. 1914. Emphasis in original. Sir David de Villiers Graaff was in London awaiting an imminent appointment as South African High Commissioner.
15 Asquith to Stanley, 4 Aug. 1914, in *Letters to Venetia Stanley*, 150.
16 Cabinet Memorandum, 4 Aug. 1914, Harcourt Papers.
17 This was the birth of the White Paper entitled *Correspondence Respecting the European Crisis* that was delivered to every member of the House of Commons on the morning of 6 August. See Pease Diary, 4 Aug. 1914, in Wilson, 'Diary of Pease', [49] 11.

18 H. Samuel to B. Samuel, 4 Aug. 1914, Samuel Papers.
19 Spender, *Life of Asquith*, II, 93.
20 Churchill, *World Crisis*, I, 178.
21 H. Samuel to B. Samuel, 4 Aug. 1914, Samuel Papers.
22 Trevelyan, *Grey of Fallodon*, 262.
23 Wilson, 'Britain', in *Decisions for War*, 202.
24 'In Downing Street', *The Times*, 5 Aug. 1914, and Clay, *King, Kaiser, Tsar*, 314.
25 Grey to Goschen, 4 Aug. 1914, *BD*, vol. XI, Doc. 594.
26 Asquith to Stanley, 4 Aug. 1914, in *Letters to Venetia Stanley*, 150.
27 Frances Stevenson, *The Years That Are Past* (London, 1967), 73–4.
28 Jerome K. Jerome, *My Life and Times* (London, 1926), 265.
29 'The Commons Resolute', *The Times*, 5 Aug. 1914.
30 Villiers to Grey, 4 Aug. 1914 (received 11.20 a.m.), *BD*, vol. XI, Doc. 584, and M. Davignon, Belgian Minister for Foreign Affairs, to the Belgian Ministers at London and Paris, 4 Aug. 1914, *Belgian Grey Book*, Doc. 30.
31 Jagow to Lichnowsky, 4 Aug. 1914, *GD*, Doc. 810.
32 *Parliamentary Debates*, Commons, 5th series, vol. 65, 1925–8 (4 Aug. 1914).
33 Margot Asquith Diary, 4 Aug. 1914, M. Asquith Papers, Ms. Eng. d. 3210. Emphasis in original.
34 'The Commons Resolute', *The Times*, 5 Aug. 1914.
35 This important point is made by Lindsay, 'Failure of Liberal Opposition', 166.
36 For example, Churchill's instructions to all Royal Navy ships, instructions sent at 2.05 p.m. that afternoon, specified: 'The British ultimatum to Germany will expire at midnight Greenwich Mean Time, August 4.' Churchill, *World Crisis*, I, 182.
37 *Parliamentary Debates*, Commons, 5th series, vol. 65, 1941–52 (4 Aug. 1914).
38 'The Commons Resolute', *The Times*, 5 Aug. 1914.
39 Lindsay, 'Failure of Liberal Opposition', 167.
40 Hankey to Adeline, 4 Aug. 1914, Hankey Papers, HNKY 3/19.
41 Wilson, 'Britain', in *Decisions for War*, 201.
42 Lloyd George, *War Memoirs of David Lloyd George* (London, 1938), I, 45–7. A Belgian plea for military aid did not reach the Foreign Office in London until 12.50 a.m. on 5 August. See Villiers to Grey, 5 Aug. 1914 (despatched at 4 p.m.), *BD*, vol. XI, Doc. 654.
43 Grey to Lichnowsky, 4 Aug. 1914, *BD*, vol. XI, Doc. 643.
44 Lancelot Oliphant, *An Ambassador in Bonds* (London, 1946), 32–3.
45 Nicolson, *Sir Arthur Nicolson*, 423–6. Nicolson's narrative of the events, from the BBC program 'Tonight: Twenty-Three Years Ago', National Program, broadcast on 4 Aug. 1937, is reproduced on the BBC Spoken Word series, J. Bourke, ed., *BBC Eyewitness: 1910–1919: A History of the Twentieth Century in Sound* (BBC Audio Books, 2004, ISBN 0–563–53091-X), CD 2, Track 2.
46 'What War Means – Great Women's Meeting at Kingsway Hall', *Common Cause*, 7 Aug. 1914, 'Women's Protest Against War', *Daily News*, 5 Aug. 1914, and Helena Swanwick, *I Have Been Young* (London, 1935), 233–9. See also Jo Vellacott Newberry, 'Anti-war Suffragists', *History*, 62, 206 (October, 1977), 414–5, and Beryl Haslam, *From Suffrage to Internationalism: The Political Evolution of Three British Feminists, 1908–1939* (New York, 1999), 41.
47 Fawcett's speech, and those that follow, are summarised in 'What War Means', *Common Cause*, 7 Aug. 1914; and 'Protest Against War – International

Meeting of Women in London, August 4', reprinted from *Votes for Women*, in *Jus Suffragii*, 1 Sept. 1914; 'Women's Protest Against War', *Daily News*, 5 Aug. 1914; and in 'Women Denounce War', *Daily Herald*, 5 Aug. 1914.

48 The original two resolutions are in 'International Crisis – Great Women's Meeting', 4 Aug. 1914, Marshall Papers, D MAR 3/37, and see 'Women Denounce War', *Daily Herald*, 5 Aug. 1914.

49 'Women's Protest Against War', *Daily News*, 5 Aug. 1914, and see 'Women Denounce War', *Daily Herald*, 5 Aug. 1914.

50 Margaret Bondfield Diary, 4 Aug. 1914, Bondfield Papers, Folder 12.2 (Vassar College), and Margaret Bondfield, *A Life's Work* (London, 1948), 142.

51 Jill Liddington, *The Road to Greenham Common: Feminism and Anti-Militarism in Britain since 1820* (Syracuse, 1989), 78.

52 The article was reprinted from *Votes for Women* in 'Protest Against War', in *Jus Suffragii*, 1 Sept. 1914. Evelyn Sharp, the former assistant editor, became editor of *Votes for Women* on 1 Aug. 1914; see Alberti, *Beyond Suffrage*, 29.

53 'What War Means', *Common Cause*, 7 Aug. 1914.

54 In Blackstone's words, the Crown held 'the sole prerogative of making war and peace'. See William Blackstone, *Commentaries on the Laws of England* (1765–69), bk. 1, ch. 7. On the Crown's prerogatives, see also Joseph Chitty, *A Treatise on the Law of the Prerogatives of the Crown* (London, 1820), 43. See especially the 'Introduction' to Walter Bagehot, *The English Constitution* (Boston, 1873), 31–2, and Alpheus Todd, *On Parliamentary Government in England* (London, 1869), vol. I, 598. On the war powers, Todd asserted that the Constitution had 'vested this right exclusively in the crown'. See also A. V. Dicey, *Introduction to the Study of the Law of the Constitution* (London, 1902), 369–70, 408–12.

55 On the King's ultimate and formal responsibility to control foreign policy and to declare war, unfettered by Parliament, see Lord Halsbury, ed., *The Laws of England*, 1st ed., vol. VI (London, 1909), 375, 386, 427–8, 440–1, 442, 444, and on the Privy Council's role endorsing documents approved by Cabinet, see ibid., 386, 427–8. This volume was written by Professor H. W. Holdsworth, E. Wavell Ridges, Meryon White-Winton and Alfred Hildesheimer.

56 Alpheus Todd, *On Parliamentary Government in England* (London, 1869), vol. II, 622–3, and see Halsbury, ed., *The Laws of England*, 1st ed., vol. VII, 51–2. The Privy Council had not been called together as a whole since in 1839. An old requirement for a quorum of seven members had fallen into disuse after Prince Albert's death in 1861. On the matter of a quorum, see also *Halsbury's Laws of England*, 4th ed., vol. 8 (2), para. 525, f.n. 1.

57 FitzRoy, *Memoirs*, II, 561.

58 'Defence of the Realm: A Royal Proclamation', *The Times*, 5 Aug. 1914.

59 'For Army and Navy: Special Prayer of Intercession', *The Times*, 6 Aug. 1914.

60 FitzRoy, *Memoirs*, II, 561.

61 King George V Diary, 4 Aug. 1914, quoted in Christopher H. D. Howard, ed., *The Diary of Edward Goschen, 1900–1914*, Camden Fourth Series, vol. 25 (London, 1980), 48.

62 Wiltsher, *Dangerous Women*, 23.

63 Beauchamp was named Lord President of the Council the next day. Second Supplement to the *London Gazette*, 4 Aug. 1914, supplement dated 5 Aug. 1914 (no. 28862).

64 Typescript headed 'AT THE COURT OF BUCKINGHAM PALACE, THE

4TH DAY OF AUGUST 1914 (AT 10.35 P.M.)', listing only The King, Granard, Beauchamp and Allendale as 'Present', appended to Almeric FitzRoy to Beauchamp, 30 Oct. 1918, in Beauchamp Papers. Also see 'Court Circular', *The Times*, 6 Aug. 1914. Two more Privy Councillors stood 'in attendance', Lieut-Colonel Sir William Carington, a guardsman, and Sir Charles Cust, the King's Equerry in Waiting.

65 See the typescript headed 'Business for the Council', listing the agenda, appended to Almeric FitzRoy to Beauchamp, 30 Oct. 1918, in Beauchamp Papers. For the full text of the two proclamations, see Supplement to the *London Gazette*, 4 Aug. 1914 (No. 28861).

66 Almeric FitzRoy to Beauchamp, 30 Oct. 1918, in Beauchamp Papers.

67 FitzRoy, *Memoirs*, II, 561.

68 George V Diary, 4 Aug. 1914, quoted in Clay, *King, Kaiser, Tsar*, 314.

69 'London and the Coming of War', *The Times*, 5 Aug. 1914.

70 'As It Was On The Night Of The Declaration Of War', *Illustrated London News*, 8 Aug. 1914.

71 'Great Britain Declares War on Germany', *Daily Mirror*, 5 Aug. 1914.

72 George V Diary, 4 Aug. 1914, quoted in Clay, *King, Kaiser, Tsar*, 314.

73 'London and the Coming of War', *The Times*, 5 Aug. 1914.

74 Foreign Office Statement, issued 12.15 a.m., 5 Aug. 1914, reproduced in 'War Declared', *The Times*, 5 Aug. 1914, and 'Why There is War', *Daily Mirror*, 5 Aug. 1914.

75 Goschen to Grey, received 19 Aug. 1914, *BD*, vol. XI, Doc. 671. Goschen reported that his interview with von Jagow on 4 August took place 'at about 7 o'clock'.

76 On the timing of the various declarations of war see Schmitt, *Coming of the War*, II, 82, 320, 327 and 374.

77 Milner Diary, 4 Aug. 1914, Milner Papers, Milner dep. 85 (Bodleian Library).

78 Cabinet Memorandum, 4 Aug. 1914, Harcourt Papers.

79 'Secret Proceedings of a sub-Committee of the Committee of Imperial Defence, assembled on the 5th of August, 1914, to consider the question of offensive operations against the German Colonies', filed with Cabinet Memorandum, 5 Aug. 1914, Harcourt Papers. The committee decided to send an expedition from India to take Dar es Salaam; that the fate of German South-West Africa should await War Office advice; that British forces should seize Togoland; that British troops in Nigeria would move against the Cameroons, but not immediately because the defences were 'formidable'; that Australia 'should be invited to send an expedition to attack the island of Yap and German New Guinea, in order to seize the cables and radio telegraph stations'; and similarly that New Zealand 'should be invited to send an expedition to attack Samoa and Nauru'. See also Hankey, *Supreme Command*, I, 168.

80 Cabinet Memorandum, 5 Aug. 1914, Harcourt Papers.

81 Ibid. Emphasis added.

82 For example, L. T. Hobhouse to Courtney, 4 Aug. 1914, Courtney Papers, vol. XI.

83 Henry Wilson's Diary, 23 May, 30 June, 1, 4, 10, 14 and 31 July 1914, quoted in Hazlehurst, *Politicians at War*, 28, 31 and 73.

84 Milner Diary, 4 Aug. 1914, Milner Papers. Emphasis in original.

85 Hankey, *Supreme Command*, I, 169–72.

86 Milner Diary, 4–6 Aug. 1914, Milner Papers.
87 Cabinet Memorandum, 6 Aug. 1914, Harcourt Papers.
88 Churchill, *World Crisis*, I, 191.
89 Cabinet Memorandum, 6 Aug. 1914, Harcourt Papers.
90 Asquith to Stanley, 6 Aug. 1914, in Brock, *Letters to Venetia Stanley*, 158.
91 Spender, *Life, Journalism and Politics*, II, 18.
92 *Parliamentary Debates*, Commons, 5th series, vol. 65, 1963–4 (5 Aug. 1914).
93 Ibid., 2074–83 (6 Aug. 1914).
94 Ibid., 2089–90.
95 Ibid., 2092.
96 Ibid., 2097.
97 Ibid., 2098.
98 C. E. Montague, *Rough Justice* (London, 1926), 193, 218.
99 H. M. Tomlinson, *All Our Yesterdays* (London, 1930), 433–4.
100 Richard Aldington, *Death of a Hero* (London, 1929), 252.

25 Radical Recriminations

1 Dillon to C. P. Scott, 12 Aug. 1914, Dillon Papers, TCD MS 6843/31.
2 *Parliamentary Debates*, Commons, 5th series, vol. 65, 2077–9 (6 Aug. 1914).
3 Ibid., 1815–6 (3 Aug. 1914).
4 Minute from Churchill to Asquith and Grey, 23 Aug. 1912, Churchill Papers, CHAR 13/10/40–42.
5 Loreburn to Hirst, 23 Dec. 1914, Hirst Papers.
6 Percy Molteno, 'European Crisis: Notes on the Situation' [typescript], 5 Aug. 1914, Molteno Papers, Box 10/40/no item number (National Library of South Africa, Capetown).
7 C. E. Montague to Scott, 11 Aug. 1914, Manchester Guardian Archive, 333/122.
8 Lord Beauchamp, 'Our Foreign Policy', *Contemporary Review*, 121, 675 (March 1922), 275.
9 Beauchamp to Percy Molteno, 31 Aug. 1928, Molteno Papers, Box 10/43/732.
10 Beauchamp to G. P. Gooch, 23 July 1930, Gooch Papers, Box 1 (University of Alberta, Calgary).
11 Ibid., Beauchamp to G. P. Gooch, 24 July 1930.
12 *Parliamentary Debates*, Commons, 5th series, vol. 150, 197 (8 Feb. 1922).
13 The original White Paper, *Correspondence Respecting the European Crisis* (London, 1914), of 159 documents was distributed to the press by the Foreign Office very late on 5 August; see 'Britain's Case', *The Times*, 6 Aug. 1914.
14 *Parliamentary Debates*, Lords, 5th series, vol. xvii, 423–4 (6 Aug. 1914).
15 'Britain's Case', *The Times*, 6 Aug. 1914. This summary reproduced only documents 85, 101 and 111.
16 *Parliamentary Debates*, Commons, 5th series, vol. 65, 2079 (6 Aug. 1914).
17 Ibid., 2100. The Vote of Credit of £100 million as supplementary estimates for the army and navy was agreed to, *nemine contradicente*.
18 For example, 'At War', editorial, *The Times*, 6 Aug. 1914, and 'Prime Minister's Eloquent Speech', *The Times*, 7 Aug. 1914.

19 R. W. Seton-Watson to Hirst, 6 Aug. 1914, Hirst Papers.

20 Grey to Goschen, 1 Aug. 1914, in *Great Britain and the European Crisis* (Doc. 123), 66. This appears as Grey to Goschen, 1 Aug. 1914, *BD*, vol. XI, Doc. 448.

21 *Parliamentary Debates*, Commons, 5th series, vol. 65, 1859 (3 Aug. 1914). Emphasis added.

22 Llewelyn Williams Diary, 9 Aug. 1914, in J. Graham Jones, ' "A Proved and Loyal Friendship": The Diary of W. Llewelyn Williams', *National Library of Wales Journal*, 34, 3 (2008), 357.

23 Lloyd George told George Riddell on Sunday 2 August that Britain was offering to remain neutral if Germany respected Belgian neutrality. See Riddell, *Lord Riddell's War Diary*, 4–5, and McEwen, ed., *The Riddell Diaries, 1908–1923*, 87. At the Cabinet of Saturday 1 August, Haldane suggested Grey should 'promise our neutrality if France [was] not invaded.' Harcourt, Cabinet Memorandum, 1 Aug. 1914, Harcourt Papers.

24 Eversley to Hirst, 12 Aug. 1914, Hirst Papers.

25 Hirst to Nicholas Murray Butler, 18 Aug. 1914, Hirst Papers.

26 J. A. Farrer to T. C. Farrer, 18 Aug. 1914, Farrer Papers, 2752/1/66 (Surrey History Centre).

27 Minute Book, 7 Aug. 1914, 11 a. m., Committee Room 9, House of Commons, in Denman Papers, Box 7, Folder 4/28.

28 Courtney to Scott, 8 Aug. 1914, Manchester Guardian Archive, 333/117.

29 Courtney to Crewe, 9 Aug. 1914, Crewe Papers, C. 9 (Cambridge University Library).

30 Eleanor Acland Diary, entry for 30 July 1914 (written up 8 Aug. 1914), Francis and Eleanor Acland Papers, 611.

31 Ibid., 9 Aug. 1914. Emphasis in original. The reference to the German reply of 'that same day' is a reference to Goschen to Grey, 31 July 1914, *BD*, vol. XI, Doc. 383, which was received at 3.30 a.m. on 1 Aug. 1914.

32 Courtney to C. P. Scott, 11 Aug. 1914, Manchester Guardian Archive, 333/121.

33 Ibid., Courtney to C. P. Scott, 14 Aug. 1914, 333/125.

34 Llewelyn Williams Diary, 9 Aug. 1914, in 'The Diary of W. Llewelyn Williams', 358.

35 William Stephens Clark to Hirst, 12 Aug. 1914, Hirst Papers.

36 Loreburn to Scott, 14 Oct. 1914, Manchester Guardian Archive, 333/154.

37 See Anna Barlow to Burns, 9 Aug. 1914, Burns Papers, Add. MSS. 46303, and Courtney to C. P. Scott, 14 Aug. 1914, Manchester Guardian Archive, 333/125.

38 Harcourt, Cabinet Memorandum, 3 Aug. 1914, Harcourt Papers, Pease Diary, 2 Aug. 1914, in Wilson, 'Diary of Pease', [43] 8–[47] 9, H. Samuel to B. Samuel, 2 Aug. 1914, Samuel Papers.

39 Morley, *Memorandum on Resignation*, 13–14. Morley recorded in his memoir that Grey had 'told us of his talk with Lichnowsky' – but he was uncertain whether this was at the Sunday morning or evening Cabinet. Morley was not specific about the offer. It is unlikely that something as remarkable as an upgraded German offer to respect Belgian neutrality, and all French territory, would have escaped Morley's exact recollection.

40 Harcourt, Cabinet Memorandum, 3 Aug. 1914, Harcourt Papers.

41 Lichnowsky to the Foreign Office [Berlin], 3 Aug. 1914, Lichnowsky, *Heading*

for the Abyss, 423–4, and Communication from the German Embassy, 3 Aug. 1914, *BD*, vol. XI, Doc. 531.

42 Scott to L. T. Hobhouse, 11 Aug. 1914, Manchester Guardian Archive, 132/179.

43 Lady Barlow, 'The Negotiations Before the War', letter to the editor, *Manchester Guardian*, 12 Aug. 1914.

44 Bertrand Russell, letter to editor, *Nation*, 15 Aug. 1914.

45 'How Germany Makes History', *The Times*, 27 Aug. 1914.

46 *Parliamentary Debates*, Commons, 5th series, vol. 65i, 123–6 (27 Aug. 1914). The government then sanctified Grey's explanations by including them in the semi-official booklet, E. Barker et al., eds., *Why We Are At War: Great Britain's Case, by Members of the Oxford Faculty of Modern History* (Oxford, 1914), 86.

47 For example, E. D. Morel, *Truth and the War* (London, 1918), 3rd ed., 26. With the publication of vol. XI of the official *British Documents* in 1926, more mysteries emerged. Five telegrams included in the White Paper were marked in the Foreign Office archives as 'Not sent – War' – without explanation. Four of these were telegrams addressed to Goschen in Berlin, three from 29 July and one from 1 August (the famous 'Doc. 123'). See *BD*, vol. XI, Docs. 284, 285, 286, 448, 282.

48 Ramsay MacDonald, 'Why We Are At War – A Reply to Sir Edward Grey', *Labour Leader*, 13 Aug. 1914.

49 *Parliamentary Debates*, Commons, 5th series, vol. 65, 2076 (6 Aug. 1914).

50 Herwig, *Marne*, 55.

51 C. V. Wedgwood, *The Last of the Radicals: The Life of Josiah Clement Wedgwood, M. P.* (London, 1951), 99.

52 Andrew Carnegie, 'The "Chief Destroyer"', *The Times*, 8 Aug. 1914.

53 Dillon to C. P. Scott, 12 Aug. 1914, Dillon Papers, TCD MS 6843/31.

54 A. Ponsonby to D. Ponsonby, 5 Aug. 1914, Ponsonby Papers.

55 Arthur Ponsonby Diary 1913–1914, Ponsonby Papers (Shulbrede).

56 Ibid., A. Ponsonby, entry for Aug. 1914, 'War Diary'.

57 Llewelyn Williams Diary, 9 Aug. 1914, 'The Diary of W. Llewelyn Williams', 359.

58 Vernon Lee to H. G. Wells, 5 Aug. 1914, H. G. Wells Papers, L 120 (University of Illinois, Champaign-Urbana).

59 Morley, *Memorandum on Resignation*, 14.

60 Ramsay MacDonald Diary, 6 Oct. 1914, MacDonald Papers, TNA: PRO 30/69/1753/1. Morley mentioned 30 July, but there was no Cabinet meeting on Thursday 30 July. For similar evidence, see Bertrand Russell to Ottoline Morrell, 24(?) Nov. 1914, Morrell Papers, 25/2, and Wilson, 'Britain', in *Decisions for War*, 176, 192, 199.

61 Irene Cooper Willis to Vernon Lee, 5 Oct. 1914, reporting the views of Howard Whitehouse, Parliamentary Private Secretary to Lloyd George, Violet Paget Papers.

62 *Parliamentary Debates*, Commons, 5th series, vol. 65, 1859 (3 Aug. 1914).

63 Jarausch, *The Enigmatic Chancellor*, 175, and Lerchenfeld to Hertling, 5 Aug. 1914, quoted in Schmitt, *Coming of the War*, II, 401. See also Mombauer, *Moltke*, 210, 219.

64 Percy Molteno, 'European Crisis: Notes on the Situation' [typescript], 5 Aug. 1914, Molteno Papers, Box 10/40/no item number.

65 Molteno draft letter to Editor of the *Manchester Guardian*, 1 Nov. 1928 (unpublished), Molteno Papers, Box 10/43/1353.

66 For example, see Zangwill to Jacob Schiff, 6 Feb. 1915, A120/38, Zangwill to Clement Shorter 13 Mar. 1915, A120/490, or the correspondence with Lucien Wolf, esp. Nov. 1914 to Oct. 1915, A120/ 608, Zangwill Papers (Central Zionist Archive, Jerusalem).

67 Vernon Lee, 'Notes to the Prologue', dated Oct. 1918, in *Satan the Waster: A Philosophic War Trilogy with Notes and Introduction* (New York, 1920), 155.

68 Morley, *Memorandum on Resignation*, 6–7.

69 *Parliamentary Debates*, Commons, 5th series, vol. 65, 1830 (3 Aug. 1914), and see ibid., Robert Outhwaite and Joseph King, 1862, 1869.

70 Ibid., 2073–83 (6 Aug. 1914).

71 Ibid., 2083–9.

72 *Parliamentary Debates*, Lords, 5th series, vol. 17, 417–23 (6 Aug. 1914).

73 Ibid., 423–5.

74 'The Declaration of War', editorial, *The Times*, 5 Aug. 1914.

75 'King and Tsar: Royal Efforts to Avert War', *The Times*, 5 Aug. 1914.

76 Ibid., 'Russo-British Amity'. Buchanan was on the balcony again on 4 August to receive cheers from a large crowd. See Michael Hughes, *Inside the Enigma: British Officials in Russia 1900-1939* (London, 1997), 59. Hirst highlighted these reports in 'Diary of the European Crisis', *Economist*, 8 Aug. 1914.

77 Compare Buchanan to Grey, 24 and 25 July 1914, in *Great Britain and the European Crisis*, Docs. 6, 17, and *BD*, vol. XI, Docs. 101, 125.

78 Buchanan to Grey, 25 July 1914, *BD*, vol. XI, Doc. 125. Emphasis added.

79 Compare Buchanan to Grey, 25 July 1914, *Great Britain and the European Crisis*, Doc. 17, and *BD*, vol. XI, Doc. 125.

80 In his post-war memoirs, Buchanan made the remarkable claim that, with just one exception (a mutilated telegram of 1–2 August to the Foreign Office), the White Paper 'recorded all the communications which passed between me and that department during those critical days'. See Buchanan, *My Mission*, vol. I, 211.

81 Buchanan to Grey, 2 Aug. 1914, *BD*, vol. XI, Doc. 490.

82 Ibid., Grey to Buchanan, 25 July 1914, Doc. 132 and accompanying note.

83 See Headlam-Morley's introduction to *BD*, vol. XI, p. vii.

84 Stephen J. Cimbala, 'Steering Through Rapids: Russian Mobilisation and World War I', *Journal of Slavic Military History*, 9, 2 (June, 1996), 383. See also the summary of the meetings of 24 and 25 July in Clark, *Sleepwalkers*, ch. 11, 'Warning Shots', and in McMeekin, *Russian Origins of the First World War*, 54–63.

85 Schmitt, *Coming of the War*, II, 244, Schuman, *War and Diplomacy*, 232, and Clark, *Sleepwalkers*, 509.

86 The White Paper, with the addition of several documents and Grey and Asquith's speeches of 3, 4, 5 and 6 August, was reprinted in late September 1914 for the public as a 'Blue Book', under the title *Great Britain and the European Crisis*, costing one penny. It came with an 'Introductory Narrative of Events' produced by the Foreign Office. Eventually, more than a million copies of the booklet were produced.

87 Aubrey Douglas Smith, *Guilty Germans?* (London, 1942), 131.

88 Quoted in Pope-Hennessy, *Lord Crewe*, 143.

89 Lord Hardinge of Penshurst, *Old Diplomacy: The Reminiscences of Lord Hardinge of Penshurst* (London, 1947), 222.

26 Conclusion

1 Hirst to Nicholas Murray Butler, 18 Aug. 1914, Hirst Papers.
2 Transcript of Norman Angell's speech to the Norman Angell Peace Dinner, Salisbury Hotel, London, 17 Sept. 1914, David Starr Jordan Papers, Box 41 (Hoover Institution, Stanford).
3 For example, Gary Sheffield, 'The Great War Was a Just War', *History Today*, 63, 8 (Aug. 2013), 6, and Max Hastings, *Catastrophe: Europe Goes to War 1914* (London, 2013).
4 Grey to Sir F. Lascelles, 18 Sept. 1907, cited by Wilson, *Policy of the Entente*, 36. Lascelles quoted the line in his reply, promising he had told the Germans that Britain could not 'leave France in the lurch' and 'that the Entente is the key-stone of our policy and that we do not intend to abandon it'. Lascelles to Grey, 20 Sept. 1907, Lascelles Papers. Lascelles, a believer in reconciliation with Germany, had previously complained about the 'anti-German current' dominating at the Foreign Office. See Lascelles to Haldane, 27 Sept. 1906, and Lascelles to Fitzmaurice, 28 Sept. 1906, Lascelles Papers, TNA: FO 800/19.
5 Typical are Sean M. Lynn-Jones, 'Détente and Deterrence: Anglo-German Relations, 1911–1914', *International Security*, 11, 2 (Autumn, 1986), 144, Jack S. Levy, 'Preferences, Constraints, and Choices in July 1914', *International Security*, 15, 3 (Winter, 1990–91), 168–70, and John H. Maurer, *The Outbreak of the First World War: Strategic Planning, Crisis Decision Making and Deterrence Failure* (Westport, 1995), 123.
6 Lichnowsky to the Foreign Office [in Berlin], 25 July 1914, [two cablegrams], Lichnowsky to the Foreign Office [in Berlin], 27 July 1914 [two cablegrams], and Lichnowsky to Foreign Office [Berlin], 29 July 1914, in Lichnowsky, *Heading for the Abyss*, 394, 395, 398–401, 405–6.
7 Grey told Ponsonby on Wednesday 29 July that 'doubt' concerning the British position helped him promote caution. Ponsonby, 'Notes of Grey's Statement to me on July 29, [19]14', Ponsonby Papers, MS. Eng. hist. c. 660, f. 43.
8 See extracts from articles in the *Daily Chronicle*, 29 July 1914, the editorial of the *Westminster Gazette*, 1 Aug. 1914, and a summary of the English press in the *Berliner Tageblatt* of 2 Aug. 1914, in *GD*, Docs. 382, 611, 661. The Kaiser's notes show that he set no great store by Radical opinion. Against the *Westminster Gazette*'s editorial expressing hope that Britain might rally all those who believed in peace, the Kaiser wrote, 'Twaddle'.
9 The Kaiser 'built so largely' on the King's reported word, writes Fischer, that the Kaiser counselled Bethmann Hollweg against offering too many concessions in his attempt to start negotiations with Britain on Wednesday 29 July. See Fischer, *War of Illusions*, 494. See also Fischer, *Germany's Aims in the First World War*, 76, and Röhl, 'The Curious Case of the Kaiser's Disappearing War Guilt' in Afflerbach and Stevenson, eds., *An Improbable War?*, 84.
10 Eleanor Acland Diary, n. d. May 1915, Acland Papers, 611.
11 Clark, *Sleepwalkers*, 512. Clark concludes: 'It is worth pausing for a moment

to ponder on the fact that the impact of a telegram from the Emperor's third cousin in Berlin was sufficient to stay an order of general mobilisation for nearly twenty-four hours.'

12 Kiesling, 'France', in Hamilton and Herwig, eds., *Origins of World War I*, 248–9, Keiger, *Poincaré*, 175, and Poincaré, *Memoirs (1913–1914)*, 221. See also Schuman, *War and Diplomacy*, 230–1, for a discussion on this and other French contacts with Russia on 30 July. Schuman concludes: '[Poincaré's] counsel always placed the obligations of the alliance before the maintenance of peace. The Russian Government was not clearly and unequivocably warned against general mobilisation, the imminence of which was still probably unsuspected in Paris.'

13 McMeekin, *July 1914*, 339–49.

14 Hirst to Nicholas Murray Butler, 18 Aug. 1914, Hirst Papers.

15 Fischer, *Germany's Aims in the First World War*, ch. 3.

16 Harcourt, 'The Spoils', 25 Mar. 1915, TNA: CAB 63/3/104-6.

17 The best is David Stevenson, *First World War and International Politics* (Oxford, 1991), ch. 3.

18 Grey's speech of 26 Jan. 1916, reproduced as *Great Britain's Measures Against German Trade* (London, 1916), 30.

19 See the balanced assessment in Kramer, *Dynamic of Destruction*, ch. 4, 'German Singularity?'

20 Lloyd George, recorded in Llewelyn Williams Diary, 6 Apr. and 13 Sept. 1909, in 'The Diary of W. Llewelyn Williams', 350, 354.

21 Vernon Lee, *Satan the Waster*, 121.

22 Caroline Playne, Diary, 24 July 1916, 27 Aug. 1916, 16 Sept. 1916, 26 Nov. 1917, 8 and 9 June 1917, 25 Aug. 1917, 16 and 31 Dec. 1917, 11 May 1918, Caroline Playne Papers (Senate House Library, University of London).

23 J. M. Winter, 'Some Aspects of the Demographic Consequences of the First World War in Britain', *Population Studies*, 30, 3 (1976), 539–52. Ruth Leger Sivard, *World Military and Social Expenditures 1991* (Washington, 1991), 23, estimates a total of deaths for Britain of 1,031,000.

24 Harcourt Cabinet Memorandum, 18 Aug. 1914, Harcourt Papers.

25 McKenna, speech on the Finance Bill, *Parliamentary Debates*, Commons, 5th series, vol. 84, c. 693 (17 July 1916); Bonar Law, 'Comparative Statement' on spending, *Parliamentary Debates*, Commons, 5th Series, vol. 95, Table A, 41W (25 June 1917); and see C. H. Oldham, 'British Finance of the War', *Journal of the Statistical and Social Inquiry Society of Ireland*, XIII, XCVI (1915–1916), 317–28, Francis Hirst, *The Consequences of the War to Great Britain* (London, 1934), 145, 159, 161.

26 R. H. Mottram, *The Spanish Farm Trilogy* (London, 1927), 46, 159, 792.

27 *Parliamentary Debates*, Commons, 5th series, vol. 65, 1851–2 (3 Aug. 1914).

Archival Material

Below are listed the archival institutions, private personal papers, and manuscript collections that have been utilised in this study.

In the United Kingdom

London: British Library, Department of Manuscripts. John Burns, Alfred Harmsworth (Lord Northcliffe), Henry Petty-Fitzmaurice (5th Marquess of Lansdowne), John Alfred Spender, Henry Wickham Steed

London: Imperial War Museum. Harold Bing (interview, with the Department of Sound Records), Lord Burnham

London: London School of Economics Archives. Edmund Dene Morel, Leonard and Kate Courtney

London: News International Record Office, Enfield. Times Newspapers Limited Archive

London: Parliamentary Archives, House of Lords. David Lloyd George, Herbert Samuel, Courtenay Ilbert

London: Senate House Library, University of London. Caroline Playne

London: The National Archives, Kew. James Ramsay MacDonald, Frank Lascelles

London: The Women's Library (now at the London School of Economics). Kathleen D. Courtney, Agnes Maude Royden, Mary Sheepshanks, National Union of Women's Suffrage Societies Archives

Oxford: Bodleian Library. H. H. Asquith, Margot Asquith, Geoffrey Dawson, Richard Denman, Francis Hirst, Lewis Harcourt, Alfred Milner, John Morley, Arthur Ponsonby, John Simon

Oxford: Ruskin College. James and Lucy Middleton

Cambridge: Churchill Archives Centre. Winston Churchill, Maurice Hankey, Reginald and Pamela McKenna

Cambridge: Fitzwilliam Museum. Wilfrid Scawen Blunt

Cambridge: Wren Library, Trinity College. Edwin Samuel Montagu

Cambridge University Library. Robert Crewe-Milnes (1st Marquess of Crewe), Charles Hardinge (1st Baron Hardinge)

Birmingham: Birmingham Central Library. Elizabeth Cadbury

Carlisle: Cumbria Record Office. Catherine Marshall
Chatsworth: The Library. Victor Cavendish (9th Duke of Devonshire)
Chichester: West Sussex Record Office. Leo Maxse
Exeter: Devon Record Office. Francis and Eleanor Acland
Haslemere: Shulbrede Priory. Arthur Ponsonby
Hull: Hull History Centre. The Union of Democratic Control Archives
Liverpool: University Library, University of Liverpool. Bruce Glasier and Katharine
    St John Conway
Manchester: The John Rylands Library, The University of Manchester. Manchester
    Guardian Archive, Francis Neilson
Newcastle: Robinson Library, Newcastle University. Charles Trevelyan, Walter
    Runciman
Woking: Surrey History Centre. Thomas Cecil Farrer
Aberdeen: Aberdeen University Library. William Robertson Nicoll
Edinburgh: National Library of Scotland. Richard Burdon Haldane, Elizabeth
    Haldane, Arthur Murray
Private family archives. William Lygon (7th Earl Beauchamp), Thomas Edmund
    Harvey

In the Republic of Ireland

Dublin: Library of Trinity College. John Dillon

In the United States of America

Austin: Harry Ransom Centre, University of Texas. Philip and Ottoline Morrell
Boston: Massachusetts Historical Society. Ellery Sedgwick
Champaign-Urbana: University of Illinois. Herbert George Wells
Muncie: Ball State University, Muncie, Indiana. Norman Angell
New York: Columbia Centre for Oral History Collection (CCOHC), Columbia
    University. Norman Angell
New York: New York Public Library, Berg Collection. Rosika Schwimmer-Lloyd
Poughkeepsie: Vassar College. Margaret Bondfield
San Francisco: Hoover Institution, Stanford University. Rosika Schwimmer, David
    Starr Jordan
Waterville, Maine: Colby College. Violet Paget (Vernon Lee)

In Canada

Calgary: University of Calgary. George Peabody Gooch

In South Africa

Cape Town: National Library of South Africa. Percy Molteno

In Israel

Jerusalem: Central Zionist Archive. Israel Zangwill

In Australia

Canberra: National Library of Australia. Ronald Munro Ferguson (Lord Novar),
    Edmund Barton

Index